Modernity at Sea

Edited by

Sandra Buckley

Michael Hardt

Brian Massumi

THEORY OUT OF BOUNDS

Modernity at Sea

Melville, Marx, Conrad in Crisis

Cesare Casarino

Theory out of Bounds   *Volume 21*

University of Minnesota Press

Minneapolis • London

Lines from "Le bateau ivre," by Arthur Rimbaud, from *A Season in Hell and The Drunken Boat*, translated by Louise Varèse (New York: New Directions Publishing Corp., 1961); copyright 1961 by New Directions Publishing Corp; reprinted by permission of New Directions Publishing Corp. Lines from "Sils Maria," by Friedrich Nietzsche, from *The Gay Science*, translated by Walter Kaufmann (New York: Vintage Books, 1974); reprinted by permission of Random House, Inc. Lines from Canto 35 in *Clarel: A Poem and Pilgrimage in the Holy Land*, by Herman Melville (Chicago: Northwestern University Press and The Newberry Library, 1991); reprinted by permission of Northwestern University Press. Lines from "John Marr and Other Sailors," by Herman Melville, from *Poems of Herman Melville*, edited by Douglas Robillard (Albany: New College and University Press, 1976); reprinted by permission of Kent State University Press. Lines from "They shut me up in Prose," by Emily Dickinson, from *The Poems of Emily Dickinson*, edited by Thomas H. Johnson (Cambridge, Mass.: The Belknap Press of Harvard University Press, 1951); copyright 1951, 1955, 1979 by the President and Fellows of Harvard College; reprinted by permission of the publishers and Trustees of Amherst College.

An earlier version of chapter 1 appeared as "Gomorrahs of the Deep; or, Melville, Foucault, and the Question of Heterotopia," *Arizona Quarterly* 51, no. 4 (1995): 1–25; reprinted by permission of the Regents of the University of Arizona. An earlier version of chapter 4 appeared as "The Sublime of the Closet; or, Joseph Conrad's Secret Sharing," *boundary 2* 24, no. 2 (1997): 199–243; copyright Duke University Press; reprinted by permission of Duke University Press.

Published by the University of Minnesota Press
111 Third Avenue South, Suite 290
Minneapolis, MN 55401-2520
http://www.upress.umn.edu

Printed in the United States of America on acid-free paper

LIBRARY OF CONGRESS CATALOGING-IN-PUBLICATION DATA
Casarino, Cesare.
Modernity at sea : Melville, Marx, Conrad in crisis / Cesare Casarino.
    p.   cm. — (Theory out of bounds ; v. 21)
Includes bibliographical references (p.   ) and index.
ISBN 0-8166-3926-4 (acid-free paper) — ISBN 0-8166-3927-2 (pbk. :
acid-free paper)
1. Melville, Herman, 1819–1891—Criticism and interpretation.   2. Conrad,
Joseph, 1857–1924—Criticism and interpretation.   3. Sea stories, American—
History and criticism.   4. Sea stories, English—History and criticism.
5. Melville, Herman, 1819–1891—Philosophy.   6. Conrad, Joseph,
1857–1924—Philosophy.   7. Marx, Karl, 1818–1883—Influence.   8. Modernism
(Literature)   9. Men in literature.   I. Title.   II. Series.
PS2387 .C37   2002
813'.30932162—dc21
2002002334

12 11 10 09 08 07 06 05 04 03 02   10 9 8 7 6 5 4 3 2 1

A mio padre
A mia madre
A mio fratello
A mia sorella

Si je désire une eau d'Europe, c'est la flache

Noire et froide où vers le crépuscule embaumé

Un enfant accroupi plein de tristesses, lâche

Un bateau frêle comme un papillon de mai.

—Arthur Rimbaud, *Le bateau ivre*

Contents

Acknowledgments

I WRITE for myself, that is, for my friends — known and unknown, past, present, and yet to come. It is you who gave me the courage to write a book about communism, love, and friendship — with what results, only you can judge. Some of you saw only the beginning, some of you saw only the end, some of you were there from the very beginning to the very end, some of you read everything, some of you never even read a word, some of you spoke much and well, some of you chose the silence that compels beyond speech, some of you I have yet to meet, some of you I might never meet. To all of you goes my gratitude for imposing on me so great a debt — a debt I can never repay.

Some creditors: Jonathan Arac, Mieke Bal, Jonathan Beller, Renu Bora, Randall Craig, Sara Danius, Cathy Davidson, Daniela Daniele, Leland Deladurantaye, Sylvia Divinetz Romero, Frederick Dolan, Ramez Elias, Barbara Gastaldello, Ambreen Hai, Susan Hegeman, Rosemary Hennessy, Caren Irr, Pierre Joris, Stefan Jonsson, Gene Kuperman, Amy Lee, Carolyn Lesjak, Barry Maxwell, Natalie Melas, Mary Moessinger, Richard Morrison, John Mowitt, Antonio Negri, Don Pease, Nicole Peyrafitte, Christopher Pavsek, Michael Rothberg, Kevin Rozario, Michael Ryan, Steven Seidman, Roy Sellars, Steven Shaviro, Barbara Herrnstein Smith, Julianna Smith, Michael Speaks, Mike Stoffel, Kenneth Surin, Neferti Tadiar, Helen

Tartar, Ernst van Alphen, Geoff Waite, Michael Watts, Philip Wegner, Joshua Wilner, Shelly Wong, Xu-dong Zhang.

Some even more generous creditors: Vitaly Chernetsky, Richard Dienst, Salvatore Ficano, Bishnupriya Ghosh, Michael Hardt, Rebecca Karl, Eleanor Kaufman, Kiarina Kordela, Gary Lombardo, Saree Makdisi, Tim Malkovich, Thomas Pepper, Ross Prinzo, Bhaskar Sarkar, Yonatan Touval.

And yet two more creditors: Fredric Jameson, Eve Kosofsky Sedgwick. If what I owe all of you is unrepayable, what I owe the two of you is altogether unthinkable.

And, above all, to the students in my seminars on Herman Melville, on Gilles Deleuze, and on the Community of Unbelonging, I am compelled to say: you might not know that you are creditors, too — but I do.

Philopoesis: A Theoretico-Methodological Preface

> Method is a digression.
>
> Walter Benjamin, *The Origin of German Tragic Drama*

The Question

WHAT IS LITERARY CRITICISM? I begin this preface and this whole book by posing this exhausted and exhausting question as if it had never been asked before. Indeed, I find that no less than a hubristic ruse of *tabula rasa* is needed to revive and to think this question at all (the reasons why one should want to revive it and to think it anew in the first place will, I hope, become clear below). This question could have been posed differently. As if inquiring after the health of a loved one who has been very ill for a long time, and who has been absent from one's daily life but all the more present because of it in one's daily thoughts, one could have asked: how is literary criticism? Or, one could have asked: when and where was literary criticism? And in this latter avatar of that question, literary criticism would have been marked as the name of a spatio-temporal locus that no longer exists as such and that has long since been evacuated of its autochthonous populations and colonized by more properly postmodern settlers and usurpers, such as, for example, theory, cultural studies, or area studies. For the time being, however, I will proceed as if this question had nothing to do with love and history, only so as to come to love and history in the end via an arduous detour. For the time being I have chosen to pose this question in the most banal possible way, only so as to reveal in the end the Trojan horse it had been all along. In the end, it will be a question of witnessing whether one's first love—which has remained one's true love all along—can rise from its own ashes, not as the eternal return of the identical love or as the eternal return of a different love, but rather as the eternal return of the love of the same, that is, as the eternal return of ever-different ways of loving the very same thing and of loving that thing such as it is. And here the thing itself will bear the paleonymic name of *literature*. And the love of the thing, that is, the love of literature, will bear the untimely and neologistic name of *philopoesis*.[1]

Now the question can be posed again and differently: what is philopoesis? In a sense, this whole book constitutes an implicit attempt to formulate and to answer precisely this question. I leave it to the introduction to articulate the central argument of this book regarding the nineteenth-century sea narrative understood as a crucial chapter in the history of the representational forms of modernity—an argument that will be revealed immediately as a heuristic postulate for a series of literary-philosophical investigations whose urgent concern ultimately is that which is not narrative in sea narratives, that which is not representational in representational forms, and that which is not modern in modernity. (The more impatient reader interested in hearing immediately about this argument is advised to begin reading from the introduction and to return to this theoretico-methodological statement at the end.) Here, in this digression in the guise of a preface, however, I wish to pose the question of philopoesis explicitly. I find that as good a way as any to begin to explicate such a question is to assert that in this book I read literary texts as if I were a philosopher who is trying to read as if he were a literary critic (but who cannot help himself also to read as if he were a philosopher), and I read philosophical texts as if I were a literary critic who is trying to read as if he were a philosopher (but who cannot help but also to read as if he were a literary critic). Clearly, what is most crucial in such a characterological merry-go-round of reading is the nature of the "as if"—an "as if" that I would characterize in terms of *interference*. Philopoesis names a certain discontinuous and refractive interference between philosophy and literature.

Interferential Ontology

In order to pose the question of philopoesis and to articulate the modalities of being of such an interference, I will turn first to what has been so far a vastly underrated and underread work, one that begins by posing a similar question and ends by confronting similarly the interferences among three different practices—understood as the three central forms of thought and fundamental instances of the human mind—namely, philosophy, science, and art: the work in question is Gilles Deleuze and Félix Guattari's last effort, *What Is Philosophy?*[2] The answer they give to this question is just as disarmingly and deceivingly simple as the question itself: philosophy is "the art of forming, inventing, and fabricating concepts," while science is the production of "prospects" and "functions," and art, including literature, is the production of "a bloc of sensations, that is to say, a compound of percepts and affects."[3] The exoteric clarity and pedagogical directness with which this eminently ontological question is posed, engaged, and centrally positioned starting from the very title seem to indicate that this is indeed the crucial and defining question of this work—and, of course, it is. Contrary to what seems self-evident, however, I would like to suggest that the crucial and more properly historical-political question that this work is posing is not the question of the title but rather the question of that question, which is, under what conditions and to what effects is one to ask the question "what is philosophy?"—or, in other words, *why philosophy?* It turns out that the answer to this other and more difficult question cannot be handled with the direct sobriety and sovereign calm that characterizes the answers to the question of the title, and that the question "why philosophy?" produces instead an answer that is scattered, turbulent, impatient, and shot through with sudden bursts of thinly veiled, indignant anger: if the explicit and actual aspect of the investigation undertaken in this work bears the stamp of Kantian *askesis*, the implicit and virtual one reverberates with the ruthless scorn of Nietzschean laughter.[4] Restless and dispersed as this answer is, it does nonetheless exist in this work, and I will piece it together and sketch it here as succinctly and reductively—that is to say, perhaps, as violently and vulgarly—as possible. In brief, the question "why philosophy?" is asked nowhere in this work and yet is answered everywhere in it—thereby constituting a veritable absent cause immanent in its own effects—and the omnipresent answer takes the form of a historical-materialist dictum, the form of an impassioned defense and assertion of the primacy of philosophy as radical critique of *doxa* and as revolutionary practice of resistance to that "absolute disaster for thought" that goes by the name of "universal capitalism."[5] And if I seem so much under the spell of the double questioning of *What Is Philosophy?*, that is so because this preface proceeds in much the same spirit: at once an exposition, an apology, and a manifesto, this preface endeavors to explain what philopoesis might be, while also being troubled by the more difficult task of articulating the historical-political conditions under which philopoesis has imposed itself on me here as a necessity in the first place. The point is that, on the one hand, the answer to the question "what is philopoesis?" will at once borrow and diverge considerably from the answer Deleuze and Guattari give to the question "what is philosophy?" and, on the other hand, the answer to the question "why philopoesis?" will turn out to be in the end the very same answer they give to the question "why philosophy?" Or—by way of a preliminary formulation—philopoesis is a historical-materialist practice.

If I take Deleuze and Guattari's definitions of philosophy as production of concepts, and of literature as production of affects and percepts, to be axiomatic for my present attempt to define philopoesis, I do so above all because such definitions allow for and indeed demand zones of interference. While *What Is Philosophy?* unfolds preeminently as a detailed exposition of certain definitions of philosophy, art, and science, and as a careful staking out of the boundaries, functions, and specificities that constitute these respective practices, the very end of that work retroactively complicates these discrete configurations by considering the points of junction of those practices and by sketching three different types of interference among them.[6] Precisely because *What Is Philosophy?* is devoted to a painstaking differentiation of practices, forms, and domains of thought, the question of interference cannot be a secondary and peripheral matter here: consigned as it is to the closing chapter and especially to the last three pages of the whole work, the question of interference is suddenly revealed to have been a critical matter and a haunting presence all along. By keeping this question at bay up until its sudden disclosure at the very end, this crystalline work of distinctions at once erases and highlights the gritty preliminary process of investigation by which it came into being in the first place. And it is only by retracing such a process in an earlier text that we come face to face with the full ontological import of interference.

On the last page of his two-volume study of cinema, Deleuze writes:

> For theory too is something which is made, no less than its object. For many people, philosophy is something which is not "made," but is pre-existent, ready-made in a prefabricated sky. However, philosophical theory is itself a practice, just as much as its object. It is no more abstract than its object. It is a practice of concepts, and it must be judged in the light of the other practices with which it interferes. A theory of cinema is not "about" cinema, but about the concepts that cinema gives rise to and which are themselves related to other concepts corresponding to other practices, the practice of concepts in general having no privilege over others, any more than one object has over others. It is at the level of the interference of many practices

that things happen, beings, images, concepts, all the kinds of events. The theory of cinema does not bear on the cinema, but on the concepts of cinema, which are no less practical, effective or existent than cinema itself... Cinema's concepts are not given in cinema. And yet they are cinema's concepts, not theories about cinema. So that there is always a time, midday-midnight, when we must no longer ask ourselves, "What is cinema?" but "What is philosophy?" Cinema itself is a new practice of images and signs, whose theory philosophy must produce as conceptual practice.[7]

In the beginning was interference. (This is to say, of course, that there is no such a thing as a beginning inasmuch as interference is literally, that is, etymologically, that which strikes in between: *inter-ferire*; this is to say, hence, that every beginning always is a wound, always takes place in the middle of things.) This last page of *Cinema 2* discloses the open secret of all the preceding pages, namely, that the whole two-volume study had been coursed and innervated by interference—between philosophy as a practice of concepts and cinema as a practice of images and signs—and that it is from within such an interference that it becomes at once possible and necessary to answer the question "what is cinema?" as well as to begin to formulate the question "what is philosophy?" To the extent to which philosophy "must be judged in the light of the other practices with which it interferes," interference here is posited in effect as the criterion for the evaluation of the different modalities of being of specific practices. What transpires even more clearly from this passage than from the last pages of *What Is Philosophy?*, in other words, is not only that different practices become discernible precisely in a zone of indiscernibility from each other, not only that interference is equiprimordial with the practices it cross-fertilizes and the limits it blurs, and not only that the defining task of *What Is Philosophy?* had been tied to the question of interference even before that work had come into being, but also that the question of interference—far from being secondary or incidental—is a definitional question for philosophy. "It is at the level of the interference of many practices that things happen, beings, images, concepts, all the kinds of events" (280). Being interferes. Being is being-in-interference. Being is always and only embedded in practices. Being is the interference agitating the one and only world of praxis, the one and only world there is. And this is another way of saying not only that the question of interference is an inherently ontological question, and not only that to conceive of this question in effect as the *conditio sine qua non* for any question of being is already to understand being as a Heraclitean process of infinite differentiation, that is, to think being as becoming, but also that such an ontological investigation immediately grounds being in politics—a lavalike, groundless ground, if there ever was one. Or, as we read in *A Thousand Plateaus:* "Before being there is politics."[8] It would take an even longer digression within this digression to show exactly how such an investigation is a materialist, immanentist, and nondialectical one—but I will return to these qualifiers. For the moment I simply wish to point out that if I have sketched here the outline of what I would like to call *interferential ontology,* I have done so because any method deserving of that name needs and implies an ontology informing it—if it is not to be reduced to sheer bureaucratic procedure— and because an interferential ontology is precisely the ontology appertaining to the reading and writing practice that is philopoesis, that is, to philopoesis as method. Earlier I described philopoesis as a certain kind of interference between philosophy and literature. But if this book is a philopoetic enterprise, that is so not only because it tries to capture the multifarious interferences between philosophy and literature in Herman Melville, Karl Marx, and Joseph Conrad, but above all because its ultimate claim is that it is such an exquisitely political conception of being as becoming that Melville, Marx, and Conrad sensed—at once with exhilaration and trepidation— and experimented with in their writing practices.

Ineluctable Modalities of Interference

While I have attempted so far to assert the ontological nature of the question of interference, the specific ways in which interference manifests itself remain as yet unexplored. The three types of interference that Deleuze and Guattari hastily outline in the last few pages of *What Is Philosophy?* mark an increasing degree of indiscernibility among different practices and are identified as extrinsic, intrinsic, and nonlocalizable interferences, respectively. The first type occurs when a practice attempts to grasp from within its own domain and according to its own methods the defining features of another practice, as "when a philosopher attempts to create the concept of a sensation...or when an artist creates pure sensations of concepts or function, as we see in the varieties of abstract art or in Klee."[9] Deleuze's *Cinema 1* and *Cinema 2,* for example, articulate largely this type of interference, inasmuch as they produce the concepts appertaining to the images and signs of cinema; similarly, as we will see in chapter 4, Conrad's *The Secret Sharer* produces the affects of a concept to which Michel Foucault gives the name of heterotopia; that is, Conrad's short novel produces the corporeal and sexual states appertaining to a particular conceptualization of autotelic spaces of enclosure that find their most exemplary instantiation at the point of intersection between the space of the ship and the space of the closet.[10]

The second type occurs when a practice slips imperceptibly into the domain of another practice and begins to assume the characteristics, functions, or methods of the latter. Deleuze and Guattari identify certain moments in Friedrich Nietzsche's philosophy and Stéphane Mallarmé's poetry as emblematic of this type of interference, in which we witness a veritable becoming-philosophy of literature and becoming-literature of philosophy; similarly, as we will see in chapter 2, an experimentation with a new poetics of temporality in Melville's *White-Jacket* in effect gives rise to a concept of time that is in many ways a forerunner of Walter Benjamin's *Jetztzeit*—that time of the now whose eminent task it is historical materialism to capture and resurrect.[11]

The third type of interference is at once the most important and the most elusive, and it takes place when a practice confronts its own unthought, namely, that which definitionally "cannot be thought and yet must be thought."[12] This paradox can be grasped only if each practice is understood as constantly being agitated by the pressures of a formless outside radically distinct from any form of exteriority or interiority—that is, from any form at all—and as always sharing a boundary with such a chaotic and troubling outside "more distant than any external world because it is an inside deeper than any internal world."[13] Philosophy, for example, comprises a plane of immanence that for our purposes can be described as an integral element of philosophy functioning as the porous threshold that, on the one hand, separates philosophy from the outside, thereby ensuring that philosophy does not fall into the outside and disintegrate into sheer chaos, and that, on the other hand, allows the inescapable and irrecusable demands of the outside to filter through and make themselves felt on philosophy as a practice.[14] If philosophy is the practice of concepts, the plane of immanence is the nonconceptual space and fluctuating surface that concepts occupy without any remainder, much like waves in the sea. The plane of immanence, in other words, marks an ever-shifting immanent horizon of nonphilosophy that "is perhaps closer to the heart of philosophy than philosophy itself" exactly to the extent to which it is forever bordering on the chaos of the outside:

> Precisely because the plane of immanence is [nonphilosophical] . . . it implies a sort of groping experimentation and its layout resorts to measures that are not very respectable, rational or reasonable. These measures belong to the order of dreams, of pathological processes, esoteric experiences, drunkenness, and excess. We head for the horizon, on the plane of immanence, and we return with bloodshot eyes, yet they are the eyes of the mind.[15]

Such delirium is the condition of possibility of philosophy that philosophers may disregard or disown at their own peril, that is, at the peril of a flight into transcendence. It is from such perturbing and impure transactions with the outside, through the osmotic membrane of the plane of immanence, in fact, that philosophy derives all of its urgencies, imperatives, and necessities: philosophy repeatedly touches the outside with its plane of immanence and repeatedly recoils from it in horror and ecstasy—but this recoiling is the electrifying whiplash that drives thought, this recoiling is the production of concepts. And that is why the plane of immanence "is, at the same time, that which must be thought and that which cannot be thought" by philosophy.[16] "Perhaps this is the supreme act of philosophy: not so much to think *the* plane of immanence as to show that it is there, unthought in every plane."[17] It is philosophy's most arduous task precisely to present this unthinkable, unrepresentable, and generative point of contact with the outside—an outside that increasingly has come to echo the formless and refractory Platonic chasm that bears the name of *Khora*.[18] But what storm rages outside? What is this indomitable chaos from which philosophy, like all other practices, draws its energies? Once again, the answer to this question is better traced through an earlier text, namely, Deleuze's study of Foucault. In discussing Foucault's *The Archaeology of Knowledge* as well as "La pensée du dehors" (his essay on Maurice Blanchot), Deleuze points to the disjunction between forms of knowledge definitionally exterior to each other—namely, seeing and speaking, the visible and the articulable—and emphasizes that we "must distinguish between exteriority and the outside" since the former is the realm of forms while the latter "concerns force."[19] He writes: "forces operate in a different space to that of forms, the space of the Outside, where the relation is precisely a 'non-relation,' the place a 'non-place,' and history an emergence."[20] But it is precisely on the stormy heath of the outside, on the agitating surfaces of this placeless place that forms emerge and square off with each other. If each and every practice is a production of forms exterior to each other, be they constellations of concepts or compounds of affects and percepts, the outside is the play of forces that bursts through and animates exteriority, the outside is the field of forces that separates forms of exteriority without ever allowing them to do without each other and that binds them to each other without ever making them identical. If each and every practice is a modality of thought, thought occurs precisely on the tangent with the outside, that is, at the unthinkable point of contact with the emergent potentialities that disrupt the *status quo* of the history of forms, that take history by surprise and by storm. And that is why "the thought of the outside"—the only thought there is—"is a thought of resistance."[21] The third type of interference occurs when practices become practices of resistance by affirming rather than disavowing their perilous negotiations with the very same forces and with the very same outside:

It is here that concepts, sensations, and functions become undecidable, at the same time as philosophy, art, and science become indiscernible, as if they shared the same shadow that extends itself across their different nature and constantly accompanies them.[22]

If chapter 2 and chapter 4 primarily deal with the first and the second types of interference respectively, chapter 3 constitutes the centerpiece of this whole book precisely to the extent to which it grapples with this third type of interference by reading Melville's *Moby-Dick* and Marx's *Grundrisse* along and through each other. It is on the shadow-line of the outside that *Moby-Dick* and the *Grundrisse* meet. It is in confronting the forces of the outside that these two works become at once irreducibly different from each other and yet the very same — the same, as we shall see, being radically different from the identical. It is in tarrying with the outside that Marx and Melville produce the concept of crisis and the affect of joy (as well as several other concepts such as circulation and limit, and several other affects such as abandon and ease) as indiscernible from each other. In chapter 3, I read *Moby-Dick* and the *Grundrisse* as works that attempt to come to terms with the outside of the history of modernity — that is, with the particular ways in which the outside erupts into history as we still know it — and hence as works of resistance to modernity. If the history of modernity is above all the history of capitalism, any thought of resistance to such a history is above all thought of resistance to capital. To resist capital is to dare to think its outside, and for both Marx and Melville such an outside makes itself felt on history through the explosive corporeal potentiality of labor, through a crisis-ridden and joyous collective body of *potentia*. In the *Grundrisse*, we witness such thought of resistance in Marx's theorization of the use value of labor, namely, use value par excellence understood not as the dialectical counterpart of exchange value but rather as the radical outside of exchange *tout court*. In this sense, exchange value is a form while use value is precisely not a form and not an actual value in any sense but rather the corporeal potentiality that capital repeatedly endeavors to harness, actualize, and formalize in a dialectical process of exchange without ever being able to do so fully. In *Moby-Dick*, the thought of the outside emerges in the widening gap between two sides of an unstable dialectic, in the faults of the dialectic that increasingly fails to bind, on the one hand, the articulation of Ahab's doomed project, and, on the other hand, the corporeal experimentations with the collective body of the crew aboard the *Pequod* that find their most exemplary instance in the experiment of love between Ishmael and Queequeg. Ultimately, in both *Moby-Dick* and the *Grundrisse*, a highly complex conceptual-affective apparatus is constructed and put into motion so as to present the potentiality that constitutes the unspent remainder of dialectical processes, so as to think *potentia* as that indomitable excess of the dialectic that both Marx and Melville see incarnated in the living flesh of labor. I will leave it to the chapter itself to show how such a vitalism on their part is not a humanism. For the moment, let it be said that if Marx and Melville always run the risk of returning to or never taking leave from the very humanism they wished to leave behind, that is so because any political-ontological enterprise always runs this risk, because the risk of a flight into transcendence is the risk that any thought of being as becoming must always run if it is to think at all. To want to jettison such a thought just because it runs such impure and compromising risks is to proverbially throw out the baby with the bath-water—a recurrent situation of thought that nobody has captured better than Theodor Adorno.[23] For it is only within such a thought that it is possible to live alternatives to what he has so aptly called "damaged life."

In outlining these three types of interference, and in identifying some of the parts of this book that correspond to them, I want to show how a philopoetic discourse is one that produces the different zones of indiscernibility between philosophy and literature. If philosophy is a production of concepts and literature is a production of affects, philopoesis is the production of the interferences between philosophy and literature. It is not enough, however, to characterize philopoesis in such a manner: as I stated prematurely at the beginning of this preface, in fact, philopoesis is not merely the practice of such interferences; rather, it is itself also an interference, it is itself the product of a certain interference between philosophy and literature. What other type of interference is this? What other types of interference are there? Earlier, I identified interference qua interference as the very movement of being, that is, as becoming. The problem then is that interference by its very nature will not keep still: interferences move, metamorphose, and proliferate. Over and beyond the extrinsic, intrinsic, and nonlocalizable interferences that Deleuze and Guattari outline at the end of *What Is Philosophy?*, there are at least two more types that need to be articulated here and that I would like to call immanent interference and potential interference, respectively. Let us proceed gradually.

If the three types of interference outlined so far are more strictly ontological—in the sense that they name the different ways in which practices always come into being in interference with one another—one might think of immanent interference as onto-epistemological in nature. To think immanent interference, in other words, is to pose the question: How does a practice come to know itself?

How does a practice think itself as practice? Immanent interference is the fissure at the very heart of a practice that constitutes the latter as split: it takes place as the zone of indiscernibility between two distinct modalities of the same practice, that is, between a practice and its relation to itself as practice. I will turn first to philosophy and then to literature as examples. Having reelaborated the last few pages of *What Is Philosophy?*, we need to return now to the very first page of that work:

> The question *what is philosophy?* can perhaps be posed only late in life, with the arrival of old age and the time for speaking concretely. In fact, the bibliography on the nature of philosophy is very limited. It is a question posed in a moment of quiet restlessness, at midnight, when there is no longer anything to ask. It was asked before; it was always being asked, but too indirectly or obliquely; the question was too artificial, too abstract. Instead of being seized by it, those who asked the question set it out and controlled it in passing. They were not sober enough. There was too much desire to *do* philosophy to wonder what it was, except as a stylistic exercise. That point of nonstyle where one can finally say, "what is it I have been doing all my life?" had not been reached. There are times when old age produces not eternal youth but a sovereign freedom, a pure necessity in which one enjoys a moment of grace between life and death, and in which all the parts of the machine come together to send into the future a feature that cuts across all ages.[24]

Much ought to be said about the sovereign tone of such an introit, which is best captured perhaps with John Donne's words as a valediction forbidding mourning for philosophy. Important as the question of valediction is here, I will suspend it in order to point to the fissure that cuts across and organizes this passage. What we witness here is nothing less than the innervating fissure of philosophy, the immanent interference between two distinct modalities of philosophical practice, namely, "to *do* philosophy" and to pose the question "*what is philosophy?*" This passage at once draws a distinction and maps a zone of indiscernibility between these two modalities. On the one hand, actually to pose the question "*what is philosophy?*" is virtually also "to *do* philosophy"—in the sense that, if "to *do* philosophy" is to produce concepts, to pose the question "*what is philosophy?*" is tantamount to producing the concept of philosophy. On the other hand, that question "was asked before" and "was always being asked" while doing philosophy—even though "too indirectly or obliquely"— in the sense that the question of philosophy was always already there lying dormant in the production of concepts and indeed constituted the virtual underside of each and every concept. To do philosophy and to pose the question of philosophy are alternately the actual and the virtual aspect of each other: one of these two modalities of philosophical practice, in other words, always remains virtual in the other actual one—and the immanent interference constitutive of philosophy is the pendulum of being forever oscillating between these two distinct yet indiscernible modalities. Similarly, literature too comes into being in the immanent interference between practicing literature as the production of affects and posing the question of literature. Contrary to much received wisdom on the matter, to pose the question "what is literature?" is part and parcel of literary practice, and practitioners of literature certainly do not need philosophers, literary theorists, or anybody else to ask that question for them—let alone answer it—and to tell them what it is that they do when doing literature. This is so not only because the question of literature is a question that practitioners of literature always ask either explicitly (see, among the many famous examples, Henry James's critical prefaces to his novels or Edgar Allan Poe's essays on poetry) or implicitly (see all those moments in literary texts when the text suddenly puts itself under scrutiny as a text, such as, for example, those passages in Gustave Flaubert's *Madame Bovary* in which novels are presented as playing a crucial role in Emma's sentimental education, or those moments in *White-Jacket* and *Moby-Dick* in which Melville writes about the very process of writing those novels—moments that I will discuss in chapters 1, 2, and 3). This is so above all because the question of literature is the virtual underside of each and every word of a literary text, and because any literary text—no matter what other questions it is also asking—is always virtually asking the question of literature by drawing attention to the very fact of its own existence, by displaying its own being-there. In this sense, all writing (whether literary, philosophical, or otherwise) is always murmuring with virtual questions, and above all with the question of itself, that is, the question of what it is and of what it is that it is doing there on the page, as well as with the question of what it is that you and I become when reading it in the first place—for it is always the realm of the virtual that puts us and the whole world into question. Such, then, is immanent interference: it is the questioning movement of a practice toward itself; it is the manner in which a practice repeatedly folds back upon itself in the attempt to come to know itself; it is the fold of being by which a practice thinks itself as practice.[25]

   If immanent interference constitutes a practice as the onto-epistemological oscillation between its actual and virtual modalities, potential interference is the zone of indiscernibility between the virtual modalities of different practices. Potential interference reveals that while the actual modality of a practice belongs fully and only to that practice, the virtual modality at once belongs to that practice and yet comes from elsewhere and reaches beyond it, thereby bearing witness to a

realm of potentiality that cuts across practices. Such a potentiality is forever emerging as the silent double questioning of a practice, at once a questioning of itself and
of its practitioners as well as a questioning of all other practices and of all other
practitioners that come to interfere with it—and this double questioning is precisely
a questioning of the history of forms, a questioning of history as *status quo*. It is also
through such a transverse potentiality that practices interfere with one another: it is
in questioning itself that a practice also puts other practices into question; it is in
folding back upon itself that a practice potentially reaches beyond itself into other
unforeseeable realms of praxis. Such are the disquieting questions that travel imperceptibly back and forth from one practice to another—much like those echoes that
reverberate from peak to peak on the alpine heights of Sils Maria, where, suddenly,
"one turned into two— / And Zarathustra walked into my view."[26] Neither fully familiar nor completely alien, neither canny nor uncanny, such echoes are the open
gates of a practice—and on these thresholds one no longer knows who questions
whom, who enters, who exits, and who comes and goes. If immanent interference is
the constitution of a practice as always reverberating with and redoubled by a questioning echo, potential interference is the manner in which practices become indiscernible in such echoes. How does all this come to pass?

       We return thus to philopoesis, understood now as the potential
interference between the virtual questions that philosophy and literature cannot
help but always ask. Philopoesis is the potential interference of philosophy and literature: it is the echo chamber where the question "what is philosophy?" returns to
the same place as the question "what is literature?" and vice versa, where these questions are asked always in the same breath and never in separation from each other,
and where, in questioning each other, philosophy and literature put the whole world
into question. This is why a philopoetic discourse is at once a political and an ontological investigation, that is, an attempt to capture on the threshold between philosophy and literature that chthonic rumbling that never ceases saying, "before being
there is politics." This is why philopoesis has an elective affinity for thinkers who
question the practice that constitutes their point of departure, and who, in doing so,
at once make that practice an unavoidable problem for the other practices with
which it comes to interfere as well as reach beyond that practice so as to experiment
with as yet unthought possibilities of praxis. This is why the encounter with Marx
and Melville became inevitable here and why the former cannot be understood solely
as a philosopher just like the latter cannot be understood solely as a novelist: if chapter 3 articulates the potential interference between Marx and Melville, in fact, that is
so precisely to the extent to which they are both thinkers who found it necessary to

depart one from the practice of philosophy and the other from the practice of literature in order to experiment with whole new worlds of writing and thought, and who, in doing so, embarked on far-reaching investigations into the political nature of being that are virtually indiscernible from each other. It is in this sense that philopoesis attempts to make Marx a problem for literature and Melville a problem for philosophy as well as to make both a problem for any thought of resistance. But I will return to the historical specificity of this encounter in that chapter. In the meantime, another return needs to take place.

Amor Potentiae

In the first section of this preface, I introduced philopoesis as the love of a thing to which I gave the paleonymic name of literature—a name that is a palimpsest on which other inscriptions must now be superimposed. Such a provisional definition of philopoesis as the love of literature can be reformulated in the following manner: philopoesis loves potentiality. Philopoesis is the love of the potentiality that cuts across philosophy and literature—and this is a potentiality that makes itself manifest specifically in writing. Concepts, affects, and all their virtual undersides, after all, come into being as writing—even though they never fully and only belong to it. If philopoesis is the love of poesis—that is, of a making of words—it is above all the love of that which remains unmade in such a making, the love of words as unspent potentials. But how can one love a potentiality? And how can one invoke love at all and still be taken seriously? The love of potentiality is the only love that is worth that name, that is, the only love that might be able to revive a name by now so indentured to the commodity form that it can hardly sound more vital or compelling than the most lethal of clichés—and it goes without saying that that name has known other and more ancient indentures. (And as we will see in chapters 3 and 4, it is indeed possible for love to rise phoenixlike from the ashes of its own clichés, as in both Melville and Conrad love between men is born precisely amidst the ruins of the most reified language of definitionally heterosexual marriage and supposedly heterosexual romance.) If the love of potentiality can deliver that name, it is so because such a love is above all the exercise of a principle that is anathema to any process of reification: love of any thing or any body is mutually exclusive with possession of that thing or that body. And this is also to say that if we love our possessions, it is in spite rather than because of possessing them that we do so and it is not qua possessions but rather as unspent potentials that we can love them at all—for possession stifles all potentiality. Even though this was already Nietzsche's lesson on the question of love, and even though this lesson was well learned and reelaborated in the twentieth century by a wide variety of thinkers, such historical-materialist truisms still await their time.[27]

   The question, however, still stands. How does philopoesis love words as unspent potentials? How does it not turn them into possessions? In order to approach this question, we need to turn to Benjamin's scandalous confessions in "Unpacking My Library"—confessions that owe their relevance here to the fact that they seem to occupy the very end of a conceptual-political spectrum whose opposite end is the love of potentiality. In concluding this essay on "the relationship of a book collector to his possessions," Benjamin writes, "for a collector . . . ownership is the most intimate relationship one can have to objects. Not that they come alive in him; it is he who lives in them."[28] The perhaps perverse suggestion that this "most intimate relationship" afforded by ownership is none other than the love of potentiality is based on the peculiar appearance of the question of life in this passage. Benjamin does not speculate on what kind of life collectors live in their possessions, but I will hazard a hasty hypothesis: if these possessions do not "come alive in him," that is so because they do not need to, as they are already alive with a life of their own; if "it is he who lives in them," he does so differently, that is, he lives in them so as to live a different life. Were possessions to "come alive in him," they would slavishly reflect back to him his most cherished image, namely, the image of the successful buyer who, godlike, bestows life on inert matter through the demiurgic power of money, and whose love of objects, therefore, can only be a narcissistic gesture of self-congratulation. In this case, in other words, possessions would in effect sing his praise and reterritorialize him as bourgeois owner. For Benjamin, however, "it is he who lives in them": rather than reassuring and reconfirming everything that he is, possessions open up a whole other space to which he is irresistibly drawn and in which he may live otherwise—they literally deterritorialize him onto uncharted terrain. The secret life of objects is envisaged here as a space of potentiality in which one may become other than what one already is. The ownership that would uphold objects in such a manner is thus not only "the most intimate relationship one can have to objects" but also the most extimate. Such a relationship is one that Benjamin is not afraid to call love: "[the collector's] existence is tied to . . . a relationship to objects which does not emphasize their functional, utilitarian value—that is, their usefulness—but studies and loves them as the scene, the stage, of their fate."[29] Under the spell of a love that lies beyond the realm of instrumental reason, objects reveal the drama of time: throughout this essay, in fact, "fate" is at once the past history and the future destiny of objects.[30] If instrumental reason inevitably binds objects to the present with the chain of "usefulness," thereby realizing them in the present, this love beyond reason seizes on objects as heterochronic enclosures animated by past and future time, thereby letting the collector and his possessions never be fully realized in the present and letting both live in a state of potentiality. It is in this sense that Benjamin's essay can be regarded as a fitting parable for philopoesis. Philopoesis loves words like Benjamin's collector loves his books. We must attain to a practice of reading words and of writing words not about but alongside other words that is in keeping with Benjamin's insight.

Philopoesis, then, is a love of words that, rather than exhausting, realizing, or foreclosing the shared potentialities through which philosophical and literary texts interfere, keeps such texts *in potentia* and leaves them the same as they are, that is, to their fate. In this sense, philopoesis is driven by a desire to live in the object of love and to become its fate, or, in other words, to rewrite the text and to repeat it word by word just as it is.[31] Such a rewriting does not repeat the text by revealing the secret truth that the text itself somehow refuses to speak, it does not question the text in the hope of extracting a confession, it does not presume to perfect the text by interpreting it: such a rewriting has no questions to ask and no revelations to make, and takes from the text and adds to the text absolutely nothing. Nor does such a rewriting repeat the text according to an oedipal script, by killing it, superseding it, and usurping its former place: such a rewriting unfolds alongside the text rather than in its wake — it accompanies the text in its path and shares its fate much like a friend would. Philopoetic rewriting, in other words, is not a faithful copy of the text but rather the loving simulacrum of the text: while the copy always attempts to be more faithful to the original than the original itself, the simulacrum does not treat the text as an original at all.[32] To have mistaken the simulacrum for the copy was Pierre Menard's valiant and instructive failure. In a sense, the most exemplary articulation of the desire driving all philopoetic enterprise is found in Jorge Luis Borges's story "Pierre Menard, Author of *Don Quixote*," in which Borges famously relates how Pierre Menard wanted not "to compose another *Don Quixote*" but rather to write, in 1930s France, *"the" Don Quixote*.[33] The reason why Pierre Menard ultimately failed is not that his desire was an impossible one but rather that he tried to understand and to fulfill such a desire in the most literal of manners. It turns out that to repeat a text in the same way is not at all to make it identical to itself by producing an exact replica of it. It turns out that in order to rewrite a text one must nonetheless make it different from itself, and that one must do so, however, not for the sake of difference but rather for the sake of sameness. This is what I meant at the beginning of this preface when I articulated the question of philopoesis as the question of whether it is possible to witness the eternal return of ever different ways of loving the very same thing and of loving that thing such as it is. But before expanding on this matter, an excursus is in order.

Sameness, Identity, Difference, and the Ontological Risk of Reading

When the history of twentieth-century humanities — including philosophy and literature — is written, it will certainly be regarded as the century of the question of difference, otherness, alterity, and so on. Urgently necessary and immensely productive as the investigation of this question undoubtedly was for the twentieth century, such an investigation nonetheless occurred at the expense of conceptions of sameness that would be radically distinct from Hegelian identity. If difference is the underside of identity, sameness is what remains unthought in the relation between identity and difference. If the vicissitudes of the binarism of identity and difference have been the main protagonist of the history of modernity, and if the explosion of difference from within the bottomless depths of identity is one of the defining chapters of that history, there is a sameness that has yet to appear on the stage as the nonmodern unthought at the very heart of modernity, as the outside of the history of modernity.[34] (And it is the force of this outside that haunts Marx, Melville, and Conrad — which is why and how they came to be the heroes of this book in the first place). To think such a sameness is the urgent political-ontological task still lying ahead of us: it is necessary now to produce at once the concept and the affect of a sameness that would escape the asphyxiating dialectic of identity and difference, of isomorphism and heterogeneity, a dialectic that is now more than ever enlisted in the service of capital.[35] It should come as no surprise that the thought of such a sameness beyond identity and difference is intimately related to the question of communism: that is the case, at any rate, in *Moby-Dick* and in the *Grundrisse*, where (as we will see in the second section of chapter 3) we can find a veritable archaeology of this intimate relation that anticipates and continues to resonate in the investigations of a series of contemporary thinkers ranging from Louis Althusser to Giorgio Agamben, from Antonio Negri to Leo Bersani. I will return to sameness, communism, and their relations in chapter 3. For the moment, I also want to point out that I am not suggesting that the question of difference ought to be jettisoned *tout court* but rather that we ought to begin from this question rather than repeatedly end with it: the question of difference, in other words, ought to be recast and deployed as a springboard for future investigations into as yet unthought conceptions of sameness. And, in this sense, the works of the two twentieth-century philosophers who above all embarked for unexplored territories of difference, namely, Deleuze and Derrida — an unlikely enough duo for some, but not for me — can be read as the farthest-reaching prolegomena to a thought of sameness. We need to go further.

The problem, in other words, does not lie in the investigation of the question of difference per se but rather in a certain reification of this question that its various investigations have been at times unable to avoid despite all best intentions. One might think of such a reification as the result of an aborted deconstruction of the binarism of identity and difference — and I am using the term "deconstruction" advisedly and in a rather strict sense. One could do worse here than heed Derrida's famous warnings on the last page of "Signature Event Context":

> Very schematically: an opposition of metaphysical concepts (e.g., speech/ writing, presence/absence, etc.) is never the confrontation of two terms, but a hierarchy and the order of a subordination. Deconstruction cannot be restricted or immediately pass to a neutralization: it must, through a double gesture, a double science, a double writing — put into practice a *reversal* of the classical opposition *and* a general *displacement* of the system. It is on that condition alone that deconstruction will provide the means of *intervening* in the field of oppositions it criticizes and that is also a field of nondiscursive forces. . . . Deconstruction does not consist in moving from one concept to another, but in reversing and displacing a conceptual order as well as the nonconceptual order with which it is articulated.[36]

In recent times, we have witnessed much in the way of such a reversal and little in the way of such a displacement: the binarism of identity and difference has been repeatedly reversed and not nearly as often displaced. Moreover, to the extent to which the success of the reversal depends also on the success of the displacement, and hence on the completion of the double gesture of deconstruction, to that extent not even the reversal can be said really to have occurred, so that what we have been asked to join is merely a movement "from one concept to another" — that is, from the presumably repressive prison of identity to the supposedly liberatory shopping mall of difference — that leaves the system itself untouched and that perhaps even corroborates it by giving us all the illusion of having successfully named and done away with it. Such a partial deconstruction, which is no deconstruction at all, has resulted at once in a generalized and enthusiastic embracing of difference as well as in a triumphant recrudescence of identity, while the displacement of that binarism could at least give the lie to a system that is increasingly able to proliferate the different and the heterogeneous precisely to the extent to which it is increasingly able to reinforce the identical and the homogeneous — and the commodity form in all of its polymorphous variations on the identical theme still remains the exemplary product of such a dialectic in our time.[37] The reification in question thus finds its most advanced and deadening form in the symbiotic celebrations, on the one hand, of latter-day metonymic displacements of difference such as diversity and multiculturalism, and, on the other hand, of all their attendant and constitutive forms of identity—and it is precisely in such self-celebratory fanfare that all sorts of practices ranging from bad philosophy to good advertisement become indiscernible. Possibly the worst outcome of this process of reification has been at once a complete foreclosure of some of the most radical potentials in the question of difference as well as a profound misunderstanding regarding the political targets and stakes of such a question in the first place. Such foreclosure and misunderstanding have often taken the form of a hasty and tendentious interpretation of the philosophy of difference as a radical antifoundationalism and as a desertion from the high ranks of ontology to the rank and file of what Michael Hardt and Antonio Negri have aptly named "deontology," while a more plausible and rigorous interpretation would understand it as a momentous effort to rethink the rules by which foundations are laid as well as to rethink the very concept of foundation itself and as an epochal experiment with immanentist alternatives to the ontology of transcendence—efforts and experiments the likes of which periodically agitate the history of philosophy.[38] Besides Deleuze and Derrida, it seems to me that the two contemporary thinkers who, in different ways, have experimented most seriously and most fruitfully with the possibility of an immanent ontology have been Giorgio Agamben and Antonio Negri—and hence I find it hardly coincidental that the latter has written one of the most remarkable books on Marx and that the former has written one of the most remarkable essays on Melville. (In this context, it is important to note that even Derrida—who would probably object more than any other member of this impromptu quadrumvirate to seeing his long-standing and painstaking deconstruction of ontology so unscrupulously characterized as the work of an immanent ontologist *malgré soi*—concludes a recent exchange with Negri, in which he scolds Negri for his ontological passions, by offering "an armistice, based on a compromise," which runs as follows: "perhaps the two of us could, from now on, agree to regard the word 'ontology' as a password, a word arbitrarily established by convention, a shibboleth, which only pretends to mean what the word 'ontology' has always meant. In that case, we could, between us, use a coded language, like Marranos.")[39] What I have been referring to as interferential ontology hopes to push such efforts, experiments, and agitations even further by insisting on the necessity to think foundations as the movement of interference, by striving to think from within being the unthinkable, unrepresentable, and immanent foundations of a being that is always already in interference with itself—and if such an ontological investigation turns out to be a Marranist and paleonymic encryption, so be it. And what I have been referring to as philopoesis aims to bring such an ontology to bear on the practice of reading words and of writing words alongside other words: it hopes to reinsert ontology into the study of texts.

        For at least the past three decades—and one could definitively reach further back in history—the shared problem of so many different practices of reading has been precisely the dismissal and forgetting of ontology as something baneful or altogether irrelevant to the study of texts (and here the cantankerous Heideggerian echo is for better and for worse unavoidable).[40] The problem with the question of being, however, is that no matter how much we may try to dismiss or forget it, it certainly does not forget us—and hence such dismissals and forgettings usually result in our inadvertently falling back into those most ossified forms of ontological transcendence that we had hoped to leave behind once and for all time. In the Anglo-American world, the past three decades have been characterized by a general shift from practices of reading that emphasize the rhetorical-linguistic register of texts to practices of reading that emphasize the historical-political register of texts, that is, from what used to be carelessly called "deconstruction" to the varieties of supposedly more politically robust theoretical-methodological tendencies ranging from new historicism to cultural studies and identity-based modes of reading—while marxist and feminist practices of the text importantly preceded such a shift, but did not survive it without undergoing profound metamorphoses of their own. (I realize how hasty and vulgar such sound-bite historiography is, but I am afraid that I cannot be more diligent within the confines of this preface, whose main thrust and scope, in any case, is not historiographical.) Such a shift also marked a general decentralization of a theoretical-methodological and political-institutional landscape that was formerly dominated by the imposing and central presence of the Yale School and that is far more dispersed and diversified at present: the historical irony of such a decentralization is that it was largely contemporaneous with the Reaganite-Thatcherite demolition of the centralized welfare state and with the correlate shift towards the nearly total deregulation of capital—but I wouldn't dare draw any conclusions from such a historical homology. The point I wish to make here, however, is not immediately historical-political but rather theoretical-methodological: the practices of reading involved in this shift—and I am aware that here we are dealing neither with monolithic schools of thought nor with neatly diachronic developments—have all run the risk of reproducing forms of transcendence precisely by altogether abandoning the question of ontology. Surely, both the rhetorical-linguistic and the historical-political registers of the text can be turned into, and can return to haunt us, as yet another form of transcendence if we cast our lot with them too much or too little — and it is, perhaps, the inevitable predicament of any practice of reading to run the risk of reading for the transcendental determinations of texts. In this respect, neither invocations of the materiality of language nor invocations of the materiality of history constitute an adequate prophylaxis against transcendence if they are not also reverberating with a political-ontological investigation of being as becoming, that is, with a materialism of interferential relations.

Invocations of the materiality of language, on the one hand, have been criticized for reverting to a mechanical, pre-Marxian, and entirely idealist version of materialism that starts from the materiality of words as an a priori without asking either what kind of materiality this is exactly or how such a materiality comes to be at all.[41] To ask these questions would be to investigate how the materiality of any word, any thing, and any body is an equiprimordial effect of the materiality of practices and relations that produce words, things, and bodies; or, to put it differently, these questions should hopefully lead to an investigation of interference understood as ontologically prior to any entity in the sense of a cause immanent in its own effects — and such investigations ought to be, and yet have not always been, the point of honor and the point of departure also of any kind of historical materialism. Invocations of the materiality of history, on the other hand, have been criticized for leaving the metaphysics of representation largely unquestioned and for returning to a decidedly humanist historicism in the name of a radical cultural politics often associated with the slogans of diversity and multiculturalism.[42] The speed alone with which such slogans have also become part and parcel of the official rhetoric of corporate capital should already make any type of materialist reader suspicious. Such a speed, however, does not merely bear witness to the cooptative abilities of flexible capital but also underscores the fact that the representational logic at work in the celebration of identity or in the celebration of difference — the two are identical — is the logic that structures the commodity form at present. The practices of reading involved in such celebrations seem to have settled the account with the metaphysics of representation by advocating self-representation instead as a radical corrective.[43] A corrective to this corrective might begin from Deleuze's statement regarding Foucault as having taught us the indignity of speaking for others, and might continue by suggesting that Deleuze forgot to add that Foucault also tried to teach us the indignity of speaking for ourselves. Put differently: at a time when forms of representation have become the commodity form par excellence—as Guy Debord already understood so well thirty years ago in his prophetic *Society of the Spectacle*—self-representation can be no more than a Pyrrhic victory over the powers of reification and at best a necessary evil. Representational understandings of the historical-political register of texts ultimately miss the point: to the extent to which something is representable and nameable as such, it is already part and parcel of history as status quo, while the forces that disrupt such a status quo are refractory to any form of representation. This is not at all to say that the representational level of texts is not important and should be disregarded. This is to say, rather, that to the extent to which representation does take place, it needs to be understood and studied as the by-product of a forever incomplete and forever renewed process of exploitation of the unrepresentable; in other words, we do need to cut through representation but we cannot stop there. Ultimately, the unrepresentable beckons: for this is the black sun that puts the heliotropical task of any materialist reading to the test. But only an ontological inquiry can lead us in that direction and this is why it is indispensable to ask after being: the cause immanent in its own effects is representable only in the form of its effects but qua cause it is formless and unrepresentable. And it should be clear by now that the kind of ontological investigation I have been formulating is precisely an attempt to grapple with the force of the formless and the unrepresentable, and that philopoesis registers the tectonic tremors with which such an immanent force shakes and cracks the representational fabric of texts. (It is in this spirit that one of the recurrent tropes of this book is the textual presentation of the unrepresentable, and that, for example, in chapters 1, 3, 4, and 5, I return repeatedly to Melville's and Conrad's alternate refusals of and capitulations to the representation of love and sex between men.)

Having said all that, let me proceed with a corollary that might sound like a sudden abjuration of all of the above but is in fact an attempt to clarify something that has been implied here all along. Transcendence is at once the error that must be avoided and the risk that must be run. To avoid the error by not running the risk is no solution: to hope to avoid that error, one must nonetheless run the risk of not avoiding it. No practice of reading is exempt from such a taxing double bind if it is to read at all. Indeed, we cannot hope to avoid transcendence by not asking the question of being because, whatever else we do when reading, we are also asking after the being of texts and after being in texts; we are always already reading texts as forms of being. It is only by owning up to this basic fact of reading and by running the risk of transcendence intrinsic in any ontological inquiry that a truly immanent practice of reading might take place.

The Irreparable Perfection of the Text

We can now return to the scene of the fourth section of this preface and recapitulate the definition of philopoesis as *amor potentiae* in the following manner. That immanent practice of reading that goes by the name of philopoesis rewrites texts by saying: this poem is this poem, this novel is the way it is, this text is perfect. To say that the text is perfect in the sense that it is the way it is (a) does not mean to say that the text is perfect in the sense that it is what it is, since the text is precisely not a what but rather a way, and (b) does mean to say that the text is no more and no less than its way, that it takes place nowhere else other than in its modality of being, that the text can only be in interference. Even though such tautological propositions aspire to the brilliance of Gertrude Stein, they may nonetheless come closer to the idiocy of Jacques de la Palisse—and yet philopoesis does not stop but rather only begins here. Philopoesis does not advocate the status quo. To say that the text is perfect is to say that it cannot be perfected or chastised, but it is not to say that it should not be read and rewritten. The text is perfect and yet it summons us, it demands to be read, it asks to be rewritten. But if the text is really perfect, why does it never cease to haunt? What perfection is this that stares at us urgently from the page with its questioning, irrefragable, written gaze? In the beginning was perfection—but that was only the beginning. It turns out that the perfection of the text is the beginning of reading: where perfection ends, there reading begins—that is, at the limit. It turns out that even perfection and only perfection has its limits. Philopoesis perfects the text by not perfecting it, that is, by singing the glory of its limits. Let me illustrate this by way of a parable.

There is a Chassidic parable regarding the messianic kingdom that ricochets from Gershom Scholem to Walter Benjamin to Ernst Bloch to Giorgio Agamben: it maintains that in that redeemed world "everything will be as it is now, just a little different." In *The Coming Community*, Agamben comments on this parable:

> And yet it is precisely this tiny displacement, this "everything will be as it is now, just a little different," that is difficult to explain. This cannot refer simply to real circumstances, in the sense that the nose of the blessed one will become a little shorter, or that the cup on the table will be displaced exactly one-half centimeter, or that the dog outside will stop barking. The tiny displacement does not refer to the state of things, but to their sense and their limits. It does not take place in things, but at their periphery, in the space of ease between every thing and itself. This means that even though perfection does not imply a real mutation, it does not simply involve an eternal state of things, an incurable "so be it." On the contrary, the parable introduces a pos-

sibility there where everything is perfect, an "otherwise" where everything is finished forever, and precisely this is its irreducible aporia. But how is it possible that things be "otherwise" once everything is definitively accomplished?

The theory developed by Saint Thomas in his short treatise on halos is instructive in this regard. The beatitude of the chosen, he argues, includes all the goods that are necessary for the perfect workings of human nature, and therefore nothing essential can be added. There is, however, something that can be added in surplus (*superaddi*), an "accidental reward that is added to the essential," that is not necessary for beatitude and does not alter it substantially, but that simply makes it more resplendent (*clarior*).

The halo is this supplement added to perfection — something like a quivering of that which is perfect, a slight glowing of its limits....

> One can think of the halo, in this sense, as a zone in which possibility and reality, potentiality and actuality, become indiscernible. The being that has reached its end, that has consumed all of its possibilities, thus receives as a gift a supplemental possibility.... This imperceptible trembling of the finite that makes its limits indeterminate, that allows it to blend and to make itself whatever, is the tiny displacement that every thing must accomplish in the messianic world. Its beatitude is that of a potentiality that comes only after the act, of matter that does not remain beneath the form, but surrounds it with a halo.[44]

The exegetical perversity of invoking Scholastic theology in order to elucidate Jewish messianism, or, indeed, of finding a Chassidic parable parasitically infiltrated in the writings of Saint Thomas, is very instructive. And "instructive" is precisely the word upon which this whole passage hinges: it is literally the hinge linking the Jewish and the Christian narratives of the passage. "The theory developed by Saint Thomas in his short treatise on halos is instructive in this regard." This deceivingly unassuming sentence introduces the treatise by Aquinas and justifies what otherwise might seem an arbitrary juxtaposition with the claim that this text is "instructive": there is something "that is difficult to explain" in the parable and the treatise presumably will instruct us in that regard, will shed light on it. But what kind of light is this? It is the glowing light of halos. It goes without saying that, as Montaigne reminds us, "[w]e need to interpret interpretations more than to interpret things," and hence that what is offered here as an explanation of the parable, namely, the treatise, needs itself to be explained in the first place, which is precisely what Agamben does in the last paragraph of this passage.[45] More importantly, the explanation of the explanation reveals that the parable and the treatise are saying the same thing and in fact explain each other to the extent to which they are the same text. That which is supposed to be instructive is so precisely because it turns out to be the same as that which is supposed to be instructed. The juxtaposition of the two is instructive not only in the sense that it shows how they both clarify each other, and not only in the etymological sense that one literally builds upon the other — *in-struere* — but also in the sense that it provides the best exemplification of that tiny messianic displacement and of that halo: the treatise and the parable are each the tiny displacement of the other, each the halo that sheds light on the other and makes the other more resplendent, each the supplemental potentiality of the other. This is a potentiality that begins to shine after all is said and done and that comes into being in the wake of the act. It is the spatio-temporal limit of perfection.

One could find no better illustration of philopoesis than in both the form and the content of this passage, which become indiscernible from each other in the same way in which the parable and the treatise become indiscernible here, which is the same way in which the halo is indiscernible from the person of the blessed and in which the redeemed world is indiscernible from our unredeemed world, which is the same way in which Marx and Melville become indiscernible in chapter 3 and in which Melville and Conrad become indiscernible in chapter 1 — each the virtual simulacrum of the other actual one, and vice versa. The parable and the treatise are each the philopoetic rewriting of the other: both are perfect — that is, perfectly finished and perfectly finite — and yet both delimit each other's perfection and materialize each other's limit as a potentiality. Philopoesis surrounds the perfect text with a halo as a superfluous gift of potentiality. A rewriting that does not do that always ends up making the text either identical to itself or different from itself, that is, it forecloses its potentialities and mortifies it. But a rewriting that makes the text shine with such a halo actively leaves the text the same as it is; it highlights its potentialities and exalts it.

Before proceeding with a crucial corollary to Agamben's passage, let me offer a counterexample. If I single out Wai-chee Dimock's *Empire for Liberty: Melville and the Poetics of Individualism* as exemplary of those practices of reading at work in contemporary literary-cultural criticism that could not be any further removed from philopoesis, it is because it is in many ways an admirable and important scholarly work — certainly one of the best among the myriad of remarkable critical accounts of Melville that have appeared in the past two decades — and because I have learned much from it.[46] In my book, I return several times to this work and to some of its specific claims — especially regarding *Moby-Dick* and *White-Jacket* — with which I sometimes agree and sometimes disagree. Important as such agreements and disagreements are, however, they are also quite beside the point here. I am bringing this work to the fore here, in fact, not to support or impugn any of its arguments but rather to draw attention to the practice of reading that informs its critical project. This project is precisely that, namely, critical — and the object of the critique is first named in the subtitle and begins to be articulated in the following passage:

> In any case, as the exemplar of a "poetics of individualism," Melville emerges, in my account, as something of a representative author, a man who speaks for and with his contemporaries, speaking for them and with them, most of all, when he imagines himself to be above them, apart from them, opposed to them. . . . Given such premise, my goal obviously is not to uncover a timeless meaning in Melville's writings, but to multiply within them some measure of their density of reference: to examine them, in short, not in their didactic relation to the twentieth century, but in their dialogic relation to the nineteenth.[47]

Undoubtedly, such an account of Melville is largely accurate and such a refusal of the myth of the timeless genius working in besieged isolation from the world is entirely salutary. And yet this argument is also held hostage by an insidious dialectic: in rejecting the myth of the timeless genius, Dimock wishes to present us instead with a timely Melville, that is, with a "representative author" *malgré soi* in "dialogic relation" with his time. I don't doubt the fact that there is an only too timely Melville to be read in his works. But why read it? This is not a rhetorical question. What I want to put into question, in other words, is the desire at work in such a reading: it seems to me that this is to a large degree a reactive desire. In reacting against the myth of the timeless genius, we run the risk of rushing to the opposite pole of this binary relation — namely, the timely writer — without, however, having necessarily stepped outside of the conceptual, epistemological, and political perimeter of the binarism. This is, in other words, a reversal without a displacement. In this way, the logic at work in that binarism is at the very least left untouched and perhaps even reinforced — thereby reconfirming the fact that the pole we meant to critique and to abandon, namely, the myth of the timeless genius, still holds us very much in its oedipal sway as something against which we are made to feel we must at all costs react. It may be hard to admit and yet all the more necessary to realize that it is the binarism as a whole that is imbued with the humanist idealism of individualism rather than only one of its poles, and that hence it is its entire governing logic that should constitute the target of a radical critique.[48] Moreover, Melville himself was very familiar with both poles of this binarism, and hence, in taking him to task by merely reversing them, we are in effect taking him at his own word and fighting him on his own turf. Commenting on her account of Melville as a timely writer in spite of all his vociferous protestations to the contrary, Dimock writes:

> Melville, of course, would not be happy with such an account. Authorship, for him, is almost exclusively an exercise in freedom, an attempt to proclaim the self's sovereignty over and against the world's. To be worthy of its name, authorship must wrest free of what he calls the world's "dull common places"; it must indulge in its own "play of freedom and invention"; it must bring forth "those deep far-away things in [itself]." Indeed, the art of authorship, as he describes it in a celebrated moment in "Hawthorne and His Mosses," is none other than the art of escape: "in this world of lies, Truth is forced to fly like a scared white doe in the woodlands." Truth here assumes its characteristic Melvillean pose as the persecuted object.[49]

Leaving aside for the moment the vexing problem of such lines of flight from the world — which to my mind constitute not only the worst but also the best of Melville's political impulses — I want to point out that Melville remains the spectral superego overseeing and determining this scene of reading and that this is arguably a flattering role that he would have been quite pleased to know he was to play in the future. "Melville, of course, would not be happy with such an account." And indeed this account may well have been Melville's worst nightmare — but it was precisely his own nightmare, and hence through such an account it is still his nightmare that we inhabit and reenact in spite of ourselves. This reading, in other words, had been not only dreamt and foreseen in advance but also preinscribed and preprogrammed by Melville in his writings as the negation of all that he believed his writings to be. The filicidal father seems to have spawned whole generations of patricidal children — but who wants to be a member of this happy family? Such then is the double bind: if we uphold the myth of the timeless genius, we make Melville's text identical to itself, that is, we merely pay homage to and ventriloquize what he already thought and wanted to hear us repeat *in aeternum*; if we counter that myth with the figure of the timely writer, we make Melville's text different from itself by negation, that is, we find that his text is exactly what he thought it was not — and either way we buttress Melville's authorial wishful thinking and we foreclose the unthought.

What remains unthought in the oedipal and dialectical strictures of the binary relation between the timeless and the timely is the untimely — and the Nietzschean echo here is at once inevitable and intentional. The untimely is the temporal register of that which is nonsynchronous with its own history, of that which at once is in history and yet can never completely belong to it: the untimely is the un-historical time of potentiality.[50] Philopoesis endeavors to rewrite Melville as an untimely thinker and to highlight the potentiality of his text: an untimely Melville is neither the timeless genius abstracted from his world nor the timely writer fully belonging to his world but rather a thinker who is at once fully in his as well as in our world and yet nonsynchronous with both. And it is precisely from what Nietzsche called the unhistorical vapors of the untimely that those potentialities emerge that disrupt the status quo of history and of the world—which is why philopoesis loves potentiality. In this respect, if Dimock aims to examine "Melville's writings . . . not in their didactic relation to the twentieth century, but in their dialogic relation to the nineteenth," my book hopes to shed light on the disruptive relations that Melville's text has to both centuries: I have hoped to present us with a Melville that fully belonged to neither of these centuries and that repeatedly opposed his and our modernity, with a nonmodern Melville that produced a thought of resistance to modernity as we still know it, that is, to the modernity of capital. Enough. Dimock's text too, after all, is perfect: it is the way it is, it does what it does, and it does many good things—and if I have not been willing and able to surround it with a halo of potentiality here, that is a flaw in my practice of reading and not in hers. I hope I have done so later in this book, when I highlight and discuss some of its most valuable lessons.

Having extracted the untimely from Dimock, I want now to present it as a gift to Agamben, so as to end this preface. There is an imperceptible untimeliness, an understated nonsynchronicity in Agamben's passage quoted above. Both the Jewish and the Christian narratives of that passage dream of the morning after redemption, anticipate a redeemed world: in that world, everything will be just as it is now, and yet displaced by a resplendent halo of potentiality. The fact alone that such proleptic leaps into a redeemed world are envisioned in our unredeemed one should already alert us to a peculiar synchronicity of the nonsynchronous.[51] There is, in other words, yet another and implicit leap in Agamben's passage: this is not only a proleptic leap but also an immanent one—this is a leap of faith in immanence. What remains implicit there is that the redeemed world and the unredeemed world are paradoxically coterminous and coextensive, synchronous and nonsynchronous: they are incompossible.[52] Our world—the only world there is—includes both those worlds *hic et nunc:* the here and now of our world is riven and generated by the infinite and infinitesimal abyss between the two, by the zone of indiscernibility between the two—in short, by the potential interference of the two. The transcendence of identity and difference ignores precisely such an interferential abyss and declares the world to be unredeemed—while sameness lives in that abyss. The world we inhabit is the same as it is: as soon as that predicate folds back upon itself in a torque of interference, a displacement occurs, a halo shines, an untimeliness emerges, an affect comes forth, a concept is born, an inside deeper than any form of interiority and an outside more distant than any form of exteriority makes itself felt on the history of forms, a formless, unthinkable, unrepresentable *potentia* agitates the world—and we begin to think. Such a conception of the sameness of the world admits neither reactionary-nostalgic longings for the forever-deferred return to the world before the fall nor utopian-messianic longings for the forever-deferred event of the world after redemption: irreparably perfect and perfectly finite, the world after the fall is also the world after redemption. At once postredemptive and postlapsarian, the Marranos of philopoesis announce that the redeemed world and the redeemed word are already here and that their interference begets thoughts of resistance. All that is left to do now is to read them.

The Sea of Modernity; or, The Nineteenth-Century Sea Narrative as Heterotopian Discourse: An Introduction

This could have occurred nowhere but in England, where men and sea interpenetrate, so to speak—the sea entering into the life of most men, and the men knowing something or everything about the sea, in the way of amusement, of travel, or of bread-winning.

Joseph Conrad, *Youth*

The Argument

THE NINETEENTH-CENTURY SEA NARRATIVE constituted a crucial laboratory for that crisis that goes by the name of modernity. *Modernity at Sea* aims to produce the concept of this laboratory, in which a new historical era was problematized, that is, was turned into a problem for thought. This laboratory concerned itself with two distinct and indiscernible sets of experiments: the nineteenth-century sea narrative proliferated, on the one hand, forms of representation of modernity and, on the other hand, conceptual-affective and conceptual-perspective constellations that resisted both modernity and representation. The nineteenth-century sea narrative came into being as the interference between these two experiments, as the spatio-temporal matrix of the crisis of modernity.

Temporal Axes

RHG?. The modernity in question is above all the modernity of capital. The crisis in question is above all the crisis that cannot be acknowledged from the standpoint of capital, even as capital continuously endeavors to harness its force and exploit it. The mere fact that the critical accounts of the question of modernity constitute one of the most voluminous chapters in the history of nineteenth-century and twentieth-century thought is already an index of the difficulty that the question of crisis poses for thought. While I will refer to several of these different accounts throughout this book, I would like to begin here by introducing what has been one of the most important ones for my present project. In the following passage from *Labor of Dionysus*, Michael Hardt and Antonio Negri attempt to come to terms with modernity as crisis and anticipate many of the arguments they continue to elaborate in *Empire:*

> Modernity is not the linearity of Western rationalism; it is not the destiny of Western reason. . . . [M]odernity is the history of a permanent and permanently incomplete revolution: a contradictory development in which there has always been an alternative between the development of free productive forces and the domination of capitalist relations of production. From the Renaissance revolution onward, modernity has been characterized by an extraordinary liberation of productive forces and emancipation from every transcendental destination of human activity, to which was opposed the forces of expropriation, private wealth, and instrumental rationality. Translated into Machiavellian terms, the universality of "virtue" was opposed by the despotic particularity of "fortune." Translated instead into Spinozian terms, the *potentia* (power) of the multitude is opposed by the *potestas* (Power) of the State. Modern rationalism is not a continuity that can be described on the basis of scientific progress; it is a contradictory product of different rationalities, one insistent on the productive capacity of human cooperation in the construction of history and life itself, and the other insistent instead on the order of power and the organization of a social division of labor directed toward the reproduction of this power. Modernity should be defined within this struggle, this logical and ethical struggle over human destiny itself, over freedom and subjugation. In its most mature form, this is defined as a dialectic, or really as a systematic form of the instrumental utilization of freedom for the construction of structures of the organization of power that are continually more inclusive and efficient. The dialectic is the imposition of the transcendental supersession on the continuous conflict that the collective constituent power of the masses, of associative labor, imposes on constituted power. The dialectic understands modernity as a state of crisis that it sublimates transcendentally.[1]

For the moment, I will refer to such a dialectic in shorthand as the dialectic of capital and labor. As *Labor of Dionysus* endeavors to show—and as Negri already maintained in *Marx beyond Marx* as well as in "Twenty Theses on Marx: Interpretation of the Class Situation Today"—the gap between the two sides of this dialectic proceeds to widen throughout modernity and especially during the second half of the twentieth century, thereby giving rise at once to the increasing autonomy of the "collective constituent power...of associative labor" as well as to the renewed attempts of "constituted power" to contain, control, and exploit such an autonomy so as to make it productive for capital. I will return to these matters and to these texts specifically in chapter 3. Here, I will put forth a provisional formulation: *Modernity at Sea* reads the nineteenth-century sea narrative not only as an engagement with the multifarious manifestations of this dialectic but also as an anticipation of the breakdown of this dialectic in our time and as a foreshadowing of that historical-materialist affirmation of crisis that Walter Benjamin (in a luminous moment that reverberates throughout Hardt and Negri's version of modernity) calls *wirklich Ausnahmezustand*—a real state of emergency.[2]

In the nineteenth century, the dialectic of capital and labor was thoroughly reconfigured by the emergence of the distinctly new mode of production of industrial capitalism from the cocoon of the older mode of production of mercantile capitalism. Such an emergence was crucially enabled (among the other factors) by the overdetermined encounter between, on the one hand, an accumulation of wealth that was no longer bound specifically to mercantile and landed interests but was now purely independent capital, and, on the other hand, the creation of the wage and the attendant industrial organization of the first labor force in history that was no longer bound to serfdom—although, this latter development will be further qualified presently. Modern capitalism, in other words, emerged at the point of intersection between free labor and free capital.[3] Even though the transition from mercantile capitalism to industrial capitalism was a protracted and laborious process, one could single out the abolition of the Corn Laws in Great Britain in 1846 as the nominal marker that sanctioned a series of political-economical transformations dating at least from the last two decades of the eighteenth century. By putting an end to agricultural protectionism, the abolition of the Corn Laws dealt a decisive blow to the already beleaguered landed aristocracy and codified a governmental policy of near complete *laissez faire* that opened the doors to a period of unparalleled industrial growth and capitalist expansion worldwide from the middle of the 1840s to the middle of the 1850s, which is, significantly, the period during which several of the works examined in this book were written.[4] (Importantly, this sudden economic growth fueled at least four decades of rampant railway construction in Great Britain, continental Europe, and the United States, that was largely financed by British capital and that was to have an enormous impact especially on the political economy and on the national self-definition of the United States). The relation between these two modes of production, however, should not be understood as one of complete supersession but rather as one of strategic incorporation and selective elimination: the older practices of mercantile capitalism were variously allowed to survive as long as and up until the moment they could still be profitably employed within the newer, more dynamic, more flexible, and more complex assemblage of industrial capitalism.

This is, in any case, an old story—and here I am more interested in locating the political economy of the sea in this transition. During the emergence and consolidation of industrial capitalism, the sea became an increasingly turbulent, contradictory, and contested terrain. The world of the sea (namely, the fishing industry, sea travel, sea warfare, and, above all, sea commerce) had occupied the central position in the functioning of mercantile capitalism—a mode of production preeminently structured around exchange. The world of the sea under industrial capitalism—which was fundamentally centered around production rather than exchange—became, if anything, more important than ever for the functioning of an international political economy that was now for the first time coming into being as a tendentially global capitalist system. From the second half of the nineteenth century until the First World War, in fact, the importance of the world of the sea for industrial capitalism reached such proportions that the growth of the world merchant marine alone—which was largely dominated by Great Britain and the United States—could be safely taken as an indicator of the expansion of the global economy, thereby testifying to the crucial role played by the political economy of the sea also during the period of monopoly capitalism and high imperialism.[5] And yet, there were high prices to be paid for such continued importance, as specific sea practices soon became obsolete within a rapidly industrializing environment: for example, during the second half of the nineteenth century, the whaling industry virtually disappeared (a development that was foreseen with vivid keenness by Melville in *Moby-Dick* and that will be discussed in chapter 3) and sail shipping quickly declined due to the full implementation of steam power, which had not yet been profitable to use for ships up until that moment (and the disappearance of sail ships is a poignant refrain in Conrad as well as in the late Melville). Furthermore, precisely due to the higher degree of complexity of industrial capitalism, the world of the sea was no longer the only clearly central site in the mode of production like it had been under mercantile capitalism—the factory more than the ship constituted such a site during the period in question here—and, indeed, industrial capitalism cannot be said to have had a single central reproductive site. This relative displacement within a more decentralized system irremediably transformed the internal consistency of the world of the sea precisely according to a logic of selective elimination and strategic incorporation.

It is also important to note that from the standpoint of the constitution and organization of labor, the political economy of the sea under mercantile capitalism had anticipated two definitional and enabling features of industrial capitalism. First, sea labor had been primarily wage labor for at least three centuries before the generalized industrial implementation of the wage at the turn of the eighteenth and nineteenth centuries: the wage was invented at sea. During mercantilism, seamen were positioned in relatively new relations to capital as well as to each other: as the first free and fully waged laborers who found work and worked among a large number of similarly situated men, they were the prototype of the associative and organized labor that was to become dominant under industrial capitalism.[6] Second, alongside the very different labor force created by slavery in the New World, sea labor had been the first fully international, multiethnic, multilingual, and also increasingly multiracial labor force since at least the Renaissance, thereby anticipating developments in the constitution of labor that became increasingly relevant for industrial capitalism from the middle of the nineteenth century onward and that have become more relevant than ever in our present.[7] (Significantly, with respect to both these features, the whaling industry was at once the most archaic and the most advanced of sea practices: on the one hand, whaling traditionally had been an exception to the wage system as it harked back to the ancient and medieval tradition of shares; on the other hand, whaling had by far the most international, multiethnic, multilingual, and especially multiracial labor force of any other sea practice.) I will return to both these features several times during the course of this book. Here, I want to point out that the world of the sea constituted a set of practices that could still be and, indeed, still needed to be variously utilized and transformed by industrial capitalism. In this sense, the persistence of mercantile capitalism as one of the cogs in the machinic assemblage of industrial capitalism was largely articulated through the continued and contradictory importance of the world of the sea: these two modes of production met and interpenetrated at sea.

The relation between the sea narrative and the wider field of literary production in the nineteenth century, and the relation between the political economy of the sea and industrial capitalism in that century are structurally homologous. Or, rather, what is homologous here is the set of immanent contradictions constitutive of such relations: if the world of the sea, whose practices and centrality to political economy was largely inherited from an older mode of production, suddenly became an indispensable element in the emergence and consolidation of a new mode of production and of its imperialist enterprises, the nineteenth-century sea narrative was an archaic form of representation that suddenly began to perform according to new narrative structures and to fulfill new cultural imperatives, and that, hence, played a direct role in the production of the emergent cultures of modernity. (To the extent to which such an homology can be said to hold any validity, however, it does so exclusively for the nineteenth century: while the world of the sea remains to this day an important part of the global political economy, the sea narrative was not able to maintain its centrality in culture during the twentieth century. As the ship turned into a space-ship, many of the functions that formerly were the prerogative and the domain of the sea narrative were inherited and metamorphosed by science fiction.)

Such is the predicament of the nineteenth-century sea narrative: what narrative structures can one use when one has a new tale to tell, when one is announcing the invisible and powerful presence of something radically new that does not yet actually exist anywhere, that cannot yet be named or represented as such, and that indeed may reveal itself to be unnameable and unrepresentable? The answer to this question is that one always makes do with what one has; and, perhaps, the more familiar the narrative structures one speaks through, the more likely one is to get across the radically new — disguised as the old and coexisting with the old. The nineteenth-century sea narrative was the site where visions of the new — much like the creatures in *Alien* — came to incubate within old forms of representation so as to then explode those forms from the interior; only that — unlike the creatures in *Alien* — these premonitions of the new did not come from a space of exteriority but rather emerged from an unrepresentable, unthinkable, untimely, formless, inside-outside space.

The contradictory character that both the sea narrative and the political economy of the sea acquired in the nineteenth century signals a problematic that Ernst Bloch identified in 1932 as the synchronicity of the nonsynchronous — the potentially explosive spatial coexistence in the same time period of historically heterogeneous practices and social formations — that he believed would present conceptual challenges to dialectical thought.[8] This problematic is nothing new: one can safely suppose that any period witnesses the overlapping of historically heterogeneous elements and that history itself is always uncompromisingly heterogeneous. That crisis that goes by the name of modernity, though, is marked by a transformed relation vis-à-vis the problematic of the synchronicity of the nonsynchronous. With modernity, such a problematic became precisely that, a problematic; it was turned into a problem for thought and it was produced at once as the condition of possibility, the organizing principle, and the definitional feature of modernity. Or, in Edouard Glissant's words: "*On the notion of modernity*. It is a vexed question. Is not every era 'modern' in relation to the preceding one? It seems that at least one of the components of 'our' modernity is the spread of the awareness we have of it. The awareness of our awareness (the double, the second degree) is our source of strength and our torment."[9] It is through the articulation of such a dialectic—of its doubleness, strength, and torment—that the nineteenth-century sea narrative produced the matrix of the crisis of modernity.

Taxonomical and Interferential Axes

The beginning of the nineteenth century marked a sudden and unprecedented proliferation of sea narratives in both Great Britain and the United States that continued practically uninterrupted for the rest of the century.[10] Although *Modernity at Sea* focuses almost exclusively on novels and short stories, I have organized this whole project around the category of "sea narrative"—as opposed to, say, "sea fiction" or "sea novel"—precisely because the object of investigation here is not a genre but rather certain narrative forms of representation that coalesced in the nineteenth century around the problematic of the sea and that are found by no means only in the novel and short story (see, for instance, poems such as Samuel Taylor Coleridge's "The Rime of the Ancient Mariner," Arthur Rimbaud's "Le Bateau ivre," Herman Melville's "John Marr and Other Sailors" as well as representations of the ship and of sea life in the paintings of William Turner, John Singleton Copley, George Caleb Bingham, Caspar David Friedrich, Théodore Géricault, Winslow Homer, Edouard Manet, and others—all of which can be said to have narrative components).[11] In order to arrive at a certain selection in what is a vast and multiform field even within literary production alone, I have produced a taxonomy of sea narratives, which will be used only as a temporary and heuristic device and not as something to be further developed. The sea narratives of this period were articulated largely according to three distinct forms of narrative structure: the exotic picaresque, the *Bildungsroman* of the sea, and the modernist sea narrative. One could think of these three forms by way of Raymond Williams's categories of residual, dominant, and emergent formations, respectively—but these too are categories that I will dissolve presently. These forms need to be understood as structural and synchronic rather than generic and diachronic: all three were not only present throughout the whole century but also often operate in various combinations within the same text. Indeed, many works

were produced precisely by the tensions and contradictions arising from the interference of these three distinct forms.

The form of the exotic picaresque had its direct antecedents in
eighteenth-century works such as Daniel Defoe's *Captain Singleton*, Tobias Smollet's
Roderick Random, and Captain Cook's journals and travelogues, but also had earlier
sources in Richard Hakluyt's *Voyages and Discoveries of the English Nation*, Luis de
Camoëns's *Lusiads*, and other late Renaissance sea and travel narratives. Clearly this
is an ancient form that can easily be traced back to narrative structures already present in Homer's *Odyssey* or even in Herodotus. The exotic picaresque, however, was
resuscitated in the nineteenth century under the guise of the sea adventure novel. In
this kind of narrative, a sense of awe and wonder—both a fascination and a repulsion—for faraway, exotic, colonized, or colonizable lands and peoples is grafted onto
an episodic narrative structure that runs from one adventure to the next. Nineteenth-
century sea narratives in which this form is centrally operative would include works
such as Frederick Marryat's *Peter Simple*, James Fenimore Cooper's *The Red Rover*,
Herman Melville's *Typee* and *Omoo*, Robert Louis Stevenson's *Kidnapped*, as well as,
in some respects, Edgar Allan Poe's *The Narrative of Arthur Gordon Pym of Nantucket*
and Charles Kingsley's historical novel *Westward Ho!*

The form that I refer to as the *Bildungsroman* of the sea often
functioned in inextricable relations with the exotic picaresque. In the sea narratives
that are written predominantly in this form, a young and innocent hero is followed
through several trials and tribulations until his rite of passage into adulthood has been
successfully performed. Often a voyage through exotic or unfamiliar landscapes provided the hero with the tests of endurance indispensable for such a rite, and that is
why the form of the *Bildungsroman* of the sea frequently needed the exotic picaresque
in order to unfold, even if only to reject it. Such interferences between these two
forms are best exemplified by works such as Melville's *Redburn*, Marryat's *Peter Simple*,
Kingsley's *Westward Ho!*, Rudyard Kipling's *Captains Courageous*, and Richard Henry
Dana's *Two Years before the Mast*.

The exotic picaresque and the *Bildungsroman* of the sea are understood as residual and dominant, respectively. They functioned more or less unprob-
lematically, in fact, as sea variants of two already consolidated and popular narrative
forms: the premodern form of the picaresque and the form of the *Bildungsroman*, the
latter of which was eminently symbolic of modernity and which—though already
well-established in the eighteenth century—reached its apogee with the nineteenth
century.[12] It is precisely because both the exotic picaresque and the *Bildungsroman* of

the sea operated within preexisting narrative traditions, however, that they usually constituted the sea voyage and the world of the ship as no more than convenient backdrops and colorful literary devices—their true interests lay elsewhere. In the residual form, the central focus always remains on what is to be found beyond the sea, that is, on the adventures of discovery and contact that the exotic landscapes and natives on the other side of the ocean and at the end of the voyage are bound to offer. In the dominant mode, the focus is carefully kept on the personal development of a young hero against the backdrop of the life of a collectivity, that is, the world of the ship. Due to the subordinate and marginal roles played by the world of the ship and by the sea voyage in them, these first two narrative forms are at once the indispensable conditions of possibility for this book and yet of secondary importance within it—my true interest lies elsewhere.

    It is the emergent and entirely new form of the modernist sea narrative that constitutes the main focus of *Modernity at Sea*. The arguments outlined in the previous section of this introduction regarding the nineteenth-century sea narrative understood as a laboratory for the conceptualization of modernity, in fact, are valid mostly for this third form. The modernist sea narrative is structured precisely around what remains marginal and underdeveloped in the exotic picaresque and in the *Bildungsroman* of the sea, namely, the sea voyage and the world of the ship, which in this third narrative form are instead constructed as autarchic and self-enclosed narrative units and detailed as multifaceted and tension-ridden universes (and in this sense, even this radically new narrative form can be said to have had antecedents in more overtly allegorical works such as Sebastian Brant's *The Ship of Fools*, whose influence on post-Renaissance European literatures was considerable.) Under the spell of this emergent form, life aboard the ship becomes the central *telos* of the narrative and is revealed in all of its explosive economies of power—its disciplinary mechanisms, racial conflicts, nationalist chauvinisms, gendered roles, sexual desires and homophobic anxieties, brutal law enforcements, antinomies of work and leisure, hierarchical subdivisions and distributions of space, the whole multiform dialectic of capital and labor, and the forever impending possibility of mutiny. Even though this third narrative form can also interfere at times with the previous two forms, such an interference differs considerably from the one occurring between the other two alone: while the interference between the exotic picaresque and the *Bildungsroman* of the sea often unfolds as a seamless symbiosis, the interference between the modernist sea narrative and the other two forms gives rise to irreconcilable tensions that crack the representational fabric of the text. In some sea narratives, for example, an effort to produce a *Bildungsroman* flounders, fails, and is redirected by this third form when the personal development of the young hero is hollowed out from the inside so as to be turned into the narrative device and the interstitial aperture through which the collective life aboard the ship can be brought to the fore and into focus: Melville's *Redburn, White-Jacket,* and *Moby-Dick,* as well as Conrad's *The Nigger of the "Narcissus"* are all produced by such representational dynamics.

It is precisely such a preoccupation with the world of the ship and the sea voyage conceived as autonomous enclosures that turns the emergent form of the modernist sea narrative into a representation-producing machine for the turbulent transitions from mercantile capitalism to industrial capitalism, into a laboratory for the conceptualization of a world system that was increasingly arduous to visualize, the more multiple, interconnected, and global it became. Many of the works that are predominantly structured around this kind of sea narrative, in fact, will be shown at once to record the old and to envision the new: they are constituted by the contradictory desires to register the rapidly disappearing past of preindustrial and mercantile practices and to produce the most advanced forms of representation of the emergent future and its new social relations. Such a dialectic of historical representation made it necessary to test the structural limits of narrative itself by corroding many of its conventional strictures and to question the very viability of narrative as a form of representation. One need only consider, for example, the representational somersaults that works such as *Moby-Dick* and *The Nigger of the "Narcissus"* perform in order to maintain against all odds some sort of coherence and stability in the narrative voice—and such somersaults are often an index of deeply divided historical and class allegiance. In this and other respects, the modernist sea narrative anticipates in the nineteenth century many of the later tendencies toward narrative fragmentation and dissolution of early twentieth-century modernism.

An alternative way of conceptualizing these three forms of sea narratives, in fact, would relate them to the vexed question of literary periodization. If the modernist sea narrative constitutes some form of protomodernism, there is also a sense in which the exotic picaresque and the *Bildungsroman* of the sea can be considered the sea narrative's version of romanticism and of realism, respectively. Such schematic parallels, however, would have to be further problematized. For example, since the modernist sea narrative is also firmly rooted in some form of realism (see especially Melville), it could be said to have captured precisely those marginal and protomodernist elements in realism that were going to become indispensable for the formation of the various literary aesthetics of modernism. Furthermore, it is

TEMPORAL AXES - Basically, old ORDER Brady dies, clings to it in form while energy of new place that dissolves old form.

10,1

also the case that the realism of the *Bildungsroman* of the sea owes a great deal to romantic idealism, often by way of the figure of the Byronic hero (see, for example, Cooper's *The Red Rover*). In any case, the point here has been to show how these three distinct forms of the sea narrative interfere with one another and include zones of indiscernibility that make it impossible to categorize them in strict terms of either genre or literary periodization. Ultimately, out of all such interferences, it is the sea voyage and the world of the ship that emerge as the new and peculiarly modern problematic to which now we need to turn.

Spatial Axes

If the nineteenth-century sea narrative produced the matrix of the crisis of modernity, such a matrix in these narratives was materialized above all as the space of the ship. What needs to be conceptualized here is the historically contradictory constitution and function of this most ancient and most modern of spaces. And I want to proceed by elaborating further an attempt to conceptualize such a space that was begun by Michel Foucault. In 1967, Foucault delivered a programmatic lecture titled "Of Other Spaces" in which he developed a concept that he had first introduced a year earlier in *The Order of Things: An Archaeology of the Human Sciences* and that he abandoned thereafter: heterotopia.[13] It is important to note, however, that what Foucault abandoned was actually the term rather than the concept per se, whose echoes can be heard throughout his later works and especially in *Discipline and Punish: The Birth of the Prison*. For the moment, it is more crucial, first, to point out that, while in *The Order of Things* heterotopia is more of a linguistic concept, in "Of Other Spaces" heterotopia is a specifically spatial concept, and second, that in both these texts heterotopia emerges as an answer and an alternative to utopia. In the lecture, we read that utopias — unlike heterotopias — are forever condemned to remain "sites with no real place."[14] Heterotopias are instead characterized as follows:

Contradiction of ship

SPATIAL ALTERNATIVE to UTOPIA.

> There are also, probably in every culture, in every civilization, real places — places that do exist and that are formed in the very founding of society — which are something like counter-sites, a kind of effectively enacted utopia in which the real sites, all the other real sites that can be found within the culture, are simultaneously represented, contested, and inverted. Places of this kind are outside of all places, even though it may be possible to indicate their location in reality. Because these places are absolutely different from all the sites that they reflect and speak about, I shall call them, by way of contrast to utopias, heterotopias.[15]

1/ REAL SITE

2/ REPRESENT ALL the SPACES of A CULTURE — A TOTALITY, BUT THAT simultaneously CONTESTS the illusion of totality.

To represent, to contest, to invert: one can think of heterotopia as a particular form of spatial representation, as a special type of space from which one can make new and different sense of all other spaces—and one can immediately see why such a concept has enjoyed much fortune and sparked much debate in the critical discourses of geography for the last two decades.[16] And yet, such an account of this form of representation needs to be crucially qualified: if to represent and to invert can both be thought of as practices of representation, exactly what kind of practice is to contest? Undoubtedly, one can use representations as much as anything else in order to contest; however, is to contest itself a practice of representation, is contestation a form of representation? My provisional answer to this question is a negative one. I am suggesting, in other words, that heterotopias as forms of spatial representation comprise a discursive and a nondiscursive aspect, a mimetic and a nonmimetic aspect, or, even, a representational and a nonrepresentational aspect. Heterotopias come into being as the interference between representational and nonrepresentational practices: this is that onto-epistemological modality of interference that I referred to in the preface as immanent interference and that occurs when a practice folds back upon itself and questions both itself and all other practices. It is precisely this movement toward itself occasioned by the presence of a nonrepresentational element that enables heterotopias to question and contest all other spaces. As we will see shortly, this is of crucial importance for the conceptualization of the space of the ship—but let us continue for the moment with Foucault's lecture.

Foucault proceeds to sketch five regulatory principles of heterotopias: (1) heterotopias are "a constant of every human group"—even though there is "no absolutely universal form" of heterotopia—and they can all be subdivided into "heterotopias of crisis" and "heterotopias of deviation"; (2) "a society, as its history unfolds, can make an existing heterotopia function in a very different fashion"; (3) a "heterotopia is capable of juxtaposing in a single real place several spaces, several sites that are in themselves incompatible"; (4) heterotopias "are most often linked to slices in time—which is to say that they open onto what might be termed, for the sake of symmetry, heterochronies"; and (5) heterotopias "always presuppose a system of opening and closing that both isolates them and makes them penetrable."[17] After having discussed—among other such spaces—gardens, brothels, and colonies as heterotopias, Foucault concludes his lecture:

> Brothels and colonies are two extreme types of heterotopia, and if we think, after all, that the boat is a floating piece of space, a place without a place, that exists by itself, that is closed in on itself and at the same time is given

over to the infinity of the sea and that, from port to port, from tack to tack, from brothel to brothel, it goes as far as the colonies in search of the most precious treasures they conceal in their gardens, you will understand why the boat has not only been for our civilization, from the sixteenth century until the present, the great instrument of economic development..., but has been simultaneously the greatest reserve of the imagination. The ship is the heterotopia *par excellence.* In civilizations without boats, dreams dry up, espionage takes the place of adventure, and the police take the place of pirates.[18]

The ship is the heterotopia par excellence: *Modernity at Sea* takes its historical and conceptual cue from such an outlandish claim. This is a claim that the modernist sea narrative understood well and made into its representational credo. The modernist sea narrative in effect had already advanced such a claim — which Foucault formulates here in specifically conceptual terms — by constructing and putting into motion an elaborate and at once representational, conceptual-affective, and conceptual-perspective apparatus so as to produce the space of the ship as its central focus and telos. The preeminent exigency of the modernist sea narrative was to secure the heterotopia of the ship in textual form: this turns out to have been a double exigency, a double fold, a double questioning. If the modernist sea narrative cathexes all of its representational energies on that space which is in effect the condition of possibility of the sea narrative per se, then the modernist sea narrative constitutes that modern event in the history of an ancient form of representation when this form folds back upon itself so as to problematize and to question — in short, to think — its foundation. Under astounding historical pressures, the sea narrative in the nineteenth century folds back upon itself in the attempt to think its floating and itinerant foundation that had gone unnoticed for so long, thereby putting itself into question as a form of representation — and the modernist sea narrative is the name of this fold. If one is to follow Foucault's account, however, the heterotopia of the ship constitutes not only the foundation of the sea narrative but also the heterotopia par excellence of Western civilization since at least the Renaissance: with the modernist sea narrative, in other words, the sea narrative questions not only its own foundation but also reaches beyond itself to question the foundation of a world that for several centuries had been run in all sorts of ways by ships — in questioning itself, it questions the whole world. By focusing on the modernist sea narrative, *Modernity at Sea* aims to capture the double event of that immanent interference by which an ancient form of representation came to confront in the nineteenth century at once its own unthought as well as the unthought of the world to which it belonged.

It is hardly a coincidence, then, that Deleuze exemplifies Foucault's understanding of the unthought as the inside-outside of thought in the following way:

> The outside is not a fixed limit but a moving matter animated by peristaltic movements, folds and foldings that together make up an inside: they are not something other than the outside, but precisely the inside *of* the outside. *The Order of Things* developed this theme: if thought comes from outside, and remains attached to the outside, how come the outside does not flood into the inside, as the element that thought does not and cannot think of? The unthought is therefore not external to thought but lies at its very heart, as that impossibility of thinking which doubles or hollows out the outside.…
>
> The inside as an operation of the outside: in all his work Foucault seems haunted by this theme of an inside which is merely the fold of the outside, as if the ship were a folding of the sea. On the subject of the Renaissance madman who is put to sea in his boat, Foucault wrote:
>
>> He is put in the interior of the exterior, and inversely…a prisoner in the midst of what is the freest, the openest of routes: bound fast at the infinite crossroads. He is the Passenger *par excellence:* that is the prisoner of the passage.
>
> Thought has no other being than this madman himself. As Blanchot says of Foucault: "He encloses the outside, that is, constitutes it in an interiority of expectation or exception."[19]

By invoking the ship and by seizing on this illuminating passage from Foucault's *Madness and Civilization* in order to explain the relations between thought and unthought, inside and outside, Deleuze unwittingly draws attention also to the ways in which the ship is indissolubly bound to these questions: it is precisely because the space of the ship comes into being as the interference between thought and unthought and between inside and outside that Deleuze can make recourse to this space so as to exemplify those questions. Such inextricable relations are reconfirmed by Deleuze also in a remarkable section in *Cinema 2* in which the cinematic image of the ship is identified as a type of crystal-image—that is, as a certain interferential circuit and zone of indiscernibility between the virtual and the actual—and in which, unsurprisingly, he singles out not a filmmaker but rather Melville as having "fixed this structure for all time."[20] The point for us here is to understand the modernist sea narrative as an attempt to produce the space of the ship as the thought of an unthinkable unthought, as the inside of an unrepresentable outside, as the fold-effect through which the immanent cause of the outside comes into being as a form in the world and comes to disrupt the history of forms—in short, as an attempt to produce the space of the ship as heterotopia. If this heterotopia became so inevitable for the modernist sea narrative, that is precisely because it was in such a space that the force of the outside made itself felt most violently in the nineteenth century. And if one thinks at the tangent with the outside, and if one can only think there by repeatedly confronting the force of the outside, the modernist sea narrative is *la pensée du dehors* of the nineteenth century: it is the thought of the outside.

We can now return to that passage in *The Order of Things* in which Foucault first introduces the concept of heterotopia. In the wake of a discussion of Borges's impossible Chinese encyclopedia, Foucault writes:

> *Utopias* afford consolation: although they have no real locality there is nevertheless a fantastic, untroubled region in which they are able to unfold; they open up cities with vast avenues, superbly planted gardens, countries where life is easy, even though the road to them is chimerical. *Heterotopias* are disturbing, probably because they secretly undermine language, because they make it impossible to name this *and* that, because they shatter or tangle common names, because they destroy "syntax" in advance, and not only the syntax with which we construct sentences but also the less apparent syntax which causes words and things (next to and also opposite one another) to "hold together." This is why utopias permit fables and discourse: they run with the very grain of language and are part of the fundamental dimension of the *fabula*; heterotopias (such as those to be found so often in Borges) dessicate speech, stop words in their tracks, contest the very possibility of grammar at its source; they dissolve our myths and sterilize the lyricism of our sentences.[21]

Heterotopias are forms of representation that disturb and undermine representation: within such aphasic spaces, the fabular language of representation falters, flounders, encounters the unspeakable, faces the unrepresentable. And if this is the case for heterotopias in general, the following chapters will show how much more this is the case for that heterotopia par excellence that is the space of the ship: much like the stammering protagonist of Melville's *Billy Budd* or the whispering protagonists of Conrad's *The Secret Sharer*, language aboard the ship suddenly and continuously breaks down or gradually and literally fades into silence. To follow the wandering movement and exhausting sweep of Melville's and Conrad's sentences is to witness language itself stretching toward regions it cannot reach to look for something it cannot have. The heterotopia of the ship produces a language that gravitates toward the nether world of the nonrepresentational and that operates at the edge of its own dissolution. Indeed, one of the main goals of this book is to trace the grammatical, syntactical, and tropological contortions of language as it confronts the nonrepresentational forces that the space of the ship repeatedly summons from the storm of the outside and that hold the ship in its sway.

The historical question of why the force of the outside elected the heterotopia of the ship as one of its most befitting and preferred forms in the nineteenth century, however, has yet to be directly addressed. It will take the rest of this book to try to answer this crucial question. Here, I will only suggest that the tectonic tremors of the outside are felt more clearly and intensely in those spaces that have become most problematic in a certain historical period, and that the heterotopia of the ship was such a space in the nineteenth century. Put differently: if the modernist sea narrative found its privileged space of investigation in that heterotopia that was the foundation and condition of possibility of the sea narrative, it was so primarily because in the nineteenth century that foundation was in the process of being destabilized, dismantled, and effaced. While Foucault claims that the ship has been at once "the great instrument of economic development," "the greatest reserve of the imagination," and "the heterotopia *par excellence*" since the Renaissance, I am concerned with the end of the history of the ship as the heterotopia par excellence of Western civilization. If we follow the second regulatory principle of heterotopias that Foucault outlined in "Of Other Spaces," we can understand the modernist sea narrative as part and parcel of a radical transformation in the function of the heterotopia of the ship. And if we also consider Foucault's third and fourth principles, we will see the modernist sea narrative as a monumental effort to rewrite the space of the ship according to the logic of the synchronicity of the nonsynchronous and as a last-ditch attempt to hold together in that same space increasingly irreconcilable historicities. While recording possibly the most glorious moment in the history of the ship, the modernist sea narrative is also thoroughly imbued with premonitions of a future in which this heterotopia would be inevitably relegated to the quaint and dusty shelves of cultural marginalia. Read, for example, the opening words of *Billy Budd:* "In the time before steamships..." It is from such longing words that in 1888—at a time when sail ships were being forced rapidly into desuetude—an old Melville begins to narrate a story taking place in 1797. And an acute nostalgia for the fading world of sail ships mixed with resentment as well as awe in the face of an increasingly techno-industrial future—of which the steamship was seen as the direful herald—is also omnipresent in Conrad and especially in *The Nigger of the "Nar-*

cissus" and *The End of the Tether.* But we shall soon embark on these and other passages. For the moment it suffices to say that the modernist sea narrative freezes the world of the ship into a fleeting image flashing onto the screen of history for one last moment before its disappearance: it captures simultaneously the apogee and the end of the ship as the heterotopia par excellence of Western civilization.

O N E

Of Monads and Fragments; or,
Heterotopologies of the Ship

...the natural changes of the monads must result from an *internal principle*, since no external cause could influence their interior.... Consequently, there must be in the [monad] a plurality of affections and relations, though it has no parts.

G. W. von Leibniz, *Monadology*

WHAT MICHEL FOUCAULT CALLS HETEROTOPIA, Joseph Conrad calls *Narcissus*. What we learned about Foucault's heterotopias in the introduction will provide here the heuristic backdrop for an investigation of spatial discourses in Conrad, and what we hope to learn about Conrad in the end will also transfigure Foucault's conceptual apparatus. Conrad and Foucault are placed here side by side as two thinkers and writers who shared in the history of certain conceptualizations of space that will ultimately be revealed to have emerged in interference with modern representations of the space of empire.

> The passage had begun, and the ship, a fragment detached from the earth, went on lonely and swift like a small planet. Round her the abysses of sky and sea met in an unattainable frontier. A great circular solitude moved with her, ever changing and ever the same, always monotonous and always imposing. Now and then another wandering white speck, burdened with life,

appeared far off—disappeared; intent on its own destiny. The sun looked upon her all day, and every morning rose with a burning, round stare of undying curiosity. She had her future; she was alive with the lives of those beings who trod her decks; like that earth which had given her up to the sea, she had an intolerable load of regrets and hopes. On her lived timid truth and audacious lies; and, like the earth, she was unconscious, fair to see—and condemned by men to an ignoble fate. The august loneliness of her path lent dignity to the sordid inspiration of her pilgrimage. She drove foaming to the southward, as if guided by the courage of a high endeavour. The smiling greatness of the sea dwarfed the extent of time. The days raced after one another, brilliant and quick like the flashes of a lighthouse, and the nights, eventful and short, resembled fleeting dreams.[1]

The passage begins, and the *Narcissus* is born by parthenogenesis. This passage—both the sea voyage and this quotation describing its beginning—rests on a paradox that is most fully articulated in the opening sentence, in which the *Narcissus* is at one and the same time "a fragment detached from the earth" and "a small planet." If the image of the "fragment" implies a lack and a broken incompleteness, the "small planet" suggests at least a self-enclosed totality, if not necessarily a complete whole. To be a ship is to oscillate ceaselessly between a completely autarchic and monadic condition, and a permanently incomplete and fragmentary one. And yet, even the notion of an oscillation, of an uninterrupted movement between two polar opposites, is mystifying as it presupposes the existence of completely separate and incompatible spaces that the representation of the ship alternately occupies, from and to which the ship travels. These spaces are certainly incompatible, but they are never separate: they are distinct and indiscernible—and the ship needs to occupy them simultaneously. The ship never travels, never goes anywhere, never even moves. If there is an oscillation here between a continuously becoming-monad and a ceaselessly becoming-fragment, it is akin to the disconcerting spatial simultaneity of holograms. The space of the ship can be adequately represented only as two absolutely separate and opposite, and yet always jarringly juxtaposed and superimposed sites. What is most uncanny about this passage, after all, is that in it these two opposite conditions are articulated within the same syntactical unit, are constructed in symbiotic position vis-à-vis one another. It is precisely such a paradoxical symbiosis of fragment and monad, such an interference of identity and difference with respect to the social field, that generates the space of the ship.

The *Narcissus*—far from being constituted as just any kind of self-enclosed totality—is a fragment of exactly the same nature as the body from which it detached itself, that is, "the earth." Indeed, beyond parthenogenesis, one witnesses here a process of cloning: throughout the passage, the *Narcissus*—a satellite thrown into orbit around its larger planet—is revealed to be more and more "like the earth." The relation between "the ship" and "the earth" rests on a conception of "the earth" not as a geographical or an astronomical entity, but rather as a socio-political one: "the ship" is "like the earth" by virtue of "the lives of those beings who trod her decks" and of "the intolerable load" of their "regrets and hopes." The *Narcissus* is constructed as the miniature replica of the web of social relations that constitutes "the earth." Indeed, if the social field is by definition that which one is always en-closed in and part of, or, in other words, if the social field is precisely that which cannot be either complete or self-enclosed, it is also the case that to think such a field, to conceptualize it both as a space and as a set of relations, one must imagine it at a distance and to represent it as a self-enclosed entity one can stand out of and look into. The condition of possibility for the construction of the ship as a floating representation of the social field, therefore, is a set of characteristics that the ship and the social field cannot share: the ship can be turned into a representation of such a field precisely because it is unlike the field in that it provides a separate, closely cir-cumscribed, and self-encapsulated space. From the very beginning of the passage, the *Narcissus* is immersed into the irredeemable, encircling solitude of the monad: "the ship" "went on lonely and swift like a small planet. Round her the abysses of sky and sea met in an unattainable frontier. A great circular solitude moved with her," and "her path" had an "august loneliness." Far from being attenuated, the solitude through which the ship travels is made even more extreme by the occasional and un-approachable presence of "another wandering white speck," which, "intent on its own destiny," "appeared far off—disappeared." This solitude is the condition of the monadic experience: it is what in effect turns the ship into an isolated and self-enclosed space, thereby making it particularly available for and conducive to repre-sentations of the social field. But *how* is the *Narcissus* alone?

Its intensity and inescapability notwithstanding, this "august loneliness," this "great circular solitude" is inhabited by many eyes. The ship is, "like the earth," "unconscious, fair to see." But what could it mean to think of the ship—or, for that matter, of "the earth"—in terms of consciousness? Of what could the ship be "unconscious"? If the ship is "unconscious," who then is conscious and of what? And who is doing the seeing if the ship is "fair to see"? The rest of the pas-sage seems to suggest that what the ship is "unconscious" of is precisely the fact that it is being seen, watched, and that whoever is conscious is also the one doing the seeing, the one watching it. Far from being alone, the *Narcissus* is being scrutinized unawares by day and by night: "The sun looked upon her all day, and every morning rose with a burning, round stare of undying curiosity." Furthermore, just preceding the paragraph describing the beginning of the ship's passage, one reads:

> A multitude of stars coming out into the clear night peopled the emptiness of the sky. They glittered, as if alive above the sea; they surrounded the running ship on all sides; more intense than the eyes of a staring crowd, and as inscrutable as the souls of men.[2]

Paradoxically, this solitude needs to be inhabited by a multitude of internal audiences if it is to be a solitude at all. That solitude which is the condition of possibility for the conceptualization of the social as a circumscribed and self-enclosed space needs at the same time to produce and to be occupied by the "consciousness" which is going "to see" this space, that is, by the narrative perspectives that can apprehend such a space as circumscribed and self-enclosed. Whether in the single and "round stare" of the sun or in the "inscrutable" and multiple one of the stars, here one sees the positing of a narrative eye that stands above and outside the social field in order to watch and to represent it—since it certainly cannot visualize itself, as it is "unconscious, fair to see." The implication running through all this passage, in fact, is that the social field cannot think itself, that it cannot represent itself to itself, and that it needs to be represented by a narrator standing outside of it. Indeed, if the ship and the earth are versions of the social field, then the sun and the stars are the constructions of a metasocial narrative standpoint: they are the articulation of a narrative desire to escape the social altogether.

The point is that this solitude, crowded and alive with eyes, is itself the narrative consciousness: at one and the same time, it produces the social field and, in producing it, escapes it. The ship, "like the earth," is "condemned by men to an ignoble fate. The august loneliness of her path lent dignity to the sordid inspiration of her pilgrimage. She drove foaming to the southward, as if guided by the courage of a high endeavour." In the whole of *The Nigger of the "Narcissus"*, this is the only reference to the nature of the mission of this commercial ship bound to London from the port of Bombay. One does not suppose that such a ship would arrive empty-handed to the shores of England, and yet not even *en passant* is one informed about this whole aspect of the passage: "pilgrimage" and "high endeavour" is as far as this novel gets in representing the world of commerce and colonial enterprise because of which the ship travels.

The image of "pilgrimage," however, does go far in representing the colonial networks if one considers how such an image returns later to haunt the pages of *Heart of Darkness*, in which "pilgrimage" is associated with some of the most brutal chapters of imperialist exploitation. The ruthless speculators of the trading posts deep within the jungle of the Belgian Congo, in fact, are referred to over and over again precisely as "pilgrims," and Marlow refers to his own journey upstream as "a weary pilgrimage among hints for nightmares."[3] The point here is that the commercial and colonial "pilgrimage" of the *Narcissus* can admittedly be described, and even denounced, as having a "sordid inspiration" while still being conceived of as having the "dignity" and "courage" of a "high endeavour." This is the same double movement of simultaneous denunciation and idealization that returns in *Heart of Darkness* when Marlow reflects that:

> The conquest of the earth, which mostly means the taking it away from those who have a different complexion or slightly flatter noses than ourselves, is not a pretty thing when you look into it too much. What redeems it is the idea only. An idea at the back of it; not a sentimental pretence but an idea; and an unselfish belief in the idea.[4]

The price these narratives seem only too willing to pay for the representation of imperialism as an "ignoble" and "sordid" business is that they ultimately also find ways to redeem it. If for Marlow what can still redeem and justify the "conquest of the earth," all else notwithstanding, is "an idea" and "an unselfish belief in the idea," for the *Narcissus* what "lent dignity to the sordid inspiration of her pilgrimage" is the "august loneliness of her path." That same solitude which surrounds and encircles the ship from all sides with its multitude of eyes, and which enables its construction as a representation of the social field, also provides here legitimacy and redemption to its participation in imperialism. But why should solitude mediate the relation between the ship and the empire? What elective affinities link such a conception of solitude to the project of empire?

The whole paragraph describing the beginning of the passage ends in "fleeting dreams." The word "dreams," used here to describe the "eventful and short" "nights," occupies a highly charged narrative field. In Conrad, dreams and the act of dreaming register an impossibility of representation: they are invoked when something cannot be narrated because it escapes language altogether, or, rather, when the presence of the inexpressible needs somehow to be represented. In this sense, "dreams" cannot be but "fleeting." Much like the image of "pilgrimage," "dreams" return to haunt the narrative of *Heart of Darkness* when, in one of the most memorable moments in all of Conrad's works, Marlow runs into the impossibility of explaining exactly why Kurtz, whom he had never yet even seen, could have had so much power over him. Finally Marlow confesses:

> He was just a word for me. I did not see the man in the name any more than you do. Do you see him? Do you see the story? Do you see anything? It seems to me I am trying to tell you a dream—making a vain attempt, because no relation of a dream can convey the dream-sensation, that commingling of absurdity, surprise, and bewilderment in a tremor of struggling revolt, that notion of being captured by the incredible which is of the very essence of dreams.... No, it is impossible; it is impossible to convey the life-sensation of any given epoch of one's existence—that which makes its truth, its meaning—its subtle and penetrating essence. It is impossible. We live, as we dream—alone...[5]

What is most striking about this epiphanic interruption is the eagerness and rapidity with which Marlow generalizes his sudden discovery. Marlow realizes that to narrate his ineluctable attraction toward that undecidable space and energy which he has chosen to call Kurtz is like trying "to convey" a dream, that is, "it is impossible"; but, as soon as he has associated Kurtz with dreams, that is, with an impossibility of representation, he precipitously extends such an impossibility to the whole of "life" itself, and finally completes the triangulation by pronouncing the foregone conclusion that: "We live, as we dream—alone." Thus, the image of dreams and the act of dreaming, along with the narrative and representational dilemmas they register, ultimately elicit a notion of being "alone," a conception of solitude, which here can no longer be defined merely as the absence of others but rather as an inexpressibility and incommunicability of experience in the presence of others: one is "alone" when confronted by the unrepresentable, and, since "life" itself cannot be represented, then one is always "alone." Having invested the whole of "life," such a conception of solitude becomes itself the very condition of existence, which comes here to be redefined as a permanent condition of unrepresentability.

We have come full circle back to the monad, whose coming-into-being as a self-enclosed and necessarily solitary entity is here revealed to be dependent on an insurmountable representational impasse. Marlow's representation of his own (and everybody else's) existential condition, and the construction of the ship as a self-enclosed and solitary entity are both homologous versions of the monad. If Marlow finally admits he cannot represent the "truth," "meaning," and "subtle and penetrating essence" of his own existence, because ultimately we all "live as we dream—alone," similarly, the ship's "august loneliness" prevents any representation of her "pilgrimage" and of the latter's "ignoble" and "sordid inspiration" by enshrouding both in the "dignity" and "courage of a high endeavour." When Marlow leaps from stating that he cannot convey his feelings for Kurtz to declaring that each and every "epoch of one's existence" cannot be narrated, he dehistoricizes such a condition of unrepresentability into a universal. The leap that displaces Kurtz with "life" (the unrepresentable objects/narratives) and Marlow with an all-encompassing "we" (the unrepresenting subjects/narrators) functions as a process of radical dehistoricization of a condition of unrepresentability that is instead specifically linked to Kurtz and Marlow and to the imperialist projects they both, albeit differently, participate in and represent. *The unrepresentable is the empire.* Or, rather, the "ignoble" and "sordid" realities of imperialism are represented in Marlow's construction of a universal, narrative, and representational impasse, and in its resulting conception of "life" as a monadic and solitary condition. In this sense, the project of empire becomes a question of form: it is embedded in the textual fabric as a narrative form and as a system of representational criteria, codes, barrages, and apertures. Indeed, all these concerns are already implicit in that "august loneliness," whose etymological energies alone propel the *Narcissus* onto its imperial "pilgrimage," invest it with imperial "dignity," shroud it with the aura of empire. But if the multifarious and intertwined constructions of the ship as a representation of the social field are enabled by the open sea, by the spectacle of the immense openness of its solitude, what then becomes of all these empire-echoing images, tropes, narrative registers, and forms of representation when the *Narcissus* finally arrives in port?

A few pages before the closing of the novel, the *Narcissus* finally "enters the chops of the Channel,"[6] and the description of the shores of England emerges as an exact counterpart of the paragraph relating the beginning of the ship's passage:

> At night the headlands retreated, the bays advanced into one unbroken line of gloom. The lights of the earth mingled with the lights of heaven; and above the tossing lanterns of a trawling fleet a great lighthouse shone steadily, like an enormous riding light burning above a vessel of fabulous dimensions. Below its steady glow, the coast, stretching away straight and black, resembled the high side of an indestructible craft riding motionless upon the immortal and unresting sea. The dark land lay alone in the midst of waters, like a mighty ship bestarred with vigilant lights—a ship carrying the burden of millions of lives—a ship freighted with dross and with jewels, with gold and with steel. She towered up immense and strong, guarding priceless

traditions and untold suffering, sheltering glorious memories and base for-
getfulness, ignoble virtues and splendid transgressions. A great ship! For
ages had the ocean battered in vain her enduring sides; she was there when
the world was vaster and darker, when the sea was great and mysterious, and
ready to surrender the prize of fame to audacious men. A ship mother of
fleets and nations! The great flagship of the race; stronger than the storms!
and anchored in the open sea.[7]

Amidst an apotheosis of imperial flourishes and fanfares, England is reborn from the
waters as the ship to end all ships—the "great flagship of the race." If the *Narcissus*
at the beginning of its passage is described as "like the earth," England itself is here
constructed as a ship. Once England is sighted from the approaching vessel, the only
language available for the narrative to describe this island in all of its imperial mag-
nificence and grandeur is the language of the space of a ship. This indicates the degree to which such a space had all along been shaped and established as a representation of what in this narrative constitutes England: imperial fleets, colonial voyages
and expeditions, precious freights, or, in other words, a nation and a race of con-
querors. In this latter metamorphosis, however, the image of the ship is at least in
one crucial respect more like a ship than it has ever been before, as it is only now
that one learns that ships are indeed freighted—"with dross and with jewels, with
gold and with steel"—while the *Narcissus*, as far as this narrative is concerned, does
not seem to have any cargo. The fact that the ship of England is also described as
being immersed in solitude—"[t]he dark land lay alone in the midst of waters, like a
mighty ship bestarred with vigilant lights"—attests once again to the vital role that
solitude plays in constituting the space of the ship in this novel. This return of the
concept of solitude also reconfirms its crucial relations with the matters of empire
and of representation: England is here described as being "alone in the midst of waters" as if the other side of the Channel had not been there, as if that continental
Europe with which England was in incessant competition for the allocation and dis-
tribution of colonial territories did not exist. Solitude signals once again an impossibility of representation: given that it was precisely this competition between England and continental Europe that marked the moment of high imperialism, what
cannot be represented here is again the political-economical web of imperialist relations. England is described as being "alone in the midst of waters" not because it is
so but because it would like to be.

So much had the ship been carved into an image of empire that the
seat of the empire itself needs now to be shaped in the form of a ship. In some ways,
this passage is also a retelling of the myth of Narcissus: the *Narcissus* discovers, reflected

over the waters of the Channel in the shape of England, an image of itself far grander and more glorious than any of the previous ones in the novel. In the name of this ship, the myth of the self-cathecting ego turns into the fantasy of a self-cathecting social totality, or, rather, into the fantasy of the social representing itself to itself as a totality, seeing itself there where it is not, reflected as a totality. Unlike with the myth of Narcissus, however, here it is impossible to determine who mirrors whom over "the immortal and unresting" waters of the sea: the *Narcissus* and England are involved in a process of mutual reflection, reproduction, and repetition. Clearly, I am not interested in the question of who is the original and who is the copy, of where and when this potentially infinite process of representation and reversal begins or ends. The point is that, no matter who is mirroring whom, the space of the ship is here reconfirmed and established no longer simply as a vessel and carrier of representations of the social field but also as an epistemological apparatus that proliferates images of the social; the ship is the factory that produces and reproduces representations of the social. England is a ship that "was there when the world was vaster and darker, when the sea was great and mysterious, and ready to surrender the prize of fame to audacious men." Ultimately, the space of the ship produces versions of a world which, under the spell of imperialism, has become increasingly smaller and devoid of mysteries precisely as the web of its political-economic relations has become increasingly more complex, intertwined, and unrepresentable.

Let us now briefly return to Foucault via Conrad—or, at least, sketch the directions that such a return might take. The ship is the heterotopia of heterotopia. These readings of the construction of the ship in Conrad's *The Nigger of the "Narcissus"* derive from and elaborate Foucault's assertion that the "ship is the heterotopia *par excellence*." The prime condition of possibility and organizing principle of these readings is that paradox of representation which constitutes the a priori of any articulation whatever of the space of the ship: the paradox of a simultaneous becoming-monad and becoming-fragment. And this is also the paradox that structures the space and concept of heterotopia. The ship is in actuality what all other heterotopias are only virtually, what the space of heterotopia strives to be: "a place without a place, that exists by itself and at the same time is given over to" an "infinity."[8] If heterotopias are special sites, places that are outside of all places but that also bear a special relation to all other kinds of spaces, the heterotopia of the ship has the additional characteristic of bearing a special relation to all other heterotopias, as it constitutes their spatial-conceptual type. It is in this sense that the ship is indeed the heterotopia par excellence: the space of the ship expresses the heterotopic desire for a space completely autonomous from every other space that, at the same time, it wishes to represent. The ship embodies the desire that produces hetero-topias, that calls the space of heterotopia into being: the desire to escape the social while simultaneously representing it, contesting it, inverting it—the desire to exceed the social while simultaneously transforming it. Such a paradoxical desire functions always on the brink of its own undoing. It is precisely the dangerous dialectic of this desire that the construction of the *Narcissus* brings to the narrative forefront: while being constituted by such a dialectic, this ship also travels far in dissolving it by stretch-ing heterotopic space and its representational possibilities. In the very attempt to represent the unrepresentable space of empire, one begins to witness the crisis of that dialectic as well as the dissolution of the ship as the heterotopia of heterotopia of Western civilization. It is, in other words, at the historical moment when a ten-dentially global and increasingly unified world system comes into being that the concept of heterotopia as well as the very concept of space undergo, of necessity, other and further-reaching metamorphoses.

What Michel Foucault calls heterotopia, Herman Melville calls *Neversink*. What we learned about Foucault's heterotopias in the introduction will provide here the heuris-tic backdrop for an investigation of spatial discourses in Melville, and what we hope to learn about Melville in the end will also transfigure Foucault's conceptual appara-tus. Melville and Foucault are placed here side by side as two thinkers and writers who shared in the history of certain conceptualizations of space that will ultimately be revealed to have emerged in interference with modern representations of sexual desire between men.

The same dialectic of representation that follows the *Narcissus* through its passage haunts the *Neversink* in Melville's *White-Jacket; or, The World in a Man-of-War*:

> For a ship is a bit of terra firma cut off from the main; it is a state in itself; and the captain is its king.[9]

A "fragment detached from the earth" and yet "a small planet," "a bit of terra firma cut off from the main" and yet "a state in itself." Once again, to be a ship is to oscil-late ceaselessly between a completely autarchic and monadic condition, and a per-manently incomplete and fragmentary one—and here too the paradoxical relations between the images of the ship and of the social field are sustained and continuously reproduced through hermetic isolation. In *White-Jacket*, this problematic can al-ready be sighted through the numerous semantic apertures of the subtitle: *The World in a Man-of-War*.[10] The axis around which this world revolves is the preposition "in." The world is a semantic minefield that threatens to explode in several different directions: are all the relations and practices aboard the ship being referred to as a world, that is, as some kind of self-contained totality? Or, is it the world ashore that is seen here inside the ship, is it only in the ship that the world materializes as "The World" and that it can be represented as a world at all? The world in the subtitle evokes these different possibilities simultaneously only to leave them all undecidable and suspended in midair. Whatever the answers to these questions might be, the crux lies a priori in that preposition, which sets the terms for the semantic investigation of the world as well as directs and limits the trajectories of this investigation by placing the world inside the ship and by positing an outside and an inside in the first place. Any questioning of the world is already after the fact, since it inevitably has to start from the space of the ship represented as an inside, that is, as an enclosure and a carrier of whatever the world might be. At the same time, the locative of the subtitle already implies an outside to the world, that is, a space that envelops and circumscribes the ship, and that expresses a narrative desire to escape the world so as to survey it from above, so as to apprehend and represent it as a totality.

This subtitle establishes the narrative paradigm for the whole novel, which unfolds entirely on its terms and strictly within its boundaries: *White-Jacket* takes place entirely aboard the ship. The shore, though, does have its temptations. When the *Neversink* stops in Rio de Janeiro for provisions, the narrator relates how "the people"—that is, the sailors—were finally given "liberty":

> With Jack Chase and a few other discreet and gentlemanly top-men, I went ashore on the first day, with the first quarter-watch. Our own little party had a charming time; we saw many fine sights; fell in—as all sailors must—with dashing adventures. But, though not a few good chapters might be written on this head, I must again forbear; for in this book I have nothing to do with the shore further than to glance at it, now and then, from the water; my man-of-war world alone must supply me with the staple of my matter; I have taken an oath to keep afloat to the last letter of my narrative.[11]

With this oath the space of the ship and the whole narrative are revealed to be synonymous. This oath articulates the world of the ship as a self-sufficient narrative ecosystem, which in order to function, like all circuits and energy-fields, needs to be sealed off and shut onto itself. Furthermore, in ensuring that the ship remains a hermetic enclosure precisely at the time when it is most threatened to be opened up to other narrative spaces, the narrator is also refusing to give in to the highly predictable plot of "dashing adventures" into which "all sailors must" necessarily fall.

The construction of the ship as a hermetic space is such a central narrative condition of possibility that even easily achievable glamor and adventure must be sacrificed on its more austere altars. There could be no clearer rejection of the narrative form of the exotic picaresque in favor of a form that kept the narrative always "afloat" and that constructed the space of the ship as the sole site and apparatus of narrative production. Even when, at another point in the novel, the narrator confesses not to be able to keep his oath and proceeds to sing the praises of the bay of Rio de Janeiro, not only does he fail to relate any adventure ashore but what he presents is a detailed description of the wonders of that city that, for its panoramic sweep, is soon identifiable as a description of the bay as observed from the removed and priviliged perspective of the ship—and even this panoramic description of the world ashore, in any case, very rapidly gives way to historical rapture on naval warfare.[12]

In the last few pages of the novel, the narrator is once again tempted to break the spell of isolation with which he had thus far successfully surrounded the ship. The *Neversink* is about to reach home at night and the narrator debates whether or not to relate the actual entrance into the harbor and the final coming ashore, and hence, while debating this question, he does, if indirectly, relate all that he finally decides not to relate. Ultimately, however, he backtracks and declares:

> No! let all this go by; for our anchor still hangs from our bows, though its eager flukes dip their points in the impatient waves. Let us leave the ship on the sea—still with the land out of sight—still with brooding darkness on the face of the deep. I love an indefinite, infinite background—a vast, heaving, rolling, mysterious rear![13]

This passage constitutes the final announcement that the narrative is firmly anchored in the ship. The "infinite background" enshrouds the *Neversink* in "brooding darkness": like in a chiaroscuro effect, the darker and more "indefinite" this background is, the more definite, distinct and self-contained is the last image of the ship in contrast to it.

If it is clear by now how *White-Jacket* obstinately insists on producing the ship as a narrative entelechy, what remains to be seen is how the ship is constructed at the same time as a radically heterogeneous space. The more the ship is posited as a completely autonomous system of representation, the more highly differentiated are its representations. At one point in the novel, during a violent storm, the narrator remarks: "We rolled and rolled on our way, like a world in its orbit."[14] This is the metamorphic tempest in which the *Neversink* remains stuck throughout the duration of its passage, and in which the image of the ship spins around its own axis continuously changing the structure of its space. The narrator's unrelenting compulsion to represent the ship always as something else, to compare its spaces to other spaces, is enabled by the extreme compartmentalization and rigid subdivision of the space of the ship and by the fact that such a highly intricate system of internal boundaries is also in a mutually determining relation to hierarchical economies of power and divisions of labor. The character of specific spaces aboard the ship is inextricable from the specific categories of the people—each with distinct duties, skills, personalities, and histories—occupying them. The waisters, for example, who attend to "ignoble duties" such as the "drainage and sewerage below hatches," are thus described in relation to their location in the ship:

> Inveterate "sons of farmers," with the hayseed yet in their hair, they are consigned to the congenial superintendence of the chicken-coops, pig-pens, and potato-lockers. These are generally placed amidships, on the gun-deck of a frigate, between the fore and main hatches; and comprise so extensive an area, that it much resembles the market-place of a small town. The melodious sounds thence issuing continually draw tears from the eyes of the waisters; reminding them of their old paternal pig-pens and potato-patches.[15]

The presence of animals, potatoes, hayseed-haired "sons of farmers" and their memories suddenly transforms this extensive area of the ship into "the market-place of a small town." This same area, however, is also used for dining:

> It was on the gun-deck that our dinners were spread; all along between the guns; and there, as we cross-legged sat, you would have thought a hundred farmyards and meadows were nigh. Such a cackling of ducks, chickens, and ganders; such a lowing of oxen, and bleating of lambskins, penned up here and there along the deck, to provide sea-repasts for the officers. More rural than naval were the sounds; continually reminding each mother's son of the old paternal homestead in the green old clime; the old arching elms; the hill where we gambolled; and down by the barley banks of the stream where we bathed.[16]

Farmyards, meadows, homesteads, elms, hills, barley, streams: under the spell of a rural memory this space turns temporarily into a pastoral idyll. Everything in these memories, from the "paternal pig-pens" to the "paternal homestead," seems to be "old." It is, in fact, a premodern, patriarchal, and agricultural world that is being recollected and reconstituted aboard the ship.

On the other hand, that archaic and rural world is what one irreparably leaves behind once entering what to the uninitiated seems to be the incomprehensible chaos of a man-of-war. The narrator attempts to reproduce the first moments of the "nonplussed and confounded" sailor:

> [H]is head is half stunned with the unaccustomed sounds ringing in his ears; which ears seem to him like bellfries full of tocsins. On the gun-deck, a thousand scythed chariots seem passing; he hears the tread of armed marines; the clash of cutlasses and curses. The boatswain's mates whistle round him, like hawks screaming in a gale, and the strange noises under decks are like volcanic rumblings in a mountain. He dodges sudden sounds, as a raw recruit falling bombs....
>
> Mark him, as he advances along the files of old ocean-warriors; mark his debased attitude, his deprecating gestures, his Sawney stare, like a Scotchman in London.[17]

Far from being rural, these overwhelming sounds and sights bear a clear bellic stamp, at least up until the moment they are revealed to be also eminently urban. Descending from his rural highlands, probably driven away from his land by a clearance act, the Scotchman arrives to the English metropolis and to its already industrialized and thoroughly urban environment. The space of the ship here is apprehended not merely as a metropolitan space: it is also reconstructed according to the way in which such a metropolitan space might have looked and felt like for the first time from the perspective of the rural disposessed, who was soon to become part of the first waged and industrial labor force. The ship is recast as a metropolis through the evocation of this confounded "Sawney stare" that by the 1850s had already become a stereotypical figure for the dislocating experiences of industrialization and urbanization—experiences that by then were already familiar in the 1850s' United States. This "stare" is the gaze through which two irreconcilable historical spaces intersected and confronted each other. In the first of numerous instances in which the ship is represented as a metropolitan space, the figure of the Scotchman crystallizes the moment of encounter and overlap between an increasingly endangered pastoral and agricultural mode of production and the burgeoning mode of industrial capitalism.[18]

Such an overlap is all the more evident when the narrator comments on the regulation and regimentation of life aboard the ship:

> And here be it known ... that to a common sailor the living on board a man-of-war is like living in a market; where you dress on the doorsteps, and sleep in the cellar. No privacy can you have; hardly one moment's seclusion. It is

almost a physical impossibility that you can ever be alone. You dine at a vast *table d'hôte;* sleep in commons, and make your toilet where and when you can. There is no calling for a mutton-chop and a pint of claret by yourself; no selecting of chambers for the night; no hanging of pantaloons over the back of a chair; no ringing your bell of a rainy morning, to take your coffee in bed. It is something like life in a large manufactory. The bell strikes to dinner, and hungry or not, you must dine.[19]

The rural "market-place of a small town" returns in this passage, only to be ultimately turned into a factory. If the "potato lockers," "chicken-coops, pig-pens," assorted animal noises, and complete lack of privacy make the ship look like a rural market, the same lack of privacy, in conjuncture with other kinds of sounds, an extreme regimentation of life, compartmentalization of space, and division of labor make this same space of the ship look like a factory. An agricultural, premodern, and precapitalist formation, and a modern and industrial-capitalist one coexist here in the same space.

The narrator takes up the role of the sociologist in a chapter entitled "The good or bad Temper of Man-of-war's-men in a great degree attributable to their particular Stations and Duties aboard Ship." There we read:

A forced, interior quietude, in the midst of great outward commotion, breeds moody people. Who so moody as railroad brakemen, steam-boat engineers, helmsmen, and tenders of power-looms in cotton factories? For all these must hold their peace while employed, and let the machinery do the chatting; they cannot even edge in a single syllable.[20]

The ship here is cast into the space and era of industrial technology. If the ship could be conceived of as a factory, here it is expanded to include a wider array of technological spaces. Incongruous as the helmsmen might seem here juxtaposed to those other laborers, the juxtaposition indicates that the ship itself is being constructed as a machine, is being apprehended as an industrial-technological space.

This space that can be simultaneously described as a market, a metropolis, a factory, a machine, undergoes a myriad of other metamorphoses: throughout *White-Jacket,* the *Neversink* is also referred to as a medieval castle, a prison, a fortress, a theater, a church, a hospital, a school, and many other assorted institutions, such as "abbeys, arsenals, colleges, treasuries, metropolitan post-offices, and monasteries."[21] Moreover, the ship itself often provides images for representing other objects and spaces. The human body, for example, is a favorite target for ship metaphors: "ribbed chests" are compared to "the ribbed bows of a frigate"; a dying sailor is described as "the mere foundering hull of a man"; a face is seen as a "port-hole"; a beard is called "the flag that Nature herself has nailed to the mast."[22] What is important here, however, is not only the semiotic, semantic, and historical specificity of each of the images, figures, and spaces through which the ship is continuously reconfigured; the overlapping specificities of all these spaces owe their importance to the fact that they constitute the index of the historical pressures exerted on the space of the ship, of the historical constellations that cut across the space of the ship. What is most crucial, in other words, is precisely the fact that these separate and distinct specificities are always intersecting and overlapping, that they are at once in a position of complete semiotic autonomy and of total semantic dependence, that they are continuously restructuring and modifying one another, that they repeatedly bring each other to crisis. A space that can be simultaneously reconfigured as a rural market and as a factory is obviously different from both: such a space irreversibly transforms those other spaces by making it impossible henceforth to think of them as separate from each other. The space of the ship is definitionally constituted by the very fact that so many different forms of representation, so many irreconcilable spaces, and all their attendant historical-political conjunctures, coexist within it.

In a chapter whose title alone encapsulates the novel's recurrent preoccupations with the question of space—"A Man-of-war full as a Nut"—the narrator launches the ship into yet another metamorphic voyage:

> In truth, a man-of war is a city afloat with long avenues set out with guns instead of trees, and numerous shady lanes, courts, and by-ways. The quarter-deck is a grand square, park, or parade-ground, with a great Pittsfield elm, in the shape of the mainmast, at one end, and fronted at the other by the palace of the commodore's cabin.
>
> Or, rather, a man-of-war is a lofty, walled, and garrisoned town, like Quebec, where the thoroughfares are mostly ramparts, and peaceable citizens meet armed sentries at every corner.
>
> Or it is like the lodging-houses in Paris, turned upside down; the first floor, or deck, being rented by a lord; the second, by a select club of gentlemen; the third, by crowds of artisans; and the fourth, by a whole rabble of common people.
>
> For even thus is it in a frigate, where the commodore has a whole cabin to himself on the spar-deck, the lieutenants their ward-room underneath, and the mass of sailors swing their hammocks under all.

> And with its long rows of port-hole casements, each revealing the muzzle of a cannon, a man-of-war resembles a three-story house in a suspicious part of the town, with a basement of indefinite depth, and ugly-looking fellows gazing out at the windows.[23]

"Or"—this conjunction is the pivot around which the ship spins and changes its form at every complete revolution. Here this conjunction does not function according to an either/or dialectic; rather, it lays out a series of parallel representational planes—a series in which each successive element does not retroactively obliterate the preceding one but rather impresses itself onto it in an ever-receding chain of representational overlays. These planes are never posited as being mutually exclusive, and in this sense the "or" expresses an additive logic; and yet this "or" is not an "and," that is, a more properly additive conjunction: the "or" unfolds these representational planes one over the other, but *as if* each one of them were totally finite, isolated, self-contained, and mutually exclusive with the next. Once again, although each of the spaces articulated here has a very significant specificity, the main focus of the passage is the mesmerizing juxtaposition and rapid succession of these representational planes: the narrative takes up an image, elaborates it, and quickly tosses it aside without having exhausted its possibilities in order to turn to some other image. The narrative energies, rather than being aimed at the elaboration of any of these specific spaces, are all channeled instead into the production of a radically heterogeneous space capable of being all these irreconcilable spaces at once.

We return, thus, to the historical question that was elaborated in the introduction. The radical heterogeneity of a space that can contain historically specific sites such as a rural market and factory is symptomatic of the peculiarly modern problematic identified by Ernst Bloch as the synchronicity of the nonsynchronous—the spatial coexistence and articulation in the same time period of historically heterogeneous social formations, of profound historical rifts and dysfunctions. What both Bloch and Melville share is an understanding of modernity as constituted by the violent impact of old and new, and by the ever-growing contradictions produced by their forced cohabitation. Aboard the *Neversink* old and obsolescent formations intersect with new and dynamic ones, thus bringing each other to crisis. The space of the ship is the heterotopia of modernity as crisis.

Let us now push all this further into other directions. For one may wonder: why all this talk about space? For one may legitimately feel that space as a concept, or otherwise, is not any thing in particular. It is indispensable, though also obvious, to point out that—as Michel de Certeau is always fond of reminding us—

there is no space that is not a *practiced* space,[24] that is not thoroughly soaked in the multiple fluidities of material practices. Hence one may think of space as a magnetic force field. In this sense, a heterotopia is a site that is constituted by certain heterotopic forces and desires, that is, by practices that simultaneously wish to represent, contest, and invert all other practices in culture.

Once recast in such a way, this spatial problematic has far-reaching implications for the understanding and the production of contestatory forces in culture—and I will briefly sketch here just one of the investigative apertures that such a recasting enables and, indeed, demands. The crisis of the ship as the heterotopia par excellence came to full fruition in the passage from the nineteenth to the twentieth century. This is a period when a pervasive crisis in conceptualizations of sexuality was also rapidly unfolding.[25] It should come as no surprise that such crises crucially intersected each other, and that the ship—at precisely the same time that its place in culture as heterotopia par excellence was being fatally questioned—became among the best stages for the dramatization of paradigm shifts in conceptions and definitions of sexuality. Such intersections should come as no surprise, especially given all that has been implied so far concerning the function of heterotopias as the nodal *loci* in culture for the production and reproduction of those desires and practices which, while being vital and integral to the construction of the social field, at the same time continuously threaten to explode this field from the inside—along with its delicate equilibria, violent norms, and stabilizing strictures—if not strategically exploited and ruthlessly contained. In this sense, Melville's *Billy Budd*—a work that has been repeatedly identified throughout our century as one of the paradigmatic texts in the crystallization of discourses of male homosexuality and homophobia, and that specifically articulates the paradox of the deployment of "male-male desire" as both the "glue" and "the solvent" of "hierarchical male disciplinary order"—is also the paradigmatic text of the encounter between the crisis of the ship as heterotopia par excellence and the crisis in conceptualizations of sexuality.[26] Put differently: if heterotopias are particular conceptualizations of space, then the crisis of a heterotopia will necessitate a reconfiguration of specific social practices of space, that is, of specific articulations of bodies in space. The crisis of the all-male disciplinarian heterotopia of the ship, hence, is coterminous with a reconfiguration of the movements and articulations of desiring male bodies in space.

If Melville produces in *Billy Budd* the most paradigmatic account of the encounter and symbiosis of these crises, such an account also finds its condition of possibility in several decades of experimentation with the heterotopic energies manifested and materialized in the space of the ship. We return, thus, to *White-Jacket*, as its narrator reflects on the vices aboard the ship:

> These [evils] are undoubtedly heightened by the close cribbing and confinement of so many mortals in one oaken box on the sea. Like pears closely packed, the crowded crew mutually decay through close contact, and every plague-spot is contagious. Still more, from this same close confinement—so far as it effects the common sailors—arise other evils, so direful that they will hardly bear even so much as an allusion. What too many seamen are when ashore is very well known; but what some of them become when completely cut off from shore indulgences can hardly be imagined by landsmen. The sins for which the cities of the plain were overthrown still linger in some of these wooden-walled Gomorrahs of the deep.[27]

Such a mesmerizing conflation of medical discourses and spatial preoccupations, epistemological contradictions and sexual interdictions, homophobic anxieties and voyeuristic pleasures, biblical overtones and genocidal undertones would deserve an extended close reading. Here, I will just point out that the conflation of such a diversity of discourses is yet another instance of the problematic of the synchronicity of the nonsynchronous: in this passage, the emergence of modern epistemologies of sexuality is signaled by the recourse to discourses and images, such as the biblical and the medical ones, that are indices of jarringly different historical formations.

One ought to marvel, for instance, at the brilliant absurdity of the verb in the last sentence of this passage: sex between men is said here to "still linger" as if it was an aberration belonging to an archaic past that has naturally and gradually disappeared since then, in the name of a proto-evolutionary ethics of sexual progress. That verb's intuition, though, is not entirely misplaced, as indeed there is something still lingering here: the very image of Gomorrah, the very appeal to archaic and latent genocidal fantasies that are punctually resurrected and strategically made to linger at moments of crisis in culture. In contrast to such archaic representation of sexual practices between men, other elements in this passage offer a strikingly different conceptualization of the same problematic: "What too many seamen are when ashore is very well known; but what some of them become when completely cut off from shore indulgences can hardly be imagined by landsmen." One is struck first of all by the epistemological somersaults of these sentences: everything and nothing is revealed about what seamen "are" or what they "become." The narrator first invokes an indefinite knowledge of the world ashore so as to establish a flattering complicity with the reader: we with worldly knowledge are well aware of what seamen are when ashore, so there is no need even to mention it. Immediately thereafter, the narrator proceeds to save and blackmail the reader by stopping that knowledge just short of imagining what the reader undoubtedly knows but what, for the reader's own good, must remain unimaginable and unavailable: you members of polite society ashore cannot in any way know the depravities of seamen aboard a ship since you are, of course, completely exempt from them. It is then necessarily the narrator's task to represent—albeit via the punitive and warning image of the biblical holocaust—what the reader cannot even be asked to know. This daring act of representation can no longer backfire on the narrator after he has done the reader the favor of interrupting the assumption of a shared knowledge precisely when both that knowledge and that assumption would have turned out to be too dangerous and compromising: I know that you know, but I will not tell if you will let me represent the object of that knowing. Thus, the peculiar final implication—that, since what cannot be imagined can hardly be desired or practiced, sex between men exists exclusively among seamen aboard ships on the high seas—is both all the more reassuring and all the more threatening by virtue of being construed from its very inception as something that is not to be believed by anybody at all.

If *Billy Budd*'s epistemological novelty resides in the crystallization of the male homosexual as a recognizable type and of male homosexuality as an ontological state, the emphasis in the passage above, on the other hand, is still decidedly placed on practices rather than identities. *White-Jacket*'s seamen may indeed indulge in the "sins for which the cities of the plain were overthrown," but their indulging in such "sins" does not yet make them identifiable as *homosexuals*. And yet the world ashore is identified as the site of seamen's "being" ("What too many seamen are when ashore is very well known") while the ship is identified as the site of their "becoming" ("but what some of them become when cut off from shore indulgences can hardly be imagined by landsmen"): lurking in the folds of such a dialectic, one can already sense the coming into being of an emergent definition of sexual identity, as aboard the ship one does become—if, when, and by indulging in those "sins"— an as yet unspecified, undefinable, unnamed something. The heterotopia of the ship is constructed as the spatial condition of possibility for the emergence of a subject-position from which one may become defined by engaging in same-sex sexual practices. If the space of the ship is the heterotopia of the crisis of modernity, that is so also because such a space comes into being as a laboratory for modern epistemo-sexual experimentations.

One last specific inflection of the passage above should not go unobserved. In it, we are faced by a conceptualization of sexual practices between men as being directly caused by the very structure of space: "These [evils] are undoubtedly heightened by the close cribbing and confinement of so many mortals in one oaken box on the sea. Like pears closely packed, the crowded crew mutually decay through close contact.... Still more, from this same close confinement—so far as it effects the common sailors—arise other evils, so direful that they will hardly bear even so much as an allusion." The "common sailors"—and one wonders, of course, who the uncommon ones might be—are so squeezed in against each other aboard the ship that, well, they just can't help themselves. Such a spatial apprehension of sexual practices operates a double-edged displacement of moral responsibility—i.e. it's not really their fault—and, most importantly, of sexual desire. It might have been far more threatening, in fact, to produce an account of such practices that would stem not from space but rather from within the body itself, that is, an account of sex as something that the sailors actually desired and that the space of the ship crucially enabled rather than as something into which the sailors were inevitably driven by forced "cribbing and confinement." If such a spatial discourse is used as a way of shifting the focus away from the explosive question of desire, it also enables Melville to bring up the question of sexual practices in the first place and indirectly to present the unrepresentable. The elision of sexual desire and its substitution by spatial categories and determinations becomes here the price paid for the representation of sexual practices between men.

It is important to note how in one of the few other works in which Melville explicitly refers to "the cities of the plain" and their "sins"—that is, in *Clarel: A Poem and Pilgrimage in the Holy Land,* written between 1867 and 1876— he once again specifically relates sexual practices between men to spatial structures, discourses, and preoccupations. The cataclysmic images of the Biblical holocaust recur persistently in those cantos—from 32 to 36 of *Clarel*'s second section—in which the present-day pilgrims sit by the desert shores of the Dead Sea, look over the vast expanse where Sodom and Gomorrah used to stand, and ponder the fate of these cities and of their people. In the midst of such descriptions, and at the moment when the disconcerted pilgrims watch Mortmain (the crazed and possessed Swede) drink water from the Dead Sea, though, the poem's narrative is interrupted and canto 35—entitled "Prelusive"—ensues with the onerous task of introducing the question of the sins for which the cities were destroyed; canto 36—entitled "Sodom"—in fact continues the narration from where it had been broken off at the end of canto 34 and unfolds as a theological meditation on sexual practices between men in which it will be left conveniently to the bewildered and bewildering Mortmain to raise such contested and compromising issues. Interesting as Mortmain's ravings on death, "Science," and Sodom's "sins refined" are in and of themselves,[28] I want to draw attention here to canto 35 and its abrupt interruption of the narrative that serves at once as a warning and as an apology for what follows (namely, an entire canto about matters that contemporary common sense and decency might have thought best left unsaid). In one of Melville's most cryptic, elusive, and disturbing moments, the desolate and open expanses of the Siddim plains and of the Dead Sea are suddenly abandoned, and one is thrown into the dark dungeons and asphyxiating crypts of Giovanni Battista Piranesi's *Le Carceri [The Prisons]* — a series of etchings representing torture chambers and subterranean enclosures, or, in other words, spaces much like the ones of "close cribbing and confinement" that *White-Jacket* adduces as the direct cause of the lingering presence aboard the *Neversink* of the "sins for which the cities of the plain were overthrown." Thus opens canto 35:

> In Piranesi's rarer prints,
> Interiors measurelessly strange,
> Where the distrustful thought may range
> Misgiving still — what mean the hints?[29]

What do indeed the "[p]it under pit," "shadowed galleries," "vaulted lanes," "wards of hush," and "allusive chambers closed" of Piranesi's prisons at once allude to and hide?[30] It is not at all self-evident, in fact, that anything in these proto-Foucauldian heterotopias of punishment and surveillance does constitute a hint of anything at all. But to Melville's apprehensive gaze — a gaze always verging on the paranoiac when it comes to mapping the perilous crossroads of power and sexuality — certain "hints" indeed lurk omnipresent amidst these chambers' ominous "[r]ing-bolts" and "Rhadamantine chains"[31]:

> The thing implied is one with man,   20
> His penetralia of retreat —
> The heart, with labyrinths replete:
> In freaks of intimation see
> Paul's "mistery of iniquity:"
> Involved indeed, a blur of dream;   25
> As, awed by scruple and restricted
> In first design, or interdicted
> By fate and warnings as might seem;

The inventor miraged all the maze,
Obscured it with prudential haze;   30
Nor less, if subject unto question,
The egg left, egg of the suggestion.
        Dwell on those etchings in the night,
Those touches bitten in the steel
By aqua-fortis, till ye feel   35
The Pauline text in gray of light;
Turn hither then and read aright.[32]

Such dizzyingly suggestive verses clearly deserve to be examined in detail. Here, I would like simply to point out the following: neither these nor the canto's remaining verses at all clarify (a) *what* in Piranesi's prisons specifically constitutes the "freaks of intimation" and "egg of suggestion" of "Paul's 'mistery of iniquity'," (b) *how* such spaces actually imply the "mistery" and the "iniquity" that, apparently, much to St. Paul's chagrin, are revealed here to be "one with man," or (c) *where* in them exactly one can "read aright" the "Pauline text" of same-sex interdiction (Melville again significantly invokes St. Paul's infamous second Epistle to the Thessalonians in *Billy Budd* when attempting to "define and denominate" Claggart's "depravity"). Let me also suggest that if Melville, spurred by the most elusive and aleatory evidence, goes so far as to put forth an interpretation of Piranesi's etchings that sees their author as a victim of self-censorship or outright prohibition in representing what otherwise would surely have been a patent homosexual content, that if Melville puts into motion such a hermeneutical apparatus, he may also be implying, at once hoping and dreading, that such an apparatus could and should be employed on his own texts, even or especially when one is faced by evidence that is most elusive and aleatory. At any rate, what is by now quite clear is (a) that the sudden narrative shift to Piranesi's spaces of incarceration—spaces that are all the more confining as they are jarringly juxtaposed to the boundless desert plateaus where the narrative unfolds—is coextensive with an explicit engagement of the question of sexual practices between men, (b) that in *Clarel* as much as in *White-Jacket* the very space of an all-male disciplinarian heterotopia somehow automatically and spontaneously generates such practices, and finally (c) that the preoccupation with such a spatial structure becomes the aptest— that is, the least objectionable—epistemological apparatus for presenting that sin whose very name decrees the impossibility of either the sin or its name to exist in language: *illum crimen horribile quod non nominandum est*. The point is that the very walls and confines of such "Gomorrahs of the deep"—that is, of both subaqueous ship holds and subterranean jails—seem to emanate contagious homosexual effluvia that will inevitably infect whomever is there in "close cribbing and confinement" (and such effluvia, hence, are not unlike the purportedly noxious exhalations streaming forth from the Dead Sea that were said at times to drive people insane.) In other words, the most perturbing quality of Piranesi's *Le Carceri* is the virtually absolute absence in them of any human figure: dungeon after dungeon and crypt after crypt, one is confronted by unnerving empty spaces that, nevertheless, echo eloquently with the stifled screams and slow agonies of twisted and tortured naked bodies. It is precisely this relentless absence of human bodies in a space in which everything (instruments of torture, architectural structures, spatial partitions, and so on) points and owes its very existence to the incarceration of the human body and to the exasperation of the sensorium and of the flesh; it is this absence, which at once hides and speaks louder than any bodily presence, that must have made Piranesi's titillating and sadistic architectural visions so attractive to Melville. This is a Melville who was forever in search of images that could have at once "miraged all the maze" and "[o]bscured it with prudential haze," that could at once present and elide the body along with its needs and its desires, that could enable an offstage of representation where the body would be crying in pleasure and in pain. What is at once strategically displaced and longingly invoked by Melville's broodings on Piranesi's disciplinarian heterotopias at the threshold of a canto entitled "Sodom" is specifically an absolutely confined and crucially unfettered, desiring body: a body from whose dilated pores those contagious effluvia of sexual desire must—in the first place and in the last instance—have emanated.[33]

When I heard, shortly after William Jefferson Clinton's election to the United States presidency, a United States Navy officer speak on National Public Radio against lifting the ban on gay and lesbian soldiers in the armed forces, it occurred to me how at once uncannily similar and radically different contemporary discourses around same-sex sexual practices, desires, and identities are from Melville's mid-nineteenth-century spatio-sexual anxieties. The Navy officer maintained that, even though lifting the ban would be baneful for all divisions of the armed forces, it would be all the more so for the Navy, because aboard a ship—and even more so aboard a submarine—sailors are squeezed far more closely against each other than in any other kind of military space, and, furthermore, they are also enclosed and detained in highly claustrophobic spaces, without anywhere else to go to, for months at a stretch. Clearly, this Navy officer would never be caught surmising—like the narrator in *White-Jacket* does—that it might be precisely because of the ship's "close cribbing and confinement" that same-sex sexual practices spontaneously arise among the crew members. Moreover, the officer's conceptualization of space is different from that of *White-Jacket*'s narrator insofar as the former is radically restructured by the potential presence of the homosexual as a type. That space containing individuals that can be isolated from everyone else and interpellated as homosexuals is a space that demands to be practiced in ways radically different from the space in which individuals cannot be identified, that is, given a specific name and identity, through their practices. In this respect, the Melville of *Billy Budd* is closer to our contemporary discourses about same-sex practices, desires, and identities than the Melville of *White-Jacket* or than the far more joyous Melville of *Moby-Dick*, in which the romance between Ishmael and Queequeg is importantly enabled—along with other factors—by the absence of any definition of and preoccupation with sexual identity. And yet, both for this officer and for the narrator of *White-Jacket*, the ultimate problem is located in space—in all the unforeseeable translations into practices of its power-scarred striations. What I find most intriguing, in fact, about the officer's reasoning, assumptions, and implications, is the way in which I heard them: the officer's words reached my ears not only as fragments of contemporary homophobic discourse but also as echoes of older spatial and sexual paradigms whose energies are clearly far from being fully spent. I heard speaking through his argument a whole history of spatial and sexual epistemologies, of which Melville's remarks are also a constitutive part: this is a history in which heterotopic space is above all a terrain of social antagonism and conflict, demarcated by contestatory practices and produced by heterotopic desires, that is, that existing, present site in which the past and the future of culture face each other in continuous struggle.

T   W   O

In the Nick of Time; or,

Heterochronologies of Modernity

Economy of time, to this all economy ultimately reduces itself.

Karl Marx, *Grundrisse*

> Let us forget the scourge and the gangway awhile, and jot down in our memories a few little things pertaining to our man-of-war world. I let nothing slip, however small; and feel myself actuated by the same motive which has prompted many worthy old chroniclers, to set down the merest trifles concerning things that are destined to pass away entirely from the earth, and which, if not preserved in the nick of time, must infallibly perish from the memories of man. Who knows that this humble narrative may not hereafter prove the history of an obsolete barbarism? Who knows that, when men-of-war shall be no more, *White-Jacket* may not be quoted to show the people in the Millennium what a man-of-war was? God hasten the time! Lo! ye years, escort it hither, and bless our eyes ere we die.[1]

THIS PASSAGE speaks of memory. It begins and ends with suggestions of forgetting, images of obliteration tinged by hints of *dies irae*. And yet the fulcrum of the whole passage is the act of remembering, of recording, of preserving precisely that "obsolete barbarism" it wishes to banish from history altogether. "Let us forget the scourge and the gangway awhile, and jot down in our memories a few little things": the sec-

ond "and," far from occupying a secondary position in the articulation of the matters at hand, fulfills instead the crucial function of binding together within the same
syntactical unit the apparently unrelated acts of remembering and forgetting, while
at the same time diverting the attention from and leaving unqualified whatever kinds
of relations there might be between those two acts. Memory emerges here as the
difficult and tense interference between remembering and forgetting. It is in the
tension between the desire to remember and the desire to forget that the pages of
White-Jacket unfold: that tension is the axis around which this novel's narrative energies revolve.

      And who can blame the narrator if he wants to "forget the scourge
and the gangway"? In the pages just preceding this passage he had miraculously es-
caped being flogged at the gangway for an occurrence in which he had no fault. The
indictment of the Navy is a question that this novel takes *ad litteram*. Many chapters
are preoccupied with discussing and denouncing the naval code, particularly with regard to corporal punishment, and it has been suggested that these attacks on naval
discipline owe much to the fact that such a critique already had wide currency in
public discourse.[2] Whether or not this novel's direct intervention in these public debates contributed to the 1851 abolition of flogging in the U.S. Navy (almost a year
after its publication), I am concerned rather with the ways such debates emerge in
Melville's text and the kinds of reflections that they enable there. Much of this novel
is spent in the paradoxical process of recording exactly what one continually claims
to want to forget, of jotting down for future memory all that one wants never to
have existed—and it is then clear that the desire to forget is here shot through with
the unfulfillable dream of retroactive excision. Chronicles of disciplinarian societies,
however, have their own peculiar logic: there is hardly a page in this novel where in-
dictments of naval brutalities and abuses do not also become loving remembrances
of the life and of the men aboard the man-of-war. So it is that *White-Jacket* unravels
simultaneously as scathing critique and nostalgic paean of the Navy—not unlike
those hymns to the world of the prison such as Jean Genet's *Miracle of the Rose* or
Our Lady of the Flowers. It is precisely the nostalgia of this novel that summoned me
here; or, rather, my present focus is the images of memory, history, and writing that
such a nostalgia projects onto the text. All the more so because in these images and
nostalgia are the prolegomena that herald the risks taken and not taken in *Moby-
Dick*—but of those other risks we will read in the next chapter.

      Let us return to the opening passage and to its conceptions of
memory. The writing practice in which the narrator participates is compelled by a

very particular urgency: this is not merely a chronicle "concerning things that are destined to pass away entirely from the earth"—and one would suppose all chronicles by definition to have such concerns—this is also a preserving "in the nick of time." This chronicle records a whole world at the last possible moment, at the critical moment of its disappearance. An urgency resonates "in the nick of time" that speaks of unfathomable historical forces hovering high above the ship of this narrative like a sword of Damocles, threatening at any minute to break into its hermetic shell to then shatter it from the inside. Under these threats the narrator must operate: such threats become here the condition of possibility for the writing of history.

To preserve "in the nick of time": an eminently temporal and historical preoccupation is formulated here in spatial terms. This trope identifies the space within which historical memory functions: a space which is a "nick," an indentation in the flowing surface of time, a safe haven from its ruinous forces, a temporal hiatus, a caesura of history. And also: a nick constituted by time, a time capsule within time, a hermetic space governed by different temporal structures within dominant historical flows. One of the most vivid narrative images of such a conceptualization of an other time within an other space is to be found in Edgar Allan Poe's "Ms. Found in a Bottle." In Poe's short story, a ship becomes a temporal black hole, a proto-science-fictional time warp standing in the midst of the dominant historical flows of the time, which in this story is the early nineteenth-century world of sea commerce and colonial enterprise. The narrative, in fact, opens "in the year 18–" and aboard a ship that had been built in Bombay, boarded by the narrator at Batavia, and freighted with such unmistakably colonial goods as "cotton-wool and oil, from the Lachadive Islands . . . coir, jaggeree, ghee, cocoanuts, and a few cases of opium."[3] That the wreck of this first ship is due precisely to this colonial freight, which had not been stowed properly, is only one of the indices of this narrative's anxieties about its own history. After the shipwreck, the narrator finds himself an invisible entity aboard another and mysterious ship that contains and travels through a much earlier temporal plane—perhaps a Dutch ship of the sixteenth century, but perhaps something more foreign and more remote. Within this other ship, time has not exactly stopped; rather, it has become frozen at a particular historical moment that, from the present perspective of the narrator, is perceived as a time when sea travel was associated predominantly with adventure and discovery rather than with commerce.[4] Through the ship, a chasm opens within which time unfolds along completely different axes, within which history follows altogether different logics and routes. In other words, the fact that this ship constitutes a hiatus in the dominant currents of an early nineteenth-century narrative does not mean that it functions outside time, since indeed it has a temporal structure all its own. It exists in the sixteenth century, not as if that century were still the present, but rather as if this were a forever unfolding sixteenth century within which everything and everybody ages *ad infinitum*, as if it were an uncooptable enclosure of the past eternally unfolding within the present (the narrator, after all, continuously remarks on how impossibly old the ship and its sailors are, and repeatedly wonders how this ship can still function and how these sailors can all still be alive and able to run the vessel).[5]

To preserve "in the nick of time" means, likewise, to stop a specific historical moment in order to keep it moving within itself and according to its own particular trajectories, in order to preserve it not as the dead and spent past but as a past still living in the present, even as the memory trace of its own disappearance. For even this "nick" is not an unerasable trace. Jacques Derrida writes: "The trace is the erasure of selfhood, of one's own presence, and is constituted by the threat or anguish of its irremediable disappearance, of the disappearance of its disappearance. An unerasable trace is not a trace, it is a full presence, an immobile and uncorruptible substance."[6] In this sense, the "nick of time" is a more accurate formulation for what constitutes a trace than the term "trace" itself: they are both indentations of presence, absences in presence, but what the "nick of time" also expresses, which "trace" does not, is precisely that always already imminent threat of its own disappearance that is what constitutes a trace in the first place. The fact that Derrida is writing here in the wake of Sigmund Freud is also relevant. "Let us...jot down in our memories a few little things pertaining to our man-of-war world": memory is the site of writing, writing is what takes place in memory. Isn't "the nick of time," after all, the writing-machine of memory, that is, Freud's *Wunderblock*? Isn't what Freud finds in "A Note upon the Mystic Writing Pad," after thirty years of flirtation with a metaphor, similar to what the narrator of the opening passage produces in the notion of preserving "in the nick of time" — that is, a representation of memory simultaneously as a writing process and as a conflation of time and space?[7] If earlier I had identified precisely this persistent threat of "disappearance of its disappearance" as the very condition of possibility for that writing of history envisaged by the narrator in the opening passage, the question that needs to be addressed at this point is what kind of writing and what kind of history such threats demand and produce.

"Let us...jot down in our memories a few little things." "I let nothing slip, however small." "I feel myself actuated by the same motive which has prompted many worthy old chroniclers, to set down the merest trifles." This is a history of the minor, a minor history. The chronicler who would speak such a language bears a family resemblance to Walter Benjamin's historical materialist:

> A chronicler who recites events without distinguishing between major and minor ones acts in accordance with the following truth: nothing that has ever happened should be regarded as lost for history. To be sure, only a redeemed mankind receives the fullness of its past—which is to say, only for a redeemed mankind has its past become citable in all its moments. Each moment it has lived becomes a *citation à l'ordre du jour*—and that day is Judgement Day.[8]

Both these chroniclers share in a desire that points toward that future in which nothing will be lost for history. The difference, though, between the narrator of *White-Jacket* and Benjamin's chronicler is that the former does distinguish between major and minor events. It is precisely the minor events, the ones whose story does not get told, that *White-Jacket*'s narrator chooses to relate, as if to suggest that the distinction between minor and major events will cease to be operative only when this other and minor history will be finally written. Anticipating some of the reactions to his revelation of all that the Navy would much rather keep hidden and untold, the narrator of *White-Jacket* thus defends himself:

> Wherever, throughout this narrative, the American Navy, in any of its bearings, has formed the theme of a general discussion, hardly one syllable of admiration for what is accounted illustrious in its achievements has been permitted to escape me. The reason is this: I consider, that so far as what is called military renown is concerned, the American Navy needs no eulogist but History. It were superfluous for White-Jacket to tell the world what it knows already. The office imposed upon me is of another cast.[9]

The "office" of this narrator, who has declared to be writing a history, has nonetheless nothing to do with official "History." The narrator of *White-Jacket* wants to salvage for history precisely what is most in danger of being excised from it. "I let nothing slip, however small": this misleading and apologetic "however" does not say how it is precisely the "small things" and minor events that the narrator considers most important for his office, as these are most liable to face obliteration at hands of "History." The minor is what cannot be written in "History" and indeed what "History" would keep from being written anywhere at all. In this sense, much of this novel is written as an unofficial history of the American Navy, as the other side of that medal that on one side is inscribed with military honors and on the other is tainted by suffering and stained with blood.

One supposes minor history to tend toward heterogeneity and polymorphism, if it is to resist the centripetal pulls that will otherwise turn it into the ossified monolith of official history. The narrator's "office" in *White-Jacket*, in fact, does not consist only of a denunciatory chronicle of oppression. He is also irresistibly attracted to that world of minutiae whose importance here is attested by his insistence on the very fact that they are consigned to the ever-shifting margins of historical writing: "a few little things," "however small," "the merest trifles." The whole novel, after all, opens with the description of a jacket, which gives the name to both the novel and its narrator, and whose vicissitudes then become the most recurrent narrative refrain, the thread that loosely binds together the pieces of the novel.[10] That an object as trivial as a jacket would be invested with such a central role in the production of a novel does not seem due solely to its distinction — that, unlike most nineteenth-century seamen's garments, it is white and that this whiteness will turn it alternately into an object of ridicule and of danger. What echoes in these pages is that there is a secret relation between the jacket's triviality and its importance in the novel, that it is precisely in its commonness that this importance lies, that it is the most familiar of trifles that are liable to turn any moment into the most uncanny objects. The jacket, discarded and given over to the sea at the end of the novel, becomes the paradigmatic image of all those small "little things" that one must capture promptly, as they "are destined to pass away entirely from the face of the earth." But what precisely are these "little things"? Or, rather, what exactly is the nature of the narrator's attraction toward trifles and minutiae?

The passage quoted at the beginning of this chapter is the opening paragraph of a chapter entitled "A Man-of-war Fountain, and other Things," which is a series of fragments describing a variety of unrelated objects and places in the ship and the practices associated with each.[11] The structure of this chapter, hence, resembles closely that of an inventory. In this sense, this chapter is a miniature image of the whole novel: each successive chapter often has little relation to the preceding one and unfolds as a self-enclosed representation — almost a cameolike sketch — of a specific object and its functions, of a particular daily activity of sailors, of a certain nook in the hold of the ship and what is to be found there, and so on. In this chapter, after having outlined what amounts to a theory of historiography ("I let nothing slip, however small," etc.), the narrator proceeds to put such a theory into practice by describing the ship's scuttle-butt, that is, the ship's water fountain. He opens this description thus:

> There is no part of a frigate where you will see more going and coming of
> strangers, and overhear more greetings and gossipings of acquaintances, than
> in the immediate vicinity of the scuttle-butt, just forward of the main hatch-
> way, on the gun-deck.[12]

The peculiarity of introducing the scuttle-butt in such a fashion is that what is being
posited here as the direct object of the reader's sensorium is the "going and coming
of strangers" and the "greetings and gossipings of acquaintances," while the scuttle-
butt itself remains on the periphery of our field of vision and is mentioned only for
the bustling activity that surrounds it, as a space rather than an object, and as a locus
of all that activity. The path leading the reader to the scuttle-butt crosses the intricate web of daily social intercourse: it is through the latter that the scuttle-butt becomes visible and graspable. The narrator's predilection for objects and trifles is
never an end unto itself: each object is firmly situated in a space that is always constructed as a social field, always inextricably entangled in the networks of daily social
practices aboard the ship. That is how each and every object aboard turns into a lens
through which a certain activity is observed and recorded and through which the
sailors are remembered. Ultimately, the sailors—both as a collective class and as individual types—and their tasks, customs, and pastimes constitute the central focus
of *White-Jacket*. The narrator writes a chronicle of everyday life—a chronicle steeped
in an "everyday matrix."[13] This chronicle departs from and contests the epic, even as
it longingly harks back to the tradition of epic chroniclers. All the explicit references,
for example, to Luis de Camoëns's *Lusiads*—the Portuguese maritime national epic
of the sixteenth century—notwithstanding, in this novel there are no heroes in the
epic sense and no heroic deeds or sensibilities: *White-Jacket* belongs to the anti-epic
of realism, that is, to the modern epic of the common people and their everyday life
and labor—the epic of an age when the time of the epic has passed. And yet, what
complicates this realism here is precisely the nostalgia for archaic narrative forms
and traditions—a nostalgia that is symptomatic of this novel's redemptive historiographical project.

Such nostalgia emerges also from the specific practices that find
their catalyst in the scuttle-butt. The ship's fountain marks a site of oral exchange: it
is a place where you go to chat, to hear and tell stories. (One supposes that it is to
such a catalytic function that the word "scuttle-butt" owes its additional meaning of
"rumor," "gossip").[14] It is crucial, therefore, to note how the narrator, after his historiographical musings, chooses to "set down" the practice of storytelling, which
throughout the novel is made most emblematic of sailors' everyday life and of their

sense of custom and tradition. The practice of storytelling most attracts the narrator's attention, perhaps because he considers it the most endangered. Groups of sailors lounging around in their free time telling stories—and then questioning their veracity or using them as pivots for yet another and related story and so forth—are a constant refrain in the pages of *White-Jacket*.[15] Either on the maintop or down in the forecastle, the sailors constantly spin yarns, narrate ancient sea lore, relate their own lived experience, which in their mouths instantaneously assumes the flavor and form of legend: they are portrayed as the voices and repositories of archaic oral traditions.

Of such traditions, and of their voices, Walter Benjamin writes:

> "When someone goes on a trip, he has something to tell about," goes the German saying, and people imagine the storyteller as someone who has come from afar. But they enjoy no less listening to the man who has stayed at home, making an honest living, and who knows the local tales and traditions. If one wants to picture these two groups through their archaic representatives, one is embodied in the resident tiller of the soil, and the other in the trading seaman. Indeed, each sphere of life has, as it were, produced its own tribe of storytellers. . . . The actual extension of the realm of storytelling in its full historical breadth is inconceivable without the most intimate interpenetration of these two archaic types. Such an interpenetration was achieved particularly by the Middle Ages in their trade structure. The resident master craftsman and the traveling journeymen worked together in the same rooms; and every master had been a traveling journeyman before he settled down in his home town or somewhere else. If peasants and seamen were past masters of storytelling, the artisan class was its university. In it was combined the lore of faraway places, such as a much-traveled man brings home, with the lore of the past, as it best reveals itself to natives of a place.[16]

Before relating Benjamin's story about storytelling to *White-Jacket*, a few words need to be said about the peculiarities of such a narrative of the history of storytelling as a cultural practice. Benjamin tells his story from the point of view of the listener, of the one who stays at home and waits for the exotic tales of faraway lands with which the next batch of seamen will undoubtedly regale him when coming ashore. What such a narrative cannot take into account is that, just like artisans, sailors also combine in their storytelling "the lore of faraway places" and "the lore of the past as it best reveals itself to the natives of a place." The sea is a place too, the place where sailors spend most of their lives, a place with its past and traditions that need to be handed down from sailor to sailor. For seamen, in other words, storytelling—as a pastime, a form of socialization, and a medium of tradition—seems to have little to do with the world ashore, as it belongs first and foremost to a community of men aboard a ship on the high seas.

      The sailor in Benjamin is one of the two archetypes of story-teller. *White-Jacket*'s paradox, however, is that through the ethnographical gaze of the narrator the sailors are produced at once as precisely such archetypes and also as the last tribe of storytellers. *White-Jacket*'s sailors, after all, do not belong to the Middle Ages but to the 1840s, and if they are conceived as the inheritors of certain archetypal storytelling traditions, they necessarily apprehend and elaborate such traditions through a series of historical metamorphoses. Benjamin claims that if "peasants and seamen were past masters of storytelling, the artisan class was its university." But what was happening to such a "university" at the time *White-Jacket* is taking place? The chapter "A Man-of-war full as a Nut" thus opens:

> IT was necessary to supply the lost cooper's place; accordingly, word was passed for all who belonged to that calling to muster at the mainmast, in order that one of them might be selected. Thirteen men obeyed the summons—a circumstance illustrative of the fact that many good handicrafts-men are lost to their trades and the world by serving in men-of-war. Indeed, from a frigate's crew might be culled out men of all callings and vocations, from a backslidden parson to a broken-down comedian. The Navy is the asylum for the perverse, the home of the unfortunate. Here the sons of adversity meet the children of calamity, and here the children of calamity meet the offspring of sin. Bankrupt brokers, bootblacks, blacklegs, and blacksmiths here assemble together; and cast-away tinkers, watchmakers, quill-drivers, cobblers, doctors, farmers, and lawyers compare past experiences and talk of old times.... Frequently, at one and the same time, you see every trade in operation on the gun-deck—coopering, carpentering, tailoring, tinkering, blacksmithing, rope-making, preaching, gambling and fortune-telling.[17]

Among "the unfortunate" and "the perverse," and alongside all sorts of other derelicts and castaways, one finds represented aboard the ship virtually the whole artisan class. The relation between the discourse of perversity and social heterogeneity emerges in several instances in the novel. As one pieces together such instances, one faces the emergence of a theorization of male homosexuality that seeks the causes of homosexual behavior in the radical heterogeneity of social castaways aboard the ship and in the spatial constriction imposed on them. But I have already detailed such matters in the previous chapter. What concerns me here is that, if artisans now can be counted among the "perverse," something on shore has radically changed. Unlike Benjamin's successful and established craftsman, who makes "an honest living" and has "settled down in his home town," these artisans are "lost to their trades and the world by serving in men-of-war." We are not told the nature of the "adversity" and "calamity" that has befallen so many handicraftsmen, and indeed it might not have been the same "calamity" for all of them. What is clear, however, is that there no longer seems to be any space for so many artisans on land: the sudden acceleration in the industrialization of the United States economy during the 1830s and 1840s might have already started to drive members of the artisan class first to bankruptcy and then to the factories or the sea (the great variety of social backgrounds aboard the ship notwithstanding, one never encounters, after all, an ex-factory worker now employed as sailor).[18] In the ship and at sea, these artisans have found, either as artisans or as sailors or both, a still safe haven—for the time being. The "university" of storytelling, thus dismembered and disbanded, is again and differently pieced together on the high seas. The historical irony of such a development is that what Benjamin thought to be the later type of storyteller, namely, the artisan—who emerged from "the most intimate interpenetration" of the two archetypes of the traveling seaman and the bound serf—now finds refuge as a sailor among sailors, that is, among the repositories of the most archaic forms of storytelling. The ship becomes here one of the last sedimentary spaces for the residues of oral narrative traditions.

It is important to consider that one of the main conditions of possibility for a continued tradition of storytelling among the mid-nineteenth-century sailors of *White-Jacket* was the fact that labor at sea was still organized around long periods of inactivity and was altogether resistant to the increasingly parcelized and machinic rhythms of an industrial environment such as the factory. At a time when labor was undergoing unprecedented restructurations and when the laborer's periods of inactivity were rapidly shrinking, to be a sailor, along with being a soldier, was one of the last occupations that—inhuman treatment, extreme danger, and exhausting physical exertion aside—still allowed for long spells of idleness and boredom, such as days spent in an unexpected calm at sea. These are the spells that would then be filled by hours of storytelling and that would make storytelling possible at all.[19]

The fact that *White-Jacket* deals centrally with the question of storytelling, however, does not mean that the narrator positions himself and his own act of narrating in an unproblematical relation with the tradition of storytelling. On the contrary, this narrator, far from merely reproducing and incorporating into his overarching narration the particular stories and singular tales of the sailors, which would have been a storyteller's concern, is more preoccupied with recording the very event of storytelling and its unfolding. When the narrator does indulge in storytelling—almost as if to cater to the expectations of an audience well habituated to the generic laws of the sea narrative—the result is often contrived, as in the case, for example, of the war tales.[20] This novel's narrator, although occasionally relating his own and other sailors' stories, is primarily interested in describing how, where, and when sailors gather to hear and tell stories, in setting down for future memory the circumstances that enable the practice of storytelling. Ultimately, this novel does not merely engage in storytelling but also constitutes a meditation on storytelling: it operates simultaneously from the inside and the outside of that narrative tradition and indeed produces a narrative space that is at once such an inside and such an outside. And if it is the case—as Benjamin argues—that the "earliest symptom of a process whose end is the decline of storytelling is the rise of the novel at the beginning of modern times,"[21] then *White-Jacket*, as a novel, is strangely positioned within such a historical process: this is a text imbued with the melancholia of someone who feels responsible for the death of a loved one and who at once refuses to part and cannot but part with the memory trace of that love.

Let us return now to the scuttle-butt so as to see more clearly how such ambivalence is registered in the text. The narrator closes the description of the ship's scuttle-butt, after having compared it to a town pump, by exclaiming:

> And would that my fine countryman, Hawthorne of Salem, had but served on board a man-of-war in his time, that he might give us the reading of a *rill* from the scuttle-butt.[22]

I would like at this point to produce a sequence out of the events of the page leading to this passage, which up until now have been discussed only separately: the narrator first outlines what I have repeatedly referred to as a theory of historiography ("I let nothing slip, however small," etc.); he then proceeds to put such a theory into practice by describing the ship's scuttle-butt and the activities revolving around it; and finally he concludes such a description with an invocation of Nathaniel Hawthorne—and this is the only such reference in the novel. The question arising from such a narrative is What kind of relation there might be, if any, between Hawthorne and the narrator's historiographical reflections and impulses? The narrator invokes the Hawthorne of the *Twice-Told Tales* here, the Hawthorne of minutiae, small sketches, vignettes, and "merest trifles," the Hawthorne of chronicles of everyday life, the Hawthorne who produces a type of narrative apparently most consonant with *White-Jacket*'s historiographical projects. The specific reference is to a short story in that collection, "A Rill from the Town Pump," which unfolds as a fountain's soliloquy about its own daily life (and in this respect, the ship's scuttle-butt differs significantly from Hawthorne's town pump, as the former does not relate — and in a certain sense is not even the central focus of — its own story).[23]

What is most peculiar about such an invocation is precisely its position at the end of that sequence: the narrator, after having vowed to preserve "in the nick of time" what "must infallibly perish" and after having then proceeded "to jot down" "a few little things pertaining" the ship's scuttle-butt, declares that Hawthorne would have adopted a different solution for these problems — a solution that, evidently, he will not or cannot take. This final declaration is also the expression of an impossible wish: "And would that. . . ." A note of regret resonates in this passage, which then seems to say, I wish Hawthorne would have been in my place as a sailor on the ship and now writing these pages, as he could have written them in a way I cannot. This wish is not exactly or immediately translatable in the following way: I wish these pages could be written in the way Hawthorne would have written them. And yet this suggestion too is left to lurk freely in the above quotation. In either case, this passage is an unequivocal expression of difference, an attempt to locate and identify a certain quality of Hawthorne's writing that cannot be reproduced here.

It is clear both from the title and from the short stories that, in the *Twice-Told Tales*, Hawthorne conceives his authorial position and his own writing to be well within the long-standing oral traditions of storytelling; in his original plan, this collection of tales was actually to be entitled *The Story-Teller*.[24] Writing as if completely from within such traditions, and claiming to represent their direct extension into the present, is what the writer of *White-Jacket* feels he can no longer do. Melville, of course, also wrote short stories, just like Hawthorne also wrote novels: Melville's short stories, however, have precious little to do with storytelling, especially of the kind Hawthorne displays in *Twice-Told Tales*. "Bartleby the Scrivener," "Benito Cereno," and *Billy Budd*, for example, are texts that investigate blockages of communication, representational impasses, narrative conundrums. Ultimately, they are about the impossibility of telling a story, or at any rate the right story, the story that is able to speak the truth about itself, to reveal its own secrets, to culminate and resolve itself in anagnorisis. The point is that it is a novel — and a novel whose recurrent engagement with storytelling is at least troubled and problematic — that Melville chose as a stage from which to invoke Hawthorne at his most storyteller-like: it is on such a stage that Melville's nostalgia for storytelling could and needed to be enacted.

Reflecting on his tales, years after their publication, Hawthorne concludes that:

> They have none of the abstruseness of idea, or obscurity of expression, which mark the written communication of a solitary mind with itself. They never need translation. It is, in fact, the style of a man of society.... They are not the talk of a secluded man with his own mind and heart... but his attempts... to open an intercourse with the world.[25]

Hawthorne—who might well have had Melville in mind when invoking this "secluded man," given that these remarks date from 1851—is describing here what Benjamin later will characterize as the constitutive difference between the task of the story-teller and the task of the novelist:

> The storyteller takes what he tells from experience—his own or that reported by others. And he in turn makes it the experience of those who are listening to his tale. The novelist has isolated himself. The birthplace of the novel is the solitary individual, who is no longer able to express himself by giving examples of his most important concerns, is himself uncounseled, and cannot counsel others.[26]

Leaving aside the fact that Benjamin's as well as Hawthorne's fictions about story-telling are founded on a rather mystifying conception and valorization of experience and of its putative communicability, these two passages nonetheless outline many of Melville's dilemmas: these are the dilemmas of a writer who wished he could have been a storyteller such as Hawthorne, but for whom the craft and time of storytelling were forever gone, and for whom, hence, the only alternatives were chartless voyages in unexplored narrative waters. It is not the case that Melville—as Hawthorne seems to imply—refused to "open an intercourse with the world." It is the case, rather, *that the world with which Melville wanted to communicate did not yet exist.* The process that takes Melville from the writing of *White-Jacket* to the writing of *Moby-Dick*— his next work—spells a paradox: if he, like Ahab, was condemned to solipsism, then he would make himself solitary to an extreme; if he could no longer be a storyteller, then he would produce the first modernist novel, namely, *Moby-Dick*.[27]

In this chapter, I have tried to unfold a poetics of time. This is the poetics of preserving "in the nick of time" that emerges as an intuition in *White-Jacket* and that finds its fullest elaboration and furthest limits only in *Moby-Dick*. It is through the later novel that one needs to follow its vicissitudes. Here, I simply want to emphasize that nothing could be farther away from such a poetics than the practice of storytelling. Storytelling in *White-Jacket* is produced as the disappearing object of that preservation. Furthermore, if to record in the nick of time is to capture an object, an event, a practice at the last moment it is possible to perceive it, at that time which is the very last time, storytelling, on the other hand, needs all the time in the world, as it belongs, according to Paul Valéry, to the time when time did not matter.[28] That is the time to which Melville's poetics harks back precisely because such a poetics belongs instead to a world and a time in which time does matter, in which time, which had been your best ally, has turned into your bitterest enemy.

Of the decline of storytelling Benjamin says that it "has quite gradually removed narrative from the realm of living speech and at the same time is making it possible to see a new beauty in what is vanishing."[29] Melville is aware of such a dialectic. To reveal the secret beauty of what is vanishing, Melville writes the chronicle of whaling in *Moby-Dick*.

And exactly what does it mean for this most elusive of concepts, time, to matter or not to matter, to be your ally or your enemy? What shifts in temporality are Melville and Benjamin (and Hawthorne and Poe and Valéry) sensing and indexing? If both Melville and Benjamin regret and register the waning of storytelling, they do so from the opposite ends of a series of cataclysmic historical processes of which that waning is one manifestation. If Melville — via his preclusion from the practice of storytelling — also signals the emergence and onset of certain historical processes, Benjamin — via his preoccupation with the disappearance of storytelling as a cultural practice — also indicates the onset of those processes' full fruition. Such indexing, hence, also constitutes an attempt to think a historical faultline and an engagement in the production of a metanarrative discourse. To say that the time of storytelling — at once the historical time when storytelling was possible and the temporal structures immanent to storytelling — was the time when time did not matter, is already to identify and to name those devastating historical processes. The time that is being imaged here is the time prior to the tyranny of the clock, the time before the factory's regular working hours and mechanized labor, the time before time had been completely colonized by the logic of the wage, the time before the equation "time = money" had fully come into being as the beating heart of industrial capitalism: *this is the time when time did not matter for capital.*[30]

Time, on the contrary, does matter for capital in *Moby-Dick*. Having been unable to retrieve the time of storytelling in *White-Jacket*, Melville launches himself with *Moby-Dick* into the ever-accelerating whirlpools of an other time, which unravels at once as increasingly regularized and systematic and yet as heterochronically shot through with a multiplicity of nicks, caesurae, and enclaves. Melville's poetics of "the nick of time" needs to be understood as the assemblage resulting from the interferences between the time of capital and a time of resistance to it. This is the poetics of a temporality never synchronous with itself that unfolds along two apposite and transversal vectors: a vector of increasing homogeneity and regularization that is repeatedly intersected and intercepted by a vector of increasing heterogeneity in the form of heterochronic punctuation and indentures. Melville's realization of the impossibility of retrieving for his writing a time of storytelling, rather than indicating a full capitulation to and acquiescence in the time of capital, is articulated in *Moby-Dick* as an attempt to shatter the limits of such a time by going along with it and pushing it to its most extreme possibilities. *Moby-Dick* constitutes an attempt to rush always ahead of the time of capital, thus warping its tendential regularities and disrupting it each time that it was about to crystallize into stable patterns and structures.

Acceleration is the motor of such a poetics. If earlier I had characterized Melville's poetics of time as one of urgency, that urgency can now be recast as acceleration. Or, more precisely, the urgency of capturing in the nick of time what is about to be swept away by the storm of progress, the urgency of that practice of historical representation that must always run faster than history itself and must always be a step ahead even of itself—such an urgency is in a synecdochical relation with the experience of the time of industrial modernity as accelerated time; it is the epiphenomenon of a modernity that makes itself manifest and accessible through the sensorium only as acceleration, only as a perception of time and history itself picking up speed and taking off. In *Moby-Dick*, such an experience of modernity as acceleration is often detectable in narrative crescendos and in images of frenzied velocity. One needs only to note, for example, the increasing recurrence of verbs expressing high speed in the very last pages of the novel and the resulting convulsive textual fabric. Of Ahab's final attempt to strike Moby-Dick, Melville writes:

> The harpoon was darted; the stricken whale flew forward; with igniting velocity the line ran through the groove;—ran foul. Ahab stooped to clear it; he did clear it; but the flying turn caught him round the neck, and voicelessly as Turkish mutes bowstring their victim, he was shot out of the boat, ere the crew knew he was gone. Next instant, the heavy eye-splice in the rope's final end flew out of the stark-empty tub, knocked down an oarsman, and smiting the sea, disappeared in its depths.[31]

And a few moments later, just before the *Pequod*'s final plunge, Tashtego is sighted at the top of the mainmast in the frantic "act of nailing the flag faster and yet faster to the subsiding spar." In fact, the three days of the chase at the end of the novel constitute an accelerating vortex, within which numerous other discrete flashes of speed suddenly flare up and are all consumed in the final spinning and spiraling apotheosis of the sinking *Pequod.* Similarly, Poe's ships in *The Narrative of Arthur Gordon Pym* and in "Ms. Found in a Bottle" suddenly accelerate their course, pulled by mysterious currents, in order then to plunge and disappear precipitously into the unknown depths of the South Pole. Melville's and Poe's are the accelerating ships of modernity: they are the past of industrial capital attempting to envision through the opaque present of acceleration the future promises of techno-industrial progress—and that envisioning is an attempt to rush ahead of the inescapable, unfathomable, and ominous gravitational pulls of a history of modernity increasingly apprehended as "one single catastrophe."[32]

Such an acceleration that constitutes the experience of modernity does not increase by a constant quantity, is not constant and continuous; it proceeds instead by fits and starts, by sudden leaps forward that at times land into spells of stillness and lag only to suddenly rush off once again. Discontinuity, rather than being an impasse, constitutes the productive and organizing principle of such an acceleration. *Moby-Dick,* understood as one whole accelerating narrative vector whose terminal and sharp arrowhead is the pointed blade of Ahab's harpoon shooting into the whale, embodies such a principle of acceleration. One can think of the protracted excursus on cetology, of the historiographical and statistical passages about whaling, of the lexical elucidations on whaleman's terminology, of the stories within stories ushered in by the several other ships the *Pequod* encounters, of the romance between Ishmael and Queequeg prior to embarking on the *Pequod*—one can think of each of these and of all other narrative enclaves in this novel as functioning according to its own specific and immanent temporal imperatives and yet as constituting the productive heterochronic zones of the whole novel's vectorial impetus. This is, in other words, a somewhat different recasting of Melville's poetics of time, which comes into being here as the synartesis of a tendentially homogeneous time of capital and a time of resistance to it constituted by heterochronic nicks and indentures. To represent a homogeneous and continuous acceleration would be tantamount to playing into the hands of the time of capital and of its apologists, that is, to capitulate to what Benjamin identifies as the homogeneous, empty time of historicism that always serves and writes the history of the victors over that of the vanquished.[33]

If Benjamin's angel of history is caught and shoved forward into the future by the storm of progress, its face remains turned and drawn toward a past of "wreckage upon wreckage." Similarly, Melville's ships embody the following paradox: it is only from within the precipitous and disastrous flux of the history of modernity that one can turn a longing gaze back over the ruins of what has been destroyed, that one can brush that history against the grain. If Foucault's dictum was that the ship is the heterotopia par excellence, that dictum needs now to be reformulated: the ship is the heterochrony par excellence.

THREE

White Capital; or,

Heterotopologies of the Limit

Pars destruens: Beyond the Last Limit

The experience of our generation: that capitalism will not die a natural death.

Walter Benjamin, *The Arcades Project*

ONE DOES NOT KNOW of the existence of an ontology of writing. If it were to exist, it would have to be eminently concerned with that peculiar writing apparatus whose motor is the first gentle breezes of history heralding the future tempest of crisis. There exists a *writing of crisis:* a writing dictated by the prescience of crisis, with its laws, its desires, its sudden flashes of apodictic vision. It is the concept of such a form of writing, in which history is sensed and lived as a rush, that the present pages wish to produce.

It is of crisis that Karl Marx repeatedly wrote from London for the columns of the *New York Daily Tribune* throughout the 1850s—of an impending crisis, which would yet again and yet more pointedly expose and denounce the bourgeois conception of crisis as something exterior to capital.[1] This coming crisis, in fact, would come into being more clearly than ever before as an immanence to capital, as the explosive product and temporary resolution of the contradictions inherent in the nascent and rapidly expanding mode of production of industrial capitalism—thus implicating such a mode of production in its entirety. For example, in an 1852 article ("Pauperism and Free Trade—The Approaching Commercial Crisis"), after having outlined the financial details of the imminent crisis, Marx writes:

> I know very well that the official economical *fortune-tellers* of England will consider this view exceedingly heterodox. But when since "Prosperity Robinson," [Frederick John Robinson] the famous Chancellor of the Exchequer, who in 1825, just before the appearance of the [1826] crisis, opened Parliament with the prophecy of immense and unshakeable prosperity—when have these Bourgeois optimists ever foreseen or predicted a crisis? There never was a single period of prosperity, but they profited by the occasion to prove that *this time* the medal was without a reverse, that the inexorable *fate was this time* subdued. And on the day, when the crisis broke out, they held themselves harmless by chastising trade and industry with moral, commonplace preaching against want of foresight and caution.[2]

Crisis for the apologists of capital always comes from an unpredictable and uncontrollable exteriority—war, famine, pestilence, and so on—like a viral agent infiltrating and ravaging what otherwise was a healthy *corpus economicus*.

However, to write *of* crisis, and even to write of it as immanence, is not yet enough, is not exactly what is meant by the writing of crisis. This other writing crystallizes when writing itself is conceived in and as crisis, when writing itself becomes crisis. It is precisely this other writing that Marx goes on to produce in the *Grundrisse* as soon as the heralded crisis finally does arrive in 1857. Starting in New York City as a series of bankruptcies, a depression avalanched for the first time through all the major national economies as well as through many minor ones, and thus constituted, in terms of its global tendency and ramifications, the first but certainly not the last *modern crisis*.[3] If in the *Grundrisse* Marx needs to reinvent materialist method as "the violent breath that infuses the totality of the research and constantly determines new foundations on which it can move forward,"[4] writing itself—the upsurging wave of writing upon which method rides and through which method unfolds—is reinvented in the *Grundrisse* as historical delirium. In *Marx beyond Marx*, Antonio Negri comments on the writing of the *Grundrisse*, drawing from Marx's letters:

> There was an extreme urgency that led to the birth of this first great political synthesis of Marx's thought: "The American crisis—which we foresaw, in the November 1850 issue of the review, would break out in New York—is fantastic," Marx wrote to Engels on November 13, 1857, "even though my financial situation is disastrous; I have never felt so 'cosy' since 1849 than

with this outbreak." "I am working like a madman for whole nights in order
to coordinate my work on economics, and to get together the *Grundrisse* before the deluge." (To Engels, Decemeber 12, 1857.) "I am working like a
condemned man. Sometimes until 4 o'clock in the morning. It is a double
work: 1) the elaboration of some fundamental aspects of the economy...
2) the current crisis." (To Engels, December 18, 1857.)[5]

Such delirious writing is dictated by the political urgency of a present that had already
been conceived and encountered as *futur antérieur*. The delirium of the writing of
crisis is that form of thought which can think the future of the past: a thought that
can envision the present of crisis as the future of the past of presentiment, and the
present of prescience as the past of a determinate future of catastrophe. Such a delirium speaks of things for which there exists as yet no language and for which a language may indeed never exist. That is why one must distinguish this delirium of
writing from the delirium of the very things it addresses and by which it is addressed
in return: the former must run along and ahead of the latter, but it cannot and must
not become the latter.[6] The delirium of the writing of crisis is not the delirium of
the crisis of which it writes: if it were so, that writing would be merely another
mimetic apparatus, another process of mechanical reproduction, another form of
representation. This is what it means to say that, in the writing of crisis, writing itself
becomes crisis: in becoming crisis, writing does not reproduce that crisis, because
while it becomes crisis, that crisis has already become something else. In becoming
crisis, writing transforms both itself and the very crisis whose emanations it perceives
as being exhaled from the other side of the horizon of history. If Marx's articles in
the *New York Daily Tribune* attempt to represent a crisis in writing—albeit a crisis
that did not yet exist—the *Grundrisse* brings a crisis to method and writing, makes a
crisis *of* writing that challenges and runs ahead of the present historical one.

In such a delirium of history, precisely because of its heliotropic
proclivity for the first modern crisis, Marx cannot help but write the *Grundrisse* as an
open work. Negri returns repeatedly to the assertion that "the *Grundrisse* is an essentially open work" and that "the *Grundrisse* is the center of the theoretical development of Marx because it represents the moment where the system in its formation,
far from closing, opens up on the totality of practice."[7] One needs to reformulate such
an assessment also with respect to the very matter of writing, that is, with respect to
writing as practice. The *Grundrisse*, in fact, is an open work in at least two distinct
but related senses: it opens itself up to that modern future of a cyclical series of ca-
tastrophes (of which the 1857 crisis had been apprehended as the inauguration) as

well as to future practices of writing, that is, to the writing practices of that modernist future in which the very question of closure and its impossibility will become one of the defining questions of writing itself. Almost as a corollary, one can now add that the writing of crisis produces the open work and that, conversely, the open work presupposes the writing of crisis, that is, it presupposes a historical delirium through which the future of crisis makes itself manifest as if through the Holy Shroud, as if it just emerged from the umbrae of a prehistoric past, as if it were a fossil, as if it had been here, with us, before us, undetected, all along.

It is in such a way that a white whale had been here, undetected, all along—with us while reflecting on Marx, and before us through all the delirious pages and visions of history in *Moby-Dick*. Melville's cetacean is precisely such a live fossil: it is that future which stares at us with a prehistoric face. But at times not even prehistory can reach far enough back in time to describe such a future. Shortly after the first appearance of the white whale, we read, "a strange fatality pervades the whole career of these events, as if verily mapped out before the world itself was charted."[8] Moby-Dick is the trace of a "strange fatality," the mark of a future that emerges from the billows of a time before time. As Ishmael remarks: "I am horror-struck at this antemosaic, unsourced existence of the unspeakable terrors of the whale, which, having been before all time, must needs exist after all humane ages are over."[9] This archaic and eternal future bears a face that is not merely prehistoric and that is, in fact, hardly a face at all: "[f]or you see no one point precisely; no one distinct feature is revealed; no nose, eyes, ears, or mouth; no face; he has none proper; nothing but one broad firmament of a forehead, pleated with riddles; dumbly lowering with the doom of boats, and ships and men."[10] While the future is certain—since it has already been folded in riddles that silently and surely speak of doom and catastrophe—it is the past, whence such a future would come, that is unpredictable. (Or, in Starbuck's despairing words toward the very end of the novel: "Oh! my God! what is this that shoots through me, and leaves me so deadly calm, yet expectant,—fixed at the top of the shudder! Future things swim before me, as in empty outlines and skeletons; all the past is somehow grown dim."[11] From a dim past, the future—in the form of Moby-Dick—swims toward Starbuck and will shoot through the *Pequod*.) Such then is the leviathan's inscrutable face: a "firmament...pleated with riddles" and even a "Rock of Gibraltar."[12] The future of catastrophe issues forth from a past measured in astronomical and geotectonic time—a nonhuman, nonmodern, nonhistorical, and perhaps even atemporal time. Not even the past can save us now from this future: catastrophe emerges from that which remains unknowable and unrepresentable in the past as well as in the present, that is, the untimely.

It is essential also to grasp the temporal contortions and somer-saults that surround the entrance of the white whale into the novel. While in quest of the white whale, the *Pequod* encounters another whaler, the *Town-Ho*, which has news of Moby-Dick. The more ominous part of this news never reaches Captain Ahab, as it was "secretly" disseminated by a sailor of the *Town-Ho* to a sailor of the *Pequod* and was eventually overheard by Ishmael. The latter finally announces: "In-terweaving in its proper place this darker thread with the story as publicly narrated on the ship, the whole of this strange affair I now proceed to put on lasting record"; but, he is quick to add: "[f]or my humor's sake, I shall preserve the style in which I once narrated it in Lima, to a lounging circle of my Spanish friends."[13] It is in the context of this latter narrative that one first encounters Moby-Dick, that is, that one first reads of anybody sighting and describing the white whale. In other words, Moby-Dick first appears within a narrative of events that had taken place prior to the events related by Ishmael in the novel; this narrative, however, belongs at once to the *future* of the main temporal framework of the novel—as Ishmael recounts the *Town-Ho*'s story in the way he later narrated it in Lima—and to the *past* of Ishmael's act of nar-ration in the present. From its very first appearance in the novel, Moby-Dick can be apprehended and represented only within a *futur antérieur*, of which, from then on-wards, it proceeds to become the trace.

Melville, in reaching toward an assured future of catastrophe as if plunging into an unfathomable past, stretches the temporal fabric of his writing and produces an open work. In the chapter on "Cetology," we read: "I promise nothing complete; because any human thing supposed to be complete must for that very reason infallibly be faulty." And later: "God keep me from ever completing any-thing. This whole book is but a draught—nay, but the draught of a draught. Oh, Time, Strength, Cash, and Patience!"[14] Or, as Adorno will put it in *Minima Moralia*, "The whole is the false."[15] In Melville, one can already sense the modernist sensibil-ities and imperatives of Adorno's capsizing of Hegel. Melville's already modernist valorization of open-endedness is steeped in the realm of the quotidian and in its strictures. Doesn't that exclamation—"Oh, Time, Strength, Cash, and Patience!"—invoke the four indispensable ingredients for successful closure, for bringing "the draught of a draught" to full completion? Here, it is a world of everyday urgencies and of financial demands, an acute and materialist sense of situatedness that are brought to bear upon the open work: this is a form that arises at a particular histor-ical crossroads, that emerges from the troubled interference between necessity and contingency. Time, strength, cash, and patience delineate the contours of precisely that historical situation which Melville feels is no longer available to him as a writer.

The social locus that Melville can no longer occupy is that of the writer of leisure, of the writer who can afford all the time, cash, strength, and patience in the world. Placed as he is at the onset of mass literary production, Melville is willy-nilly cast in the new role of the professional writer, a role to which he owes his first success with *Typee* and *Omoo*, but which he will very soon find constricting and tyrannical. Melville's bitter discovery is that writing has now been subjected to the tyranny of the market—and ample evidence of such a discovery can be found in his letters. In an 1849 letter to his father-in-law, he famously writes of *Redburn* and *White-Jacket:* "They are two *jobs,* which I have done for money—being forced to it, as other men are to sawing wood. . . . So far as I am individually concerned, & independent of my pocket, it is my earnest desire to write those sort of books which are said to 'fail.'"[16] In the same year, he writes to Evert Duyckinck about *Redburn*'s success: "I am glad of it—for it puts money into an empty purse. But I hope I shall never write such a book again."[17] To all this he adds (in a letter to Hawthorne written in 1851 while *Moby-Dick* was being finally revised): "What I feel most moved to write, that is banned,—it will not pay. Yet, altogether, write the *other* way I cannot. So the product is a final hash, and all my books are botches."[18] Here, perhaps, a network of determining relations between literary form and the logic of the market is most clearly perceived: the very structure of the text seems to buckle down and crack at its seams under the enormous atmospheric pressures of capital, and the final product of such metamorphic processes might well be one of the first specimens of an as yet unrecognizable and unprecedented literary form. What to Melville looks like a "hash" and a botch might be the new form that writing needs to assume in order not to give in to the demands of capital, while at the same time necessarily operating within those demands. *Moby-Dick* is such a botch, that is, a generic and structural mess whose immanent logic derives from the double-edged desire not to surrender to the writing dictated by the logic of capital while pushing that very logic beyond its limits in writing and so beating capital at its own game.[19] And if the desire that produces *Moby-Dick* is double edged, that is precisely because such a desire demands that writing also become that which it must not surrender to. At this point the writing of crisis needs to be understood as a writing of resistance to capital within capital.

Recounting to Hawthorne in 1851 the last and feverish stages of writing *Moby-Dick*, Melville declares that the "calm, the coolness, the silent grass-growing mood in which a man *ought* to compose,—that, I fear, can seldom be mine. Dollars damn me; and the malicious Devil is forever grinning in upon me, holding the door ajar."[20] It is indeed the daemonic powers of capital that hold "the door ajar" onto the wide expanses of the future, that open up the work to the realm of history.

It is through that door that Melville sights the approaching crisis, as in the same letter he confesses, "a presentiment is on me, — I shall at last be worn out and perish, like an old nutmeg-grater, grated to pieces by the constant attrition of the wood, that is, the nutmeg."[21] The writing of crisis is an unrelenting war of attrition against a history perceived as a ruinous process enlisting to its service elemental and cataclysmic forces — the prehistoric and indeed nonhistoric forces harking back to astral revolutions and tectonic formations, harking back to that time from which the Leviathan itself dates and irrupts into our present. And does it matter what this "presentiment" announces and exactly what form the impending crisis will assume? It does — but only inasmuch as it is not any one crisis, any one form. Prescience of crisis so thoroughly infuses each and every page of *Moby-Dick* right from the very opening lines — the first chapter is appropriately entitled "Loomings," and the first paragraph is imbued with intimations of melancholia and suicide — that, when the long-expected catastrophe does arrive, one is left with a sensation of excess of crisis. The sinking of the *Pequod* somehow does not safely exhaust and account for the intensity of all the delirious foreboding and visionary force that the novel had carefully built up and built itself upon. In this sense, prescience of crisis functions like a pharmacon that starts affecting an organism only after a certain amount has been accumulated in it, and that will then make its effects felt far after the interruption of its intake. In the end, there is no anagnorisis and no fulfilling catharsis, but only a dangerous surplus of crisis. In the end, the writing of crisis rushes through and after the end. After the shipwreck of the *Pequod* and after the end of *Moby-Dick*, one is left with a world that has become permanent crisis. If it is the case that the "tradition of the oppressed teaches us that the 'state of emergency' in which we live is not the exception but the rule,"[22] it is precisely such an image and conception of history that surfaces after the sinking of the *Pequod* — along with regurgitated detritus and wreckage. Constant "state of emergency" and permanent crisis: this is what on the last page of the novel becomes visible to Ishmael, who is left "floating on the margin of" history "and in full sight of it."[23]

How to conclude these prolonged prefatory remarks to a reading of *Moby-Dick* and of the *Grundrisse* as one and the same work? Would it be enough to suggest that both are differently dictated not only by the same first modern crisis of 1857 but also by the same new conception of crisis, by the very concept of modern crisis?[24] Would it be enough to maintain that they both write the crisis of modernity? And would it be just too visionary to imagine Melville in 1852, just over the exertions of *Moby-Dick*, reading the scathing commentaries on the coming crisis by one Karl Marx, the London correspondent of the *New York Daily Tribune*?[25] Idle questions? Perhaps. The point is that the writing of crisis lends a new form to a little-understood desire: the delirious desire to exceed, to overcome, to abolish history as we know it.

> And thus have these naked Nantucketers, these sea hermits, issuing from their ant-hill in the sea, overrun and conquered the watery world like so many Alexanders; parcelling out among them the Atlantic, Pacific, and Indian oceans, as the three pirate powers did Poland. Let America add Mexico to Texas, and pile Cuba upon Canada; let the English overswarm all India, and hang out their blazing banner from the sun; two thirds of this terraqueous globe are the Nantucketer's. For the sea is his; he owns it, as Emperors own empires; other seamen having but a right of way through it. Merchant ships are but extension bridges; armed ones but floating forts; even pirates and privateers, though following the sea as highwaymen the road, they but plunder other ships, other fragments of the land like themselves, without seeking to draw their living from the bottomless deep itself. The Nantucketer, he alone resides and riots on the sea; he alone, in Bible language, goes down to it in ships; to and fro ploughing it as his own special plantation. *There* is his home; *there* lies his business, which a Noah's flood would not interrupt, though it overwhelmed all the millions in China. He lives on the sea, as prairie cocks in the prairie; he hides among the waves, he climbs them as chamois hunters climb the Alps. For years he knows not the land; so that when he comes to it at last, it smells like another world, more strangely than the moon would to an Earthman. With the landless gull, that at sunset folds her wings and is rocked to sleep between billows; so at nightfall, the Nantucketer, out of sight of land, furls his sails, and lays him to his rest while under his very pillow rush herds of walruses and whales.[26]

Moby-Dick, or, *The Nantucketiads*. The heroes of Melville's epic are the Nantucketers whose glorious deeds constitute the world of whaling. However, all the imperialist fanfare and expansionist rhetoric notwithstanding, these heroes and their deeds are much unlike Luis de Camoëns's navigators and their feats of exploration in the *Lusiads*, or Virgil's founders of future empires and their exploits of bellic valor and filial piety in the *Aeneid*. Ultimately, Melville's epic is no epic at all — even though, in passages such as this, it seems to wish to be precisely that.[27] More than setting an epic tone and announcing this work as the epic of whaling, this passage claims a uniqueness for whaling that exceeds (that bears little relation, even, to) the claims of whaling as a heroic and epic activity. "Merchant ships are but extension bridges; armed ones but floating forts; even pirates and privateers, though following the sea as highwaymen the road, they but plunder other ships, other fragments of the land like themselves, without seeking to draw their living from the bottomless deep itself. The Nantucketer, he alone resides and riots on the sea. . . . *There* is his home; *there* lies his business." Here we return to the unstable dialectic between the ship as monad and the ship as fragment that was explored in chapter 1. If in that chapter we learned that these two distinct constructions of the ship, far from being mutually exclusive, are completely interdependent, we can safely surmise that to the degree to which the monadic construction is upheld as the sole image for whaling and for the *Pequod*, this ship and its world will also swing to the other dialectical pole and will be revealed as fragments of the world ashore — fated and damned as they are by the latter's history. For the moment, however, the point is that the sea is perceived here as being no more than incidental for all sea practices and for all types of ships, other than whaling and whalers. Undoubtedly, this is Melville's way of saying that after a novel on the merchant marine and a novel on the navy — namely, *Redburn* and *White-Jacket* — he has finally found what he had been looking and preparing for in those other two novels (both those novels, after all, were the "*jobs . . .* done for money," while *Moby-Dick*, evidently, was written from the outset as one of those "books which are said 'to 'fail.' ") Whether or not one is to surrender to Melville's evolutionary conception of his own literary trajectory, what is clear is that the exceptional nature of whaling is highly unclear. It is not clear why the uniqueness of whaling should become so crucial for Melville in *Moby-Dick* nor what new and unexplored narrative waters whaling provides for him in this novel. Before going too far with this investigation, let us first put such questions to Ishmael — for he is very familiar with them.

After a series of introductory speculations regarding the peculiar magnetic energy of the sea, Ishmael asks himself, why whaling?

> But wherefore it was that after having repeatedly smelt the sea as a merchant sailor, I should now take it into my head to go on a whaling voyage; this the invisible police officer of the Fates, who has the constant surveillance of me, and secretly dogs me, and influences me in some unaccountable way — he can better answer than anyone else. And doubtless, my going on this whaling voyage, formed part of the grand programme of Providence that was drawn up a long time ago. It came in as a sort of brief interlude and solo between more extensive performances. I take it that this part of the bill must have run something like this:
>
> "*Grand Contested Election for the Presidency of the United States.*
> "WHALING VOYAGE BY ONE ISHMAEL.
> "BLOODY BATTLE IN AFFGHANISTAN."

... though I cannot tell why this was exactly; yet, now that I recall all the circumstances, I think I can see a little into the springs and motives which being cunningly presented to me under various disguises, induced me to set about performing the part I did, besides cajoling me into the delusion that it was a choice resulting from my own unbiased freewill and discriminating judgement.[28]

Between fate perceived as police ("the invisible police officer of the Fates") and history treated as farce ("a sort of brief interlude and solo between more extensive performances"), whaling unfolds as a (temporary) escape from both. The jocular tone notwithstanding, Ishmael's whaling voyage is retrospectively posited in between historical events.[29] Is Ishmael's whaling voyage in some way also being turned into a historical event, given that it is situated between the election of a United States President and a war in foreign lands? Or are these two events somehow made to partake of the (putatively) inconsequential import of whaling? Clearly, the point is that these three acts on the bill of history need to be viewed as contiguous and related, and that whaling here is positioned in a context of matters historical and of the public sphere — after all, this bill reads, not coincidentally, like a newspaper. And if whaling is encased in between historical events, it is also geographically placed in between the United States and the world outside of it, almost as an element of mediation, or, perhaps, as the United States' own arrowhead launched into the world. (And as I will discuss later, during the first half of the nineteenth century whaling was the entrepreneurial and expansionist face that the United States most often showed to the world outside.) However, this historical bill, too, has been written and completely overshadowed by fate ("the grand programme of Providence"), just like every motive for going whaling — which might have been otherwise feasibly attributed to Ishmael's own "unbiased freewill and discriminating judgement" — is finally ascribed to the predetermined schemes of fate. But it is precisely when everything — both the personal and microhistorical as well as the "more extensive" historical "performances" — is explained in terms of fate's "surveillance" and coercion, thus leaving Ishmael a pawn at once powerless and free from blame or responsibility, that one ceases to believe his elaborate disclaimers.

There is someone else who understands the matter of fate far better than Ishmael, or, rather, who is willing to call it also by another name. Throughout the passage quoted above — and, indeed, at several other points in *Moby-Dick* — one hears echoes of Poe's Nantucketer, Arthur Gordon Pym, another melancholy character, who describes thus his attraction to the life of the sea:

For the bright side of the painting I had a limited sympathy. My visions were of shipwreck and famine; of death or captivity among barbarian hordes; of a lifetime dragged out in sorrow and tears, upon some gray and desolate rock, in an ocean unapproachable and unknown. Such visions or desires— for they amounted to desires—are common, I have since been assured, to the whole numerous race of the melancholy among men—at the time of which I speak I regarded them only as prophetic glimpses of a destiny which I felt myself in a measure bound to fulfill.[30]

Fate is desire. To catch a glimpse of the future one feels fated to fulfill is here understood as the form taken by the desire for that future, as a claim-staking over its as yet "unapproachable and unknown" territories: to foresee and to want are produced here as the Janus-headed process propelling the discourse of fate. Once reread through Pym's stark lucidity, Ishmael's retrospective illumination—the fact that now he can somehow suddenly recognize "the springs and motives" for setting sail on a whaler as having been the "cajoling" of fate—is also revealed as fulfilling a double function of representation. For Ishmael, fate is produced both as the materialization and as the displacement of a desire too great and unconfessable to be made manifest any form other than a policing exteriority, a panomphean deus ex machina hovering and looming high above the stage on which the drama of whaling is about to unfold. But can one name Ishmael's desire for whaling?

Ishmael's inquiry "into the springs and motives which being cunningly presented to [him] under various disguises" cajoled him into choosing whaling above other sea practices thus continues:

Chief among these motives was the overwhelming idea of the great whale himself. Such a portentous and mysterious monster roused all my curiosity. Then the wild and distant seas where he rolled his island bulk; the undeliverable, nameless perils of the whale; these, with all the attending marvels of a thousand Patagonian sights and sounds, helped to sway me to my wish. With other men, perhaps, such things should not have been inducements; but as for me, I am tormented with an everlasting itch for things remote. I love to sail forbidden seas, and land on barbarous coasts. Not ignoring what is good, I am quick to perceive a horror...

By reason of these things, then, the whaling voyage was welcome; the great flood-gates of the wonder-world swung open, and in the wild conceits that swayed me to my purpose, two and two there floated into my inmost soul, endless processions of the whale, and, mid most of them all, one grand hooded phantom, like a snow hill in the air.[31]

It is crucial to note that "[c]hief among these motives was" *not* "the great whale himself" but rather "the overwhelming *idea*" of it. Right from the outset, the prime motor of the whole novel is identified as a mental image and located in the realm of the abstract, until later when it is also and more precisely cast in terms of the fantastic and phantasmal. Ishmael, in fact, is finally swayed to his purpose when he (fore)sees "the great whale" as "one grand hooded phantom" floating "like a snow hill in the air." "The great flood-gates of the wonder-world swung open" and visions of a fated future came rushing in — but they did so as phantoms, that is, in the form elected by the past for haunting the present. What ultimately seals Ishmael's fate to this whaling voyage, what finally provides his desire for whaling with its most accurate form, is a vision of the return in the future of the past, a vision of a future haunted by ghosts of the past. Right from its introduction in the novel, whaling as a practice is put up against overwhelming, unfathomable, and phantasmal powers, is inextricably and fatefully related to the logic of the *futur antérieur.* So it is that Ishmael can say of the *Pequod* that it "blindly plunged like fate into the lone Atlantic," without relating — as one might think — its disastrous end, but rather the very beginning of its passage.[32] It is no common whaling ship and no common whaling voyage that Melville chooses in this novel, unlike the very ordinary voyages on which he had purposely focused in *Redburn* and *White-Jacket.* In *Moby-Dick,* one sets sail for the whaling voyage to end all whaling voyages, to end all whaling. *Moby-Dick* is written as whaling's last passage.

Unsurprisingly, when it came to finding a whaling ship for his voyage, Ishmael's desire emerged from the waters of Nantucket harbor as the return of the repressed. He chooses the *Pequod* without hesitation: it is a "noble craft, but somehow most melancholy!"[33] Like Pym, who belongs to "the whole numerous race of the melancholy among men," Ishmael is drawn to the melancholy: such irresistible melancholy is one of the many spellbinding mechanisms that are sent from the future both as baits and heralds of catastrophe. It turns out, however, that this melancholy may also emanate from the past: for the *Pequod* too is a ghost. After describing the ship still lying at anchor, Ishmael adds offhandedly: "*Pequod,* you will no doubt remember, was the name of a celebrated tribe of Massachusetts Indians, now extinct as the ancient Medes."[34] One wonders about the ideological somersaults, political contortions, and plain stoppage of intelligence that went into the making of such an astounding sentence and into recasting (recent) genocide as (ancient) extinction — and one can safely assume that such theatrics of historical obliteration were not unique to Melville.[35] And yet there is something eerily accurate in having the ghost of an ancient mass extinction preside over Ishmael's fated whaling voyage, for the *Pequod* is not only the return of the repressed from the primal scene of the United States' political unconscious but also a return that is now put to new tasks. Such a return of the repressed is mobilized in a desperate attempt to at once anticipate and stave off a future of catastrophe, to at once call such a future into being — before it calls you — and defer it for as long as possible. If to reconstruct the disappearance of the Pequod Indians as an extinction is to erase the historical fact of extermination and to deny the existence of an exterminating community — to which both Melville and Ishmael belong — the historical fiction of extinction may well be for both of them the only viable form of representation for apprehending another, albeit very different, extermination that takes place in *Moby-Dick*. The return of the repressed, in its incarnation as the *Pequod*, is invoked here to represent the end of the world of whaling and indeed to rush such a world to its end — a ruinous end that is a willed political-economical execution made historically available to Melville only as extinction. Such a representational complexity is undoubtedly also due to the fact that, while the former extermination found Melville fully within the exterminating community, in the case of the passing away of whaling, his allegiances are continuously renegotiated between the exterminated and the exterminator. The historical forces actively at work in the disastrous downfall of whaling are perceived to be so immense and multifarious, so decentralized and omnipresent that they have become thoroughly rarified and naturalized; they are perceptible only as transcendent, ominous loomings and doom. *Moby-Dick* formulates a representational paradox: it conjures up the future image of the destruction of whaling — at the hand of as yet unfathomable and unidentifiable forces — as the natural extinction of a historical form.

But what are these unfathomable forces that cast from the future their inescapable net and ensnare and annihilate in it the world of whaling? What is so wrong with whaling that it needs to be terminated? One ought to put these questions to the discourse of extinction; after all, what is said to have become extinct is precisely that which was no longer able to adapt its ossified structures to a radically transformed historical situation, that is, that which was no longer needed and which was an impediment for successfully effecting such radical transformations. What is said to have become extinct is that which actually was directly and ruthlessly hunted down and destroyed by the historical forces that had started such transformations. In *Moby-Dick*, whaling is perceived as precisely such an obsolescent relic of an ancient artisanal world that is to be swept away by the forces of progress. In this sense, the unfathomable and invisible powers responsible for whaling's downfall are only too easily recognizable as the usual culprits of the increasingly dominant assemblages of industrial capitalism. Having said this, however, one has said barely anything —

and certainly nothing interesting yet! The point is not to discover in *Moby-Dick* the historical forces responsible for the annihilation of whaling as a practice—for that would indeed be tantamount to wanting to extract from *Moby-Dick* the truth about whaling. The point is, rather, to push this text to that limit beyond which it will tell us altogether different stories about itself and about its own relation to the world of whaling, beyond which this relation will be clearly articulated as a representational paradox of antagonism and complicity.

It is undoubtedly because he sensed this to be whaling's last passage, its flight beyond the precipice of extinction, that Ishmael was inevitably drawn to whaling and to the *Pequod*. Being thus set from its inception, this novel's relation to whaling cannot but unfold as one of elegiac celebration forever oscillating between mourning and melancholia. *Moby-Dick* is recast here as a chronicle that captures the world of whaling in the nick of time, that records whaling at the very last moment in which it is possible to record it, at the crucial moment of its disappearance. And if this has started to sound like a refrain, you may be reassured that it is one. We have returned here to the poetics of the nick of time and to its historical pressures and representational urgencies that were explored in chapter 2. In this respect *White-Jacket* initiated a process whose fruition and consequences were to be fully felt and elaborated only here in *Moby-Dick*. In *White-Jacket*, Melville focuses on the representation of certain specific practices (such as storytelling) that are perceived to be threatened by historical effacement, while the entire world housing this and many other practices—that is, the navy—was and is under no immediate threat. In *Moby-Dick*, on the other hand, Melville found what he had been looking for all along: a whole dying world urgently demanding representation—with all of its specific minutiae. The mesmerizing complexity and infinite detail of the world of whaling transform Melville's historical-representational projects, so that in *Moby-Dick* the poetics of the nick of time take radically different turns.

Indeed, the very practice of writing is continuously transfigured and reconfigured by its encounter with the wild and refractory matter of whaling: the world of whaling exerts crucial pressures on the very structure and fabric of writing in *Moby-Dick*. I would go as far as to say that, even though in this novel we read numerous, intertwined, and very diverse narratives, *Moby-Dick* is ultimately not very concerned with narrative per se. In *Moby-Dick*, Melville has taken up nothing less than a world, nothing less than a whole historical formation, which needs more than the unfolding of narratives to be narrated in its untrammeled entirety and to be produced anew in writing. Hence the cross-generic and cross-disciplinary wilderness of this text: to conjure up this whole world of whaling, and to trace all of its future ramifications and past genealogies, Melville needs to produce and to combine with each other very different types of writing: zoological taxonomies; etymological investigations; cetacean anatomies; literary and pictorial histories of the whale; political economies of whaling along with attendant financial-statistical analysis; numberless manual-like lists; descriptions and explanations of whaling equipment, of customs and discipline, of etiquette, and even of victuals, and so on. In Ishmael's own words:

> One often hears of writers that rise and swell with their subject, though it may seem but an ordinary one. How, then, with me, writing of this Leviathan? Unconsciously my chirography expands into placard capitals. Give me a condor's quill! Give me Vesuvius' crater for an inkstand! Friends, hold my arms! For in the mere act of penning my thoughts of this Leviathan, they weary me, and make me faint with their outreaching comprehensiveness of sweep, as if to include the whole circle of the sciences, and all the generations of whales, and men, and mastodons, past, present, and to come, with all the revolving panoramas of empire on earth, and throughout the whole universe, not excluding its suburbs. Such, and so magnifying, is the virtue of a large and liberal theme! We expand to its bulk. To produce a mighty book, you must choose a mighty theme.[36]

One wonders if anybody after St. Thomas Aquinas has ever wished—let alone attempted—to write such a *Summa Totius Philosophiae*. What is being invoked here, however, may well be the very opposite of the book of the world and of all knowledge, the converse of a veritable *summa mediaevalis*. If one is to believe this passage, in fact, *Moby-Dick* does not wish to reproduce and to shut the world inside its pages, as if in a gilded philosophical-representational cage; it does not wish to firmly control and dominate the world via the yoke of one homogeneous and perfected type of writing (and such a wish is indeed what drives and produces the *summa*, the synthesis of all things.) In *Moby-Dick* writing magnifies and "expands" itself; it rises and swells with the sweep of the universe and reaches out toward its unreachable boundaries; it stretches its own limits so as to adapt itself to the matter that it must confront; it extends and superimposes itself onto such a matter much like a film, to the point that it becomes other than itself; it opens itself up to and lets itself be transformed by the world (of whaling) and to its practices; it opens itself up to the very problem of praxis. In *Moby-Dick*, the world is not forced to become the book; rather, it is the book that, in running after and in attempting to become the world, becomes something other than either the world or itself. This is nothing short of a revolution in writing.

This is all to say that *Moby-Dick* is not a novel. Or, rather, I am not interested in whether or not one calls it a novel, as long as one does not succumb to the mystifying conclusion that, having called it a novel, one can comprehend how it functions by placing it as a novel among other novels: it is not as a novel or because it is a novel that one will be able to reconstruct the modalities of being of its writing and of its novelty. To grasp *Moby-Dick*'s writing revolution, one needs also to posit it within the history of the production and emergence of new types of critical discourse that needed to be cross-generic and cross-disciplinary—and often even antidisciplinary—if they were to make anything at all of that crisis which is modernity. In this respect, one also ought to understand Melville's desires and efforts in *Moby-Dick* alongside the texts of other thinkers who felt that the traditional epistemological and disciplinary instruments at their disposal were inadequate for the emergent problematic they faced, and who therefore had to produce whole new worlds of praxis, language, and writing to engage with what they perceived as the world, that is, in order to produce the world. If the *Grundrisse* constituted the product of, as well as the escape from, the representational impasses and epistemological breakdowns that philosophy and political economy faced when confronted with the emergent world of industrial capitalism, *Moby-Dick* constituted the product of, as well as the escape from, the representational impasses and epistemological breakdowns that the novel—and indeed literature and high culture *tout court*—faced when confronted with the dying world of whaling. Before elaborating these suggestions any further, however, we need to return to the narratives and chronicles of the dying world of whaling in *Moby-Dick*.

Nowhere else are Melville's chronicling imperatives more intense than in the chapters illustrating the activities and objects constituting the practice of whaling.[37] In such chapters, the question of the fated narrative and historical obliteration of whaling is posited as a more urgent condition of possibility for writing than in the chapters that explicitly articulate the presentiments of future crisis and catastrophe. These are the least understood and most easily overlooked pages of the novel: the pages that students don't like to read and that are notoriously expurgated by editors in juvenile editions or other such ravagings of *Moby-Dick*. These are pages of the microscopic. These are pages driven by a passion for minutiae and spent in painstakingly detailed, protracted, and impersonal descriptions of whaling artifacts and the practices associated with each. Such a microscopic writing is always verging on the didactic (echoes of Virgil's *Georgics*), always infused with reverence in the face of congealed labor time and of labor time yet to come, always directed by an uncompromising representational *dictat:* that no trifle go overlooked, that nothing be lost for history. This is a writing *en apnée:* a writing thoroughly submerged in the very matter of whaling, thoroughly immured in its diverse materials and multiple materialities—a writing that rarely surfaces from its complete absorption in the elaboration of whaling as praxis. However, it is in the rare, sudden, and temporary emersions that one needs to look for this writing's modalities of being.

It would be foolish to assert that it is here and only here, in these descriptive and expository chapters on whaling, that one finds the true Melville. It may not be as misguided, however, to believe that it is in the *relation* between such chapters and the other types of writing in the novel that one finds the articulation of Melville's historical-representational projects. These descriptive chapters and sections of chapters are usually linked to the surrounding narrative fabric via justificatory passages and apologetic circumlocutions. Thus, for example, Ishmael introduces the whale-line:

> With reference to the whaling scene shortly to be described, as well as for the better understanding of all similar scenes elsewhere presented, I have here to speak of the magical, sometimes horrible whale-line.[38]

At other times, such explanatory words follow the narratives they are meant to elucidate:

> The allusion to the waifs and waif-poles in the last chapter but one, necessitates some account of the laws and regulations of the whale fishery, of which the waif may be deemed the grand symbol and badge.[39]

And again:

> Out of the trunk the branches grow; out of them, the twigs. So, in productive subjects, grow the chapters.
> The crotch alluded to on a previous page deserves independent mention.[40]

The arborescent metaphor notwithstanding, this novel grows rather by fits and starts, and in rhizomatic ruptures and deviations. The "subjects" of *Moby-Dick*, though, are indeed "productive" of each other and dependent upon each other—and so are their attendant chapters. Ultimately, one witnesses here a veritable symbiosis of distinct forms of writing. Even though the burden of proof is repeatedly put on the passages illustrating specific elements of whaling (whose existence is predicated solely on the fact that they clarify the preceding or ensuing narratives aboard the *Pequod*), and even though the pages devoted strictly to the matter of whaling are continually deemed secondary or auxiliary to the more properly narrative parts of the novel, one often gets the sense that those narratives may instead exist so as to necessitate the elucidations about whaling, so that the world of whaling be explored as praxis, so that whaling's ruinous fate also be told from the perspective of all of its specific materials and practices.

Ishmael, on the other hand, may be capsizing and transfiguring these relations—which he himself had first established in passages such as the ones just cited—when he concludes a detailed account of the whale-line in this fashion:

> Again: as the profound calm which only apparently precedes and prophesies of the storm, is perhaps more awful than the storm itself; for, indeed, the calm is but the wrapper and envelope of the storm; and contains it in itself, as the seemingly harmless rifle holds the fatal powder, and the ball, and the explosion; so the graceful repose of the line, as it silently serpentines about the oarsmen before being brought into actual play—this is a thing which carries more of true terror than any other aspect of this dangerous affair.[41]

Ishmael here has sensed the immanence of the virtual—an immanence that implies the virtual as the material horizon of the object. The virtual here is felt pulsating within the fabric of the momentarily still and silent object: it is the terrifying stillness and serpentine silence of that object, it has collapsed into and it is the very fabric of that object. The "explosion" of the virtual, the looming "storm," the ruinous fate that can be felt through folding surfaces of temporality such as the patient, expectant, and springlike coilings of the whale-line: all this is apprehended as the material constituting the "profound calm" and the "graceful repose" of a present that no longer "precedes," "prophesies," signifies, or represents anything other than itself, or even anything at all, as it is thoroughly saturated with representation and knows itself to be already the past of a copresent future of crisis. What we witness here is the breakdown of the signifying chain and of representation altogether—a breakdown due not to their failure but rather their success, that is, to an excess of signification and to a surplus of representation. The calm does not stand for, represent, or signify the storm; the calm has exceeded itself within itself: it *is* the storm. (And here Melville crosses the boundaries of the always tendentially transcendent dominion of mimesis and reaches into the realm of immanent ontology). Such a past-present-future of crisis is not only a temporal structure but also a spatial one: such a relentless spatialization of time enables the production of the chronicles of whaling and allows Melville to capture whaling in the nick of time. Objects such as the whale-line—those objects of whaling perceived to have the undoing, of everything surrounding them as well as themselves, curled up within them in a state of hibernation—are the magnets that attract the writing of crisis. Or, rather, the writing of crisis turns everything it touches into precisely such "magical, sometimes horrible" objects of temporal copresence, it turns any minutia into a crystal ball. This is how *Moby-Dick*'s recurrent and protracted excursus on the matter of whaling ought to be read: as the world of "actual play" already hosting the realm of the virtual, as a writing already imbued with and driven by the "terror" of catastrophe, as the writing of crisis. In this sense, the last three days of the chase—along with all the other narratives of this novel—constitute the excursus and the escapes from the exegetical chronicles of whaling, while such chronicles constitute instead the fruition and explicative elaboration of a catastrophe that was already implicit there where one would least expect to find it, namely, in the most serene and mundane writing of whaling.

 Whaling in *Moby-Dick* never really stood a chance: it was a world that was conjured up precisely so as to be constructed right from the beginning as its own living end, as its own catastrophe. The fate of whaling in *Moby-Dick* is undoubtedly the proverbial fate worse than death. We have returned here to the troubling equation of fate and desire. But while fate had been identified earlier as a policing transcendence, here it has also been located as immanence. Now we can reconfigure both these constructions more accurately by understanding the fate of desire and the desire of fate in *Moby-Dick* as a transcendence-in-immanence, that is, as a transcendence-effect within the object, as that immanence that, in opening itself up to distinct yet indiscernible temporal planes simultaneously, becomes apprehensible only as transcendence. The equation between fate and desire, however, turns out also to have contained an unknown quantity all along, namely, history. What is most emblematic about Melville's chronicle of whaling as a doomed world is the fact that he wrote it from the very height of the golden age of whaling. Melville's whaling travels took place during the early 1840s and *Moby-Dick* was written between 1850 and 1851: these years are completely contained within the most florid period of United States whaling, which spanned roughly from the mid-1830s to the late 1850s and which had its apogee during the 1850s—and it is important to note that by the 1830s the United States had by far the most prosperous and powerful whaling fishery in the world.[42] Melville watches whaling at its zenith through the melancholy gaze of anticipated loss. In this crack between history and representation—at once an aperture and a discrepancy that undoes both history and representation—one may catch a glimpse of Melville's desire *in fieri:* a desire for the obliteration of whaling that is at once all the more determinate for having to run counter to all the present circumstances of whaling, and yet all the more dependent on such circumstances of unparalleled prosperity as they implicitly formulate questions of historical direction (namely, whereto—and how and why—from such a present?). While Melville's desire for the obliteration of whaling is formulated as fate and reinserted back as immanence into the very matter of whaling, such a desire also and conversely formulates the hope against hope of staving off indefinitely this catastrophic fate—or, as a last resort, of striking alliances with it—as soon as such a fate is perceived as historically inescapable. In other words, lest one get caught in a chicken-or-the-egg rut regarding the relations between fate and desire, it is imperative to realize that fate and desire here are both forms for the thinking of history: they are both onto-epistemological apparatuses through which Melville attempts to capture, identify, and materialize history's elusive logic. Once again, it is a question of excess—but also of betrayal. The love Melville feels for each and every practice, object, and body of whaling is expressed as a betrayal of precisely that object of love, a betrayal that takes the form of an excess of desire for the death of the loved object as soon as that death is for the first time understood to be inescapable, if not also imminent. Melville is the Judas Iscariot of the world of whaling, who delivers it to the policing hands of the ruinous powers of history so as not to remain caught in its fated downfall, and who, therefore, also enables its resurrection and secures it in writing. In this sense, *Moby-Dick* is the chronicle of a ruthless historical becoming: the becoming-executioner of the one who feels he is about to be executed, that is, the complete betrayal of a socio-historical *locus*. *Moby-Dick* is the chronicle of the struggle to achieve such a betrayal—a betrayal that a priori entails the difficult task of accurately identifying the exterminating agents with whom one may ultimately need to side.

Melville could not have foreseen the specific historical convergences that marked the sudden decline and fall of whaling as a practice. If the financial crisis of 1857 signaled the beginning of the end of whaling, it did so not in and of itself—whaling had indeed recovered before from such severe crises—but primarily because it subtracted vital funds from whaling that, a few years later, were going to be needed to face new and unforeseeable challenges. The discovery of petroleum in 1859 quickly provided a new series of far cheaper substitutes for all the products derived from sperm whale oil. The Civil War also dealt significant blows: the slow and unarmed whaling ships became prime targets for Confederate attacks as well as objects of the Union's sacrifices (for example, in 1861 the Union deliberately sank a whole whaling fleet in an attempt to blockade the ports of Savannah and Charleston). Most important and insidious, perhaps, was an increasing and irreversible flight of investment capital from whaling that started taking place in the very center of whaling shipping as soon as whaling was perceived to be a sinking ship. In New Bedford, Massachusetts, in fact, the investment of whaling profits had been crucial in the commencement of the industrial manufacture of cotton goods since 1846; the cotton industry, however, proceeded to benefit even further from and indeed speeded up whaling's downfall during the following decades when textiles were seen to offer a steadier yield to capital than a whaling industry in crisis...Whaling was kept alive until it fulfilled its historical mission of supporting the New Bedford cotton industry to the point of its complete, self-sustained, and self-reproducing financial independence. Whaling was "the wrapper and envelope" and indeed the cocoon of industrial capitalism.[43] Finally, with the mid-nineteenth-century push into the continental expanse, the sea had to abdicate to the West the role of frontier for United States expansionism—a role that the sea had fulfilled since at least the victorious war of 1812–1815 against England, which had been predominantly a naval war. Brave new worlds had been opened that whaling was not equipped to explore.

Few of these developments could have been available to Melville. Because the historical conjunctures of the ruinous fate of whaling were still rarified and unfathomable, they could be materialized in the novel only as belonging to whaling, as whaling's self-victimization and self-destruction (and in this case Ahab would be seen as the embodiment of such an immanence). It rests then with the whale to constitute the only (apparently) external force through which the causes of that fate can take a form at all—albeit not an intelligible one: it is only as the whale that the historical apparatus that was to do away with whaling is at all perceived and crystallized. I am not saying that the whale is an allegory for the emerging forces of industrial capitalism: I am suggesting, rather, that in the whale Melville produced not the metaphor but rather the concept of the logic governing historical formations that did not yet fully exist, even though they peeped and threw random clues and cryptic messages into his present from the privileged and heavy-curtained balconies of future history. It is perhaps due to its paradoxical constitution—that is, its coming-into-being as the concept of necessarily abstract historical formations that were not yet in existence—that Moby-Dick inhabits this novel at once as the most material and the most abstract of bodies, at once as the bulkiest, heaviest, largest of all living beings and as a "phantom," a vision, and a fleeting mental image.

In other words, even though Melville could not have been privy to many of the complex historical conjunctures outlined above, he did nonetheless sense the generalized and almost gaseous presence of an as yet uncoalesced series of contingencies and logics that would negate the necessary preconditions of the artisanal world of whaling and that would demolish its foundations. What he did perceive was that a machinic apparatus had been put into motion which would eventually capture and process whaling through its merciless cogs—not unlike the machine that swallows Charlie Chaplin in *Modern Times*. Machines are indeed relevant here: that apparatus which Melville perceives as the primary agent in the destruction of whaling, in fact, will turn out to constitute itself precisely as a regime of machines, as an emergent techno-industrial imperative. That is why, perhaps, in this novel the concept of the machine and the discourse of the machinic are at times invoked when writing runs up against the ineffable and the unintelligible. Of Ahab one reads that "without using any words [he] was meanwhile lowly humming to himself, producing a sound so strangely muffled and inarticulate that it seemed the mechanical humming of the wheels of his vitality in him."[44] Of madmen and poets it is said that they hear voices. Here Melville hears instead the wordless, "muffled and inarticulate" humming of the inscrutable machine of future history, whose distant thunder echoes through its chosen and oracular automata.

> To have *circulation*, what is essential is that exchange appear as a process, a fluid whole of purchases and sales. Its first presupposition is the circulation of commodities themselves, as a natural, many-sided circulation of those commodities. The precondition of commodity circulation is that they be produced as *exchange values*, not as *immediate use values*, but as mediated through exchange value. Appropriation through and by means of divestiture *[Entaüsserung]* and alienation *[Veraüsserung]* is the fundamental condition.... Circulation is the movement in which the general alienation appears as general appropriation and general appropriation as general alienation. As much, then, as the whole of this movement appears as a social process, and as much as the individual moments of this movement arise from the conscious will and particular purposes of individuals, so much does the totality of the process appear as an objective interrelation, which arises spontaneously from nature; arising, it is true, from the mutual influence of conscious individuals on one another, but neither located in their consciousness, nor subsumed under them as a whole. Their own collisions with one another produce an *alien* social power standing above them, produce their mutual interaction as a process and power independent of them. Circulation, because a totality of the social process, is also the first form in which the social relation appears as something independent of the individuals, but not only as, say, in a coin or in exchange value, but extending to the whole of the social movement itself. The social relation of individuals to one another as a power over the individuals which has become autonomous, whether conceived as a natural force, as

chance or in whatever other form, is a necessary result of the fact that the point of departure is not the free social individual.[45]

Circulation appears. Of circulation one cannot say that it is, only that it appears. The concept of circulation is held hostage as well as released into circulation by a difficult, demanding verb: *erscheinen*—at once to appear, to seem to be as well as to appear, to arise, to become manifest, to come into being. This is a verb of being and not being at one and the same time. What such a verb and its appearance in almost all the sentences of the above passage demands of us is that we immediately cast circulation into the phantasmal, that we think circulation right from the beginning as that which appears to be when and what it actually is not, as well as that which appears, emerges, "arises spontaneously from nature" and hovers above us—the itinerant and circulating *Erscheinung* of the social. The immanent interference constitutive of this verb identifies, delimits, and charts that space within which the social can think itself as a whole. One catches Marx here in the attempt to conceptualize the social's own process of self-constitution and subjectification through the act of seeing itself reflected there where it is not—in a fluid and smooth process and as a seamless and continuous whole. Marx here is already elaborating a theory of a shared, collective, social imaginary. It is only in the realm of such an imaginary that the whole would appear as more than the sum of its parts and that the repeated and cumulative collisions of the singular and specific moments of the social process would produce a representational surplus in the form of an autonomous and transcendent social entity. This is an entity that cannot just sit still: in order to continue to materialize itself it needs to be reproduced and realized all over again in each singular and successive moment of exchange. Circulation, in other words, appears as a transcendent social form that is apprehensible and operative only as an immanence in the singular moment of social relation, only as the structuring and enabling principle in that epiphenomenical moment of relation. Circulation appears as its own material condition of possibility, as the absent effect of its own just-as-absent cause.

If I say that the white whale in *Moby-Dick* is precisely such a self-reproducing process of transcendence-in-immanence, I mean to say above all that Melville's cetacean and Marx's circulation share the same modalities of appearance. "[T]he great flood-gates of the wonder-world swung open, and in the wild conceits that swayed me to my purpose, two and two there floated into my inmost soul, endless processions of the whale, and, midmost of them all, one grand hooded phantom, like a snow hill in the air."[46] Moby-Dick suddenly bursts forth from a "wonder-world" and materializes as a phantasmal presence emanating from and hovering above an endless process(ion) of relations in and by twos, as an alien and transcendent entity that nonetheless resides in the "inmost soul." Its appearance having been established in such a fashion at the beginning of the novel, the white whale will proceed to haunt the rest of this novel as a ghost, will continue to live in it as an autonomous and terrible power that—like Marxian circulation—"arises spontaneously from nature." And yet this is indeed a *social* power: Moby-Dick functions as the cement and ultimately also as the solvent of the social relations in the novel. Each and every single moment of relation and exchange aboard the *Pequod* at once produces and is mediated by the looming vision and absent presence of the white whale. Most emblematic in this respect is the foundational event of the voyage, namely, the moment when Ahab extracts from and exchanges with the whole crew the vows to kill Moby-Dick in "The Quarter-Deck" chapter: the white whale is posited in these vows, which become the prime social contract constitutive of the *Pequod*'s unique mission, as an invisible but nonetheless binding power, as the repeatedly invoked, yet repeatedly unavailable, structure of this ship's hierarchical relationality.[47] Moby-Dick embodies the paradox of a social power that can be imaged and materialized only "as a natural force, as chance or in whatever other form"—other, that is, than a social and historical one.

The white whale needs to appear in the novel not only as an absent but also as a circulating presence if it is to keep the *Pequod* and its special mission itinerant and afloat, if it is to provide continuously both the lubricant and the fuel of that ship's internal systems of relation and of their attendant narrative forms. Both Moby-Dick and Marxian circulation, over and beyond their common appearance, are concepts articulating a particular type of movement. Figures of circulation and circular movement with regard to the whale abound throughout the novel (and the most emblematic moment, in this respect, is perhaps the end of the first day of the chase, when Moby-Dick, having capsized Ahab's boat, starts furiously and inexplicably to swim in circles around its wreckage as if under a spell—and the center of this circular spell is the head of barely afloat Ahab.)[48] What is specific and unique to such figures is that circulation is conceptualized in them as tendentially and potentially infinite. Much like Marx understands circulation as that which "[a]t first sight...appears as a *simply infinite* process" and which ought to appear that way if it is to function at all as circulation,[49] Melville at first posits the white whale as possibly perpetual and uninterrupted circulation, as being caught—and as catching the *Pequod* along with it—in a potentially infinite and continuously repeated circumnavigation of the globe. But as soon as this problematic is articulated in such a manner, one faces a foregone conclusion: as soon as Marx writes "at first sight" and as soon as Melville opens the whole novel and continues to saturate it thereafter with loomings of catastrophe, one knows that Marxian circulation had been posited from the very beginning as discontinuous, potentially finite, and internally fractured by contradictions, and that Moby-Dick's circular and circulating line of flight had already been doomed to be brutally interrupted. After such beginnings, the only real question that remains for both texts is to find out what the costs involved are in arresting the work of seamless and endless circulation and bring it to a grinding halt. It follows that both these texts are ultimately also formulating questions about what it might mean as well as what kind of world it would take to undo the very concept of a self-legitimizing "alien social power" and to explode from within the social's own foundational concept of itself.

    Ahab is the embodiment of that anomalous desire that is thrown into the machinery of circulation in order to send it haywire: he is the agent of that desire charged with the mission of sabotaging and shutting down the process of circulation. Ahab had already broken away from circulation long before attempting to stop it in its specific form as the white whale. Ahab is the obsolete remnant of an archaic, nonsynchronic, premodern, and perhaps even precapitalist desire to refuse to engage in exchange—a desire to flee from the logic of exchange altogether. In this sense, Ahab ought to be regarded as the relic that the whole novel conspires to do away with or, rather, that the novel needs to put in the situation of having to do away with itself so that the new may come into being. Dimock, for example, shows how Ahab is constructed as an Oriental despot and a participant in feudal formations who "has no use for substitution and exchange," as he seeks only vengeance for its own sake, namely, not a kind of vengeance that—as Starbuck might have suggested— could be justified by being exchanged "for a different set of terms, like its value on the Nantucket market."[50] Ahab, hence, is in a directly antagonistic and doomed position with respect to the emergent and concerted logics of capital, which is founded on concepts of exchange and circulation, and of liberal democracy, which is founded on concepts of political representation. C. L. R. James had already advanced similar hypotheses when he stated that, in hunting the white whale, Ahab "says, in effect, to hell with business and money," and that thus he has "trumpled upon" and "derided" the "sacred principles" of United States civilization, that is, of capitalism.[51] Such interpretations of Ahab, however, are only partially accurate inasmuch as they are not dialectical enough in assessing what are highly dialectical dynamics. If Ahab has indeed wrested himself away from the logic of capital, in doing so, he also still functions completely within that logic—and for at least two related reasons. First, the very act of breaking away is already contained, determined, and anticipated by the conceptual presuppositions through which the logic of capital operates: to reject and negate a dialectical process of constitution is merely to pave the way for a higher level of subsumption within such a process rather than to escape it. Second, as we will see later in this chapter, Ahab's attempt to break away from the logic of capital ultimately turns out to be necessary for the further development of that logic. For the moment, it suffices to say that such a desire to reject exchange and to terminate circulation wedges Ahab right in the middle of the contradiction of circulation. Far from instituting circulation as an infinite and seamless whole, such a contradiction produces circulation as a discontinuous and fractured process right from its inception. It is the modus operandi of this productive contradiction that needs to be explored now.

Money: that is the paradox Marx sights in that crack which is the contradiction of circulation. For our present purposes, the lengthy and intricate arguments regarding the money-form in the *Grundrisse* can be summarized by saying that money is understood there as having three, perhaps four, semiautonomous and, under special circumstances, simultaneous functions: (1) money as measure; (2) money as medium of circulation; (3) money as money and (3a) as capital.[52] "As measure, its amount was irrelevant; as medium of circulation, its materiality, the matter of the unit, was irrelevant: as money in its third role, the amount of itself as of a definite quantity of material is essential."[53] Later in this chapter, I will consider this "third role," in which money negates the other two and transcends the process of circulation in order to become the independent and general form of wealth; or, as Marx puts it: "[money f]rom its servile role, in which it appears as mere medium of circulation . . . suddenly changes into the lord and god of commodities [as it] represents the divine existence of commodities, while they represent its earthly form."[54] For the moment, it is money in its second role—as medium of circulation—that concerns me. In this second role, money is itself the material form of the constitutive contradiction of circulation. Marx writes:

> At first sight, circulation appears as a *simply infinite* process. The commodity is exchanged for money, money is exchanged for the commodity, and this is repeated endlessly. . . . In this way, commodity is exchanged for commodity, except that this exchange is a mediated one. . . . It is entirely wrong, therefore, to do as the economists do, namely, as soon as the contradictions in the monetary system emerge into view, to focus only on the end results without the process which mediates them; only in the unity without the distinction, the affirmation without the negation. The commodity is exchanged in circulation for a commodity: at the same time, and equally, it is not exchanged for

> a commodity, in as much as it is exchanged for money. The acts of purchase
> and sale, in other words, appear as two mutually indifferent acts, separated
> in time and place. . . . In so far as purchase and sale, the two essential moments
> of circulation, are indifferent to one another and separated in place and time,
> they by no means need to coincide. Their indifference can develop into the
> fortification and apparent independence of the one against the other. But in
> so far as they are both essential moments of a single whole, there must come
> a moment when the independent form is violently broken and when the in-
> ner unity is established externally through a violent explosion. Thus already
> in the quality of money as a medium, in the splitting of exchange into two
> acts, there lies the germ of crises, or at least their possibility.[55]

Money here is above all the expression of a contradictory and potentially explosive social relation. As long as the buying and the selling of commodities are conceived as unrelated transactions — that is, as long as the exchange of X for money and the exchange of that money for Y are not regarded as transactions that at once negate each other and are dependent on each other — it is the case (a) that money is just another commodity and that a money economy is no more than barter, (b) that exchange is always free and equal exchange, and (c) that the contradiction in circulation is ignored. To highlight the contradiction that money incarnates due to its special position vis-à-vis all other commodities, on the other hand, would mean to expose that social relation upon which exchange is founded and to reveal exchange to be unequal exchange by definition. Marx here pushes the very matter of contradiction toward that social *locus* in which it might become other than itself, that is, irresolvable contradiction. If that contradiction that is implicit in an understanding of buying and selling as unrelated transactions enables the smooth functioning of circulation, what that contradiction becomes when one understands buying and selling as synchronic and antithetical is contradiction that can no longer be used by the system of circulation and that may indeed effect the breakdown of that system: what that contradiction becomes is no longer a contradiction at all. Money is precisely that *locus* where contradiction may multiply into an unco-optable surplus of contradiction, where it may saturate and exceed the subsumptive capabilities of dialectical relations. In the money-form, the dialectical process of circulation gets more than it bargained for, more than it can take. Such then is the explosive corollary to Marx's investigation of the money-form: circulation functions thanks to and in fear of forever impending but continuously deferred crisis — what circulates is precisely the possibility of crisis. Marx writes of circulation as "completion," as "the return of the point of departure into itself."[56] If the possibility of crisis is what impels and guides such a return, the actuality of crisis in the end impedes returns, explodes completions, and forbids any end.

But we have not yet seen money at work, nor do we know yet exactly what it is. If circulation was described earlier as constituting at once its own cause and its own effect, one can be sure to find a similar structuring principle within the mechanisms of the money-form:

> As a mere medium of circulation, in its role in the constant flow of the circulatory process, money is ... the mere *representative* of the price in relation to all other commodities, and serves only as a means to the end that all commodities are to be exchanged at equivalent prices. It is exchanged for one commodity because it is the general representative of its exchange value; and, as such, as the *representative* of every other commodity of equal exchange value, it is the general representative; and that is, as such, what it is in circulation itself. It *represents* the price of the one commodity as against all other commodities, or the price of all commodities as against the one commodity. In this relation it is not only the *representative* of commodity prices, but the *symbol* of itself; i.e. in the act of circulation itself, its material, gold or silver, is irrelevant. ... Hence, in this process, its reality is not that it is the price, but that it represents it, is its representative — the materially present representative of the price, thus of itself, and, as such, of the exchange value of commodities. ... From this it follows that money as gold and silver, in so far as *only* its role as means of exchange and circulation is concerned, can be replaced by any other *symbol* which expresses a given quantity of its unit, and that in this way symbolic money can replace the real, because material money as mere medium of exchange is itself symbolic.[57]

Marx encounters and confronts in the money-form a particularly vexed philosophical question, namely, the question of representation. The question of money and the question of representation are produced here as one and the same: the uniqueness of money among commodities is located in the work of representation and yet the potential breakdown of any representational system is implied here in the unique character of money as the symbol of itself. If money within the process of circulation functions as the representation of exchange value and thus of itself, how does representation function when faced by that which ultimately represents only itself — above and beyond all else it also can, must, and does represent? What does it mean to say of money that it is its own symbol? It is to say that it no longer means anything at all. To say such a thing virtually identifies money as an excess of signification, tendentially locates money in a realm beyond representation. And what is the color of money? White, of course. The color of money is white.

Ishmael thus concludes his protracted meditations on the color white:

> But not yet have we solved the incantation of this whiteness, and learned why it appeals with such power to the soul; and more strange and far more portentous — why, as we have seen, it is at once the most meaning symbol of spiritual things, nay, the very veil of the Christian's Deity; and yet should be as it is, the intensifying agent in things the most appalling to mankind.
>
> Is it that by its indefiniteness it shadows forth the heartless voids and immensities of the universe, and thus stabs us from behind with the thought of annihilation, when beholding the white depths of the milky way? Or is it, that as in essence whiteness is not so much a color as the visible absence of color; and at the same time the concrete of all colors; is it for these reasons that there is such a dumb blankness, full of meaning, in a wide landscape of snows — a colorless, all color of atheism from which we shrink? And when we consider that other theory of the natural philosophers, that all other earthly hues — every stately or lovely emblazoning — the sweet tinges of sunset skies and woods; yea, and the gilded velvets of butterflies, and the butterfly cheeks of young girls; all these are but subtile deceits, not actually inherent in substances, but only laid on from without; so that all deified Nature absolutely paints like the harlot, whose allurements cover nothing but the charnel-house within ... —pondering all this, the palsied universe lies before us a leper. ... And of all these things the Albino whale was the symbol. Wonder ye then at the fiery hunt?[58]

White is among colors what money is among commodities: the material presence of both the absence and the representation of itself — always more than itself and not itself at all. Just like white in Melville is "the visible absence of color" and "at the same time the concrete of all colors," money in Marx is the "*précis de toutes les choses*"[59] as well as the site where commodities appear absent and where all one can see is their exchange value leveling and standing in for their singularity. White and money are different names for the same place: this is the place in which both colors and commodities, as if by magic, become equivalent and dissolved, in which "their particular character is erased," in which they are revealed to have always been "merely accidental existences."[60] This is the place not only where the "particular" becomes the "accidental" and where both become void of any meaning and value, but also where everything else becomes meaningless and valueless too, since it is that which can only mean itself. The whiteness of a landscape covered with snow becomes a "dumb blankness, full of meaning": this is a landscape that is so full of meaning that it can no longer speak, that it can no longer mean anything at all. This landscape is the final horizon of hermeneutics: it is precisely "the palsied universe" of the system of value—a paralyzed system in which value has been brought to a standstill. Melville here, after all, invokes possibly the most powerful signifying structure for the production of value in Judeo-Christian traditions, namely, the binarism of good and evil: as soon as the color white is understood both as "the most meaning symbol of spiritual things, nay, the very veil of the Christian's Deity" and as "the intensifying agent in things the most appalling to mankind," a gaping abyss of indiscernibility opens up in which the opposite values of good and evil cease to signify since they begin looking too much like each other, since their meaning had been posited on their radical difference from each other. (And this is undoubtedly that Nietszchean abyss that goes by the name of the transvaluation of all values, that abyss of which Nietzsche writes in *Beyond Good and Evil* that "when you look long into" it, it "also looks into you."[61]) In this sense, the endless literary-critical disputes over this or that specific meaning of whiteness and over what exactly the white whale symbolizes seem to miss the point: neither the white whale nor its color mean anything at all—and this is precisely what is so terrifying about both for Ishmael. There are, of course, several critics who do come to similar conclusions.[62] The problem, however, is that usually such conclusions are reached precisely as conclusions, that is, as an all-meaningful moment of epiphany at which one can stop and rest and contemplate—being much fatigued by the exertions of having finally reached what should have been the point of departure of the investigation in the first place. If upheld as the conclusion of the investigation rather than as its starting point, the realization that both the white whale and its color in *Moby-Dick* cannot readily be recruited for the production of meaning and for any system of value can easily lead to either reveling or despairing in the face of the meaninglessness of the universe and of all things. Such reveling or despairing, of course, are identical to each other, and ultimately they constitute a terminally humanist move, that is, humanism's last-ditch effort to recuperate for meaning that which would resist any such recuperation, that which Wallace Stevens might have called "the nothing that is." This is humanism's last call for boarding yet again onto the sinking ship of hermeneutics.[63] The question that such critical accounts finally do not formulate is: How do such an absence of meaning and such an impossibility of value function in Melville? What powers do they serve and why?

For both Melville and Marx the question of whiteness and the question of money at once presuppose and generate the question of value—and what is at stake in both cases is an attempt to identify the possibility and the site of crisis. For Melville, whiteness is a crisis in meaning, value, and representation. For Marx, "already in the quality of money as a medium... there lies the germ of crises, or at least their possibility"—or, as Negri puts it, in the *Grundrisse* money is posited "*as the crisis* of the law of value."[64] What both Marx and Melville have detected, in other words, is the virtual breakdown of different systems of value: they have discovered, in money and in whiteness, the secret and shared mechanism—all the more secret and invisible precisely because it stands there in public and for all to see—through which those systems operate and in which those systems have poured all of their contradictions. They have sensed where and what one should strike for value to ultimately turn its violence against itself, to be forced to undo itself by itself.

And yet, this picture needs to be complicated further: Melville, in fact, is fundamentally ambivalent regarding what he has discovered in whiteness. Money in its third role of "money as money and as capital"—when it "independently steps outside of and against circulation"[65]—comes even closer to that certain whiteness so dreadful to Ishmael. Of this third and final stage in Marx's analysis of money, Negri writes:

> The dominion of money has the appearance and the indifference of mobility and fluidity; money exercises its dominion under the paradoxical form of *evanescence*. It is everywhere and it dilutes itself in persistence, but at the same time it recovers itself as a sign of the totality. Its intermediation is as supple as it is rigid. But that is how this paradox is materialized: the evanescent power of money attacks things and transforms them in its own image and resemblance. It is a *demiurgic power* which through a sign modifies reality. It is clear that in this Marx, money is a *tautology for power*. A power that extends everywhere.[66]

If one were to indulge in a most unphilological game of substitution throughout this passage (namely, substituting in it "whiteness" for "money"), one would nonetheless go a long way in tracing the contours of Ishmael's dread. Whiteness is dreadful precisely because its power is embodied in the paradox of present absence, "of evanescence": it disappears, dissolves into, and lives buried within all colors and within all objects as their common and prime material principle; it also, hence, "attacks things and transforms them in its own image and resemblance," as it touches them "with its own blank tinge"; it is "a demiurgic power" that produces reality and produces it empty of any meaning and value, produces it as "the charnel-house within." This is indeed a tautology for omnipresent power: "a monumental white shroud that wraps all prospect around" us. This is indeed "a power that extends everywhere." *White Power*.

To say that the obsession with the color white in the literatures of the United States—which is present already with Charles Brockden Brown's *Wieland*, haunts Poe in the *Narrative of Arthur Gordon Pym* and Melville in at least *White-Jacket* and *Moby-Dick*, and returns to constitute itself as a veritable poetic tradition through Emily Dickinson, Wallace Stevens, Robert Frost, and so on—is eminently driven by anxiety regarding the question of race is to state the obvious.[67] At one point in his excursus on the color white, Ishmael reflects on how this color's "royal pre-eminence" "applies to the human race itself, giving the white man ideal mastership over every dusky tribe."[68] Although this fairly nonchalant reference to the question of race indicates that Melville knows exactly what he is inevitably also talking about when discoursing on whiteness, it is not here that one ought to look for the racial impulse of Melville's obsession with the color white. Such an impulse becomes more manifest in Ishmael's dread in the face of whiteness, or, more precisely, in the irresolvable representational impasse he runs into when attempting to explicate and justify that dread. Even as it complicates racist discourse by exposing the impasse upon which it is founded, Ishmael's horror of whiteness is not readily explained as antiracist sentiment. What appalls him about this "colorless, all color of atheism" is the realization that the suffocating and ubiquitous power of such a "monumental white shroud that wraps all the prospect around him" is in a symbiotic relation with its "heartless voids and immensities," its "blankness, full of meaning," its inability to signify, its unwillingness to represent or be represented. That the supreme power of the white race might function through self-negation and self-dissolution, might signify only and exclusively itself, might indicate no intrinsic, stable, and essential value of superiority, and might hence be treading dangerously on the brink of an incommensurable and unfathomable historical abyss—these are indeed the components of Ishmael's horror at the dizzying sight of whiteness, this is what causes his "Descartian vortices."[69] Melville here has sensed the constituting contradiction of power that rules by decree, of self-teleological power that exploits and annihilates simply because it can and exclusively because it exists. Ultimately, it is not even the brutal *modus operandi* of such a power that terrifies Ishmael as much as the fact that, already implicit in its very modalities of being, he can sense the possibility of its self-destruction, that is, the virtual, violent, and complete dissolution of that power and of its attendant social order. What horrifies Ishmael, in other words, is not that white power is violent and absolute and meaningless and valueless, but that one day it may finally collapse, thus leaving the door open to as yet unimaginable historical possibilities. The urgent question one can hear echoing in Ishmael's dread of whiteness is how and for how long can absolute power last as a tautology for itself? Or, what will finally be the modalities and the schedule of disintegration of such a power?

Before proceeding any further, a clarification is in order. It might seem, in fact, that I have conflated two distinct conceptions of value and that I have leveled, on the one hand, the economic specificities of Marx's investigation, and, on the other hand, the ethical-religious and hermeneutical-representational specificities of the discourses with which Melville is engaging. Here, I will limit myself to three brief points. (1) Even though Marx's and Melville's conceptions of value are distinct and irreducible to each other, they nonetheless share zones of indiscernibility (e.g. both money and whiteness are seen as posing problems for representation) and, more importantly, they share in a common genealogy. John Guillory's reminders regarding the ways in which "*both* aesthetics and economics were founded in contradistinction to the concept of 'use value'" and in which both these discourses derive their distinct conceptions of value from the same source—namely, eighteenth-century moral philosophy—are relevant here.[70] Such zones of indiscernibility and common genealogies, however, are not my immediate concern. (2) Even though Marx and Melville engage with different discourses on value, what they attempt to put into question as well as to escape in such discourses is arguably the same thing, namely, the logic of exchange. Marx and Melville discovered this same increasingly dominant logic in different discourses: this is the logic of equivalence and commensurability, the logic that decrees it possible and necessary to produce the equivalent representation of something that is resistant to any form of representation. What both Marx and Melville attempt to conceptualize through different discourses is this nonrepresentational, asignifying, asubjective, incommensurable something. By way of a paleonymic encryption, this something can be identified for the moment with that use value which constitutes the unthought of both aesthetic and political-economical discourses. While the second part of this chapter deals with this vexed question in detail, here I would like to anticipate that if Marx and Melville attempt to think the unthinkable—namely, use value—that is so because use value is not value at all, because value qua value exists exclusively within the logic and the world of exchange, because use value resides in the realm of potentiality. (3) What has concerned me, however, is something other than what I have sketched in (1) and (2), and that can be thought of as a series of structural homologies. What has been most important so far is not that

Marx and Melville are writing about the same kinds of things—even though that is precisely what I will argue in a moment—but rather that they are writing about whatever they are writing about *in the same way:* they are mobilizing the same conceptual apparatus for confronting matters that only at first sight are radically different from each other. Such a conceptual apparatus is part and parcel of that form of thought that goes by the name of the dialectic and yet attempts to bring the dialectic to the point of crisis so as to disengage itself from it. Marx and Melville confront the specific forms they do confront (money, whiteness, and so on) also because such forms can be effectively conceptualized only through a crisis in dialectical thought, which crisis, then, is revealed as more of an object of investigation than even the specific forms that are apprehended through it.

The structural homologies between *Moby-Dick* and the *Grundrisse* that I have outlined so far can now be summarized through a mathematical proportion.

Circulation : The White Whale = Money : Whiteness

Each of the four terms of this proportion is internally fractured: Marx's and Melville's Hegelian intuition is that it is thanks to and not in spite of such fractures that these terms function, both on their own terms and within that proportion. Marx and Melville, in other words, discovered that these terms function dialectically—but they did not stop at such a discovery. Negri writes of "crisis" in the *Grundrisse* "as the form of circulation."[71] Crisis is a form of discontinuous movement, and, as if by a law of transitiveness, it constitutes not only circulation but also the other three terms of that proportion: this is a form of movement defined by that fracture, by that site of contradiction that runs through the middle of each of those terms and keeps them revolving around their own axes and metamorphosing at each complete revolution. Crisis intended as the form of movement and change of each of the terms in that proportion is the ever-renewing contradiction in the dialectic. This is a crisis that ought to be at all times carefully monitored if it is to enable the smooth functioning of the system that enslaves it: crisis must resist its potentially ever-widening centrifugal pulls and gyrations, must not overperform, must not lead to catastrophe. It is precisely such a centrifugal path of escape from the dialectic that Marx and Melville are trying to trace, as they spell out the formula for catastrophe, that is, for the surplus of crisis, for the overperforming crisis of crisis. Or, as Negri puts it— paraphrasing Roman Rosdolsky: "Marx's 'catastrophism' is a keynote of revolutionary music."[72] It is in this sense that both Marx and Melville confront the urgent question of the dialectic. Such a confrontation became unavoidable at a time when the dialectic was rapidly becoming the dominant conceptual apparatus for the production and reproduction of everything everywhere. In *Moby-Dick* and in the *Grundrisse*, they formulate at once the conditions of possibility as well as the conditions of impossibility and catastrophe of an era founded on the dialectic and of the dialectic itself. Marx and Melville make history a problem for philosophy and philosophy a problem for the history of the material world.

The moment has arrived for those structural homologies to be discarded, as they have served their heuristic function. In the face of such a crisis of crisis even homology is too timid and fragile. We need to go further. In non-Euclidean geometry, parallel lines do meet at infinity: one ought to stretch the limits of thought and of writing toward that unreachable infinity; one ought to reach that point of interference where Marx and Melville address and are addressed by the same force, namely, capital — that is, capital as the law of crisis. And what is the tenet of this law? Its tenet is the limit. And what is the modality of being of this law? Its modality of being is a Sisyphean production and expansion of limits.

If crisis is the form of circulation, circulation cannot stop expanding. Marx writes:

> A precondition of production based on capital is therefore *the production of a constantly widening sphere of circulation*, whether the sphere itself is directly expanded or whether *more points within it are created as points of production*. While circulation appeared at first as constant magnitude, it here appears as a moving magnitude, being expanded by production itself. . . . The tendency to create the *world market* is directly given in the concept of capital itself. Every limit appears as a barrier to be overcome.[73]

Negri, thus, draws the conclusions that circulation "is a capitalist victory over the crisis" and that capital "must extend outward and multiply in the process of circulation in order to normalize the crisis . . . which constitutes it and which is constantly about to explode — more and more impetuously."[74] This is a victory that is not won only once and for all time but rather that needs to be won over and over again, and each time with higher stakes, and that in the long run may reveal itself to be a Pyrrhic victory. "Every limit appears as a barrier to be overcome." From within circulation, each and every limit needs to appear as the last limit — until the next round of expansion. From the standpoint of crisis, however, limits appear in a different light: during the tendentially global expansion of circulation, crisis may trace its line of flight through and across all possible limits. A few pages later, after having described in detail the plethora of traditional social relations and formations dissolved by capitalist circulation on its irrevocable march to the world market, Marx adds:

> It is destructive towards all of this, and constantly revolutionizes it, tearing down all the barriers which hem in ... the expansion of needs, the all-sided development of production, and the exploitation and exchange of natural and mental forces.
>
> But from the fact that capital posits every such limit as a barrier and hence gets *ideally* beyond it, it does not by any means follow that it has *really* overcome it, and, since every such barrier contradicts its character, its production moves in contradictions which are constantly overcome but just as constantly posited. Furthermore. The universality towards which it irresistibly strives encounters barriers in its own nature, which will, at a certain stage of its development, allow it to be recognized as being itself the greatest barrier to this tendency, and hence will drive towards its own suspension.[75]

Each and every limit is posited as the last limit and already points to yet another last limit. Capital treats each and every limit at once as the last one and as the one before the last: it confronts limits merely by displacing them and setting them farther along. If the last limit implies infinite seriality and is posited as a form of exteriority, however, beyond all possible last limits there is yet another and altogether different kind of limit, that is, *the other limit:* an event of immanence and singularity.[76] Unlike the last limit, the other limit is not exterior to capital and resides "in its own nature," in its irresistible rush toward "universality," in its irrevocable will to power, which will eventually "drive towards its own suspension." The last limit is the expression of capital's dread in the face of the other limit. The expansionist march of capital — its serial strategy of confrontation and deferral of last limits — unfolds a trajectory that constitutes the converse projection of the other limit's furious and expectant stillness within each drumbeat of that very march. In each and every last limit, capital acts as its own exorcist: in positing the last limit, capital attempts the impossible task of conjuring up and expelling from within itself the other limit, that is, the absent presence of its own unthought. It is through the other limit that the force of the outside from time to time makes itself felt on the history of capital and dictates to capital its inescapable ultimatum: you either play a different game or lose this one, you either metamorphose or die.

Enough. One gets the drift. One knows too well by now the history of these metamorphoses, that is, the history of the costly restructurations capital undergoes as a last resort in order not to collapse when pushed beyond that other limit: the colonial genocides, the imperialist wars, the implementation of more efficient forms of exploitation, the termination of certain industries and of their workers for the coming-into-being of new and more profitable industries and of kinder, gentler, and cheaper workers. This history is carved into the backs of labor much like the sentence is carved into the back of the prisoner in Franz Kafka's penal colony.

It is such a history that elected Melville as one of its chroniclers when he undertook the immense task of writing the book of the world of whaling. His was the task of composing the untimely elegy of a soon-to-be-defunct set of practices whose yielded capital was being reinvested not into them but rather into industrial production in its earliest and most emblematic form, as was discussed earlier in this chapter, the cotton industry. His was the task, in other words, of writing a volume in the history of last limits: the limit that whaling came to constitute for capital was overcome by being set farther along in the form of the cotton industry — and it is in this transition that *Moby-Dick* came into being. Ahab wished to overcome and to abolish such a history of limits. But let him speak — for he has not yet spoken:

> ["] But what's this long face about, Mr. Starbuck; wilt thou not chase the white whale? art not game for Moby-Dick?"
>
> "I am game for his crooked jaw, and for the jaws of Death too, Captain Ahab, if it fairly comes in the way of the business we follow; but I came here to hunt whales, not my commander's vengeance. How many barrels will thy vengeance yield thee even if thou gettest it, Captain Ahab? It will not fetch thee much in our Nantucket market."
>
> "Nantucket market! Hoot! . . . If money's to be the measurer, man, and the accountants have computed their great counting-house the globe, by girdling it with guineas, one to every three parts of an inch; then let me tell thee, that my vengeance will fetch a great premium *here!*"
>
> "He smithes his chest," whispered Stubbs, "what's that for? methinks it rings most vast, but hollow."
>
> "Vengeance on a dumb brute!" cried Starbuck, "that simply smothe thee from blindest instinct! Madness! To be enraged with a dumb thing, Captain Ahab, seems blasphemous."
>
> ". . . All visible objects, man, are but as pasteboard masks. But in each event — in the living act, the undoubted deed — there, some unknown but still reasoning thing puts forth the mouldings of its features from behind the unreasoning mask. If man will strike, strike through the mask! How can the prisoner reach outside except by thrusting through the wall? To me, the

white whale is that wall, shoved near to me. Sometimes I think there's naught beyond. But 'tis enough. He tasks me; he heaps me; I see in him outrageous strength, with an inscrutable malice sinewing it. That inscrutable thing is chiefly what I hate; and be the white whale agent, or be the white whale principal. I will wreak that hate upon him. Talk not to me of blasphemy, man; I'd strike the sun if it insulted me....Who's over me? Truth hath no confines.["][77]

Masks through which one ought to strike, prisons outside of which one must reach, walls through which one has to thrust, and, finally, beyond all these limits, one comes to a truth that has no longer any "confines," no longer any limits at all. Ahab must have known all along that the bitter truth in the end was actually an inescapable abyss, that beyond all these limits he was to find only a centripetal vortex of whiteness: "Sometimes I think there's naught beyond. But 'tis enough." The inevitable catastrophe aside, however, one might think that the most important feat that he had set for himself has been accomplished all the same: namely, that he break loose from the "great counting-house" of "the globe" whose very circumference can now be measured only by money, that he escape the logic of exchange upon which capital is founded. Not so. Ahab is the nth avatar of crisis, he is the crisis of capital made flesh: he embodies that crisis of value which is value itself frozen for an instant at the very moment when it can either be revalued, reused, and realized in a new form or be done away with once and for all time. For forty years, Ahab had been the most efficient and committed believer in the enterprise of whaling and in capitalist ethics; then his dismemberment and mutilation, at the hand of fate materialized as the white whale, began a crisis, re-formed him as his own and capital's condition of permanent crisis: instead of retiring to shore to wife, children, and business, as any other zealous citizen of capital would have done, he embarks on that (only apparently) aberrant voyage of unexchangeable vengeance that is *Moby-Dick* — thus revealing the fracture he had borne all along. He reemerges through that fracture as the crisis of capital momentarily gone awry, as the sudden acceleration and line of flight of that crisis through and beyond what appears to him as the other limit of capital and of the whole world, capital and the world having collapsed for him into the same entity. The white whale — that truth that "hath no confines," that can no longer know or mean anything since it means and knows no bounds, that can no longer be comprehended since it is infinity itself, that is no longer of any value because it is the beyond of all value, that is no longer either true or false — emerges for Ahab as the other limit of capital. And what does such a limit say? It says, metamorphose or die. And the white whale as the form of the other limit ended up marking a metamorphosis for capital and a death for Ahab. For Ahab was needed by capital; his crisis had been exploited all along, and even his attempt to finally bring about a real crisis and a real state of emergency—namely, that unexploitable surplus of crisis that would have saturated the system of value and that would have constituted a catastrophe for capital—results in the termination of the world of whaling so that entirely new forms of capital might come into being. Ahab is the archaic arrowhead shooting through the other limit and into the future of capital: he is that nonsynchronous element of resistance within capital that finally does the bidding of capital far better than any of its fully synchronous elements. Ahab had wanted to stop and abolish circulation *tout court*, and instead he enables its new beginning somewhere else in another form: Ishmael/Melville, after all, is spared the final hecatomb, goes back home, writes down the tale, and eventually becomes a clerk regulating the international circulation of commodities and immigrant labor.[78]

In "The Song of the Sirens," Maurice Blanchot writes:

> Of Ahab and Ulysses, the one with the greater will to power is not the more liberated. Ulysses has the kind of deliberate stubbornness which leads to universal domination: his trick is to seem to limit his power; in a cold and calculating way he finds out what he can still do, faced with the other power. He will be everything, if he can maintain a limit, if he can preserve that interval between the real and the imaginary which is just what the Song of the Sirens invites him to cross. The result is a sort of victory for him, a dark disaster for Ahab. We cannot deny that Ulysses understood something of what Ahab saw, but he stood fast within that understanding, while Ahab became lost in the image. In other words, one resisted the metamorphosis while the other entered it and disappeared inside it. After the test, Ulysses is just as he had been before, and the world is poorer, perhaps, but firmer and more sure. Ahab is no longer, and for Melville himself the world keeps threatening to sink into that worldless space towards which the fascination of one single image draws him.[79]

This is all true. However, the devastating moral of this story—a moral Blanchot infinitely defers—is that ultimately both Ulysses and Ahab do the bidding of the value of the world and of the world of value: the former does so by affirmation, while the latter does so by negation. This marks a success for Ulysses, who wanted nothing better than to reassert the stability of the world, and a failure for Ahab, who wanted to undermine that stability. Ahab's failure was a failure of the imagination: he had learned so well the lesson of capital and had absorbed so completely its logic of exteriority that, when he attempted to trace his own line of flight, all he was able to see was the path traced and retraced by capital in its continuous attempts to transcend itself and its own contradictions, namely, the path delimited by the constant displacement and repositing of outer limits. The secret was that the white whale never really marked the other limit. (Ulysses, in his Dantean and Tennysonian reincarnations, seems to have known this secret vis-à-vis the song of the sirens, and that is why he needs to restart his voyage after his return to Ithaca, although he commits Ahab's same mistake in the end.) The white whale was yet another last limit of capital. Ahab should have looked for the other limit inside his ship: the virtual other limit of capital was right there for all to see in the myriad practices, bodies, and contradictions constituting the world of whaling to which Ahab was systematically oblivious throughout his careful staging of a failure foretold. And yet, no failure can fail to express a desire. His failed desire to escape from the logic of capital has a symbiotic counterpart in Melville's successful and paradoxical desire to escape that very logic in writing the book of the dead of the world of whaling—a world swept away not by a storm but rather by "the profound calm which only apparently precedes and prophesies of the storm" and which "is perhaps more awful than the storm itself."[80] It was from within such a profound and profoundly devastating calm that Marx and Melville could not fail to hear the roar of "the really *modern crises*, in which [the] contradiction of capital discharges itself in great thunderstorms which increasingly threaten it as the foundation of society and of production itself."[81]

Pars construens: At the Other Limit

... nobody as yet has determined the limits of the body's capabilities: that is, nobody as yet has learned from experience what the body can and cannot do.

Baruch Spinoza

In the world of commercial exchange, he who gives over the measure is in the wrong; whereas the lover is always he who loves beyond measure.

Theodor Adorno and Max Horkheimer

At the other limit of capital unfolds the writing of joy. It is the concept of such a mode of writing, in which the body is sensed, lived as *potentia* and *multitudo*, that these pages wish to produce. For one has forgotten to say that *Moby-Dick* and the *Grundrisse* are also joyous books. For one has forgotten to say that at the other limit crisis is also joy, that the other limit is that body which incarnates crisis as joy, that body whose collective utterances speak crisis and joy as one and the same historical affect. One must return, hence, to the other limit and to its demands one last time.

I have written of capital so far as the subject of its own history of crisis, as the agent of its own sudden expansions, as the force igniting and propelling the repeated *Aufhebung* of the last limit. I have endowed capital with a life that is ultimately not its own. It is the borrowed life and time of capital and their provenance that concern me here, for such a life and such a time are plundered from that body of *potentia* and *multitudo* whose very flesh flexes around and embodies the absent presence of the other limit.

Here I may be doing nothing more yet than translating into my own corporeal idiom what ought to be a historical-materialist truism, namely, that the restructurations periodically undergone by the mode of production are always reactions against and attempts to contain and dominate class struggle. Capital's cyclical process of simultaneously surpassing and resetting farther along the forever receding outer horizon of the last limit is a process initiated and commanded by the always virtually insurgent life animating that immanence which is the other limit. Such are also the conclusions that Negri reaches in *Marx beyond Marx* and that he encapsulates even more poignantly perhaps in his "Twenty Theses on Marx: Interpretation of the Class Situation Today." In thesis twelve, which states that the "struggles precede and prefigure social production and reproduction," he writes:

> The transformations of the machinery, the restructuration, the new norms of the customs and the new arrangement of the institutions, all follow there where the struggle has been—where, that is, living associative labor has been freed and has thrust forward its own autonomous project.... [Living associative labor] is also the real entrepreneur of history, because history, industry and civilization are constrained to modify themselves in a way which is complementary, functional, organic to the contents, to the needs, to the tendencies, to the forms of organization of the proletarian struggles. This is the boss' curse: those who learn most from the class struggle get ahead. This paradox is the shame of the boss—the perennial spy, who borrows and represses. The proletarian struggle, the workers' struggle and now the thousands of figures of the every-day revolt of social labor have—within the order—dominated (and that is put in motion, formed, prefigured, anticipated) the epochs and the phases of capitalist civilization, of the industrial civilization which we know.[82]

The "autonomous project" of "living associative labor" unfolds precisely at the other limit of capital. If the paradox of capital consists in the fact that its reproduction is dependent upon having to foster and muster those social energies that, once constituted and organized, will forever after threaten to do away with capital altogether — if *this* is the boss's paradoxical curse, the paradox of that "autonomous project" as it unfolds at the other limit consists rather in its coming-into-being, on the one hand, as an impasse constitutionally internal to capital, and, on the other hand, as an immense reservoir of social knowledge and social experimentation separate from and inimical to capital. While from capital's own perspective the other limit is a forever menacing immanence, from the point of view of the historical agents of that project the other limit is an autonomous zone of antagonism to capital. While capital, in other words, is cursed with having to consider the other limit as irremediably internal to itself, "living associative labor" does not need to conceive of itself as structurally symbiotic to capital — which is another way of saying that if the master is nothing without the slave, the slave without the master and in getting rid of the master may become more powerful even than the entire master-slave dialectical assemblage. However, any project unfolding at the other limit — due to its paradoxical position of being construed by capital as an immanence to capital and by its own agents as transcendent of capital — while fatally threatening capital with the final explosion of its contradictions, also unwittingly provides capital with invaluable political lessons as well as with the social energies needed for the continuous displacement of the last limit in the form of new technologies, new industries, and new geopolitical and noo-corporeal areas to colonize. It is precisely the paradoxical forms through which this "autonomous project" makes itself manifest in what are the most passionate and affirmative pages of *Moby-Dick* and of the *Grundrisse* that concern me here. My insistence on the body as a privileged site of experimentation for such a project and its forms will soon become clear. For the moment, I want at least to extract a corollary from Negri's formulations: what he identifies as the "autonomous project" of "living associative labor" not only lives in the body — which is, of course, to be understood always as a fiercely collective entity — but also necessarily implies, projects, and demands unexpected and unforeseeable ways of moving, living, and loving bodies.

Ahab's failed line of flight from capital, due to his mistaking the last limit for the other limit, had been governed by an obstinate blindness to precisely this body, that is, the body of the living labor of whaling. It is this body of the other limit that continuously tantalizes Ahab with its presence — a presence he does sense but ever so readily interprets as the siren-like magnetism of the forever distant white whale. In witnessing Ahab's torments throughout the fated passage of the *Pequod*, one often feels that their source must surely be quite near rather than impossibly distant. The novel's own way of imaging the tyrannical proximity of such a source of haunting, however, is to force Ahab to completely internalize it. Among the countless instances in which Ahab's agony is conveniently represented as self-originating and self-inflicted, one stands out as most exemplary: at the end of chapter 44 ("The Chart"), Ahab is mesmerizingly described at once as having turned himself into a Prometheus and as having created inside himself the vulture that devours Prometheus alive — and this vulture, of course, turns out to be the idea of the white whale.[83] Because in the original Greek myth, it is Zeus who sends the vulture (as a punishment for having stolen fire from the gods and given it to human beings), we are given to surmise here that Zeus, too, along with both Prometheus and the vulture, has been collapsed and molded into Ahab. This should come as no surprise, given that throughout the novel Ahab repeatedly arrogates to himself divine attributes, powers, and status, as when, for example, he declares himself "proud as a Greek god."[84] What is all the more striking in Melville's rewriting of this myth, therefore, is the fact that while all of the myth's agents (namely, the divinity, the sinning outcast, and the vehicle of punishment in the form of the vulture) can be incorporated into the one single body of Ahab, the dangerous and never completely tractable force constituting both the human and the divine object of desire (namely, fire) cannot be made to fit inside Ahab and is implicitly posited as prior to and autonomous from everything and everybody — autopoetic divine omnipotence included. I will return to Ahab's Zarathustrian leanings: this self-made, flawed, fated, and fallen god, in fact, declares himself to worship fire as a higher divine principle and even as his progenitor.[85] It suffices to say here that in worshipping fire Ahab is as close as he will ever get to sensing the presence of an indomitable and autonomous power that, nonetheless, has generated him and continues to generate him even as he deliriously addresses himself to it.

Such a compulsory internalization may have been the only historically viable and politically safe way to comprehend and govern in Ahab an entire phenomenology of anger, anguish, and unrest determined by an other entity that was indeed very near, but not so near as to coincide with and be generated by that same affective range, which instead constituted the most furious epiphenomenon of that entity in the first place. One ought to de-existentialize such a peculiarly bourgeois, idealist, romantic, and at once Kantian and Hegelian phenomenology of interiority, of which Ahab is a prime expression. This is a phenomenology according to which the other and sublime limit of capital is first apprehended as transcendent and exogenous, and henceforth reconceptualized as immanent and endogenous, and thus finally made controllable and exploitable to a degree. This is a phenomenology, in other words, according to which such an other limit can never be comprehended as paradoxically exogenous and immanent with respect to capital, that is, *as autonomous from capital*. Autonomy from capital is the condition of being at once exogenous and immanent with respect to capital, at once integral to and constitutive of capital as well as not generated by it.[86] It is such an irreducible paradox that constitutes the explosive potential of the other limit: it is because of the nonnegotiable and indeed antinomial nature of such an ontological conundrum that the other limit, unlike the last one, finally cannot be appeased or recuperated by any—however flexible and acrobatic—dialectical process of *Aufhebung*. Such is the paradoxical law of the other limit whose clandestine existence and operations aboard the *Pequod* agitate that unwitting and tragic agent of capital that is Ahab. Ahab's blindly egocentric and proud vanity never let him see that the cause of the cankerous fury corroding his hollow insides was not of his own making and did not belong to him but resided rather in an other body upon which he vitally depended, a body that was indeed too near for comfort and for words. To have seen all that would have shattered the bourgeois mythology of parthenogenesis that Ahab ultimately shared with the social class which he most despised.[87]

And yet, somewhere beyond all these solipsistic impasses, there is another Ahab wanting to be saved from himself, another Ahab waiting to be written. At times, Ahab comes uncannily near to abjuring the white whale as that which possesses him and to acknowledging the autonomous proximity of that other body which tantalizes him. It is just a fleeting moment, but one for which it will have been worth waiting:

> With a wild whimsiness, [Queequeg] now used his coffin for a sea-chest; and emptying into it his canvas bag of clothes, set them in order there. Many spare hours he spent in carving the lid with all manner of grotesque figures and drawings; and it seemed that hereby he was striving, in his rude way, to copy parts of the twisted tattooing on his body. And this tattooing had been the work of a departed prophet and seer of his island, who, by those hieroglyphic marks, had written out on his body a complete theory of the heavens and the earth, and a mystical treatise on the art of attaining truth; so that Queequeg in his own proper person was a riddle to unfold; a wondrous work in one volume; but whose mysteries not even himself could read, though his own live heart beat against them; and these mysteries were therefore destined in the end to moulder away with the living parchment whereon they

were inscribed, and so be unsolved to the last. And this thought it must have been which suggested to Ahab that wild exclamation of his, when one morning turning away from surveying poor Queequeg — "Oh, devilish tantalization of the gods!"[88]

If Ahab is a modern Prometheus, he is also a modern Tantalus. Given how relentlessly throughout this novel Ahab molds himself into a self-ordained, if fallen, divine principle, this "wild exclamation" cannot but index also his own condition of being tantalized by the mystery of Queequeg's exposed, superscribed, and laboring body — which is here both the body of the other limit of capital as well as the limit marked by the body of the racial and cultural other. (And here Queequeg is not to be understood as a symbol of the body of the other limit, of the body of the living labor of whaling; he is, rather, one of its most exemplary material forms.) In this passage as well as in many other parts of the novel, Queequeg is constituted as the autonomous inverse of Ahab (and "autonomous" here is meant first of all in the literal sense that while Ahab clearly is affected enough by Queequeg first to want to survey him and then to turn away from him in despair, the latter, if one is to go by his behavior throughout the novel, is probably quite unconcerned with Ahab's scrutinizing, tantalized, and disturbed presence.) Whereas Ahab incarnates a hyperpsychologized hollow interiority that wishes to swallow and thus annihilate itself in the whole universe like a black-hole of consciousness, Queequeg's body is presented here as a "living parchment" entirely superscribed with an unfathomable cosmogony, that is, as a full surface and indeed as the nonpsychological fullness of surfaces. Furthermore, for Ahab both meaning and value need first to be posited as real entities if they are then to be dialectically reconceptualized and revealed as empty and nonexistent — and such a revelation leads him to angst and *horror vacui*. For the Queequeg of this passage — who is in the midst of an activity and in the fullness of a time autonomous vis-à-vis the world of value, as he is carving during what are "spare hours" — there is, on the other hand, no meaning and no value to start with. Or, rather, for this Queequeg meaning and value can exist only frozen in a perennially virtual state, not only because nobody — including himself — can interpret the "hieroglyphics" on his body but also because the mimetic practice in which he is so laboriously involved evidently places no value in meaning at all, as he seems to be concerned rather with the very act of reproducing the material form itself of such a cosmogony, that is, what Ishmael perceives as its "grotesque figures" and "twisted" shapes. Queequeg is engaged in a paradoxically antimimetic mimetic practice: he reproduces the scriptures of his body onto the surfaces of his coffin not because they supposedly mean, explain, and represent "the heavens and the earth"—for even if such a hermeneutical level does exist, it will never be available to him—but because they are the world made flesh, because they are the point of contact and interference between corporeal surfaces and the surfaces of the world, the point at which any distinction between such surfaces is not exactly erased but rather suspended in a state of infinite and osmotic proximity. While Ahab's cult of psychological depths and "Descartian vortices"—which is the emblematic expression of a humanist nihilism—leads him to blindness to and autotelic isolation from the world and finally to his own and everybody else's death, Queequeg's radically nonhermeneutical and nonpsychological stance leads him to unfold his body inside out (to the point that it becomes pure outside), leads him to reproduce and superimpose its surfaces onto other surfaces, leads him to produce and multiply the planes of tangency with the world (so as to reconstitute interaction with the world as contact.) In *Moby-Dick*, Queequeg marks a site of experimentation with whole new worlds of corporeal praxis and affect—and it is precisely the virtual presence of these worlds that Ahab finds so tantalizing in Queequeg's body. The fact that Queequeg's behavior throughout this novel is characterized as a concentrate of fatalistic stoicism and pagan impassibility always verging on the catatonic is clearly an index of irrecuperable racism and cultural prejudice. However, one should not fail to see because of such a racism that, in constructing such an (apparently) unaffective body of surfaces, this novel is also taking risks with its own cultural notions of bodies, affects, and social relationality, and that Ishmael's complex physical, affective, and political relations with that body constitute elements toward an as yet not fully articulated asubjective and asignifying corporeal praxis.

One final corollary to these speculations may consist in pointing out that one has already implicitly located Ishmael in them. If in this novel Queequeg is constructed as the autonomous inverse of Ahab, then Ishmael is throughout silently torn between these two asymmetrical poles. In this sense, C. L. R. James's understanding of Ishmael as "the modern young intellectual who has broken with society and wavers constantly between totalitarianism and the crew" is not irrelevant, even though it is founded upon dialectical notions of mediation that do not entirely capture the position of Ishmael in this novel.[89] *Moby-Dick* may indeed be the chronicle of Ishmael's impossible double romance, may indeed be the modern and tragic version of Carlo Goldoni's proverbial and comical situation of the servant of two masters: between the body of the other limit of capital and the unwitting but relentless body of capitalist domination, Ishmael ultimately finds himself betrayer of and orphaned by both the political bodies he most loved. But we have, thus, finally abandoned Ahab to his own fate. For one had wanted to give him here one last chance to trace the line of flight he had so much wanted to trace, to find the escape from capital he had so much wanted to find. For one had instead come to these last pages with a different promise: to stop spying on the other limit from behind the envious jalousies of capital and to start producing the other limit from its autonomous other side.

If the borrowed life of capital is extracted daily from the other limit, what actually lives at the other limit and how? And why is it that one senses with absolute certainty that the life of the other limit is what drove both Melville and Marx to writing, that the other limit is the absolute passion of both the *Grundrisse* and *Moby-Dick*, that the other limit is embodied in them as an absolute? Indeed, if the other limit in the *Grundrisse* and *Moby-Dick* is anything at all, it is a *corpus absolutus:* a body that has broken away and freed itself—even if for just an instant—from the myriad forms of its domination and exploitation, that is, that body in which life can no longer be bought or sold as it is absolutely expended in itself, in its own singular and autonomous form. *Moby-Dick* and the *Grundrisse* are the living epiclesis of such a *corpus absolutus* of the other limit and of its always potentially revolutionary life: these two antinarratives of modernity in crisis are love songs to that body and to that life.[90]

And are the incarnations of this *corpus absolutus* in the *Grundrisse* and *Moby-Dick* specifically male? Are these two works hymns to the male body as the other limit of capital? Can one find in these two texts elements toward a male homoerotics that may trace lines of flight from the composite assemblage of patriarchal-capitalist misogyny from which it may nonetheless be inextricable? What is certain is that the body of Queequeg as well as the interracial and cross-cultural romance between Ishmael and Queequeg constitute some of the most exemplary trajectories traced by the desires of the other limit in *Moby-Dick*—though by no means the only ones.[91] As far as Marx is concerned, it is important to note that *Capital* is a far more explicitly corporeal work than the *Grundrisse*, and that in *Capital* the body of the worker is often a specifically gendered one inasmuch as it is not exclusively or by default a male body but also and importantly a female and a child one (see especially, in *Capital, Volume One*, the chapters on "The Working Day," on "The Division of Labour and Manufacture" and on "Machinery and Large-Scale Industry"). But while the body of *Capital* is most usually a suffering and defeated one—since in this work Marx is often concerned with analyzing, detailing, and denouncing the torments inflicted by capital on the body of the worker—the apparently far more absent, abstract, nongendered, and by default often male body of the *Grundrisse* is more often a potentially insurgent and autonomous one, that is, a body at the other limit of capital.

In other words, it is only there where Marx is not immediately interested in tracing the other limit of capital and where the body of the worker is an invariably bound and crushed body that a specifically female body is at all allowed to be present. Furthermore, one wonders about what kind of erotic investments might be implicit in a project that Luce Irigaray has characterized thus:

> Marx defined the origin of the exploitation of man by man as the exploitation of woman by man, and he affirmed that the first human exploitation stems from the division of labor between man and woman. Why did he not devote his life to resolving this exploitation? He perceived the root of the evil but he did not treat it as such.[92]

Marx must have been aware that—as Leo Bersani reminds us—a new division of labor and a new community "in which it would no longer seem natural to define all relations as property relations"[93] would need an altogether new erotics: the fact that he "perceived the root of the evil but . . . did not treat it as such" may indicate, among the other things, that, for better and for worse, the new erotics of the body at the other limit of capital is implicitly inscribed in Marx as a specifically male homoerotics.

For love of the insurrectional body, for love of life: such are the passions of the *Grundrisse*. In the process of analyzing the relation between capital and labor, Marx conceptualizes the use value of labor "not as *a* use value but as *the* use value pure and simple"[94]—much like earlier he had identified money not as one commodity among other commodities but rather as "the lord and god of commodities." For Marx, such use value par excellence is incarnated in the body of the worker. He writes:

> The use value which the worker has to offer to the capitalist, which he has to offer to others in general, is not materialized in a product, does not exist apart from him at all, thus exists not really, but only in potentiality, as his capacity. . . . As soon as it has obtained motion from capital, this use value exists as the worker's specific, productive activity; it is his vitality itself, directed toward a specific purpose and hence expressing itself in a specific form.[95]

And later:

> For the use value which [the worker] offers exists only as an ability, a capacity *[Vermögen]* of his bodily existence; has no existence apart from that.[96]

And again:

As against capital, labour is the merely abstract form, the mere possibility of value-positing activity, which exists only as a capacity, as a resource in the bodiliness of the worker.[97]

And, finally, in a moment of dizzying synthesis:

> *Separation of property from labour* appears as the necessary law of this exchange between capital and labour. Labour posited as *not-capital* as such is: (1) *not-objectified labour [nicht-vergegenständliche Arbeit], conceived negatively*.... As such it is not-raw-material, not-instrument of labour, not-raw-product: labour separated from all means and objects of labour, from its entire objectivity. This living labour, existing as an *abstraction* from these moments of its actual reality (also, not-value); this complete denudation, purely subjective existence of labour, stripped of all objectivity. Labour as *absolute poverty*: poverty not as shortage, but as total exclusion of objective wealth. Or also as the existing *not-value*, and hence purely objective use value, existing without mediation, this objectivity can only be ... an objectivity coinciding with his immediate bodily existence.... In other words, not an objectivity which falls outside the immediate presence *[Dasein]* of the individual himself. (2) *Not-objectified labour, not value*, conceived *positively*, or as a negativity in relation to itself, is the *not-objectified*, hence non-objective, i.e. subjective existence of labour itself. Labour not as an object, but as activity; not as itself *value*, but as the *living source* of value.... Thus ... the in-every-way mutually contradictory statements that labour is *absolute poverty as object*, on one side, and is, on the other side, the *general possibility* of wealth as subject and as activity, are reciprocally determined and follow from the essence of labour, such as it is *presupposed* by capital as its contradiction and as its contradictory being, and such as it, in turn, presupposes capital.[98]

Use value is the body as absolute *potentia*. In the body of the worker—that is, in use value par excellence, in use value incarnate—capital is confronted by life itself, given, presented, and exposed as potential. This body contains a capital lesson: life cannot be; it can only become. Paradoxically, if it is—that is, if it has been frozen as exchange value and realized as objectified labor—then it already has ceased to exist; it has ceased to become, since becoming is its only modality of being. Such a use value—constituted as immanent in the very "bodiliness" of a body whose "vitality" itself is repeatedly exhibited here as "resource," "ability," "capacity," "possibility," and "potentiality"—can be used and exploited but not comprehended by capital. For capital, such a use value remains ultimately a non-sense and a nonvalue that can be grasped only as "abstract chaos" and as "madness," that is, as an incomprehensibly alien force.[99] Such a force that constitutes at once "absolute poverty" and the "living source" of value—that is, that which produces all value but which itself is not value at all—is the unthought of value. In this sense, Jean Baudrillard's famous critique of the metaphysics of utility in what he calls Marx's "use-value fetishism" is at once *accurate* on its own terms and *misplaced* here.[100] Baudrillard's claim that use can be at all conceptualized as a value only within an economy of exchange, and that, hence, use value is dependent upon and indeed provides the naturalizing ideology for such an economy rather than constituting an ontologically prior and revolutionary alternative to it— such a claim is not applicable to a definition of use value as the unthought of value and as *potentia*. In other words, Baudrillard's critique is valid only to the extent that use value is constituted in a dialectical relation with respect to exchange value. In the passages quoted above, however, Marx is precisely in the process of disengaging use value from such a relation so as to think the unthought of that dialectic: he is not merely reversing the dialectical binarism of exchange value and use value, he is also attempting to displace it altogether.[101] Ultimately, such a use value is no longer the object of Baudrillard's critique and goes well beyond that idealist anthropology through which Marx, according to Baudrillard, purportedly fixes use value as the moral teleology, that is, the natural essence, at the heart of both subject and object.[102] *Potentia* is neither teleological nor essential. For this Marx, it is not a question of positing a priori that while "people are not equal with respect to goods taken as exchange value . . . they would be equal as regards goods taken as use value."[103] Once Marx has presented use value as *potentia*, he is no longer able to posit it as a universal equalizer: the fact that such a potentiality is shared by the collective body of labor does not make such a body equal and identical to itself; the fact that *potentia* is and can only be in common does not mean that it is commensurable and representable. Marx, rather, attempts to sense the force of that incommensurable and unrepresentable potentiality in any and every body: he attends to the modalities of being of that which remains historically unknowable in the body and yet is already lived in it as *potentia* as well as realized—that is, killed before being born—as objectified labor. Marx in effect reformulates and expands the question posed by Spinoza in the *Ethics*: "nobody as yet has determined the limits of the body's capabilities: that is, nobody as yet has learned from experience what the body can and cannot do."[104]

Ultimately, it is only a question of time. The corporeal force of use value is steeped in temporality: what capital faces in the body as absolute *potentia* is the presence of a future that, if governed by "the necessary law" of "[s]eparation of property from labour," shall be a regulated future of objectified labor, but that, if governed by the spiraling and exponential intensification of that very same law, will be an unforeseeable future of catastrophe and revolution. The body as absolute *potentia* is already the past of a copresent future of crisis: it already contains the *corpus absolutus* of the other limit in the same way that "the graceful repose of the line" already contains the final catastrophe of Ahab's strangulation; it is "the profound calm which only apparently precedes and prophesies of the storm," which "is perhaps more awful than the storm itself," and which "is but the wrapper and envelope of the storm" of the other limit.[105] Marx's discovery in these pages is that capital's invention and implementation of the wage has re-formed the body of the worker as time, that under the regime of the wage such a body has been temporalized, and that, hence, the floodgates of history have swung open to whole new forms of body politic(s): the body has become time, that is, at once labor-time and a time-bomb. Marx's exhilarating epiphany is that, if one attunes one's ears to certain peculiar and almost imperceptible corporeal rhythms and rumblings, one will be able to hear the inexorable ticking of the timer of history directly in the machinic mechanisms of use value, that is, in "the worker's muscular force"[106] and in the very flesh of collective, living labor.

The *Grundrisse* contains the seeds of an other time. If the body of labor is given as *potentia* — as the nonvalue that is the potential of all value — that is so because such a body has come into being by definition as separate from and opposed to capital. Here, we witness Marx's first attempt to descry that law of separation and opposition that I identified earlier as the paradoxically immanent and exogenous autonomy of the other limit. Although such a law is already implicit in the last two passages quoted, Marx continues to expand his argument:

> The first presupposition is that capital stands on one side and labour on the other, both as independent forms relative to each other; both hence also alien to one another.[107]

And again:

> [T]he opposite of capital cannot itself be a particular commodity... it is not this commodity or that commodity, but all commodities. The communal substance of all commodities... as *commodities* and hence *exchange values*, is this, that they are *objectified labour*. The only thing distinct from *objectified* labour is *non-objectified labour*... *labour* as subjectivity. Or, *objectified* labour, i.e. labour which is *present in space*, can also be opposed, as *past labour*, to labour which is *present in time*. If it is to be present in time, alive, then it can be

present only as the *living subject*, in which it exists as capacity, as possibility; hence as *worker*. The only *use value*, therefore, which can form the opposite pole to capital is *labour*.[108]

And finally:

> [A]s *the* use value which confronts money posited as capital, labour is not this or another labour, but *labour pure and simple*, abstract labour; absolutely indifferent to its particular specificity *[Bestimmtheit]*, but capable of all specificities.... This economic relation—the character which capitalist and worker have as the extremes of a single relation of production—therefore develops more and more purely and adequately in proportion as ... [labour's] particular skill becomes something more and more abstract and irrelevant, and as it becomes more and more a *purely abstract activity*, a purely mechanical activity, hence indifferent to its particular form; a merely *formal* activity, or, what is the same, a merely *material [stofflich]* activity, activity pure and simple, regardless of its form.[109]

Before commenting on what already implicitly constitutes a theory of revolution and of revolutionary bodies, I want to consider also the conclusions Negri draws from this last passage:

> [This] is a dialectical development of an exceptional intensity: *the opposition determines subjectivity and this subjectivity of labor is defined as a general abstraction. The abstraction, the abstract collectivity of labor is subjective power (potenza).* Only this abstract subjective power *(potenza)*, this prolonged refinement of the labor power in its entirety which destroys the partiality of labor itself, can permit labor to be presented as a general power *(potenza)* and as radical opposition. In this passage, the separation of labor from capital becomes the quality which defines labor.[110]

To all this, I want to add that what I find also of crucial importance in Marx's formulations is their *rhythm* (which is probably what Negri has in mind when commenting on the "exceptional intensity" of the "dialectical development"). If "capital stands on one side and labour on the other" as forms that are "independent" from, "relative," and "also alien to one another," as forms that are the "opposite poles" and "the extremes of a single relation of production," it is also the case that such a dialectical relation cannot reach an equilibrium and a standstill: "more and more purely and adequately"; "more and more abstract and irrelevant"; "more and more a purely abstract activity." *For Marx, the logic regulating such a relation of autonomy is that of an ever-widening gap, which is also to say that ever-increasing autonomy is posited here as the tendential law of the breakdown of the dialectic.* If the "opposite" and "extreme" poles of "a single relation" do come into being as dialectically related to one another, one wonders just how high a degree of exponential autonomy such a dialectical relation will be able to accommodate and how far such poles will have to get from each other before altogether different kinds of relations will emerge. Or, *the biorhythm of the body of labor is a crescendo of history.* In this context, the labor "subjectivity" that both Marx and Negri see resulting from such a tendential law is not to be confused with the bourgeois ideal of the purely monadic and solitary subject—a solipsistic ideal of which Ahab, all his premodern archaisms notwithstanding, still is a most exemplary embodiment. The "non-objectified labour" that is "labour as subjectivity" constitutes the collective converse and indeed the unthought of the bourgeois subject, inasmuch as it is forged in the heat of struggle and inasmuch as it is generated by a historical dynamic of vertiginously spiraling and expanding autonomy. This collective body of subjectivity is both *potentia* and *multitudo*—and as such it implies and needs no interiority. *This is a subjectivity without subjects.*

It is precisely such a subjectivity—and its tendential and antagonistic autonomy that immediately posits labor as a dynamic entity parallel to capital—that we find in the collective body of the living labor of whaling in *Moby-Dick.* The entrance of such a body onto the narrative stage takes place very early in the novel. This is Ishmael's first night in New Bedford at the Spouter-Inn, where in a few hours he is to meet Queequeg in bed:

> Presently a rioting noise was heard without. Starting up, the landlord cried, "That's the Grampus's crew. I seed her reported in the offing this morning; a three years' voyage, and a full ship. Hurrah, boys; now we'll have the latest news from the Feegees."
>
> A tramping of sea boots was heard in the entry; the door was flung open, and in rolled a wild set of mariners enough.[111]

Or, labor as flood. These "rioting," "tramping," and rolling sailors, who fling the doors of the novel open and thus avalanche their way into the reader's sensorium, constitute the emblematic figure and form of labor in *Moby-Dick:* they are a dynamic force, a "wild" *potentia.* Such a sweeping ingress, however, bears a peculiar resemblance to the first entrance in *Moby-Dick* of what I identified earlier as the powers of circulation. It is thus that visions of the white whale first invaded Ishmael's body and permanently settled there:

> By reason of these things, then, the whaling voyage was welcome; the great
> flood-gates of the wonder-world swung open, and in the wild conceits that
> swayed me to my purpose, two and two there floated into my inmost soul,
> endless processions of the whale, and, midmost of them all, one grand hooded
> phantom, like a snow hill in the air.[112]

Resonating in the alliteration of the letter "w," one can hear the omnipresence of the
white whale: these are indeed the echoes of "a power that extends everywhere," of a
power in process. This omnipresent power that is circulation and that dynamic force
that is labor are posited from their first appearance in the novel as parallel entities
and in parallel ways: in both passages, one witnesses a set of bodies in motion bursting
through a limit and flooding onto the scene according to uncannily similar lexical
dictions, namely, to fling open, to swing open. Moreover, both these sets of unar-
restable bodies are experienced as "wild" powers: "a wild set of mariners enough";
"in the wild conceits that swayed me to my purpose" (and the adjective "wild" is also
frequently used throughout the novel to describe both Queequeg and Ahab, as we
saw in a passage discussed earlier, when Ishmael refers to Queequeg's "wild whimsi-
ness" and to Ahab's "wild exclamation").[113] Clearly, such a parallel structure of redoubling separates as much as it relates: readapting Marx's formulations, one might
say that the first presupposition of *Moby-Dick* is that the powers of circulation stand
on one side and the body of labor on the other, both as independent forms relative
to each other and both hence also alien to one another.[114] From the very beginning
of the novel, sailors and whales are juxtaposed as the real contending sides of the ensuing agon. Melville here has sensed and captured autonomy as a form of antagonistic relation. The central agon in *Moby-Dick* is not located in the struggle between
Ahab and the white whale or between Ahab and the dominant logic of exchange:
Ahab is at best an unwitting agent of that whale as well as of capital, and his "monomaniac" desire and fate is, after all, to become indistinguishable from and lose himself in both whale and capital. The secret, subterranean antagonism of *Moby-Dick* is
to be found at the other limit, that is, in that body of labor whose life itself is the
only life in the world of whaling, a body that goes largely unacknowledged in this
novel but whose "rioting" presence is nonetheless felt throughout its pages.

      And yet, Melville has also captured here a subtle and fundamen-
tal difference in the constitution of limits. Sailors and whales are not exactly each
other's doubles after all. If in the above passages the geometrical configurations and
even the verbs expressing the sudden movement of ingress are almost the same, the
conjugations of these two verbs are each other's opposite, as one is faced in the first

passage by a passive voice while in the second passage by an active voice: "the door was flung open"; "the great flood-gates of the wonder-world swung open." In both cases, the grammatical subject of the sentence is constituted by a limit, and, more specifically, by a limit meant to maintain a boundary and to keep an irruptive force out of an enclosed and presumably safe space. The difference lies in the ways in which this limit is confronted and overcome by such a force: whereas "the door" of the inn was forcedly "flung open" by the collective hurtling body of the "Grampus's crew," the "flood-gates" of Ishmael's "wonder-world" "swung open" all by them-selves—as if by magic—at the sudden appearance of "endless processions of the whale" headed by the "grand hooded phantom" of Moby-Dick himself. The sailors confront "the door" as a boundary to be overcome and soon thereafter forgotten—so that they can get on with their own more impelling matters and programs, which in this specific case consist of getting drunk.[115] The haunting "processions of the whale" that have come to invade Ishmael's life, on the other hand, seem to be an-nounced and welcomed by these "flood-gates," which act as if they had known in ad-vance of their arrival, which hence are not in an antagonistic relation vis-à-vis these powers, which hence cannot be forgotten and left behind once they have been en-tered, and which hence might be found farther along the road swinging open again and again. Once the powers of circulation and the body of labor have come, they are here to stay; but while those powers will continue to confront and be able to over-come only their own last limits, that body—which itself is at the other limit—will confront only limits that are not of its own making, only limits that it can either ex-ceed and destroy completely or be limited by and succumb to. Melville's intuition in these first few pages of *Moby-Dick* is that while the body of the living labor of whal-ing is itself that other limit from whose standpoint any other real limit is necessarily experienced as an external, foreign, alien imposition and is dealt with accordingly, the powers of circulation are at the very least in a mutually determining position vis-à-vis any successive limit they encounter and re-encounter.[116] And if to extract so much from just the grammatical voice of a verb might seem a hyperbolic and hyper-hermeneutical gesture, it may be necessary to reiterate here that everything in this novel develops exponentially: in that voice as well as in the voice of the *Grampus's* crew, it is already possible to hear all the words spoken and not spoken by the crew of the *Pequod*.

Among the words not spoken aboard the *Pequod*, there are some that stand out clearest and loudest: never do we hear a word against Ahab and his mad purpose coming from the crew. This may seem to contradict all that I have been trying to suggest. If it is the case that the body of the living labor of whaling is potentially constituted from the very beginning of the novel as the antagonistic and autonomous counterpart of the powers of circulation and of their crazed and unwitting agent—if it is the case, in other words, that that body was immediately posited as the virtual other limit of capital, why is it, then, that the crew of the *Pequod* follows Ahab in his fated designs of revenge? Why didn't they rebel—especially considering that Ahab had in effect provided them with the perfect reasons for doing so, even with the full support of the law?[117] Answers to these questions that invoke Ahab's promise of the gold doubloon to whomever would first sight the white whale, or that appeal to Ahab's charismatic presence, rhetorical skills, and disciplinarian tyranny do no more than reiterate Ahab's own opinion in the matter and reassert a conception of the crew as a bunch of gullible simpletons who are unable to know either what they want or what they should want. Ahab clearly believes he has settled the matter of the crew's loyalty entirely by virtue of his own manipulative cunning: at one point he presumptuously boasts that revealing the real purpose of the passage and convincing the crew to swear their allegiance to it "was not so hard a task," and that his "one cogged circle fits into all their various wheels and they revolve."[118] In this respect, C. L. R. James—all his good intentions notwithstanding—does no more than reiterate the boss's point of view when he declares that "Ahab, the totalitarian, bribed the men with money and grog and whipped them up to follow him on his monomaniac quest."[119] For all of his unabashed worship of the body of labor (which for him is at once "tension . . . and skill and grace and beauty," "sweat and beauty," "splendid physique, unconquered spirit and spontaneous generosity,")[120] or, perhaps, precisely because of such a worship, James has little to say about either the motives or even the possibility of the existence of any motive whatsoever that the crew might have had in complying with Ahab's request. Far from trivializing or reprimanding James's intensely romanticizing and homoerotic gaze when repeatedly watching the scenes of manual labor aboard the *Pequod*, I want to take such a gaze very seriously.[121] It seems to me that James has forgotten that "beauty" is indeed in the eye of the beholder and that hence it speaks solely of that beholder's desires—desires that may or may not find correspondence and resonance in the gazed-upon body's own desires and self-imaging. Ultimately, James only expresses his own homoerotic desire rather than addressing the potential presence of homoeroticism within the very constitution of that body of labor—a homoeroticism that may not have much in common with James's own. If, as James unwittingly suggests, the beauty of the body of labor contains and expresses a potentially revolutionary homoeroticism, that is certainly not so because James is able to homoerotically look at and desire such a body. As it turns out, and as I will discuss later, such a homoeroticism finds no

revolutionary realization in James whatsoever, as it is also fueled and crippled by homophobia. It suffices to say here that James's dialectical-materialist and homoerotic
paean to the body of labor in *Moby-Dick* is far closer to Conrad's reactionary nostalgia and longing for that very same body throughout his works—and especially in
The Nigger of the "Narcissus"—than it is to the just-as-intense but differently articulated homoeroticism that does indeed exist aboard the *Pequod*. I will return to this
matter. For the moment, it is important to note that James's homoerotic romanti-
cization of the body of labor leaves Ahab's version of the events intact and does not
translate into an investigation of the crew's own projects in the novel.

Some may object that if so many readers of *Moby-Dick* fail to account for the reasons why the crew readily accepts Ahab's terms of this fated passage, that is so because we hardly get to hear the crew in this novel and hence have
no textual bases on which to even begin speculating about their desires and aspira-
tions.[122] While this is literally the case, it is also the case that the crew is actually
omnipresent in this novel and that their bodies—whether in labor or at rest—inhabit virtually each and every page of *Moby-Dick*. It is precisely such a discrepancy of
representation that ought to provide the basis for an investigation of the body of the
living labor of whaling in *Moby-Dick*. It is not a question of chastising Melville for
representing the crew without giving them much chance to represent themselves,
since, obviously, that would have constituted only a self-representation effect, that
is, yet another form of authorial representation of the crew. What is at stake here,
rather, is the possibility that the presence of the crew, unlike Ahab's presence, is of a
type that cannot be forced to represent itself because it structurally resists self-representation, because there is no self in it either to do the representing or to be represented. Our most cherished hermeneutical habits may be quite inadequate when it
comes to asking questions about the crew because such habits engender modes of
reading that can read exclusively (for) subjects and that hence will be systemically
blind to asubjective presences. To ask what admittedly might well turn out to be
unanswerable questions about the possible motives—or lack thereof—that the crew
might have had in swearing and keeping their loyalty to Ahab's "monomaniac revenge" is already to ask questions about the modalities of being of precisely such
asubjective presences. The fact that there is strictly speaking only one subject in this
novel—that is, Ahab—does not mean that there is nothing and no body else in it:
as we shall see, there is no such body that would be subject of the other limit—for
such a limit is eminently a limit for the subject.

Before proceeding any further with this line of investigation, we
need to locate the position that Ishmael occupies in the body of labor aboard the

Pequod. His unique function within the novel notwithstanding, it is undeniable that Ishmael considers himself and indeed is an integral part of the crew. "I, ISHMAEL, was one of the crew; my shouts had gone up with the rest; my oath had been welded with theirs"—he declares.[123] In other words, I would like to warn against overemphasizing Ishmael's purportedly educated and upper-middle-class provenance to the point of turning him into an entity completely separate from the crew, and I would like to insist on the purported nature of such a provenance because, after all, one is given very little about Ishmael's social background and because such a scarcity of information should not be taken as a sign that his background is identical to Melville's own, even when their respective biographies seem to coincide. Whether or not Melville's class condition—namely, that of a suddenly impoverished member of the American elite—was the same as Ishmael's is actually beside the point. There is no homogeneity within such a crew of "mongrel renegades, and castaways, and cannibals"[124] who have nothing in common other than their presumed gender and the labor of whaling itself; that is, they do not belong to the same *ethnos*, race, nationality, language, religion, culture, age group, or class—and hence Ishmael cannot be the odd one out in such a diverse group of social rejects and ostracized bodies. Moreover, one needs also to remember that—if not exactly in *Moby-Dick*, then certainly in *White-Jacket* and in others among Melville's sea narratives—the seemingly autobiographical narrator is by no means the only educated and literary-minded member of the crew. This is not to say that Ishmael is just like any other member of the crew; this is to say, rather, that there is no crewman who would be just like another—and this in no way implies that they are all equally different from each other either. All this may sound quite obvious but it has perhaps not so obvious an implication: the collective subjectivity of the body of the living labor of whaling is not a shared class *Weltanschauung*, or what used to be called class consciousness, but rather a shared potential for the overcoming of capital (in and as whaling) that cannot be adequately expressed in terms of class. This is not to say that the body of labor cannot constitute a class; it is rather to assert that it is not qua class—and not even as an oppositional and struggling class—that such a body is necessarily dangerous to capital, as the latter, during at least the past two centuries, has given ample evidence that it actually *needs* both such a constitution of class as well as the realities of class struggle in order to function, to modernize itself, and to continuously overcome its last limits. In overcoming the very concept of class, and in forging altogether different ways of being-in-common which would completely bypass the dialectical logic of struggle, the body of labor may become dangerous and indeed fatal to capital. Inevitably, what sprouts on the bloody fields of class war after each battle is a more advanced and efficient form of capital, and that is so because the military topography of such fields is well known to capital — for the fields of class war constitute capital's own territory. Other fields and other wars are needed for the body of labor to make itself unrecognizable to capital by not appearing in the familiar form of class and by not acting in the ways capital expects that which it created to act. To put all of the above in terms more consonant with Moishe Postone's extensive investigation of similar theses: communism consists not at all in the dictatorship of the proletariat but rather in the self-abolition of the proletariat.[125]

Let us return now to Ishmael and the crew — from whom we have not strayed too far. All I have been saying here could not be farther removed from the reading undertaken by C. L. R. James — a reading that shuttles back and forth between the mutually determining poles of the homoerotic glorification of the crew-as-proletariat and of the stigmatization of the modern-intellectual-as-faggot in the figure of Ishmael. We have already seen James at work on the crew's body of labor — a body that for James "remain[s] sane and human" throughout the novel. To complete the picture, we also need to see how Ishmael for James is kept apart from the crew by "his intellectualism, his inability to embrace reality spontaneously, the doubt and the fear and guilt and isolation from people" which are characteristic of the "guilt-ridden," "modern, young, intellectual" for whom "life consists of nothing else but fine cambrics and tea on the piazza," and who "begins by clinging to the powerful Queequeg" so that "in typical modern fashion, his relationship with him on land has all the marks of homosexuality."[126] Such an unfortunate characterization of both crew and Ishmael has nonetheless the great merit of sensing a fundamental relation between "homosexuality" and modernity. As I will argue later, however, the relationship between Ishmael and Queequeg is neither "modern" nor does it bear any "marks of homosexuality."

But we have yet to hear Ishmael finally ask these questions:

> Such a crew, so officered, seemed specially picked and packed by some infernal fatality to help [Ahab] to his monomaniac revenge. How it was that they so aboundingly responded to the old man's ire — by what evil magic their souls were possessed, that at times his hate seemed almost theirs; the White Whale as much their insufferable foe as his; how all this came to be — what the White Whale was to them, or how to their unconscious understandings, also, in some dim, unsuspected way, he might have seemed the gliding great demon of the seas of life, — all this to explain, would be to dive deeper than Ishmael can go. The subterranean miner that works in us all, how can one tell whither leads his shaft by the ever shifting muffled sound of his pick?

Who does not feel the irresistible arm drag? What skiff in tow of a seventy-four can stand still? For one, I gave myself up to the abandonment of the time and the place; but while yet all a-rush to encounter the whale, could see naught in that brute but the deadliest ill.[127]

If Ahab in his blinding arrogance has understood nothing about the crew, Ishmael at least does admit of not understanding the crew, that is, of not understanding that of which nonetheless he is a part. Ishmael's quick surrender to the fact that the crew's motives and behavior are for him finally unfathomable, however, is quite extraordinary given that it comes as the conclusion to a chapter in which he dives into the somehow perfectly fathomable depths of Ahab's madness and explains in detail exactly what Ahab's compulsions are in "chasing with curses a Job's whale round the world."[128] The fact that Ishmael can ultimately understand Ahab far better than he can understand either the crew or himself qua member of that crew should give one pause. What kind of dead end has Ishmael reached here? In this passage, Ishmael's narrative has run aground on the sharp rocks of an unexpected barrier reef: in it, the novel itself has found its immanent other limit, namely, that which it cannot grasp without undoing itself, that beyond which it structurally cannot go without having to become something else and without having to overcome itself altogether. The white whale, the shipwreck of the *Pequod*, the final catastrophe and hecatomb: all these outer boundaries that had loomed ominously over the unfolding of the whole novel like some fated and unsurpassable narrative horizon marked in the end only a series of narrative last limits, which the novel was able to survive and beyond which the novel was able to reconstitute itself in some other form—as the postapocalyptic last chapter and Ishmael's lone survival demonstrate.

Far from not understanding the crew, Ishmael in this passage has captured possibly the only thing that there is to understand about them, namely, that they cannot be understood (within narrative parameters and in narrative terms). Ishmael's attempt "all this to explain" is symptomatic of that analytical and psychologizing mode of thought that he had just successfully employed to reconstruct and interpret Ahab's "monomania"—a mode of thought that turns out to have been adequate and necessary exclusively for the coming-into-being, articulation, and deciphering of a subject such as Ahab. Here "to explain" is an exquisitely narrative enterprise: it means to dive into psychologized and existentialized depths so as to excavate, extract, and tell the true story of the subject, that is, the story of his origins; it means to produce such depths as the original repository—at once the original factory and the original warehouse—of the subject intended as narratable, that is, of the subject intended as inextricable from narrative; it means to narrate the subject into being as depth. Such a depth is precisely what Ishmael here has realized the crew cannot have or be. Ishmael here has sensed in the crew *that collective body of subjectivity without either subjects or the Subject* — a body that constitutes the other limit not only for the powers of circulation and its agents but also for narrative *tout court*.

Lest these assertions remain articles of faith, let us also read from Ishmael's psycho-archaeology of Ahab. In the pages directly preceding the passage in which Ishmael fails to fathom the crew's "unconscious understandings," he extricates and explains Ahab's "monomania," "delirium," "direful madness," "full lunacy," and "frantic morbidness" in what constitutes a proto-psychoanalytical case study.[129] Even in the case of Ahab, however, analysis turns out to be interminable. After having crowned the etiology of Ahab's "madness" with what he calls a "furious trope" — namely, by stating that Ahab's "special lunacy stormed his general sanity, and carried it, and turned all its concentrated cannon upon its own mad mark" — Ishmael images thus that which he ultimately cannot reach and resolve:

> This is much; yet Ahab's larger, darker, deeper part remains unhinted. But vain to popularize profundities, and all truth is profound. Winding far down from within the very heart of this spiked Hotel de Cluny where we here stand — however grand and wonderful, now quit it; — and take your way, ye nobler, sadder souls, to those vast Roman halls of Thermes; where far beneath the fantastic towers of man's upper earth, his root of grandeur, his whole awful essence sits in bearded state; an antique buried beneath antiquities, and throned on torsoes! So with a broken throne, the great gods mock that captive king; so like a Caryatid, he patient sits, upholding on his frozen brow the piled entablatures of ages. Wind ye down there, ye prouder, sadder souls! question that proud, sad king! A family likeness! aye, he did beget ye, ye young exiled royalties; and from your grim sire only will the old State-secret come.[130]

Beam me down, Herman! In what is one of the more delirious visions of this delirious book, we are led down a spatio-temporal passageway that links medieval Paris directly to ancient Rome, and at the end of our descent we are brought face to face with the unconscious. For it is no less than the unconscious that Ishmael has discovered in the guise of this captive and royal father buried beneath the ruins of history. Anticipating those memorable pages in which Sigmund Freud will resort to Rome's millennial and highly stratified architectural topography for representing how the psychic past is forever preserved and is always virtually retrievable if one is able to go "back far enough,"[131] Ishmael here bids us to descend in space and time to discover and question among ancient Roman architectural structures this immemorial "awful essence" that at once engenders and supports the whole edifice of the subject as well as guards and embodies its most profound secrets. What is most remarkable about such a version of the unconscious—Melville's even more than Freud's—is that in it the unconscious is never allowed to crystallize as private and individual: even in the case of that most consummate of solipsists that is Ahab, we confront in the end an uncompromisingly collective unconscious—that is, the shared and originating "essence" of all those "prouder" and "sadder" souls such as Ahab. This unconscious is immediately made into a problem for history, politics, and the State, as many of the images invoked here—from "the piled entablatures of ages" to the ancient architectures, from the "captive king" to the "old State-secret"—indeed suggest. Moreover, if this is an unmistakably oedipalized unconscious, it is so in ways that nonetheless index a desire to circumvent oedipalization altogether: if the unconscious here manifests itself in the mutually reinforcing patriarchal forms of a father and a king, it is also a broken, captive, mocked, and altogether pitiable father-king into whose presence we are ushered by Ishmael. This, of course, is also the fate that is allotted to Ahab himself: the only two men aboard the *Pequod* who may be said to entertain at times an oedipalized relation vis-à-vis that "proud and sad" father-king that is Ahab—namely, Ishmael and Starbuck—ultimately feel for him only infinite pity rather than classically oedipal hatred (see, for example, Starbuck's filial entreaties the day before the white whale is first sighted.)[132] Pity, however, is not completely outside the realm of oedipalization: such an affect in this novel often indexes a paradoxical attempt to use a process of oedipalization as a stepping-stone for escaping that very process (and, in this sense, Ishmael's and Starbuck's positions with respect to Ahab in *Moby-Dick* are quite similar to the position that Deleuze and Guattari attribute to Kafka vis-à-vis his own father.)[133]

Though collective and shared rather than private and individual, and though at once oedipal and on its way to eluding oedipalization, what we face in the above passage is still an unconscious—and one that is typically imaged through the discourse of profundity and its attendant spatial tropology of depth. My earlier claim (that such a discourse and such tropes are precisely what Ishmael tries to but cannot muster for inquiring into the crew's motives) can be rephrased now by saying that Ishmael's discovery of the unconscious in Ahab is simultaneous with his discovery of that other body for whom the unconscious is simply not a germane analytical category—germane, that is, to any understanding of its political constitution, projects, and praxis. This is a body for whom the unconscious is already obsolete before being fully born as a concept. Or, by way of diminishing the purism of such claims, one could say that if the crew has an unconscious, it is one that is structured even more atypically than the already somewhat unorthodox unconscious of Ahab. Let us return, then, to Ishmael's attempt at sounding the crew's nonexistent depths and "unconscious understandings." After declaring that he is not able "all this to explain," Ishmael continues thus:

> The subterranean miner that works in us all, how can one tell whither leads his shaft by the ever shifting muffled sound of his pick? Who does not feel the irresistible arm drag? What skiff in tow of a seventy-four can stand still? For one, I gave myself up to the abandonment of the time and the place; but while yet all a-rush to encounter the whale, could see naught in that brute but the deadliest ill.

It seems as if the figure of this "subterranean miner" might constitute some sort of unconscious as well as a trope of psychological depth, after all. The analogies with the previous imaging of Ahab's unconscious, however, go no further (exception made, of course, for the fact that both that king and this miner share the same gender and that they are both associated with traditionally all-male spaces—the miner with mines, and the king with a medieval monastery as well as with ancient Roman public baths.) First of all, while there we had a father-king, here we have a miner—as if to stress that this version of the unconscious cannot be so readily enlisted in oedipal-familial triangulations as well as to suggest that each social station has its own unconscious. Second, while there we were made to descend from "the fantastic towers" of consciousness to its very bowels and dungeons, here the metaphoric vector has been inverted, as we start instead from subterranean enclosures only to be dragged upward by an "irresistible arm" that delivers us to the boundless expanses of the sea on which a mere "skiff" is being pulled away by a warship—as if to warn us that this unconscious, try as we may to reach it and address it in its subterranean burrows, will keep sending us right back up to face instead the world and its wide-open surfaces, as if to say, in other words, that this unconscious forces us open to the world rather than luring us into that trap which is the desire for interiority. Third, while there we were able to reach, see, and even question that father-king, here we can only hear the "ever shifting muffled sound of [the miner's] pick" and hence we are not even able to locate his exact position within us at any given moment. But here lies perhaps the most crucial difference: while that father-king was "buried," "captive," "frozen," "patient," and "like a Caryatid," this miner is "ever shifting" and only becomes perceptible through the shock waves that his movements and his work send through the very frame of consciousness. Starting from such a miner, the whole passage is henceforth steeped in movement, as each successive sentence unfolds as a series of moving images. There can no longer be any doubt: while Ahab's unconscious is the static "awful essence" of being, in and about the crew we are confronted instead by dynamic forces and by the very rush of becoming.

That is why Ishmael, in the attempt to apprehend such movement, relinquishes any conventional notion of understanding and in the end opts instead for abandon: "For one, I gave myself up to the abandonment of the time and the place." The dynamic forces of becoming are apprehended here as that which cannot be understood but to which one can only abandon oneself, or, rather, that which can only be understood *by* abandoning oneself to it — and not in the least because abandoning oneself to anything at all means abandoning one's self in the first place, that is, deflating or renouncing *tout court* any notion of self as well as any notion of that attendant buffer zone of being commonly known as critical distance. (And Ishmael's solution here, one might add, is radically different from the classical Kantian one vis-à-vis the dynamical sublime). The onto-epistemological shift is thus complete: what is at stake here is nothing less than the valorization of what is at once a mode of knowing and a mode of being that has been systemically dismissed as imperfect, insignificant, and altogether inferior throughout the history of Western metaphysics. In the opposition between abandon (to a flux of becoming) and understanding (of depths and interiority), Ishmael is reelaborating the philosophical distinction between perception and apperception. If reliance on mere bodily perception has traditionally been deemed an index of stunted onto-epistemological growth, while apperception — beginning at least with René Descartes — has been granted the seat of honor in the convened assembly of being, Ishmael, in facing the body of the other limit and as a member of that very body, renounces precisely that self-reflexive mode of thought which is the hallmark of apperception and of rational consciousness.[134] Such a renunciation constitutes neither a defeat nor a regression on Ishmael's part; it is, rather, an affirmation of abandon as a form of thought in its own right and as the *modus vivendi* and the constitutive praxis of what I called earlier the collective body of a subjectivity without either subjects or the Subject. Abandon is thought lived as affirmative praxis, that is, thought as *potentia* and *multitudo*. Abandon is thought *tout court*.

If Ishmael's shift from rational understanding to abandon indexes the affirmation of a form of thought that is intrinsically collective as well as always unrealized, Giorgio Agamben, in fact, goes even further by identifying in such a form of thought the only possible definition of thought itself:

I call thought the nexus that constitutes the forms of life in an inseparable context as form-of-life. I do not mean by this the individual exercise of an organ or a psychic faculty, but rather an experience, an *experimentum* that has as its object the potential character of life and human intelligence....

Only if I am not always already and solely enacted, but rather delivered to a possibility and a power, only if living and intending and apprehending themselves are at stake each time in what I live and intend and apprehend—only if, in other words there is thought—only then a form of life can become, in its own factness and thingness, form-of-life, in which it is never possible to isolate something like naked life.

The experience of thought that is here in question is always the experience of a common power....

That is why modern political philosophy does not begin with classical thought, which had made of contemplation, of the *bios theoreticos*, a separate and solitary activity ("exile of the alone to the alone"), but rather only with Averroism, that is, with the thought of the one and only possible intellect common to all human beings, and, crucially, with Dante's affirmation—in *De Monarchia*—of the inherence of a multitude to the very power of thought....

Thought is form-of-life, life that cannot be segregated from its form; and anywhere the intimacy of this inseparable life appears, in the materiality of corporeal processes and habitual ways of life no less than in theory, there and only there is there thought.[135]

In this radical rejection of any philosophical tradition—ranging from ancient Platonic idealism to modern Cartesian and post-Cartesian rationalism—that ascribes to thought a transcendentalizing power and that indeed conceptualizes the act of thinking as a separation, an elevation, and a flight into transcendence, Agamben never alludes to either the term or the concept of abandon. Ishmael's act of abandoning himself to "the abandonment of the time and the place," however, is an answer to precisely that problematic of separation that constitutes Agamben's main preoccupation in this passage and that leads him to the formulation of the concept of form-of-life in the first place.[136] For Ishmael, abandon is a praxis of inseparability from the modalities of being and material conditions of possibility of one's own environment, that is, a praxis constitutive of form-of-life. Such a political imperative of inseparability—in Melville no less than in Agamben—is no humanist and reactionary nostalgia for a long-lost organic unity with nature or for a populist rapprochement and communion with the multitude and the working class; this is, rather, the affirmation of a radically experimental attitude vis-à-vis the world perceived in a profoundly

Heraclitean way, that is, perceived as being always already a multitude in flux bursting forth with unrealized potential. In this sense, Ishmael's attitude toward the crew in general is no different from his attitude toward Queequeg in particular as well as toward the whole question of whaling: Ishmael's way of abandoning himself to whaling, to Queequeg, and to the whole crew is time after time an experiment in which the whole of living is inseparable from each new form of social relation that comes into being, an experiment in which life itself is always at stake. Remember, for example, how whaling for Ishmael is literally a last try in the face of suicide,[137] or how his first overtures to Queequeg are directly preceded by this revealing remark: "I'll try a pagan friend, thought I, since Christian kindness has proved but hollow courtesy."[138] Ishmael always puts everything on the line in his each and every gesture precisely because he cannot foresee the exact trajectory and outcome of those gestures — and that is why these are gestures of pure possibility, that is, the urgent gestures of an abandon without reserve. But such is, of course, Melville's own attitude vis-à-vis writing itself in *Moby-Dick* — an attitude that can be properly understood only as "an *experimentum* that has as its object the potential character of life and human intelligence." *Moby-Dick* is a book written with abandon, that is, not unthinkingly, but rather in the midst and in the plenitude of a thought that is inseparable from its material forms and from its historical conditions of possibility: in each and every successive experiment in this book's writing — which is to say, on virtually every page — the very possibility of writing is always at stake.

Premature as such speculations on abandon might seem at this point, it should be clear at least that the being-in-common indexed by Ishmael with the notion of abandon is in a nonoedipal and nondialectical relation vis-à-vis Ahab. Whatever else one might say about the fact that mutiny was never so much as considered by the crew, even when the situation was so favorable to it (given that the law would have been on their side and that the first mate had come out very strongly against Ahab's designs), one can at least say that such a complete lack of interest in the very possibility of mutiny should not necessarily be interpreted as loyalty to Ahab or as a sharing in his designs; rather it is a forgetting of Ahab, that is, a radical refusal of any engagement whatsoever with Ahab as the oedipal bearer of the Phallus. While any act of rebellion would have inevitably locked the crew in a dialectical struggle with their captain, abandon is posited instead as an act of delinking, that is, as a going adrift toward other zones of praxis and affect so invisible from the heights of Ahab's depths that he will not be able to see them even as they are being mapped under his very eyes. The crew's abandon is not at all an abandon to Ahab's authority but rather an abandon to their own being-in-common: throughout the novel, they are always abandoning themselves to themselves, that is, to that unrealized *potentia* and that immanent *multitudo* which is their body of living labor. (Ishmael, after all, does not merely say that he abandoned himself to the situation aboard the ship; more accurately, he says that he gave himself "up to the abandonment of the time and the place," or, in other words, that he abandoned himself to what was already a generalized condition of "abandonment.") Such an abandon without reserves—that is, without any interest in safeguarding some however minimal *terra firma* of value on which to land in case of catastrophe—is an abandon to abandonment itself, namely, an abandon to a state of having abandoned the familiar and familial dominion of the father-king as well as the interpellating and mesmeric spell of the Subject: this is an abandon to that radically exilic and orphan condition which is the only possible be-ing-in-common of a *corpus absolutus*.

Excursus of Fire

All things are an equal exchange for fire and fire for all things, as goods are for gold and gold for goods.

Heraclitus

Before tracing the modalities of being of such a condition of abandon throughout the pages of *Moby-Dick*, it is essential to realize that the ambivalent Ishmael does not always abandon himself to it: at those times when he best perceives the overwhelm-ing transformative force of the body of living labor, he may suddenly back away in fright at the sight of his discovery—thereby indexing the presence of such a force and the force of such a presence all the more vehemently. The time has come, in other words, to speak of fire—the protean force Ahab worships but ultimately does not understand. If earlier I alluded to how Ahab, in worshipping fire as well as in de-claring himself the progeny of fire, is as near as he will ever come to perceiving the presence of that autonomous and intractable force that constitutes his very condi-tion of possibility, we need to look more closely now into this novel's experiments with fire—and not exactly because of Ahab, but, as we shall see, because of Ishmael's very different role within such a process of experimentation.

In the chapter entitled "The Candles," we read of a rare phe-nomenon: while the *Pequod* is struggling to stay afloat in the middle of a typhoon, the surrounding air is so overcharged with electricity that—much to the terror of everyone but Ahab—long, tapering flames of white fire suddenly sprout from each mast-end and yardarm-end. This is the point at which Ahab madly forbids the use of lightning rods so as to address himself directly to the "speechless, placeless power" of the flames with delirious words of worship and defiance.[139] Predictably, Ahab treats the "clear spirit" and "supernal power" of fire in ways that immediately signal a flight into transcendence.[140] As soon as fire is turned into a sign of the divine, Ahab rapidly comes to the inevitable conclusion that the true source of its power is to be found somewhere outside of it: so it is, then, that Ahab shifts his all-consuming passion from fire to a purported "unsuffusing thing," "incommunicable riddle," and "unparticipated grief" that lie surely but unreachably beyond it. To transcendentalize fire, however, is to have understood precisely nothing about it: thus, Ahab's hermeneutic-paranoiac gaze—much like Don Quixote's—is forever turning the world and its forms into mere symbols of the all-important and forever inaccessible otherworldly, thereby emptying the only forms in which the world takes place out of all the life they have and dismissing them as ultimately irrelevant.

While Ahab is too busy seeking the true being of fire in a transcendental beyond to be able to notice anything or anybody else around him, Ishmael's attentive eyes are on the crew:

> While this pallidness was burning aloft, few words were heard from the enchanted crew; who in one thick cluster stood on the forecastle, all their eyes gleaming in that pale phosphorescence, like a faraway constellation of stars. Relieved against the ghostly light, the gigantic jet negro, Daggoo, loomed up to thrice his real stature, and seemed the black cloud from which the thunder had come. The parted mouth of Tashtego revealed his shark-white teeth, which strangely gleamed as if they too had been tipped by corpusants; while lit up by the preternatural light, Queequeg's tattooing burned like Satanic blue flames on his body.[141]

Seen here under a new and different light, the whole crew—and especially its supreme embodiments, namely, the harpooners—seem to be not only reflecting the flames but also producing their very own flames. The fire burning up in the spars is then turned here into the mere catalyst of a sudden epiphany: the crew is revealed to be burning of a fire of its own. Ishmael's powerful similes express the discovery of an isomorphic relation between the crew and fire: while Ahab worships in fire a power that he then attributes to a transcendence, Ishmael has detected in fire the same logic that is at work in the body of living labor. "Satanic" as the "blue flames on" this body might be, however, they are still not Satanic enough: Ishmael does not seem much perturbed at the sight of his discovery and is still able to represent the crew via such stunning yet distancing images as "a faraway constellation of stars." We witness here an osmotic transaction between the power that has just been detected in the crew and the power of representation: Ishmael is readily able to translate and displace the former into the latter, as he produces a series of extremely powerful images whose effect is to provide with forms as well as to tame or distance to a degree a force that, like fire, is formless and perilous to handle or even to approach.

The igneous body of living labor does appear at times in far more demonic, disturbing, and intractable incarnations. In the chapter entitled "The Try-Works," Ishmael—after having presented with his usual painstaking zeal the technical details of the process by which the whale's blubber is turned into oil by being cooked in enormous pots fitted into a furnace—thus describes the crew:

> The hatch, removed from the top of the works, now afforded a wide hearth in front of them. Standing on this were the Tartarean shapes of the pagan harpooneers, always the whale-ship's stokers. With huge pronged poles they pitched hissing masses of blubber into the scalding pots, or stirred up the fires beneath, till the snaky flames darted, curling, out of the doors to catch them by the feet. The smoke rolled away in sullen heaps. To every pitch of the ship there was a pitch of the boiling oil, which seemed all eagerness to leap into their faces. Opposite the mouth of the works, on the further side of the wide wooden hearth, was the windlass. This served for a sea-sofa. Here lounged the watch, when not otherwise employed, looking into the red heat of the fire, till their eyes felt scorched in their heads. Their tawny features, now all begrimed with smoke and sweat, their matted beards, and the contrasting barbaric brilliancy of their teeth, all these were strangely revealed in the capricious emblazonings of the works. As they narrated to each other their unholy adventures, their tales of terror told in words of mirth; as their uncivilized laughter forked upwards out of them, like the flames from the furnace; as to and fro, in their front, the harpooneers wildly gesticulated with their huge pronged forks and dippers; as the wind howled on, and the sea leaped, and the ship groaned and dived, and yet steadfastly shot her red hell further and further into the blackness of the sea and the night, and scornfully champed the white bone in her mouth, and viciously spat round her on all sides; then the rushing Pequod, freighted with savages, and laden with fire, and burning a corpse, and plunging into that blackness of darkness, seemed the material counterpart of her monomaniac commander's soul.[142]

The Satanic crew of this hell on water is not merely mirroring the light coming from the flames of the try-works but rather is "strangely revealed" as sharing in the very physics of fire: "their uncivilized laughter forked upwards out of them, like the flames from the furnace." Indeed, the fire and the crew here mirror each other, that is, they mirror in each other that which they have in common: a forbidding and barely controllable power that is always about to overflow, break loose, and exceed all limits—much like the flames darting out of the furnace or the boiling oil that is "all eagerness to leap" out of the cauldrons. If the rhetorical figure of the pathetic fallacy does not quite capture the metaphoric contortions of this passage—since here one would have to speak not only of pathetic fallacy but also of pathetic fallacy in reverse—that is so because the fire, the ship, the crew, the wind, the sea, and the night are all partaking of and being driven by such a potential for centrifugal excess. It would be incorrect to understand this passage in terms either of a naturalization of the crew or of an anthropomorphosis of the crew's surrounding environment or of both: one does not find here that essential difference between the forces of nature and the forces of human labor that constitutes the ontological entablature of many a binarism, in which such opposite forces are inevitably posited as forever engaging in a dialectical combat with each other. While Ahab's struggle against the white whale can in some way still be enlisted in the service of that humanist binarism par excellence which is the Man-Nature dialectic, the relation between the crew and the so-called natural elements can no longer be made to serve such a humanist project. Each of these forces—that is, the crew, the fire, as well as everything else surrounding them—comes into being by being caught and participating in a transformative process of becoming whose exemplary form here is at first the transmutation of the whale into oil but whose object and scope seem ultimately to encompass no less than the whole universe.

The writers of *Anti-Oedipus* are not far from Melville in this passage. In one of the most crucial and exhilarating moments of over twenty years of collaboration, Deleuze and Guattari write:

> It is probable that at a certain level nature and industry are two separate and distinct things: from one point of view, industry is the opposite of nature; from another, industry extracts its raw materials from nature; from yet another, it returns its refuse to nature; and so on. Even within society, this characteristic man-nature, industry-nature, society-nature relationship is responsible for the distinction of relatively autonomous spheres that are called production, distribution, consumption. But in general this entire level of distinctions, examined from the point of view of its formal developed structures, presupposes (as Marx has demonstrated) not only the existence of capital and the division of labor, but also the false consciousness that the capitalist being necessarily acquires, both of itself and of the supposedly fixed

elements within an over-all process. For the real truth of the matter—the glaring, sober truth that resides in delirium—is that there is no such thing as relatively independent spheres or circuits: production is immediately consumption and a recording process *(enregistrement)*, without any sort of mediation, and the recording process and consumption directly determine production, though they do so within the production process itself. Hence everything is production.... This is the first meaning of process as we use the term: incorporating recording and consumption within production itself, thus making them the productions of one and the same process.

Second, we make no distinction between man and nature: the human essence of nature and the natural essence of man become one within nature in the form of production or industry, just as they do within the life of man as species. Industry is then no longer considered from the extrinsic point of view of utility, but rather from the point of view of its fundamental identity with nature as production of man and by man.... This is the second meaning of process as we use the term: man and nature are not like two opposite terms confronting each other—not even in the sense of bipolar opposites within a relationship of causation, ideation, or expression (cause and effect, subject and object, etc.); rather, they are one and the same essential reality, the producer-product. Production as process overtakes all idealistic categories and constitutes a cycle whose relationship to desire is that of an immanent principle.[143]

Too many are the points of intersection between this "delirium" and Melville's own—and I have already implicitly sketched some of the possible intersections in the above readings of Ishmael's description of the crew at the try-works. Here I will limit myself to just two further observations. First, it is precisely the composite, self-reproductive, and cyclical nature of the productive process that Ishmael is pondering when he describes how "after being tried out, the crisp, shrivelled blubber...still contains considerable of its unctuous properties [and is hence used to] feed the flames," and when he concludes by remarking, "Like a plethoric burning martyr, or a self-consuming misanthrope, once ignited, the whale supplies his own fuel and burns by his own body."[144] Second, it ought to be clear by now that Melville's name for the immanent principle invoked here by Deleuze and Guattari—immanent, that is, in the general process of production of the universe—is nothing other than fire. Such, then, is the uncompromising and radical antihumanism of Ishmael's ruminations: in the isomorphism of the bodies of fire and of living labor—bodies that are here accomplices in an industrial metamorphosis—he has sensed and captured the universe as a universe of production.

This, however, is no easy capture. It is precisely when they are seen in the light of production — and hence at their most protean, dynamic, and transformative — that the body of fire and the body of living labor also appear most demonic, uncontrollable, and excessive: the extraordinary diction of this passage alone speaks unmistakably of a too-close encounter with radical otherness as absolute evil: "Tartarean," "pagan," "snaky," "barbaric," "unholy," "uncivilized," "begrimed," "hissing," "howled," "groaned," "leaped," "blackness," "darkness," "savages," "tawny features," "matted beards," "red hell," "wildly gesticulated," "scornfully champed," "viciously spat," "tales of terror." In the episode of "The Candles" the isomorphism of crew and fire can still be reined in by a masterful representational hand, whereas in the violent heat of the productive moment — a moment that Ishmael starkly sums up as the "burning of a corpse" — the images are possibly even more powerful and far more numerous, so that their cumulative effect signals an epistemological state in Ishmael that might be described as representational panic. It is almost as if Ishmael, having suddenly come face to face with too awesome and ubiquitous of a kinetic force, frantically proliferates one series of images after another in the attempt to contain such a force's centrifugal motion that might otherwise exceed him and sweep him away with it. Even though this is a textual conceit — because, strictly speaking, there is no gap or residue between that force and the images that represent and indeed produce it in the text — such a conceit does have an urgent indexicality all its own: a trace of the extratextual presence of that force — which is to say, an extratextual textual effect — is nonetheless detectable here.

Such a trace is most visible in this passage's syntactical acrobatics: its syntax is forever straining at the leash of representation as if possessed by an invisible force greater than the linguistic forms through which alone the effects of such a force can be felt in the text in the first place. In particular, the last sentence of the passage is a veritable battleground for such a syntactical-representational tug of war:

> As they narrated to each other their unholy adventures, their tales of terror told in words of mirth; as their uncivilized laughter forked upwards out of them, like the flames from the furnace; as to and fro, in their front, the harpooneers wildly gesticulated with their huge pronged forks and dippers; as the wind howled on, and the sea leaped, and the ship groaned and dived, and yet steadfastly shot her red hell further and further into the blackness of the sea and the night, and scornfully champed the white bone in her mouth, and viciously spat round her on all sides; then the rushing Pequod, freighted with savages, and laden with fire, and burning a corpse, and plunging into

that blackness of darkness, seemed the material counterpart of her monomaniac commander's soul.

Or, syntax-in-flight. Much like the rushing *Pequod*, this sentence is shot to hell. Its
Romance length alone speaks of an attempt to reach further and further toward an
unreachable limit as well as to stretch the very linguistic unit to its furthest limits.
This is not simply a question of length; more importantly, it is a question of structure. Over and beyond the fact, for example, that most of the verbs of this sentence
signify violent motion already in and of themselves, it is the syntax itself here that
rushes along with them and is always a step ahead of them. This syntactical rush,
however, is in one crucial respect much unlike the flux in which the *Pequod* as well as
everything and everybody in and around it seem to be caught: while the latter appears to be continuous and without pause, the syntax that would structure the representation of such an image of flux—though itself no less in flux—is radically discontinuous, as it proceeds by fits and starts, and is always stopping and beginning
again. Considering that when a sentence begins with a subordinate clause reading
habits lead us to expect the principal clause to follow immediately after it, in this
sentence those expectations are repeatedly aroused and disappointed, as we are made
to go through a series of no less than ten subordinate clauses before we reach the
pivotal "then" heralding that resolution is finally at hand and introducing the principal clause ("then the rushing Pequod..."). Just when we think to be surely in the
presence of the principal clause, however, the forever-imminent resolution is again
repeatedly postponed, as four attributive phrases ("freighted with savages, and laden
with fire, and burning a corpse, and plunging into that blackness of darkness") are
interposed between the grammatical subject and the verb ("seemed the material
counterpart of her monomaniac commander's soul"). Furthermore, if we consider
that the four attributive phrases do not introduce radically new elements in the passage as a whole but rather recapitulate much of the imagery already elaborated in
the subordinate clauses, it should be clear that the main function of such phrases is
one of interruption by means of repetition and intensification. This is, in other
words, a syntax of deferral and liminality—a syntax that unfolds at one and the
same time by overcoming limits and by adding new ones further along.

   And yet this syntax seems also to be strangely divided against itself
and pulled in different directions at once—almost as if the tensions and discrepan-
cies between syntax and representation are being played out in different ways inside
the syntax itself. In this respect, the use of conjunctions is illuminating. While the
first few subordinate clauses are introduced by the properly subordinating "as," there

is then a rapid switch to the coordinating "and" not only to connect nouns within a clause but also to introduce the clauses themselves: while the "as" begins by promising a hierarchical structure that will deliver closure and meaning in the end, the "and" threatens instead to establish a potentially infinite seriality that might delink completely from the intertwined questions of closure and meaning by pushing both of them beyond reach. Take, for example, the last series of subordinate clauses just before the principal is announced: "as the wind howled on, and the sea leaped, and the ship groaned and dived, and yet steadfastly shot her red hell further and further into the blackness of the sea and the night, and scornfully champed the white bone in her mouth, and viciously spat round her on all sides; then the rushing *Pequod...*" This series of subordinates is introduced by an "as" but is then stretched and turned into a plane of coordinates by the repeated use of the "and" that simply produces more and more parallel images rather than ordering and ranking them, and that seems destined therefore to get us farther and farther away from the syntactical gravitational center of the sentence, which, in fact, can finally emerge only abruptly and arbitrarily. (In this sense, it is remarkable that Deleuze and Guattari resort to precisely such a use of the conjunction "and" in order to exemplify the functioning of the general process of production, as they write that the "productive synthesis, the production of production, is inherently connective in nature: 'and...' 'and then...'.")[145] The "as" and the "and" answer to two different spatio-temporal imperatives: while the logic of the "as" functions according to a teleological a priori (that is, it immediately and proleptically announces a future resolution in the form of a principal clause, after which the whole process of subordination and eventual resolution can begin all over again), the logic of the "and" does not function according to an eschatology of signification, as it could well continue to unfold *ad infinitum* without any resolution whatsoever. But we should be quite familiar by now with such dynamics, which have been found ensconced and pulsating here in the most micrological levels of Melville's poetics. What is being registered in the syntactical fabric of this passage by means of the different pulls and functions of the "as" and of the "and" is nothing other than a form of the antagonism between capital and labor: on the one hand, such a simultaneous proliferation, deferral, and overcoming of limits indexed by the "as" is the very *modus operandi* of capital; on the other hand, such an accretive and connective logic indexed by the "and" is the very *modus vivendi* of an infinitely productive universe, that is, of that universal process of production that capital seeks to harness and exploit — and whose life and time capital continuously borrows.

Ishmael's discovery of an intractable, immanent, and infinitely productive power in the isomorphism of the bodies of fire and of living labor, and his perilous capture of this power in a passage whose syntactical tensions bear witness to the difficulty involved in containing, representing, and exploiting such a power in any way—such a discovery and such a capture cannot go unpunished (much like Prometheus's sin, which Ishmael must have surely had in mind, if one is to judge from the fact that a few sentences earlier he had remarked on "the fierce flames" of the furnace "which at intervals forked forth from the sooty flues, and illuminated every lofty rope in the rigging, as with the famed Greek fire.")[146] Following the description of the crew at the try-works, in fact, we learn that Ishmael, who had been watching the scene at some distance while at the ship's helm, is the protagonist of a strange occurrence:

> So it seemed to me, as I stood at her helm, and for long hours silently guided the way of this fire-ship on the sea. Wrapped, for that interval, in darkness myself, I but the better saw the redness, the madness, the ghastliness of others. The continual sight of the fiend shapes before me, capering half in smoke and half in fire, these at last begat kindred visions in my soul, so soon as I began to yield to that unaccountable drowsiness which ever would come over me at a midnight helm.
>
> But that night, in particular, a strange (and ever since inexplicable) thing occurred to me. Starting from a brief standing sleep, I was horribly conscious of something fatally wrong. The jaw-bone tiller smote my side, which leaned against it; in my ears was the low hum of sails, just beginning to shake in the wind; I thought my eyes were open; I was half conscious of putting my fingers to the lids and mechanically stretching them still further apart. But, in spite of all this, I could see no compass before me to steer by; though it seemed but a minute since I had been watching the card, by the steady binnacle lamp illuminating it. Nothing seemed before me but a jet gloom, now and then made ghastly by flashes of redness. Uppermost was the impression, that whatever swift, rushing thing I stood on was not so much bound to any haven ahead as rushing from all havens astern. A stark, bewildered feeling, as of death came over me. Convulsively my hands grasped the tiller, but with the crazy conceit that the tiller was, somehow, in some enchanted way, inverted. My God! what is the matter with me? thought I. Lo! in my brief sleep I had turned myself about, and was fronting the ship's stern, with my back to her prow and the compass. In an instant I faced back, just in time to prevent the vessel from flying up into the wind, and very probably capsizing her. How glad and how grateful the relief from this unnatural hallucination of the night, and the fatal contingency of being brought by the lee![147]

Rather than reasonably putting this strange event at rest as a mere lapse due to exhaustion, Ishmael quickly blames it on the preceding scene and hence proceeds to draw an even stranger moral from what now has suddenly and retrospectively become a story:

> Look not too long in the face of fire, O man! never dream with thy hand on the helm! Turn not thy back to the compass; accept the first hint of the hitching tiller; believe not the artificial fire, when its redness makes all things look ghastly. To-morrow, in the natural sun, the skies will be bright; those who glared like devils in the forking flames, the morn will show in far other, at least gentler, relief; the glorious, golden, glad sun, the only true lamp—all other but liars!
>
> Nevertheless the sun hides not Virginia's Dismal Swamp nor Rome's accursed Campagna, nor wide Sahara, nor all the millions of miles of deserts and of griefs beneath the moon. The sun hides not the ocean, which is the dark side of this earth, and which is two thirds of this earth. So, therefore, that mortal man who hath more of joy than sorrow in him, that mortal man cannot be true—not true, or undeveloped. With books the same. The truest of all men was the Man of Sorrows, and the truest of all books is Solomon's, and Ecclesiastes is the fine hammered steel of woe. "All is vanity." ALL. This willful world hath not got hold of unchristian Solomon's wisdom yet. But he who dodges hospitals and jails, and walks fast crossing grave-yards, and would rather talk of operas than hell; calls Cowper, Young, Pascal, Rousseau, poor devils all of sick men; and throughout a care-free lifetime swears by Rabelais as passing wise, and therefore jolly;—not that man is fitted to sit down on tomb-stones, and break the green damp mould with unfathomably wondrous Solomon.
>
> But even Solomon, he says, "the man that wandereth out of the way of understanding shall remain" (*i.e.* even while living) "in the congregation of the dead." Give not thyself up, then, to fire, lest it invert thee, deaden thee; as for the time it did me.[148]

These three successive passages (that is, the description of the crew, the description of Ishmael's momentary lapse, and the resulting exhortations and reflections) are linked by a relation of causality and constitute some sort of cause-effect-and-moral-of-the-story or thesis-antithesis-synthesis triad. In effect, one is faced here with a narrative strategy of containment as well as with the abjuration of too dangerous an epiphany: Ishmael discovers fire, plays with it, gets burned, promises not to do it ever again, and warns us all against its treacherous nature. But what a confusing and bombastic narrative mise en scène for such a simple tale! If it is difficult to find one's way in these labyrinthine passages, that may well be an index of the difficulties encountered by Ishmael here. What exactly is, in fact, the moral of this story? Let us try to unravel at least some of its main threads.

In the end, Ishmael—who had been staring for so long at the "fiend shapes" of the crew "capering half in smoke and half in fire" in front of him while at the helm that he had fallen into a trance-like sleep and had turned away from the helm and compass as well as from the crew and the try-works, thereby endangering the ship and all aboard—denounces the "artificial," "unnatural," "ghastly," false, inverting, and deadening powers of fire (as opposed to the "natural," "true," "bright," "gentler," "glorious, golden, glad sun"). This whole diatribe against fire is posited on an equivalence—or, at the very least, on a causal relation—between inversion (from the true to the false, from the natural to the unnatural) and death: Ishmael's act of turning his back to his duty at the helm and threatening everybody with sure death is transmogrified and allegorized via Solomon's words into a turning away from "the way of understanding" and toward "the congregation of the dead." And it is fire that is singled out as the cause of nothing less than such a cataclysmic existential inversion-unto-death. Given that "inversion" was one of the few figures available in the 1850s for what a few decades later will be baptized as homosexuality, such a grandiose allegorization of a mere loss of bearing into a fatal moment of universal inversion (that is, into a momentary inversion of all that is true, natural, and good) may also betray Ishmael's homosexual panic at the realization of having turned his defenseless back to the demonic forces of the fire and the crew. Improbable as such a reading of this scene might seem, one ought at least to consider the peculiar diction of Ishmael's sudden realization of what had happened:

> Convulsively my hands grasped the tiller, but with the crazy conceit that the tiller was, somehow, in some enchanted way, inverted. My God! what is the matter with me? thought I. Lo! in my brief sleep I had turned myself about, and was fronting the ship's stern, with my back to her prow and the compass.

As soon as he comes to, Ishmael discovers that the tiller was no longer where it was supposed to be and immediately imagines this occurrence as an inversion: "the tiller was...inverted." Rather than more predictably prompting him to ask what had happened to the tiller, the realization of this inversion prompts him rather to ask: "My God! what is the matter with me?" This occurrence, in other words, implicates and indicts *him* rather than the tiller or whatever magic force had caused its inversion in the first place. Ishmael does not even ask: what is the matter with the tiller? or, even, what has happened to me?—he asks, rather: "what is the matter with me?" Such a question may seem innocuous and unobtrusive enough, if it weren't for the fact that this same phraseology returns to haunt Melville several decades later in one of the most crucial moments of *Billy Budd*. The opening line of chapter 11 of that short novel reads thus: "What was the matter with the master-at-arms?" This is the piv-otal chapter in which the narrator attempts to fathom the "hidden nature"—that is, the pathological depths—of Claggart, the master-at-arms aboard Billy Budd's ship. Claggart—who, according to the narrator, is "the direct reverse of a saint"—is identified here as the exemplary specimen of a certain "Natural Depravity: a deprav-ity according to nature." But I have already discussed in chapter 1 the arguments re-garding the paradigmatic position that this short novel occupies in the late-nineteenth-century discursive emergence of the homosexual. Here, I simply wish to draw attention to the fact that for Melville the matter of the question "what is the matter?" may be inseparable from questions concerning "depravity," "inversion," and what he calls "the deadly space between" the natural and the unnatural.[149]

The contraindications that are finally called for in the face of such a fire-induced "unnatural hallucination," however, lock Ishmael into insoluble contradictions. "Look not too long in the face of fire, O man!... Turn not thy back to the compass.... Give not thyself up, then, to fire, lest it invert thee, deaden thee; as for the time it did me." The problem with Ishmael's prescriptions is that they are, strictly speaking, impossible for him to follow. How is he *not* to look "too long in the face of fire" as well as *not* turn his "back to the compass," if he cannot help facing the fire when facing the compass? Wasn't he actually already following his advice to not look "too long in the face of fire" when turning away from it in his sleep? Isn't such a deadly inversion the solution to the problem of not giving himself "up...to fire" rather than the problem caused by such a deadly abandon to fire in the first place? Isn't self-defense here at one and the same time also self-destruction? Ishmael is caught in a lethal double bind, that is, in "the deadly space between." In the preced-ing scene he had discovered the demonic power of production embodied in the crew and in fire—and after that discovery he cannot but continue to give himself up to that power which he has sensed might well invert and destroy him, because not to give himself up to it would mean to be inverted and destroyed all the same. Look not too long in the face of fire, O Ishmael! *But look not too short either.*

Having been momentarily placed outside the crew by his duty at the helm, Ishmael looks over them at a distance and is able to see them literally in a different light and, as it were, for the first time: "So it seemed to me, as I stood at her helm, and for long hours silently guided the way of this fire-ship on the sea.

Wrapped, for that interval, in darkness myself, I but the better saw the redness, the madness, the ghastliness of others." In the light of fire and in the heat of the moment of production, Ishmael's fellow sailors have become "others." Ishmael here is in the presence of the collective body of the other limit: that nonvalue that is potentially productive of all value and that can be imaged from a distance only as "abstract chaos" and as "madness" — "madness, however, as a moment of economics and as a determinant of the practical life of peoples."[150] The double bind in which Ishmael is caught throughout the chapter on "The Try-Works" is the paradox beating at the very heart of capital: the capital paradox of having to continue to harness, exploit, and foment precisely that immanent power of production that — much like the "snaky flames" darting out of the furnace, the "boiling oil" leaping out of the cauldrons, or the "uncivilized laughter" that "forked upwards out of" the crew — might at any given moment overflow beyond its confines, spin out of control, exceed itself, and bring about the catastrophe of a crisis beyond crisis. In these difficult experiments with the isomorphism of the bodies of the crew and of fire, Melville is already elaborating what will be one of Marx's crucial intuitions in the *Grundrisse:* "Labour is the living, form-giving fire; it is the transitoriness of things, their temporality, as their formation by living time."[151]

But let us finally leave both crew and fire to their metamorphic labors, and turn a final time to the last passage quoted above. In that passage, Ishmael feels compelled to ponder "joy" and "sorrow" in ways that cannot remain unquestioned here. Having first contrasted the false light of fire and the only true light, that is, the light of the sun, Ishmael reflects on the fact that not even the sun can hide the sorrows of the world, and proceeds to draw the following conclusions:

> So, therefore, that mortal man who hath more of joy than sorrow in him, that mortal man cannot be true — not true, or undeveloped. With books the same. The truest of all men was the Man of Sorrows, and the truest of all books is Solomon's. . . . But he who dodges hospitals and jails, and walks fast crossing grave-yards, and would rather talk of operas than hell; calls Cowper, Young, Pascal, Rousseau, poor devils all of sick men; and throughout a carefree lifetime swears by Rabelais as passing wise, and therefore jolly; — not that man is fitted to sit down on tomb-stones, and break the green damp mould with unfathomably wondrous Solomon.

It will remain unclear till the end why exactly the preceding discourse on fire should spark these literary reflections on "joy" and "sorrow." What is clear, however, is that *this* book — that is, *Moby-Dick* — partakes neither of that riskless optimism of the will that here bears the name of "joy" nor of that nihilistic pessimism of reason that here bears the name of "sorrow." Beyond the dialectical polarities of such a "joy" and such a "sorrow" lie an altogether other joy and other sorrow that are always one (in) crisis: that joy that is always at stake in the sorrow of crisis, that promise of an other history that quivers in the wounded flesh of the *corpus absolutus*, that Benjaminian imperative of a *wirklich Ausnahmezustand* to which we must now turn.

In an incomparable essay on Melville, Leo Bersani asks, "Is there a *subject* of homosexual desire in *Moby-Dick*?"[152] While his answer to this crucial question is an emphatic *no*, my answer to the same question will be a qualified *yes*—and it will turn out that, far from contradicting each other, these two answers are actually coterminous. The time has come, in other words, to return to that condition of abandon that is the only possible ontological state of the *corpus absolutus* as well as to that earlier claim regarding the romance between Ishmael and Queequeg intended as the most joyous and exemplary trajectory traced by the desire of the other limit in *Moby-Dick*. For if there is no subject of homosexual desire in *Moby-Dick*, and furthermore, if there is, strictly speaking, no sexual subject of any kind to be found anywhere in it, there certainly reigns omnipresent, intense, and rarefied in this novel what could be provisionally termed a *homosexual subjectivity*. This is another way of saying that that subjectivity without either subjects or the Subject that is the collective body of living labor of whaling finds its primary form of expression and moment of constitution in a continuous experimentation with corporeal abandon. What new forms of being-in-common might arise when male bodies abandon themselves to each other? Such is the question of the other limit in *Moby-Dick*.

After having discussed the relation between Queequeg and Ishmael, Bersani writes:

> Is there a *subject* of homosexuality in *Moby-Dick?* Far from representing either unequivocal homosexuality or surfaces of heterosexual desire troubled by repressed homosexual impulses, Melville's characters have no sexual subjectivity at all.... Interiority in *Moby-Dick* is almost entirely philosophical; each character is a certain confluence of metaphysical, epistemological, and social-ethical positions. Homoeroticism can enter the novel so easily because, psychologically, there is nothing at stake.... Ishmael's marital metaphors [describing his relation to Queequeg] reveal nothing about him because there is nowhere in the novel an Ishmael about whom such metaphors can be revealing.

This does not mean that they are unimportant: their very signifi-
cance depends on *not* providing an intelligible alternative to Ahab's despotism.... Only something that does not enter into logical opposition can be
"opposed" to Ahab. Politically this means that in order to escape the antide-
mocratic consequences inherent in the democratic ideal, a type of social relation must be imagined that is neither autocratic nor democratic.

Ishmael's response to Queequeg and the crew is the testing of this
other relation.... But ... the introduction of homoeroticism in the novel prevents his representation of Queequeg and the crew from being one of a society united in the bonds of friendship created by communal work. This homoeroticism, however, never settles into what would be merely another type
of oppositional grouping. By figuring what I have called a nonpsychological
homosexuality, Melville proposes a social bond based not on subordination
to the great personality embodied by Ahab, not on the democratic ideal of
power distributed according to intrinsic worth, not on those feelings binding
either two friends or the partners in a marriage, not, finally, on the transgressed homage to all such legitimated social bonds in conventional images
of homosexual desire.[153]

Is it because this passage emerges from and yet still squarely belongs to the eleventh
hour of the Cold War that Bersani is uninterested in taking the next logical step and
argue that the nonautocratic and nondemocratic "social relation" envisaged by such
a "nonpsychological homosexuality" is precisely that alternative to capitalist relations
of exchange that at least since the July Revolution of 1830 bears the little-understood
and much-betrayed name of communism? Presumably, Bersani's essay—published
in *The Culture of Redemption* in 1990—was still being written around the time of
what has become the nominal marker for the end of the Cold War, namely, the
1989 fall of the Berlin Wall. It is important to draw attention to these dates here because, if during the Cold War it might have been difficult to think communism due
to the monopoly over that concept exercised by a long tradition of teleologically-
inclined utopian Marxism, after the demise of the Soviet experiment communism
has regained for some of us a crucial validity as a heuristic concept for thinking the
multifarious past and present practices of antagonism to capital precisely because
such a concept has now been freed from the oppressive doctrinal monopoly and historical referent of the Soviet State, which was, if anything, a cruel travesty and a terminal betrayal of communism in the first place.[154] However the case may be, what is
certain is that that "social relation" is unintelligible only from the standpoint of the

forever-expanding spiral of last limits in which "Ahab's despotism" is caught, but it is precisely what becomes intelligible and what constitutes the very index of revolutionary intelligibility when considered and posited from the standpoint of the other limit. Bersani, after all, is himself caught in a paradox here: no matter how unintelligible he claims this new "type of social relation" to be, it surely must be intelligible in some positive form or other—and not merely as the negation of all existing forms of relationality—for him to be able to sense it and to write about it at all. For Bersani, such a "social relation" is at the very least *potentially* intelligible, that is, intelligible as *potentia*.

The further proof of such a paradoxical intelligibility lies in reading Bersani's reading of *Moby-Dick* retroactively as a prelude to a series of arguments that he fully elaborates five years later in his *Homos*, a work in which that purportedly unintelligible new "type of social relation" becomes intelligible enough for Bersani to bestow a name upon it and to turn it into the center of that work's entire investigation. That name is "homo-ness" and this is the calling of that name:

> It is perhaps unfortunate, but no less true, that we have *learned to desire* from within the heterosexual norms and gendered structures that we can no longer think of as natural, or as exhausting all the options for self-identification. Since deconstructing an imposed identity will not erase the habit of desire, it might be more profitable to test the resistance of the identity from *within* the desire. Although there are valid grounds for questioning the assumption that desire between men, or between women, is desire for "the same," it is also true that because our apprenticeship in desiring takes place within that assumption, homosexuality can become a privileged model of sameness—one that makes manifest not the limits but the inestimable value of relations of sameness, of homo-relations. Perhaps inherent in gay desire is a revolutionary inaptitude for heteroized sociality. This of course means sociality as we know it, and the most politically disruptive aspect of the homo-ness I will be exploring in gay desire is a redefinition of sociality so radical that it may appear to require a provisional withdrawal from relationality itself....
>
> The writers I discuss are—in sharp contrast to contemporary gay and lesbian theorists—drawn to the *anticommunitarian* impulses they discover in homosexual desire. For them, otherness is articulated as relay stations in a process of self-extension. [They]...are nonetheless relevant to [contemporary] debates in demonstrating how desire for the same can free us from an oppressive psychology of desire as lack (a psychology that grounds sociality in trauma and castration). New reflection on homo-ness could lead

> us to a salutary devalorizing of difference—or, more exactly to a notion of difference not as a trauma to be overcome...but rather as a nonthreatening supplement to sameness....
>
> ...If homosexuality is a privileged vehicle for homo-ness, the latter designates a mode of connectedness to the world that it would be absurd to reduce to sexual preference. An anticommunal mode of connectedness we might all share, or a new way of coming together: that, and not assimilation into already constituted communities, should be the goal of any adventure in bringing out, and celebrating, "the homo" in all of us.[155]

While I will return to the question of same-sex desire intended as desire of the same in the next chapter, it is crucial now to emphasize that the trajectory of thought traced by Bersani from *The Culture of Redemption* to *Homos* completes a shift from a negative to a positive ontology. Homo-ness emerges here fully as a form-of-life in its own right and as a concept for thinking those experiments with social relations that had already been sensed in the political possibilities of a "nonpsychological homo-sexuality" in *Moby-Dick*. It is not merely the case that an articulation of "otherness" "as relay stations in a process of self-extension" and "a notion of difference not as a trauma to be overcome...but rather as a nonthreatening supplement to sameness" describe accurately Ishmael's modes of attraction to and engagement with Quee-queg; or, that the rhetorical somersaults of Ishmael's marital metaphors can be seen precisely as an attempt "to test the resistance of" "an imposed identity" "from *within*" "the heterosexual norms and gendered structures" of desire; or, that what Bersani calls "the most politically disruptive aspect of...homo-ness"—namely, "a redefini-tion of sociality so radical that it may appear to require a provisional withdrawal from relationality itself"—is virtually coextensive with what I have identified as an ontological state of abandonment to the condition of having abandoned the at once autarchic and democratic realm of "Ahab's despotism" and all its social contracts. More importantly, after reading in *Homos* how one of the most exemplary instantia-tions of homo-ness—namely, Michel's "pederasty" in André Gide's *The Immoral-ist*—leads Bersani to speculate that "if a community were ever to exist in which it would no longer seem natural to define all relations as property relations (not only my money or my land, but also my country, my wife, my lover), we would first have to imagine a new erotics [without which] all revolutionary activity will return, as we have seen it return over and over again, to relations of ownership and dominance," we are then more than authorized to re-read that third term escaping both autarchic and democratic social relations in *Moby-Dick* as a communist *potentia*.[156] In paying my own "transgressed homage" to Bersani, in other words, I do not mean merely to out him as a crypto-communist *malgré soi* and draw attention to the numerous points of intersection between his work and my own project; I want, rather, to outline how his identification of a revolutionary impetus in *Moby-Dick*'s "nonpsychological homosexuality" led him uncoincidentally to formulations about anticommunitarian forms of community that closely resemble a series of recent attempts to rescue that desire that goes by the name of communism from political disrepute and historical oblivion. These include Maurice Blanchot's *The Unavowable Community* (1983), Giorgio Agamben's *The Coming Community* (1990), Antonio Negri and Félix Guattari's *Communists Like Us* (1985–1990), Negri and Michael Hardt's *Labor of Dionysus* (1994) and *Empire* (2000). That Bersani has elaborated these formulations with the added benefit of recognizing the importance of the question of same-sex desire for any kind of communist praxis, and that he has come to such formulations via an encounter with the intense homo-ness of *Moby-Dick*, is also a testimony to the revolutionary energies intrinsic in the experiments with corporeal abandon that animate Melville's work. And if I have embarked here on the perhaps entirely presumptuous project of pushing Bersani's passion to the other limit, I have done so also because in the end I want to return with such a reelaboration of his passion to that future which is the Marxian theory of communism and revolution implicit in the *Grundrisse*, so as to find love between men there—where it has been all along.

We have not yet seen with our own eyes, however, the love that courses through Ishmael and Queequeg and that binds them to each other in such indeterminable relations. The unfolding of their love constitutes the narrative centerpiece of the first twenty-one chapters—roughly one fifth of the whole novel—which take place on land before the *Pequod* "blindly plunged like fate into the lone Atlantic."[157] Once aboard, the story of their relationship all but goes underground, almost as if to make space for Ahab's obsession which immediately turns into the official story of the *Pequod*'s whole passage. It goes underground, but it does not disappear. Melville draws attention to the unchanged persistence of the special relation binding Ishmael and Queequeg by letting it resurface from time to time aboard the *Pequod* in the form of Ishmael's terms of endearment: "my Queequeg"; "my particular friend Queequeg"; "my own inseparable twin brother"; "my brave Queequeg"; "my poor pagan companion, and fast bosom-friend, Queequeg"; and—when deciding to draft his will—" 'Queequeg,' said I, 'come along, you shall be my lawyer, executor, and legatee.' "[158] Moreover, there are several moments during the passage when a specific task requires Ishmael and Queequeg to work together, thereby bringing their special friendship back onto the narrative stage once more. Clearly, the fact

that the encounter between Ishmael and Queequeg is at first foregrounded in the
land chapters and is then narratively marginalized and yet never abjured—and, in
fact, periodically reasserted—in the sea chapters is of crucial importance for understanding not only the nature of the Ishmael-Queequeg relationship but also the structural development of the whole novel. Far from ever being forgotten or negated, the
narrative primal scene of that first encounter could be said to constitute the continued condition of possibility for the rest of the novel, that is, the fuel propelling the
Pequod and all aboard in their fated peregrination.

It is from one of those moments in which the Ishmael-Queequeg
relationship reappears aboard the *Pequod* that I want to begin to ask after the specific
nature of their bond, so as to return later on land to those pages in which they first
meet and became "fast bosom-friends." In a chapter entitled "The Mat-Maker," we
find Ishmael and Queequeg "mildly employed weaving what is called a sword-mat."[159]
As is often the case with the objects and practices of the world of whaling, this activity becomes the catalyst for Ishmael's metaphysical broodings:

> I was the attendant or page of Queequeg, while busy at the mat. As I kept
> passing and repassing the filling or woof of marline between the long yarns
> of the warp, using my own hand for the shuttle, and as Queequeg, standing
> sideways, ever and anon slid his heavy oaken sword between the threads, and
> idly looking off upon the water, carelessly and unthinkingly drove home
> every yarn; I say so strange a dreaminess did there reign all over the ship and
> all over the sea, only broken by the intermitting dull sound of the sword,
> that it seemed as if this were the Loom of Time, and I myself were a shuttle
> mechanically weaving and weaving away at the Fates. There lay the fixed
> threads of the warp subject to but one single, ever returning, unchanging vi-
> bration, and that vibration merely enough to admit of the crosswise inter-
> blending of other threads with its own. This warp seemed necessity; and
> here, thought I, with my own hand I ply my own shuttle and weave my own
> destiny into these unalterable threads. Meantime, Queequeg's impulsive, indif-
> ferent sword, sometimes hitting the woof slantingly, or crookedly, or strongly,
> or weakly, as the case might be; and by this difference in the concluding
> blow producing a corresponding contrast in the final aspect of the completed
> fabric; this savage's sword, thought I, which thus finally shapes and fashions
> both warp and woof; this easy, indifferent sword must be chance—aye, chance,
> free will, and necessity—no wise incompatible—all interweavingly working
> together. The straight warp of necessity, not to be swerved from its ultimate
> course—its every alternating vibration, indeed, only tending to that; free
> will still free to ply her shuttle between given threads; and chance, though

restrained in its play within the right lines of necessity, and sideways in its motions directed by free will, though thus prescribed to by both, chance by turns rules either, and has the last featuring blow at events.[160]

Who exactly is the mat-maker here? And why is the chapter containing this passage entitled "The Mat-Maker" rather than "The Mat-Makers"? One may want to begin to excavate this passage by noting that the singular of the chapter's title does not correspond to the plural of the activity described in it. Does that title indicate that there is only one mat-maker here and that his name is Queequeg, given that Ishmael is a mere "attendant or page"? Or, are we to surmise instead that the co-operation that is necessary for this activity has turned Ishmael and Queequeg into one single laboring apparatus that goes by the name of the mat-maker? In either case, that title indicates that Ishmael is being dissolved and incorporated into a complex laboring body in which his identity is either indiscernible or heteronomous or both. The discrepancy between what the title announces and what this passage describes already anticipates the anagnorisis of Ishmael's allegorical drama: in these interweavings of necessity, free will, and chance, the latter ultimately has the last word, as Ishmael in his double role of necessity and free will is finally subordinated to "the last featuring blow" of Queequeg in the guise of chance. That chance is the prevalent force here is also confirmed by the fact that Ishmael's free will proves to be weak and discontinuous at best. Immediately following this passage, we see that the activity in which they are both engaged is suddenly disrupted by a call signaling the first sighting of a whale: "Thus we were weaving and weaving away when I started at a sound so strange, long drawn, and musically wild and unearthly, that the ball of free will dropped from my hand, and I stood gazing up at the clouds whence that voice dropped like a wing."[161] And later in "The Monkey-Rope" chapter, we see the two friends tied together by the waist in a perilous, life-threatening task—and this predicament inevitably leads Ishmael to the following reflection: "So strongly and metaphysically did I conceive of my situation then, that while earnestly watching [Queequeg's] motions, I seemed distinctly to perceive that my own individuality was now merged in a joint stock company of two; that my free will had received a mortal wound."[162] Ishmael's free will in this novel is always already dead or dying, and his individuality is best described by Jonathan Arac when he writes, "In *Moby-Dick*, individuality is neither a goal nor a premise. At best, it is a puzzling possibility."[163] Whatever unrealized promise this possibility may hold for Ishmael, it is clear that his life and universe—including his relation to Queequeg—are ruled by principles other than the ones constituting the point of honor of bourgeois secular modernity.

If Ishmael is no Hegelian believer in the primacy of necessity, his tentative denials of free will do not make him a crypto-Jansenist either. What is at stake in Ishmael's allegorical reading of the weaving of the mat is an understanding of "events" as overdetermined, that is, as the product of the mutually determining relations of necessity, free will, and chance — in which chance, however, is always determining in the last instance. And if an Althusserian echo is heard troubling these formulations, you can rest assured that this is not a coincidence. If I turn now to that late interview in which Louis Althusser endeavors to define as well as to trace the genealogy of what he calls "aleatory materialism," that is because I believe that a crucial aspect of the love that binds Ishmael and Queequeg will emerge here if one dares to place Melville within that genealogy. This is Althusser's philosophical gamble:

> — Do you conceive of aleatory materialism as a possible philosophy for marxism?
>
> — Yes.... Now we can return to Democritus and to the worlds of Epicurus...: before the formation of the world, an infinite number of atoms were falling parallel to each other through the void. The implications of such a statement are important: 1) before there ever was a world, absolutely nothing existed that had a *form*, and, at the same time, 2) all the elements of the world already existed separately and for all eternity before any world had come into being.
>
> The implication of all of the above is that before the formation of the world there existed no cause, no end, no reason, and no unreason. This is the negation of all teleology — whether rational, moral, political, or aesthetic.... [This is] the materialism of a process without a subject that governs the order of its own development, without any assignable end....
>
> And then the *clinamen* suddenly appears: an infinitesimal declination that one doesn't know whence, when, or how it originated... [and that] causes the atom to deviate the course of its fall through the void and causes an *encounter* with the nearest atom — and from encounter to encounter... a world is born.
>
> — Are we to deduce that the origin of the whole world and of reality, of all necessity and sense is due to an aleatory deviation?
>
> — Exactly. What Epicurus posits is that this aleatory deviation is at the origin of the world rather than the First Cause or rather than Reason. It is crucial to understand, however, that the encounter does not create any of the world's reality and that it provides atoms themselves with their own reality; without any deviation or any encounter, in fact, atoms would be no more than abstract elements without either consistency or existence. It is only after

the world is constituted that the realm of reason, of necessity, and of sense is established. . . .

Rather than thinking of contingency as a modality of necessity or as an exception to necessity, one ought to think of necessity as the becoming-necessary of the encounter of contingencies.

It is my intention here to insist on the existence of a materialist tradition that has not been acknowledged by the history of philosophy. This is the tradition of Democritus, Epicurus, Machiavelli, Hobbes, the Rousseau of the second discourse, Marx, and Heidegger—along with all its attendant categories, such as void, limit, margin, absence of centre, displacement of the centre to the margin (and vice versa), and freedom. This is a materialism of the encounter and of contingency, in other words, a materialism of the *aleatory*, that opposes itself to those materialisms that have been acknowledged as such, including that materialism that is commonly attributed to Marx, Engels, and Lenin. The latter is a materialism of necessity and teleology, which is to say, a form of idealism in disguise.[164]

Here it is not only a question of noting how this radical attempt to provide Marxism with a non-Hegelian philosophical foundation also goes a long way in tracing the contours of Ishmael's world, it is also very much a question of emphasizing how Ishmael seems to be pushing these Althusserian formulations even further: "chance, though restrained in its play within the right lines of necessity, and sideways in its motions directed by free will, though thus prescribed to by both, chance by turns rules either, and has the last featuring blow at events." In other words, if it is the case, as we read in Althusser, that "[i]t is only after the world is constituted that the realm of reason, of necessity, and of sense is established," it is also the case that contingency will not disappear once this fated realm is established, and that it will continue to exert its sudden, eruptive, and epiphanic force on that realm up to—as Marx would say—that realm's blessed end.[165] Chance—Ishmael seems to be saying—has not only the first blow but also the very last.

The figure in the mat is none other than the love that binds Ishmael and Queequeg. Ishmael's hermeneutic exercise in the face of what could be called the mat-event, which leads him to an assertion of the primacy of chance incarnated in Queequeg's activity, ultimately provides a key to the aleatory nature of their relationship. If the powerful bonds that link these two friends assume and retain throughout the novel the ineluctable modality of necessity, that is so precisely in terms of a necessity lived as "the becoming-necessary of the encounter of contingencies." Such is the encounter of Ishmael and Queequeg in this novel—an encounter that becomes all the more necessary and cherished for having been a chance encounter in the first place. If—as Bersani recognizes—this friendship is so difficult to define, that is so because it is brought about and it continues to unfold under the aegis of chance and therefore does not have what Althusser calls an "assignable end." Their friendship is open-ended as well as end-less: it is not oriented toward any preordained *telos* and does not function according to any predetermined rules. When Queequeg passionately expresses his feelings for Ishmael as early as the day after they had first met and slept together, in fact, a flattered yet cautious Ishmael remarks: "In a countryman, this sudden flame of friendship would have seemed far too premature, a thing to be much distrusted; but in this simple savage those old rules would not apply."[166] In this early and pivotal moment, Ishmael already knows he is leaving familiar forms of propriety behind and embarking on a journey through unmapped territories of male-male sociality—and by declaring those rules "old" he already envisages new rules to come. The difference between "those old rules" and the new ones is crucial: unlike the old, the new rules do not preexist and determine a social relation but rather coexist with and run along that as-yet-uncharted relation in the first place. These new rules are going to be made up as they go along, are generated by that relation's intrinsic urgencies, and are posited as immanent to the relation itself. But only a game of chance, that is, a game that begins as a chance encounter and that proceeds under the sign of chance, can admit and sustain rules such as these—rules that in effect are made answerable to the game's own potentials rather than functioning as the harness that would direct such potentials toward the actualization of an a priori goal. For Ishmael and Queequeg, the only rules of the game are those that constitute their game as the becoming-necessary of a chance encounter and that preserve the necessity of such an encounter as unrealized and unrealizable *potentia*.

In this sense, Bersani's entirely accurate assessment—that "[h]omoeroticism can enter the novel so easily because, psychologically, there is nothing at stake"[167]—still needs to be modified. For if there is no sexual psychology at stake in the ease with which homoeroticism slides into the pages of *Moby-Dick*, that ease is nonetheless an index of the becoming-necessary of a chance encounter in which absolutely everything that matters is at stake. This is not the ease with which one performs a gesture that does not matter. This is the ease with which one performs a gesture after the point at which nothing any longer matters, that is, the ease of a gesture that matters only too much because it is now the only thing that matters and, in fact, because it is now all that can truly matter as if for the very first time. The ease with which Ishmael—referring to his feelings for Queequeg—remarks on "how elastic our stiff prejudices grow when once love comes to bend them"[168] is the ease one feels in the face of a last chance, that is, the ease with which one abandons oneself to the sudden appearance of chance when all "our stiff prejudices" have betrayed us and when all else is lost. For it is only with such a reckless, desperate ease that one can turn an arbitrary contingency into an absolute necessity and put one's very being at stake in a single gesture of love. Such are the poignant ease and the urgent gestures of love: they befall like chance — always for the very first time and always after the very last. And if there is indeed an inexorably teleological impetus in *Moby-Dick* — since this novel unfolds from its earliest pages as the chronicle of a catastrophe foretold — there is also in it a just-as-powerful nonteleological undertow constituted by a refractory, necessary, and aleatory love that dares not speak its end.

And if Ishmael and Queequeg deviate the course of their fall through that void which is their orphan and exilic life, and eventually encounter each other in bed on a cold winter night, what stroke of chance caused such a deviation and such an encounter? Where is the *clinamen* that made them collide into each other in the first place? Peter Coffin is the name of the *clinamen* in *Moby-Dick*. We need to return to the beginning of the novel and greet Ishmael on his arrival in the whaling capital of the world: New Bedford. After searching in vain for lodgings cheap enough for his purse, Ishmael finally comes across the Spouter Inn: "It was a queer sort of place," he remarks — and just how queer it was, we will see presently.[169] Here is Peter Coffin — landlord of the Spouter Inn and master of irony, innuendoes, and ambiguities:

> I sought the landlord, and telling him I desired to be accommodated with a room, received for answer that his house was full — not a bed unoccupied. "But avast," he added, tapping his forehead, "you haint no objections to sharing a harpooneer's blanket, have ye? I s'pose you are goin' a whalin', so you'd better get used to that sort of thing."[170]

But just what "sort of thing" is that? This seems to be the question that puzzles and unnerves Ishmael while waiting tensely for the arrival of the mysterious harpooner, if one is to judge by his repeated remonstrations:

> I told [the landlord] that I never like to sleep two in a bed; that if I should ever do so, it would depend upon who the harpooneer might be, and that if he (the landlord) really had no other place for me, and the harpooneer was not decidedly objectionable, why rather than wander further about a strange town on so bitter a night, I would put up with the half of any decent man's blanket.[171]

No man prefers to sleep two in a bed. In fact, you would a good deal rather not sleep with your own brother. I don't know how it is, but people like to be private when they are sleeping. And when it comes to sleeping with an unknown stranger, in a strange inn, in a strange town, and that stranger a harpooneer, then your objections indefinitely multiply. Nor was there any earthly reason why I as a sailor should sleep two in a bed, more than anybody else; for sailors no more sleep two in a bed at sea, than bachelor Kings do ashore. To be sure they all sleep together in one apartment, but you have your own hammock, and cover yourself with your own blanket, and sleep in your own skin.

The more I pondered over this harpooneer, the more I abominated the thought of sleeping with him. It was fair to presume that being a harpooneer, his linen or woollen, as the case might be, would not be of the tidiest, certainly none of the finest. I began to twitch all over. Besides, it was getting late, and my decent harpooneer ought to be home and going bedwards. Suppose now, he should tumble in upon me at midnight—how could I tell from what vile hole he had been coming?[172]

All other kinds of "objections" to sleeping "two in a bed" notwithstanding, the appearance in both these passages of the sexually and morally surcharged adjective "decent" as a hopeful attributive description of the would-be bedmate seems to indicate that the undecidable ambiguity of Peter Coffin's reference to "that sort of thing" has triggered in Ishmael the fear that this unknown harpooner might indeed be indecent. The sexual-moral discourse of decency is reinforced in the second passage by the surreptitious emergence of the even more surcharged discourse of abomination, which is indirectly articulated via a verbal rather than a substantive form: "The more I pondered over this harpooneer, the more I abominated the thought of sleeping with him"—a sentence that here sounds much like the anamorphosis of another and more revealing sentence that may have gone as follows: "The more I pondered over this harpooneer, the more I thought of the abomination of sleeping with him, that is, the more I thought that sleeping with him would be or would involve an abomination." And although Ishmael's most defensive protestation—namely, that as a sailor "you . . . sleep in your own skin"—is being presented here as a comical hyperbole, this protestation nonetheless cannot be read so hyperbolically in the context of such sexual-moral discourse, and indeed constitutes an attempt to at once expose and answer back to Peter Coffin's comment by saying, as it were, that if "that sort of thing" involves sleeping in each other's skins, the reader can rest assured that sailors would have none of it.

Such reassuring words regarding the sleeping habits of sailors and the inviolability of their skins, however, are immediately revealed to be pious and wishful thoughts that not even Ishmael seems to be taking too seriously, given his final objection to the sleeping arrangements: "Suppose now, he should tumble in upon me at midnight—how could I tell from what vile hole he had been coming?" Here it is not merely a question of noting that the verb choice—namely, to tumble, followed by a penetrative preposition, which is itself followed by a preposition denoting contact—already conjures up fearful images of forced physical contact and, perhaps, of rape *tout court*. It is above all a question of emphasizing how the image of this possibly drunken sailor tumbling in upon Ishmael in bed after what the latter seems to be implying might have been the usual rounds of taverns and brothels is also overdetermined by the preceding rebuttal of Peter Coffin's insinuation that sailors somehow sleep in each other's skins, thereby indicating that what Ishmael fears above all is that the unknown harpooner might be in the habit of entering and coming out of holes so "vile" as to be unmentionable, and hence that he might indeed want to sleep in Ishmael's skin—which is to say, perhaps, also in Ishmael's hole. But one ought also to question the peculiar internal logic of Ishmael's statement: is he implying that, had this sailor been coming from anywhere else other than a "vile hole," it would have been then perfectly fine for the latter to "tumble in upon" him? And why is it that what Ishmael finds most objectionable about this sailor tumbling in upon him at such a late hour is the fact that Ishmael wouldn't be able to tell whence he had come rather than the fact that he would be tumbling in upon Ishmael in the first place? And had the sailor come earlier, how exactly would Ishmael have known "from what vile hole he had been coming" anyway? And so on. The point here is not to try and find answers to all these questions but rather to note that a discourse that proliferates so many unanswerable questions and that raises far more questions than it answers points to undercurrents of troubling as well as inexpressible affect. Or, Ishmael's ruminations in the wake of Peter Coffin's ambiguous jab unwittingly outline a state of mind that could be characterized as acute homosexual panic.

The reason for pausing here on this not-so-joyous prelude to the encounter between Ishmael and Queequeg is to return to and amend Bersani's only partially accurate assessment of the sexual politics of *Moby-Dick*—an assessment whose main thrust went as follows: "Is there a *subject* of homosexuality in *Moby-Dick*? Far from representing either unequivocal homosexuality or surfaces of heterosexual desire troubled by repressed homosexual impulses, Melville's characters have no sexual subjectivity at all."[173] But if Ishmael's reactions to Peter Coffin's comment cannot be said to attest a fully formed sexual subject, they do bear witness at the very least to the presence of a sexual subject *in fieri*. And like all subjects, that would-be sexual subject that is Ishmael is a negatively posited subject as well as an entirely secondary subject, that is, a subject that comes into being as the by-product of a host of mechanisms of interdiction, prohibition, and interpellation (and, of course, one ought to keep in mind that just because the subject is a mere residue of processes and articulations of power, it does not mean that it is any less of a noxious little shit). Ishmael's tentative sexual subjectivity surfaces here solely as a function of the repeated negation of certain unmentionable acts of abomination, a negation that is articulated even in the absence of the usually concomitant—that is, attendant and constitutive—affirmation of heteronormative sexual acts such as, say, the expression of sexual attraction toward members of the opposite gender. (And this heteronormative sexual attraction, by the way, is conspicuously absent not only from the all-male sea chapters, in which one supposes that Ishmael could have perhaps given vent to his pining for a female love ashore, but also, with the exception of a very brief and perfunctory episode,[174] from the land chapters, in which plenty of opportunities could have been found for inserting and expressing such an attraction, given the fact that the world ashore is commonly construed within sea narratives as the site of romance, family, and domesticity, that is, as the place where women are). Admittedly, the pages preceding the encounter between Ishmael and Queequeg constitute the only instance in which an emergent sexual subject can be seen lurking in the narrative folds of this novel; such an instance, however, acquires all the more import precisely due to its being an isolated one. But what exactly is so important about such an isolated, temporary, and underdeveloped crystallization of sexual subjectivity in Ishmael? What is most remarkable here is certainly not the psychological content of this barely emergent sexual subject—a content whose makeup we have seen to consist of a very common, predictable, and ultimately uninteresting mix of homosexual panic and paranoia. What is far more crucial and revealing than either its psychological interiority or its having emerged in the first place is this subject's modality of arrest and disappearance.

After many more ambiguous exchanges between an increasingly anxious Ishmael and an increasingly teasing Peter Coffin, who "chuckled with his lean chuckle, and seemed to be mightily tickled at something beyond [Ishmael's] comprehension," Ishmael eventually gives in to the idea of sharing the unknown harpooner's bed and finally gets to meet him there.[175] The comical and riotous scenes of this first encounter—in which Ishmael's shock at discovering that his bedfellow "must be some abominable savage or other shipped aboard of a whaleman in the South

Seas"[176] is matched only by Queequeg's shock at finding someone else in his bed —
come to a conclusion with the intervention of Peter Coffin as *deus ex machina:*

> But thank heaven, at that moment the landlord came into the room light in
> hand, and leaping from the bed I ran up to him.
>
> "Don't be afraid now," said he, grinning again, "Queequeg here
> wouldn't harm a hair of your head."
>
> "Stop your grinning," shouted I, "and why didn't you tell me that
> that infernal harpooneer was a cannibal?"
>
> "I thought ye know'd it... but turn flukes again and go to sleep.
> Queequeg, look here — you sabbee me, I sabbee you — this man sleepe you —
> you sabbee?"
>
> "Me sabbee plenty" — grunted Queequeg, puffing away at his pipe
> and sitting up in bed.
>
> "You gettee in," he added, motioning to me with his tomahawk, and
> throwing the clothes to one side. He really did this in not only a civil but a
> really kind and charitable way. I stood looking at him a moment. For all his
> tattooings he was on the whole a clean, comely looking cannibal. What's all
> this fuss I have been making about, thought I to myself — the man's a human
> being just as I am: he has just as much reason to fear me, as I have to be
> afraid of him. Better sleep with a sober cannibal than a drunken Christian....
> Queequeg... again politely motioned me to get into bed — rolling over to
> one side as much as to say — I won't touch a leg of ye....
>
> I turned in, and never slept better in my life.[177]

Much could be said about the dialectical interplay between the discourse of cannibalism and the Defoeian-Rousseauian discourse of the noble savage in this passage
as well as in the pages immediately preceding it — an interplay which Melville had
already amply experimented with in *Typee* and which recently has also been shown to
be shot through with the matter of same-sex desire.[178] What is even more crucial
here is the fact that this passage constitutes at one and the same time the *terminus ad
quem* and the *terminus ad quo* of Ishmael's same-sex education in *Moby-Dick:* this is,
in fact, the pivotal moment at which, on the one hand, the short-lived formation of
Ishmael-as-sexual-subject is abruptly stopped, and, on the other hand, the joyous experimentation with corporeal abandon that is the primary form of expression and
moment of constitution of a subjectivity without either subjects or the Subject is
suddenly begun. In this sense, the process of self-persuasion that brings Ishmael to
the conclusion that to share Queequeg's bed might not be such a bad idea after all
culminates in a doubly revealing epiphany: "Better sleep with a sober cannibal than

a drunken Christian." This final clincher reconfirms that what had at once sparked Ishmael's homophobic anxieties as well as put the complex apparatus of subject-formation into motion was the expectation that the unknown harpooner would be a drunken sailor. At the same time, Ishmael's critical turning point reveals that the condition of possibility for the complete overcoming of his "stiff prejudices" regarding the possibility of sleeping "two in a bed" is the encounter with "a sober cannibal," which is to say, the encounter of the unexpected.

As soon as the last hesitation has been overcome, Ishmael's turnabout is unrestrained and his enthusiasm is unbounded: "I turned in, and never slept better in my life." Such a triumphant declaration at the end of a whole chapter that had seen Ishmael repeatedly mired in the muck of paranoia marks a sudden and exponential leap into altogether different realms of desire and affect: never again will the fears and anxieties of the previous pages come back in this novel, and never again will the interpellating shadows of subject-formation return to haunt Ishmael. From now on, Ishmael abandons himself to Queequeg, and the affective register of their experimentation with new forms of male-male sociality unfolds along the lines of what Bersani has characterized as a "non-psychological homosexuality." This is all to say that such a "non-psychological"—and indeed asubjective—"homosexuality" was not there to begin with as a narrative a priori, and that its emergence and development throughout this novel ought to be regarded as a political achievement of the highest order: there could have very well been in *Moby-Dick* what Bersani refers to as "a subject of homosexuality"—and indeed such a subject had already begun to come into being in "The Spouter-Inn" chapter. This process of subject-formation, however, was arrested by Ishmael's encounter with the unexpected, that is, by a chance encounter, by the encounter with Queequeg-as-chance. The fact that this chance encounter also constitutes the return of the cannibal-as-noble-savage from the pages of *Typee*, in which this figure had been associated with Edenic forms of sociality,[179] does not make such a return any less novel or unexpected in *Moby-Dick*. Unlike both the narrator of *Typee* and the South-Pacific Islanders whose captive guest he is in that novel, in fact, Ishmael and Queequeg have completely delinked from homes to which they are both painfully aware they will never be able to return: of Ishmael's radically maladjusted and disaffected condition we immediately learn in the opening pages of *Moby-Dick*; as far as Queequeg is concerned, Ishmael relates that, once asked if he would ever return to his native Kokovoko so as to take the place of his father as ruler of that island, he "answered no, not yet; and added that he was fearful Christianity, or rather Christians, had unfitted him for ascending the pure and undefiled throne of thirty pagan Kings before him."[180] Clearly, the fact that both Ishmael and Queequeg have irreparably quit the realm of the father-king constitutes the crucial condition of possibility of their loving each other in ways that would be unrecognizable in each of their originary realms.

Once the last limit has been left behind by virtue of the encounter with the unexpected, the world of the other limit suddenly becomes manifest as the necessary stroke of chance. "I turned in, and never slept better in my life." This sentence ends "The Spouter-Inn" chapter by also marking a new beginning: this is the first time that the world of the other limit and its uncharted possibilities make their appearance in *Moby-Dick*. Ishmael never explains what made that first night with Queequeg so remarkable and indeed unrepeatable. The first sentence of the following chapter, however, may be as good an explanation as any: "Upon waking next morning about daylight, I found Queequeg's arm thrown over me in the most loving and affectionate manner. You had almost thought I had been his wife."[181] I will refrain for the moment from inquiring into the question of the recurrent matrimonial rhetoric of these pages. Here, I simply wish to draw attention to the fact that the juxtaposition of these two sentences—that is, the last sentence of the previous chapter and the first sentence of the following chapter—seems to indicate that the reasons why Ishmael slept so incomparably well that night may have to do with that "most loving and affectionate" physical intimacy. But perhaps there is nothing to explain and really nothing to say here. The following excerpt, from a chapter significantly entitled "A Bosom Friend," speaks for itself without any explanations, justifications, or apologies for the *fait accompli* of love that it presents:

> As I sat there in that now lonely room...I began to be sensible of strange feelings. I felt a melting in me. No more my splintered heart and maddened hand were turned against the wolfish world. This soothing savage had redeemed it. There he sat, his very indifference speaking a nature in which there lurked no civilized hypocrisies and bland deceits. Wild he was; a very sight of sights to see; yet I began to feel myself mysteriously drawn toward him. And those same things that would have repelled most others, they were the very magnets that thus drew me. I'll try a pagan friend, thought I, since Christian kindness has proved but hollow courtesy. I drew my bench near him, and made some friendly signs and hints, doing my best to talk with him meanwhile. At first he little noticed these advances; but presently, upon my referring to his last night's hospitalities, he made out to ask me whether we were again to be bedfellows. I told him yes; whereat I thought he looked pleased, perhaps a little complimented....

If there yet lurked any ice of indifference towards me in the Pagan's breast, this pleasant, genial smoke we had, soon thawed it out, and left us cronies. He seemed to take to me quite as naturally and unbiddenly as I to him; and when our smoke was over, he pressed his forehead against mine, clasped me round the waist, and said that henceforth we were married; meaning, in his country's phrase, that we were bosom friends; he would gladly die for me, if need should be. In a countryman, this sudden flame of friendship would have seemed far too premature, a thing to be much distrusted; but in this simple savage those old rules would not apply.

After supper, and another social chat and smoke, we went to our room together....

How it is I know not; but there is no place like a bed for confidential disclosures between friends. Man and wife, they say, there open the very bottom of their souls to each other; and some old couples often lie and chat over old times till nearly morning. Thus, then, in our hearts' honeymoon, lay I and Queequeg—a cosy, loving pair.[182]

And this later passage unfolds in similar ways:

We had lain thus in bed, chatting and napping at short intervals, and Queequeg now and then affectionately throwing his brown tattooed legs over mine, and then drawing them back; so entirely sociable and free and easy were we, when at last by reason of our confabulations, what little nappishness remained in us altogether departed, and we felt like getting up again, though day-break was yet some way down the future.

Yes, we became very wakeful; so much so that our recumbent position began to grow wearisome, and by little and little we found ourselves sitting up; the clothes well tucked around us, leaning against the head-board with our four knees drawn up close together, and our two noses bending over them, as if our knee-pans were warming-pans. We felt very nice and snug, the more so since it was so chilly out of doors; indeed out of bed-clothes too, seeing that there was no fire in the room.... Nor did I object to the hint from Queequeg that... he felt a strong desire to have a few quiet puffs from his Tomahawk. Be it said, that though I had felt such a strong repugnance to his smoking in the bed the night before, yet see how elastic our stiff prejudices grow when once love comes to bend. For now I liked nothing better than to have Queequeg smoking by me, even in bed, because he seemed to be full of such serene household joy then....I was only alive to the condensed confidential comfortableness of sharing a pipe and a blanket with a real friend. With our shaggy jackets drawn about our shoulders, we now passed the Tomahawk from one to the other, till slowly there grew over us a blue hanging tester of smoke, illuminated by the flame of the new-lit lamp.[183]

After many years of reading and re-reading all these words of "serene household joy," I still feel that I have absolutely nothing to say about them—and this will prove to be indicative of more than just my lack of critical imagination. "As I sat there in that now lonely room. . . . I began to be sensible of strange feelings. I felt a melting in me. No more my splintered heart and maddened hand were turned against the wolfish world. This soothing savage had redeemed it." In describing his falling in love with Queequeg, Ishmael also reveals the nature of the serene joy that imbues these passages. For this is the joy of redemption—and redemptive pages are these that glisten with that joy. If modernity has repeatedly found in the discourse of re-demption one of its most definitional forms of expression, there is instead some-thing peculiarly non-modern in the articulation of that discourse in these passages. Unlike most modern versions of that discourse, the pages that present the love that binds Ishmael and Queequeg are not spent on the question of waiting for the eter-nally deferred event of redemption: for they are pages written literally the morning after that event has taken place. (And, of course, in Ishmael's post-eschatological version of this discourse, that other and "wolfish" world does not simply cease to exist just because a redeemed world has come into being: these two incompatible worlds coexist and interact, and the complex modalities of such coexistence and interaction are articulated in the sea chapters as the relation between the world of Ahab, that is, the world of the powers of circulation, and the world of the crew, that is, the world of the living labor of whaling—a relation that has been already discussed in detail.) But this is why there is nothing to say *about* these pages, and why one ought to un-learn here many of our hermeneutical reading habits so as to approach these pages with that intentionless spirit of the scholastic treatise of which Benjamin writes in his work on the Baroque.[184] For there is nothing to explain and nothing to say about pages presenting the *fait accompli* of an already redeemed world of love, of a world that is no longer waiting: one can only write alongside with them and in their mar-gins, that is, one can only write in their praise.

"We had lain thus in bed, chatting and napping at short inter-vals, and Queequeg now and then affectionately throwing his brown tattooed legs over mine, and then drawing them back; so entirely sociable and free and easy were we." Indeed, what has always struck me above all else in these passages is the ease with which they reverberate — an ease that, as I have already pointed out, is indistinguishable here from the very urgency and intensity of loving. The ease with which Ishmael and Queequeg commune and with which the joy of love-as-redemption is being presented in these pages is no mere rhetorical ornament or stylistic redundancy: this is an ease that ought to be regarded not only as a discursive form of expression but also as a specific modality of being in its own right that was started by what Ishmael refers to as Queequeg's "last night's hospitalities." There is indeed something essentially ontological at stake in such an ease that constitutes it at once as a mode of hospitality and a mode of being: a mode of hospitality that undoes both host and guest by virtue of a chance encounter, or, more precisely, a mode of being-in-common in the chance encounter of and in the mutual abandon to the other. (And in the next chapter we will face another, more cruel version of such a mode of being and of hospitality in Conrad's *The Secret Sharer*).

If Ishmael in these passages weaves an intricate ontological web out of ease, love, joy, friendship, redemption, hospitality, as well as racial and cultural otherness, there is somebody else who has woven such a web out of these very same threads. In a chapter entitled "Ease" in *The Coming Community*, Giorgio Agamben writes:

> According to the Talmud, two places are reserved for each person, one in Eden and the other in Gehenna. The just person, after being found innocent, receives a place in Eden plus that of a neighbor who was damned. The unjust person, after being judged guilty, receives a place in hell plus that of a neighbor who was saved....
>
> In the topology of this Haggadah of the Talmud, the essential element is not so much the cartographic distinction between Eden and Gehenna, but rather the adjacent place that each person inevitably receives. At the point when one reaches one's final state and fulfills one's own destiny, one finds oneself for that very reason in the place of the neighbor. What is most proper to every creature is thus its substitutability, its being in any case in the place of the other.... [T]he great Arabist Louis Massignon, who in his youth had daringly converted to Catholicism in the land of Islam, founded a community called Badaliya, a name deriving from the Arabic term for "substitution." The members took a vow to live *substituting themselves* for someone else, that is, to be Christians *in the place of others*.
>
> This substitution can be understood in two ways. The first conceives of the fall or sin of the other only as an opportunity for one's salvation: A

loss is compensated for by an election, a fall by an ascent, according to an economy of compensation that is hardly edifying. (In this sense, Badaliya would be nothing but a belated ransom paid for Massignon's homosexual friend who committed suicide in prison in Valencia in 1921, and from whom he had had to distance himself at the time of his conversion.)

But there is also another interpretation of Badaliya. According to Massignon, in fact, substituting oneself for another does not mean compensating for what the other lacks, nor correcting his or her errors, but *exiling oneself to the other as he or she is* in order to offer Christ hospitality in the other's own soul, in the other's own taking-place. This substitution no longer knows a place of its own, but the taking-place of every single being is always already common—an empty space offered to the one, irrevocable hospitality.

The destruction of the wall dividing Eden from Gehenna is thus the secret intention that animates Badaliya. In this community there is no place that is not vicarious, and Eden and Gehenna are only the names of this reciprocal substitution. Against the hypocritical fiction of the unsubstitutability of the individual, which in our cultures serves only to guarantee its universal representability, Badaliya presents an unconditioned substitutability, without either political or philosophical representation—an absolutely unrepresentable community. . . .

Ease is the proper name of this unrepresentable space. The term "ease" in fact designates, according to its etymology, the space adjacent *(ad-jacens, adjacentia)*, the empty place where each can move freely. . . . The Provençal poets . . . make ease a *terminus technicus* in their poetics, designating the very place of love. Or better, it designates . . . love as the experience of taking-place in a whatever singularity.[185]

If "when one reaches one's final state and fulfills one's own destiny, one finds oneself for that very reason in the place of the neighbor," then the final state is not final and the fulfillment of one's own destiny is neither fulfilled nor fulfillable: after redemption, history does not end but rather continues in an other direction; after redemption, one receives an other life to live, which is to say, a necessary chance to live otherwise. This supplemental gift that one receives in the end as the "adjacent place" of the other is "common" in the sense that one can no longer be either one or oneself in it, and is "empty" in the sense that one can never fill it, know it, or determine it. To go on to be in such an "empty" and "multiple common place" of intractable otherness constitutes in every sense an afterlife: a life in the wake of the death of one's unsubstitutable self, a life in the wake of the undoing of one's onto-political boundaries and borders, a life left wide open to the turbulence of possibility and to the necessary encounter of the-other-as-chance, a life without any predestined and fore-seeable end(s). This other life cannot be known and yet must be lived—that is, it can only be lived in common as a shared experiment without any teleological horizon. To live "in the place of the other" is to live as *potentia* and *multitudo*.

After the redemptive event of mutual love has taken place, Ishmael and Queequeg go on to live this other life, go on to live in the place of the other. Their Badaliya unfolds as a double exile: at once an exile *from* their respective homes and an exile *to* the other as he is. Queequeg's vow to exile himself to Ishmael is clearly articulated in the trajectory that takes him from his night "hospitalities" to the matrimonial declaration of eternal friendship: "he pressed his forehead against mine, clasped me round the waist, and said that henceforth we were married; mean-ing, in his country's phrase, that we were bosom friends; he would gladly die for me, if need should be." In this vow, Queequeg articulates at once a translation, a trans-position, and a transgression: the translation of "his country's phrase" into a linguis-tic and conceptual idiom that might be comprehensible to Ishmael, and the transpo-sition of "his country's" ritual of friendship in a foreign land and on a foreign body constitute here an event of cultural transgression. We have already seen how Ishmael's cautious reaction to this vow ("In a countryman, this sudden flame of friendship would have seemed far too premature, a thing to be much distrusted") immediately turns into a transition from "old" to new "rules" ("but in this simple savage those old rules would not apply"). What remains to be noted here is that this vow marks also a similar transition for Queequeg: in translating and transposing this ritualized seal of friendship, Queequeg, too, is abandoning his "old rules" for new interpretations and applications of them; or, at the very least, he is taking risks with his "old rules" by bestowing the honor of this seal of friendship outside of its validating cultural space and upon a Christian other for whom such a seal and such rules may well turn out not to be binding. This is all to say that there is no indication here of an attempt on Queequeg's part to turn Ishmael into his countryman or to convert Ishmael to "his country's" cultural rituals, and that his gesture ought to be regarded rather as a giving hospitality to Ishmael as he is in Queequeg's own transgressed, transplanted, and exiled cultural space: Queequeg exiles himself to Ishmael by offering Ishmael hospitality in his own exile. To the extent to which Queequeg declares that "he would gladly die" in the place of such a Christian other, he is also expressing his de-sire to live in the place of that other: this is a desire for a being-with-the-other that can take place only in what culturally and otherwise constitutes a placeless place of love and friendship—a place Ishmael and Queequeg can enter and inhabit only to-gether and only as they are.

While Ishmael does not explicitly take such vows, his exiling himself to Queequeg is no less intense and resolute. Much in the above passages indicates that Ishmael abandons himself to Queequeg because of all that Queequeg is. In this sense, Ishmael's realization that it is "[b]etter [to] sleep with a sober cannibal than a drunken Christian" is only the beginning of a process of total abandon to unco-optable otherness that culminates in these remarks: "Wild he was; a very sight of sights to see; yet I began to feel myself mysteriously drawn toward him. And those same things that would have repelled most others, they were the very magnets that thus drew me. I'll try a pagan friend, thought I, since Christian kindness has proved but hollow courtesy." Such are the unmistakable confessions of a race traitor and a cultural deserter. Among the numerous expressions of Ishmael's exilic love for Queequeg, I have always been most drawn to this one stunning sentence: "I was only alive to the condensed confidential comfortableness of sharing a pipe and a blanket with a real friend." Here Ishmael indicates not only that the ease of this sharing is the only thing of which he was aware at the time, but also that his only life to live was at stake in that ease and in that sharing. In this "multiple common place" of hospitality, the only modality of being is being-in-common; in this redeemed world of love beyond both Eden and Gehenna, to be is to share. The ease that reigns sovereign in this space of sharing is indeed a "condensed" ontological state: for Ishmael, to be in such a space entails nothing less than a condensation of being—at once a concentration and an intensification of experience intimating that there can be no being for him other than a sharing that allows no remainders. If in "The Mat-Maker" chapter we saw how Ishmael's tentative relation to free will makes him an unlikely candidate for the dialectical fiction of individual unsubstitutability and universal representability that is the point of honor of the modern political and legal subject, here we witness a further undoing of such a fiction not only in the coextensiveness of being and sharing but also in the alliterative cluster of that sentence. In that "condensed confidential comfortableness" one can hear an echo of the title of Melville's work that is most directly concerned with the substitutability of identity and with the shattering of self, namely, *The Confidence-Man*. And this echo can be heard at least twice here: in the adjectival cognate "confidential"—which also appears earlier in the passage when Ishmael declares that "there is no place like a bed for confidential disclosures between friends"—as well as in the syllabic repetition "con...con... com." More importantly, this syllabic repetition indexes the presence of the problematic of sharing already at the level of etymon: what is being repeated in this alliteration, in fact, is the Latin preposition *cum*—corresponding to the English "with," or, "together"—from which each of the syllables in the cluster "con...con...com" derives. This "condensed confidential comfortableness" spells thrice over the ease of a being-with-the-other, and hence the whole sentence unfolds as a tautological series in which virtually each and every element—to be "only alive to," "condensed," "confidential," "comfortableness," "sharing," "with a real friend"—repeats and reinforces all the others, thereby emphasizing over and over again that Ishmael can only be in the being-in-common of friendship.

So it is that Ishmael and Queequeg, while "sitting up" next to each other in bed with their "clothes well tucked around" them and with their "four knees drawn up close together," delineate a "multiple common" space of adjacence— at once, an "empty space offered to the one, irrevocable hospitality" and an "empty place where each can move freely." This is indeed that "unrepresentable space" of ease and that "absolutely unrepresentable community" of love that Agamben finds in Massignon's Badaliya. Earlier we discovered how the body of the living labor of whaling is in effect unrepresentable. But how exactly is Ishmael and Queequeg's Badaliya unrepresentable? And how is one to speak of unrepresentability with regard to these joyful pages that present such a space and such a community so openly, eloquently, and unapologetically? These questions impinge on the vexed relation between two specific modes of representation: the relation between, on the one hand, political-legal representation intended as the apparatus by which the subject is spoken for as well as identified and interpellated in the Law and in the State, and, on the other hand, philosophical-aesthetic representation intended as the apparatus by which images are articulated in and as signification, that is, are made meaningful and readable as signs. While it would be impossible to rehearse here the complex vicissitudes of this problematic, it is necessary at least to note that in Agamben the community of Badaliya is unrepresentable in both senses of that concept: "Against the hypocritical fiction of the unsubstitutability of the individual, which in our cultures serves only to guarantee its universal representability, Badaliya presents an unconditioned substitutability, without either political or philosophical representation—an absolutely unrepresentable community." Such a characterization of this community by no means conflates these two specific modes of representation; rather, this passage constitutes an acknowledgment at once of the distinctions and discontinuities between them as well as of the possibility of a space of sociality situated beyond both these modes, that is, the possibility of a mode of being-in-common outside both signification and subjectification.[186] It is precisely in this sense that Ishmael and Queequeg's Badaliya is doubly unrepresentable: on the one hand, it escapes the realm of signification, which is the hallmark of philosophical-aesthetic modes of representation, by virtue of being presented as an already redeemed world of love, thereby defeating so many of our hermeneutical reading habits that have been honed on the inscrutable signs of a world stuck in a perpetual state of waiting for an eternally deferred event of redemption; on the other hand, it escapes the realm of subjectification, which is the hallmark of political-legal modes of representation, by virtue of being constituted as a space in which the subject cannot crystallize and in which new forms of being-in-common are experimented with that are unrecognizable to the Law and to the State. All this notwithstanding, there is a crucial difference between Agamben's and Melville's articulations of this unrepresentable community: a difference that marks Ishmael and Queequeg's Badaliya also as a mise en scène of the repeated and repeatedly failed attempts of this double apparatus of representation to subject such an unrepresentable space.

This difference is to be found in the ubiquitous matrimonial tropology that enwraps Ishmael and Queequeg in these pages. Or, more precisely, this difference emerges most clearly here in the continuous oscillations between the rhetoric of marriage and the rhetoric of friendship. While many readers of *Moby-Dick* have focused their critical attention on the presence and the deployment of matrimonial rhetoric in this novel, I believe it is far more important to focus on the *relation* between these two different rhetorics in it. We have already witnessed numerous instances of both rhetorics in the passages quoted earlier and I will not cite them again or analyze them individually here. The point is not only that several of the matrimonial metaphors occur in a chapter entitled "A Bosom Friend" but also that the rhetoric of marriage and the rhetoric of friendship are most often articulated in combination with each other throughout, as it is best exemplified in the final paragraph of that chapter: "How it is I know not; but there is no place like a bed for confidential disclosures between friends. Man and wife, they say, there open the very bottom of their souls to each other; and some old couples often lie and chat over old times till nearly morning. Thus, then, in our hearts' honeymoon, lay I and Queequeg—a cosy, loving pair." What needs to be stressed, in other words, is that friendship here is no less a metaphor than marriage and that both are imperfect metaphors for this "cosy, loving pair." These sets of metaphors function in relation to each other precisely because neither of them adequately represents, in both senses of that concept, the new forms of being-in-common that are being produced in the chance encounter between Ishmael and Queequeg. The pages presenting this encounter repeatedly mix their metaphors. And what else is the discourse of mixed metaphors—so unduly denigrated by many of our teachers from elementary to graduate school and beyond—if not an urgent attempt to draw attention to the fact that any one metaphor is imperfect and that one has come up against the power of the unrepresentable? Or, to put all of the above in Austinian terms: although these pages unfold mainly on the level of the performative, they also stage the powerlessness of the constative when faced by the unrepresentable. If these pages produce heavily overdetermined social signifiers such as marriage and friendship, they produce them only as failed ones, that is, as signifiers that fail to signify anything socially recognizable. And it is precisely in the staging of this failure that the difference between Agamben's and Melville's articulations of this unrepresentable community of love lies: while in the former we witness a performance of love, in the latter we witness that performance staged alongside the joyous failure of that love to signify or to represent itself in any way whatsoever. The ease of these pages presents the joy of its own unrepresentability—and in so doing it speaks far more than any of the metaphors that would represent it. In between the rhetoric of marriage and the rhetoric of friendship, Ishmael and Queequeg move freely and at ease: they orchestrate their *ad-agio* by using phrases from both, only so as to carve out and open up a space beyond both.

This is all to say that the mixed metaphors of these pages fulfill an important function precisely to the extent to which they are being used improperly, that is, precisely to the extent to which they are being conjured up, mixed together, and played against each other so as to highlight the inadequacy of each and to make space for a world of which they cannot speak. Such a function is not unlike the proverbial one of the Wittgensteinian ladder. This is Ludwig Wittgenstein in proposition 6.54 of the *Tractatus Logico-Philosophicus*, but it could have well been a metanarrator in *Moby-Dick:*

> My propositions are elucidatory in this way: he who understands me finally recognizes them as senseless, when he has climbed out through them, on them, over them. (He must so to speak throw away the ladder, after he has climbed up on it.)
>
> He must surmount these propositions; then he sees the world rightly.[187]

Similarly, the intertwined tropologies of marriage and friendship in *Moby-Dick* fulfill their purpose by being surmounted and left behind. Almost all the occurrences of these tropes are crammed into four of the land chapters at the beginning of the novel, and rarely do such tropes reappear in the sea chapters, which instead elaborate the space that has been opened up by surmounting those tropologies. (As was pointed out earlier, after those four chapters, the rhetoric of friendship is retained solely in some of Ishmael's occasional terms of endearment for Queequeg, and the rhetoric of marriage returns only once more in "The Monkey-Rope" chapter, while the bond between Ishmael and Queequeg is articulated throughout in far more complex and unconventional ways, such as the ones we saw in "The Mat-Maker" chapter). To see Melville's world "rightly" one must not remain trapped in those mixed metaphors, that is, not look at this world through the signifying and subjectifying categories of the Law and of the State.

Lest one think that along with this tropological ladder we have also left behind the question of same-sex desire, let me emphasize that to see Melville's world "rightly" entails also seeing same-sex desire in it as well as seeing such a desire as part and parcel of the unrepresentable. Regarding the matrimonial metaphors, Bersani remarks that "[t]here is no ambiguity whatsoever in all these eroticizing allusions" and that, although "[t]hey clearly instruct us to think of the bond between Ishmael and Queequeg as not unlike marital bonds" without any "suggestion of homosexual desire," "we might also say that homosexual desire is precisely what is signified by those conjugal signifiers."[188] As we have already seen, this representational double bind leads Bersani to theorize at once the absence of "a *subject* of homosexual desire in *Moby-Dick*" as well as the presence in this novel of an asubjective and "nonpsychological homosexuality"—a "homosexuality" that, for our present purposes, could be characterized precisely as an unrepresentable form of same-sex desire, inasmuch as representation is always, strictly speaking, representation of and for subjects. The point, however, is that, although in these pages both the rhetoric of marriage as well as the rhetoric of friendship are replete with unambiguously "eroticizing allusions," neither of these rhetorics constitutes the exclusive domain in which such "allusions" are produced and elaborated. The erotic energies of the Ishmael-Queequeg encounter do not originate either from any one of those rhetorics or from the complex admixture of them—and, in fact, it would be impossible as well as irrelevant to locate such an erotogenic origin in the first place. Such energies cut across all those mixed metaphors and spill over onto the adjacent textual fabric: many of the moments of physical intimacy in those passages are not expressed via any of these metaphors, and this suggests that the erotic coziness of this "cosy, loving pair" should not be understood as being in a necessary relation of cause and effect vis-à-vis either the rhetoric of marriage or the rhetoric of friendship. The erotic energies of these pages come from the outside of those rhetorics and, in fact, constitute the outside—that is, the affective surface—of the text. If one can see same-sex desire in these highly eroticized pages, that is not due to the presence of marriage and friendship in them; rather, we are faced here with an erotic *stimmung* that does not seem to originate from anywhere or from any body in particular and that is the visible and palpable textual epiphenomenon of a desire that—much like the great whale—"must remain" unrepresented and "unpainted to the last."[189]

   We have also seen, however, that on occasion Melville is perfectly willing and able to represent explicitly sexual practices between men—if not the desire of those practices—and that he does so always by making recourse to the censuring moral-religious discourse of abomination.[190] The fact that same-sex desire in *Moby-Dick* is presented at once as joyous and unrepresentable could be taken as an ultimate political failure to represent such a desire explicitly in a positive light—almost as if the price paid for investing same-sex desire with joy is to bar its official entrance into the Law and the State and to prevent it from becoming socially consecrated in any way. By the same token, however, such a purported failure has the inestimable advantage of showing that to trace a line of flight from the Law and the State is not only possible but also indispensable, and that it is from such a flight rather than from any plea or struggle for integration that same-sex desire derives its political power, which is to say, its joy. Melville's political sensibility in *Moby-Dick* vis-à-vis the question of same-sex desire is very far from, say, the present and ongoing struggles for gay and lesbian marriage—and this is a nonrepresentational sensibility to which anybody who cares for the revolutionary energies of that desire needs to return and reelaborate. Such is the political sensibility that Bersani pursues in *Homos* and that he inherits not only from the triad of Gide, Proust, and Genet—who constitute the focus of the last and most important chapter of that work—but also undoubtedly from Melville. The opening paragraph of that last chapter presents us with one of the possible avatars and reelaborations of this political inheritance:

> Should a homosexual be a good citizen? It would be difficult to imagine a less gay-affirmative question at a time when gay men and lesbians have been strenuously trying to persuade straight society that they can be good parents, good soldiers, good priests. Though I find none of these options particularly stimulating, we should certainly defend people's rights to serve whatever worthy or unworthy cause inspires them. And yet, given the rage for respectability so visible in gay life today, some useful friction—and as a result some useful thought—may be created by questioning the compatibility of homosexuality with civic service.[191]

Such "rage for respectability" and desire for integration is precisely what Ishmael and Queequeg do not have—especially if one considers the joyous and dismissive obliviousness with which they meet the disapproving eyebrows that their intimate and interracial relation manages to raise among those who are watching them.[192]

And so it is that in *Moby-Dick* Melville provides us with much "useful friction"—and he does so in effect by capsizing and transforming a cornerstone of United States political culture, as the once revolutionary slogan of "no taxation without representation" is metamorphosed here into a rather different injunction: no love between men with representation.

Ishmael and Queequeg may have no desire to become "good parents, good soldiers, good priests," or good citizens of any sort; nonetheless, neither their radically exilic and orphan condition nor their love for each other prevents them from becoming at the very least good sailors and good workers, that is, from being fully compatible with the world of capital-labor relations. But we have already seen how such a compatibility is by no means mutually exclusive with an exponential and centrifugal movement of autonomy from capital, that is, with that "autonomous project" of living labor that constitutes itself as the other limit of capital. And if in this novel the body of the living labor of whaling is given as unrepresentable, that should be attributed in no small measure to the fact that Ishmael and Queequeg had already laid down the presuppositions for such unrepresentability in the first place. Indeed, the unrepresentable space of ease and community of love that Ishmael and Queequeg carve out at the beginning of *Moby-Dick* is the first instance of such an "autonomous project" and, as such, it inaugurates further experiments with corporeal abandon aboard the *Pequod*. We return, thus, to what had been identified earlier as the fundamental question of the other limit in *Moby-Dick*: what new forms of being-in-common might arise when male bodies abandon themselves to each other? And we need to embark aboard the *Pequod* one last time to see where such questioning and such experiments might lead.

In the chapter entitled "A Squeeze of the Hand," we find Ishmael and other fellow sailors engaged in the sublime task of squeezing "sperm":

> It had cooled and crystallized to such a degree, that when, with several others, I sat down before a large Constantine's bath of it, I found it strangely concreted into lumps, here and there rolling about in the liquid part. It was our business to squeeze these lumps back into fluid. A sweet and unctuous duty! No wonder that in old times sperm was such a favourite cosmetic. Such a clearer! such a sweetener! such a softener; such a delicious mollifier! After having my hands in it for only a few minutes, my fingers felt like eels, and began, as it were, to serpentine and spiralize.
>
> As I sat there at my ease, cross-legged on the deck; after the bitter exertion at the windlass; under a blue tranquil sky; the ship under indolent sail, and gliding so serenely along; as I bathed my hands among those soft,

gentle globules of infiltrated tissues, wove almost within the hour; as they richly broke to my fingers, and discharged all their rich opulence, like fully ripe grapes their wine; as I snuffed up that uncontaminated aroma,—literally and truly, like the smell of spring violets; I declare to you, that for the time I lived as in a musky meadow; I forgot all about our horrible oath; in that inexpressible sperm, I washed my hands and my heart of it; I almost began to credit the old Paracelsean superstition that sperm is of rare virtue in allaying the heat of anger: while bathing in that bath, I felt divinely free from all ill-will, or petulance, or malice, of any sort whatsoever.

Squeeze! squeeze! squeeze! all the morning long; I squeezed that sperm till I myself almost melted into it; I squeezed that sperm till a strange sort of insanity came over me; and I found myself unwittingly squeezing my co-laborers' hands in it, mistaking their hands for the gentle globules. Such an abounding, affectionate, friendly, loving feeling did this avocation beget; that at last I was continually squeezing their hands, and looking up into their eyes sentimentally; as much as to say,—Oh! my dear fellow beings, why should we longer cherish any social acerbities, or know the slightest ill-humor or envy! Come; let us squeeze hands all round; nay, let us all squeeze ourselves into each other; let us squeeze ourselves universally into the very milk and sperm of kindness.[193]

Such a visionary, spermophilic paean to corporeal abandon constitutes a boundless expansion of Ishmael and Queequeg's space of ease, an exponential amplification of the joy we heard in their chance encounter. The phraseology, diction, and affective state of this passage are at once remarkably similar to the ones we found in those earlier pages as well as an intensification of all that we witnessed there. "As I sat there at my ease. . . . I felt divinely free from all ill-will, or petulance, or malice, of any sort whatsoever." We are not far here from those moments of ease when Ishmael confesses the redemptive effect of Queequeg's presence ("I felt a melting in me. No more my splintered heart and maddened hand were turned against the wolfish world. This soothing savage had redeemed it") as well as of Queequeg's touch ("and Queequeg now and then affectionately throwing his brown tattooed legs over mine, and then drawing them back; so entirely sociable and free and easy were we.") We are not far from those moments, and yet . . . where is Queequeg here?! We are not told who Ishmael's "co-laborers" are, and hence nothing excludes the possibility that Queequeg might be among them. However, even if Queequeg is not one of the sailors whose hands Ishmael is squeezing so enthusiastically and whose eyes Ishmael is "looking up into" so "sentimentally," he is nonetheless virtually omnipresent here. Queequeg, or, rather, Queequeg's name lies at the very center of the mantra that is repeated no less than thirteen times within this passage: "squeeze," "squeezing"—a mantra that even provides the whole chapter with its title ("A Squeeze of the Hand"). The reason for such a symptomatically insistent repetition may well be that the syllabic cluster "quee" is shared by both the proper name "Queequeg" and the verb "to squeeze"—a syllabic cluster, therefore, that indissolubly binds Queequeg and this activity to each other. Undoubtedly, this activity is linked back to Queequeg also because he had been the first one to squeeze: we might recall Ishmael waking up the morning after their first encounter only to find Queequeg "hugging" him "tightly" with a "bridegroom clasp" as well as Queequeg's sudden embrace and vow of friendship on that same day.[194] This is one of those proverbial cases in which the student excels the teacher: Ishmael has learned Queequeg's lesson and applies it here not only to "those soft, gentle globules" of sperm but also to all his other fellow sailors, while Queequeg's echoic presence still supervises the mise en scène of what Freud might have called an "oceanic" squeeze.[195]

This passage's intensification of the Ishmael-Queequeg encounter, in fact, consists primarily in the further collectivization of this activity of squeezing and in the corporeal metamorphoses that emerge in it. If in Ishmael and Queequeg's Badaliya we witnessed a loss of self—in the sense that no subject was allowed to crystallize there and that the only viable modality of being in it was the being-in-common and the sharing of hospitality—here we are faced with a loss of body *tout court*, or, at the very least, with a fluid redrawing of bodily boundaries. As soon as Ishmael dips his hands in the magic fluid, his "fingers felt like eels, and began, as it were, to serpentine and spiralize." This exquisitely Ovidian sentence is only the beginning of a metamorphosis that climaxes in an orgiastic scene of corporeal abandon, as Ishmael "almost melted into" the sperm itself and is overcome by "a strange sort of insanity" that finds him "unwittingly squeezing" his "co-laborers' hands" and indeed "mistaking" them "for the gentle globules." A paroxysmal series of exhortations to melt and, indeed, to meld crowns this scene, as Ishmael's enthusiasm reaches a feverish pitch: "Come; let us squeeze hands all round; nay, let us all squeeze ourselves into each other; let us squeeze ourselves universally into the very milk and sperm of kindness." What is being so joyfully lost in this fusion and confusion of bodies, in other words, is not the body per se but rather its representability. The very presence in this passage of ten exclamation marks—which attempt to reproduce the high pitch and stress of speech when grappling with the inexpressible—already speaks of a linguistic-representational failure in the face of an emotive, expansive body that no longer knows exactly where or what it is, that is forever reaching beyond, spilling over, and exceeding itself, and that seems, in fact, to have acquired by sympathy or osmosis the liquid state of the fluid in which it bathes. But what this body seems to have acquired above all from this fluid is its uncompromising inexpressibility—especially if one considers how Ishmael, after a series of lyrical similes attempting to describe this fluid ("as [those soft, gentle globules] richly broke to my fingers, and discharged all their rich opulence, like fully ripe grapes their wine; as I snuffed up that uncontaminated aroma,—literally and truly, like the smell of spring violets"), still can do no better than referring to it as "that inexpressible sperm." Ishmael's loving injunction to his fellow sailors not only to "squeeze" themselves "into each other" but also to "squeeze" themselves "universally into the very milk and sperm of kindness" stands here as the expression of an urgent desire for an absolutely unrepresentable and unidentifiable collective body. In this sense, I find this passage to be an unlikely forerunner of a text that is possibly the most sustained and furthest-reaching experiment with precisely such a fluid, interpenetrative, loving, joyous, unrepresentable, collective body. I am referring to Monique Wittig's *The Lesbian Body*, in which one can find many pages remarkably congruent with Melville's corporeal experiments in "A Squeeze of the Hand." Ishmael's eel-like and spiralizing fingers, for example, bear an uncanny resemblance to these other fingers: "M/y fingers grow at a crazy speed each of them reaching a length fifteen times greater than its original length. I abandon m/yself to a gentle exploration of your body at first uncertain insidious then increasingly insistent."[196]

In Wittig, however, such a collective and unrepresentable body is very often an unabashedly sexual one. Is the body of "A Squeeze of the Hand" also a sexual body? Are we indeed in the presence here of some sort of sexual act or performance with multiple partners? If these questions seem at once banal and redundant as well as unanswerable and irritating, that may have to do with the fact that while, on the one hand, it would be hard not to read the passage from "A Squeeze of the Hand" as highly eroticized and sexualized, it is, on the other hand, vexingly difficult to say exactly what form of sexuality we are dealing with here. In describing this passage, Bersani writes that "the homoeroticism itself is merely the expression of a comically anarchic sensuality that is so idiosyncratic, so frankly irreducible to any viable social bond—that it can only be *described*—accommodated by language as a joke."[197] In a sense, this remark is a very apt analysis of the pan-erotic and pansexual character of "A Squeeze of the Hand"—exception made for the adjective "viable," which I would rather substitute with "known." Bersani seems to have declared defeat too soon in the face of the admittedly "idiosyncratic" nature of this passage and of whatever "social bond" may well be envisaged in it. We need to go further. What "can only be . . . accommodated by language as a joke," after all, can only be a matter of the most serious kind—and indeed I have already remarked on the peculiarly confessional character of Melville's sense of humor. In order to take this joke seriously, one would have to begin by saying that if this "anarchic sensuality" seems so "idiosyncratic," that is so because it is unrecognizable and because something is taking place here that requires some shifting and fine-tuning of our sexual registers and expectations. Or, in other words, "A Squeeze of the Hand" marks not only an experimentation with the body but also an experimentation with the sexual body and with sexuality *tout court*.

       If I have described this "oceanic" event as orgiastic, that is so because something of a bathhouse *ambiance* permeates this scene of squeezing—a scene that could have been lifted out of Petronius's, or, indeed, Federico Fellini's *Satyricon*. One does not need to stretch the textual fabric of this passage too much to find in it an echo of that male homosocial and homoerotic space par excellence that is the ancient Roman baths—a space and a figure that has fuelled many a same-sex phantasmagoria in modern literary, pictorial, and cinematic iconography. Ishmael informs us that he "sat down before a large Constantine's bath" of sperm—and the reference here is to the fourth-century statue of the Roman emperor Constantine, whose famed colossal size is being metaphorically displaced to the bathtub containing the "delicious mollifier." The fact that this reference to ancient Rome is being mobilized to describe a bathtub full of sperm may lead one to suspect that this whole sentence reaches beyond this mere bathtub and resonates also with the figure of the Roman baths—especially if one considers that Ishmael is not foreign to this figure, which we already came across when he spoke of "those vast Roman halls of Thermes."[198] Once evoked, this "Constantine's bath" becomes important enough to act as the trigger of a series of related expressions, as the noun "bath" is turned into a verb and is then repeated several times throughout this passage: "as I bathed my hands among those soft, gentle globules" and "while bathing in that bath." In this sense, such a refrain and its concomitant echo of the ancient Roman baths are congruent with and corroborate Ishmael's orgiastic visions of male bodies squeezing into each other and squeezing themselves into sperm. And yet, if this was all that was being attempted in "A Squeeze of the Hand," one could hardly uphold this text as an example of sexual experimentation, as we would be left then with an undoubtedly pleasurable and arguably risqué vignette denoting vaguely pornographic leanings and inspired by rather conventional images of Roman antiquity—a vignette with the likes of which the nineteenth century was replete.

The point is that Ishmael's orgiastic entreaties to his fellow sailors are part and parcel of a pan-erotic and pan-sexual ecstasy that seems to index anything but either sexual arousal or sexual climax. What takes place in "A Squeeze of the Hand" may be orgiastic but is certainly not orgastic: this passage unfolds as a highly sexualized vision without exhibiting, however, any of the usual accoutrements of a sexual teleology that structures sexual practices as well as sexual desire around the achievement of the final, all-consuming, all-important, and all-meaningful event of orgasm. The key to such a paradox lies in the material condition of possibility of this scene of squeezing, that is, in the very sperm that these sailors have convened to squeeze. The fact that sperm is what they are squeezing and bathing in is precisely what enables the articulation of modes of sexual expression that bypass that sexual teleology altogether: it is almost as if the very presence of this sperm testifies that an enormous orgastic event had already taken place somewhere behind the scenes, and that what takes place in this scene of squeezing is to be understood instead as the expression of a post-coital and post-orgastic type of sexual pleasure. In this sense, Ishmael's invitation to his fellow sailors—"Come; let us..."—is not to be taken as an injunction to come again but rather as an even lovelier postcoital entreaty: come here, hold me, play with me, be with me. Sperm is here at once the catalyst and the lubricant of sexual games and of a sexual playfulness that emerge in the wake of—rather than as the foreplay leading to—a collective, cosmic, and, indeed, "oceanic" ejaculation. Such playful games do not acquire their importance and do not derive their pleasure from being prelusive and subordinated to that telos, that is, from being a means to that orgastic end; rather, they are posited here as an end unto itself and indeed they constitute their own end as immanent in the very means. Much like the pages of the Ishmael-Queequeg encounter—which describe an already redeemed world of love that is no longer waiting for the arrival of an eternally deferred event of redemption—this passage circumvents any privileging discourse of the end, and presents us with a nonteleological sexuality and a posteschatological sexual world. Even the decidedly anticlimactic lesson that Ishmael draws from this scene of squeezing nonetheless bears witness to such a world. Immediately following the passage quoted above, Ishmael declares:

> Would that I could keep squeezing that sperm for ever! For now, since by many prolonged, repeated experiences, I have perceived that in all cases man must eventually lower, or at least shift, his conceit of attainable felicity; not placing it anywhere in the intellect or the fancy; but in the wife, the heart,

the bed, the table, the saddle, the fire-side; the country; now that I have perceived all this, I am ready to squeeze case eternally. In thoughts of the visions of the night, I saw long rows of angels in paradise, each with his hands in a jar of spermaceti.[199]

Even though the world of heteronormative domesticity and of reproductive sexuality reenters the scene, reasserts itself, and dampens the visionary enthusiasm of the previous paragraphs, such a world is also unmistakably denounced here as a very poor alternative to that other world in which one might have kept "squeezing that sperm for ever." Even as the previous paragraphs are being implicitly slighted here as a mere product of "the intellect or the fancy" and as a nonviable "conceit of attainable felicity," the last word is still made to rest with a beatific vision of spermophilic "angels." This decidedly unorthodox image of "paradise" as well as the other invocations of eternity in this paragraph ("Would that I could keep squeezing that sperm for ever!" and "I am ready to squeeze case eternally.") reconfirm and reinforce the hypothesis that what is being envisaged in this whole passage is precisely a high plateau of sexual pleasure—or, rather, a reconceptualization of sexuality as a high plateau of pleasure—unfolding after any event of redemption and without any foreseeable end(s). The risks taken with the sexual body and with sexuality in "A Squeeze of the Hand" consist precisely in having produced a vision of sexual pleasure after sex and without sex—an unrecognizable and unco-optable excess of pleasure that is cherished above any sex whatsoever.[200]

Of course, the sexual teleology that is being circumvented in "A Squeeze of the Hand" is by and large sexuality as we still know it. This is also to say that such a teleology structures and defines not only heteronormative and reproductive forms of sexuality but also many of the nonreproductive and, indeed, homonormative dialectical counterparts of those forms. Such a teleology, which asserts and enforces the primacy of sex for any definition and comprehension of the sexual body, is the main organizing principle of all modern dialectical sexuality (where the latter is understood as that normative double bind which produces heterosexuality and homosexuality as the asphyxiating symbiotic structures through which alone one's multiplicity of sexual pleasures and affects can come into being and be recognized at all as pleasures and as affects within modernity).[201] In "A Squeeze of the Hand," Melville bypasses that subjectivizing as well as subjectifying apparatus that is sex and offers in its stead a vision of sexual pleasure and a conception of same-sex desire that cannot be made to work for and be recognized from within that dialectical double bind, and that hence cannot be said, strictly speaking, to be homosexual or modern in any way.

The uniqueness, novelty, and radical potential of such an experimentation with the sexual body should not be underestimated, and I will let Foucault underscore more precisely what is at stake here in a passage whose political sensibility is not far from Melville's. In the first volume of *The History of Sexuality*, after having discussed at length how we "must not place sex on the side of reality, and sexuality on that of confused ideas and illusions," since sexuality is that "very real historical formation" that "gave rise to the notion of sex, as a speculative element necessary to its operation,"[202] Foucault thus details the tyranny of sex:

> It is through sex ... that each individual has to pass in order to have access to his own intelligibility ... to the whole of his body ... to his identity.... The Faustian pact, whose temptation has been instilled in us by the deployment of sexuality, is now as follows: to exchange life in its entirety for sex itself, for the truth and sovereignty of sex....
>
> By creating the imaginary element that is "sex," the deployment of sexuality established one of its most essential internal operating principles: the desire for sex—the desire to have it, to have access to it, to discover it, to liberate it, to articulate it in discourse, to formulate it in truth. It constituted "sex" itself as something desirable. And it is this desirability of sex that attaches each one of us to the injunction to know it, to reveal its law and its power; it is this desirability that makes us think we are affirming the rights of our sex against all power, when in fact we are fastened to the deployment of sexuality that has lifted up from deep within us a sort of mirage in which we think we see ourselves reflected—the dark shimmer of sex.... We must not think that by saying yes to sex, one says no to power; on the contrary, one tracks along the course laid out by the general deployment of sexuality. It is the agency of sex that we must break away from—through a tactical reversal of the various mechanisms of sexuality—to counter the grips of power with the claims of bodies, pleasures, and knowledges, in their multiplicity and their possibility of resistance. The rallying point for the counterattack against the deployment of sexuality ought not to be sex-desire, but bodies and pleasures.[203]

It is precisely "the truth and sovereignty of sex" as well as "the agency of sex" that are undermined in "A Squeeze of the Hand" by being in effect completely ignored: what these joyous pages implicitly contest is the by now commonsensical truth that sex is the necessary and inevitable route for any articulation of the sexual body and of its pleasures. Far from grounding same-sex desire in "the desire for sex—the desire to have it, to have access to it, to discover it, to liberate it, to articulate it in discourse, to formulate it in truth," Melville produces same-sex desire as a constellation of bodies in pleasure. In the end, rather than being left with sex as the sacrosanct repository of identity and as the complicitous consignor of the sexual body to the agencies of the Law and the State, it is the "claims of" "bodies and pleasures" that emerge here as the urgent and irrecusable demand of a desire that has yet to be contended with.

It is from within the "rallying point" of "bodies and pleasures" that I wish to return to Marx—who was never too far from this prolonged inquiry into the corporeal experiments of *Moby-Dick*, and who does articulate a strikingly similar "rallying point" in the *Grundrisse*. While discussing the relation between the wage and necessary labor, Marx wages a powerful critique of the discourse of "*self-denial*"—that is, of the capitalist injunction that the worker ameliorate his condition by (a) "saving, cutting corners in his consumption" as well as by (b) "denying himself more and more rest, and in general denying himself any existence other than his existence as worker, and being as far as possible a worker only."[204] Marx draws attention to the crucial difference between these two forms of self-denial. From the point of view of capital, the injunction to save and to cut consumption should not really be implemented by workers "generally... and as a rule" because, if workers were to comply with this injunction to the letter, there would be catastrophic consequences for capital, given the damage that this "would do to general consumption... and hence to production."[205] Such an injunction, hence, serves mostly the ideological function of supporting the myth that it was precisely by practicing such a form of self-denial that the capitalist became a capitalist in the first place. The form of self-denial that enjoins the worker to be nothing other than a worker, on the other hand, would be, if implemented fully, the proverbial dream come true of capital, as this would rechannel all of necessary labor—that is, the labor necessary to reproduce the bodily existence of the worker—back into the process of production. In the context of a critique of both forms of self-denial, Marx writes:

> The most he can achieve on the average with his self-denial is to be able to better endure the fluctuations of prices—high and low, their cycle—that is, he can only distribute his consumption better, but never attain wealth. And that is actually what the capitalists demand. The worker should save enough at the times when business is good to be able more or less to live in the bad times, to endure short time or the lowering of wages.... That is, the demand that they should always hold to a minimum of life's pleasures and make crises easier to bear for the capitalist etc. Maintain themselves as pure labouring machines and as far as possible pay their own wear and tear. Quite apart from the sheer brutalization to which this would lead—and such a brutal-

ization itself would make it impossible even to strive for wealth in general form, as money, stockpiled money—(and the worker's participation in the higher, even cultural satisfactions, the agitation for his own interests, newspaper subscriptions, attending lectures, educating his children, developing his taste etc., his only share of civilization which distinguishes him from the slave, is economically only possible by widening the sphere of his pleasures at the times when business is good, where saving is to a certain degree possible), [apart from this,] he would, if he saved money in a properly ascetic manner... conserve his savings and make them fruitful only by putting them into banks etc., so that, afterwards, in times of crisis he loses his deposits, after having in times of prosperity foregone all life's pleasures in order to increase the power of capital; thus has saved in every way *for* capital, not for himself.[206]

The rallying point for the counterattack against capital is a crisis of pleasure. The appearance of the question of pleasure in the *Grundrisse* is indissoluble from the question of crisis: if by practicing self-denial workers "ultimately make crises easier to bear for" capital, by "widening the sphere of [their] pleasures" they would instead bring about a real crisis, namely, that crisis of the other limit, that Benjaminian *wirklich Ausnahmezustand,* that real state of emergency for which we have been waiting. In commenting on this passage, Negri elaborates further the notion of such a "widening" and identifies it as an essential moment in the movement of autonomy from capital: "the workers' opposition, the proletarian struggle, tries continually to broaden *the sphere of non-work,* that is, the sphere of their own needs, the value of necessary labour."[207] For Negri, such a "widening" is ultimately tantamount to "the ontological broadening of ... use value, through the intensification and elevation of the value of necessary labour."[208] And it is precisely such a broadening of "*the sphere of non-work,*" such an "ontological" intensification, and such a vision of indomitable crisis that we encountered in the pages of "A Squeeze of the Hand"—in which a moment of work is made to yield an excess of sexual pleasure that spirals away from the task at hand, and that turns such a task inside out and reconstitutes it as a moment of nonwork and as a vision of collective abandon beyond both sex and capital. "I forgot all about our horrible oath; in that inexpressible sperm, I washed my hands and my heart of it." Deep from within the realm of work, Ishmael acts against the injunction to deny himself "any existence other than his existence as worker": he forgets the "oath" that binds all aboard to the hunt of the white whale and to the powers of circulation, widens "the sphere of his pleasures," metamorphoses into a joyous body of crisis, and, indeed, produces both joy and crisis as the collective body of the other limit.

Admittedly, as opposed to the immediately corporeal pleasures offered by Melville, all of the "life's pleasures" to which Marx specifically refers in the preceding passage fall under the humanist aegis of the purportedly civilizing influence of education and culture. Marx does not indicate whether the realm of the sexual body and of its pleasures can or ought to enter the antagonistic political arena he has outlined—even though, one might add, he certainly does not suggest anything that would exclude such a realm from being articulated there either. It turns out, however, that to expand Marx's conception of pleasure is not a difficult task, and that one can easily enlist Marx himself for this very purpose. If "widening the sphere of...pleasures" constitutes an "ontological broadening of...use value," we need only recall how Marx conceives of the worker's use value—that is, of use value par excellence—as a *potentia* incorporated in the very "bodiliness" and "muscular force" of the worker, in order to assert that the body ought to be upheld as a critical *locus* for "widening the sphere of...pleasures" in the first place. Furthermore, it is also a question of excess. The "ontological broadening of...use value" must pass through an excess of corporeal pleasure—that is, an excess that cannot be reined in or even accounted for by that subjectivizing apparatus which Foucault identifies as "the desire for sex"—if it is not to run the risk of being continuously turned into an only too cooptable and complacent form of bourgeois hedonism, which has become the very fuel of our present culture of rampant and unbridled consumerism. At a time when such a culture has done much to harness or quell the radical political potential of any experimentation with pleasure at once by counteracting the demand for pleasure with more or less available forms of pleasure-as-commodity as well as by subtracting from such a demand the intrinsic impetus toward forms of sociality that would not fall under exchange relations—at such a time, it is all the more crucial that any "widening [of] the sphere of...pleasures" contend with pleasures that money cannot buy or that immediately constitute themselves as new forms of being-in-common, or both. At a time when capital has learned to readjust itself continuously to such a "widening" demand for pleasure by capturing the sexual body and by producing all of its pleasures exclusively through the deployment of sexuality and through its ancillary discourse of sex—at such a time, it is all the more imperative that the sexual body be reclaimed for revolutionary projects over and against "the desire for sex," and that the "claims of" "bodies and pleasures" be attended to from within the very logic of profit and work in which they remain buried alive. At such a time, Marx and Melville can once again provide us with trenchant dissent and untimely dissonance as well as with the example that it is possible and indeed indispensable to think and live a space of autonomy from capital, even while the only existence that is granted us by the present historical conjuncture unfolds, Jonah-like, right in the belly of the beast.

I would like to conclude this reading of *Moby-Dick* and the *Grundrisse* by returning to Negri and to the question of "the ontological broadening of . . . use value," for this question is still rife with potentials that are yet to be fully discerned and articulated. And I will look for the ramifications and reverberations of this question in what might seem an unlikely place. In a postscript to a letter written from prison three years after having delivered his lectures on the *Grundrisse*, Negri writes:

> P.S. Cher David, in these last few letters I have told you of Raniero. Of a pedagogical relationship. Of his love and of his seduction. But I have done so still abstractly. I can't manage to do any better. I happen to entertain or to undergo a pedagogical relationship—I avoid to speak concretely of the other, of the disciple or of the master. Thereby evading the intersection of affections, sensations, perturbations, enthusiasms. I establish and satisfy relationships that are laden with sensuality in purely conventional terms. How unjust this is! How much sensuality there is in political pedagogy! Here, in my narration, there are no passions, betrayals, or abandonments—and wrongly so, since the abstraction of the concept does not take away the concreteness of *cupiditas* from politics. And from the point of view of a peeping Tom, it could seem that you and I, as well as Raniero and I, are entangled in a homosexual relationship that we hypocritically do not recognize. Perhaps it's true. But it's not completely true: because the bristly peeping Tom spies on us in private and with all his resentful and whiny inconsistency, while we entertain, and while I have happily undergone other times, that *aufklärische Erziehung*, that relationship of communist education that unravels sensuality in a universal, schizophrenic, collective, and joyous relationship. It is the space of the private that makes experience prurient, while the concept can replenish itself with free sensuality. No matter how much I try to write about the erotic complexity of political relationships, I can't manage it. But I believe that to formulate unresolved problems is also the task of enlightened education. This undoubtedly means that some of my arguments are insipid. But. . . . Writing is a limit: perhaps it is precisely this achieved, mature eros of the concept that shows how this world of writing is ancient, surpassed, and obsolete. Eros asks life to build denser and more complex forms of expression. Couldn't my poverty of expression be an index of a (historically net) deficit of narrating by writing? A deficit of the impossibility not to relate eros in writing but to relate it collectively, publicly, corporally, like something

belonging to all of us? Like something interchangeable, full, and concrete in its collective relation? End of the Gutenberg galaxy? By now, books are able to teach only after experience has given itself. There are increasingly fewer useful books, increasingly fewer... allusions, traces. But then, why do I write?[209]

If I borrow and affix this postscript here—thereby marking it also as the postscript to this whole chapter—it is because in it Negri attempts against all odds to form a constellation out of what have also been the most insistent components of my elaborations on *Moby-Dick* and the *Grundrisse*. This constellation comprises five stars: communism, desire, representation, writing, limit. This constellation also has a name or a *Stimmung*, that is the ether in which the stars are suspended and which enables any relation among them. And the name of this *Stimmung* and the name of this constellation is: crisis, or, joy—for in this postscript, as well as in *Moby-Dick* and the *Grundrisse*, crisis and joy name the very same affective concretion and indeed are the very same thing. But how can one write of a constellation? How can one translate an uncompromisingly synchronic cluster of relations into an irreparably diachronic movement of signs? Such a highly imperfect translation entails drawing and highlighting at least some of the possible sets of relations among the elements of this constellation. Here I will attempt such a translation by way of drafting what will turn out to be at once a conceptual précis of the present project as well as a series of prolegomena to projects that are yet to come—and it is perhaps regretful that I will limit myself to doing so without providing the full philological proof and the indispensable textual articulation of what I hope will nonetheless illuminate and be illuminated in return by my reading of *Moby-Dick* and the *Grundrisse*. Set 1: communism, desire. What this suffered postscript does make clear is that the desire of communism is corporeal, erotic, sexual; that if this desire is not lived in the body, it is not lived at all; that this desire opens the body up to the space of collectivity rather than entrapping it into the private prison of interiority; that this desire is always a desire for new forms of being-in-common and for new modes of moving, living, and loving bodies; that in the historical conjuncture that goes by the name of modernity these new forms of being-in-common and these new modes of moving, living, and loving bodies manifest themselves principally as forms and modes of same-sex desire; that "the ontological broadening of... use value" entails contending with same-sex desire as the exemplary manifestation of the desire of communism. Set 2: communism, desire, representation. The crucial problem this postscript grapples with is that the desire of communism is unrepresentable; that such a desire is unrepresentable precisely because it constitutes a world of praxis that lies beyond representation; that it is nonetheless the task of writing to present such an unrepresentability. Set 3: writing, limit. This postscript is an exemplary instantiation of writing in crisis as well as of the joy of writing. This postscript constitutes the writing of crisis and the writing of joy as one specific form of writing—a form that can now be named the writing of the other limit. Writing is a limit in the sense that its urgency always comes from elsewhere—an elsewhere that writing nonetheless never ceases to index. Writing always points to its unthought, to its unreachable underside, to its immanent outside, to that world of passion, affect, and desire that leaves its traces in writing like so many scars. Writing, in other words, is its own limit. (Much like capital, writing confronts only its own limits, which it continuously pushes further along and infinitely defers by more and more writing). Writing can try to hide its limit, its scars, its failure to reach its outside; or, it can try to foreground its limit, to wear its scars on the surface, and to show the process by which it repeatedly comes to its failure. The writing of the other limit does the latter and indeed constitutes an exemplary revelation of the fundamental relation that binds all forms of writing to their outside. In this sense, the writing of the other limit is the presentation of the unrepresentability of the desire of communism.

Such, I believe, are also the lessons that have been drawn from the juxtaposition of *Moby-Dick* and the *Grundrisse*. And this juxtaposition—which I have presented throughout as a *fait accompli* and indeed as the necessary postulate upon which this whole chapter has been built—can finally, if anticlimactically, be granted its raison d'être: the material and historical condition of possibility of reading *Moby-Dick* and the *Grundrisse* together is that they both share and are driven by that desire that goes by the name of communism.

F O U R

The Sublime of the Closet; or, Heterotopologies of the Male Body

O, not from memory lightly flung,

Forgot, like strains no more availing,

The heart to music haughtier strung;

Nay, frequent near me, never staleing,

Whose good feeling kept ye young.

Like tides that enter creek or stream,

Ye come, ye visit me, or seem

Swimming out from seas of faces,

Alien myriads memory traces,

To enfold me in a dream!

Herman Melville, *John Marr and Other Sailors*

Preliminary Remarks on Emily Dickinson's Last Laugh

> They shut me up in Prose —
> As when a little Girl
> They put me in the Closet —
> Because they liked me "still" —
>
> Still! Could themself have peeped —
> And seen my Brain — go round —
> They might as wise have lodged a Bird
> For Treason — in the Pound —
>
> Himself has but to will
> And easy as a Star
> Abolish his Captivity —
> And laugh — No more have I —[1]

LIKE ONE OF THOSE STARS whose light continues to puncture our night skies long after its astral source has ceased to exist, Dickinson's image of absolute-freedom-in-captivity continues to haunt and guide all that one ever thinks in and about the closet. The now fully extinct source of such an image is a historical conjuncture whose imperatives are evidently still with us. This is that conjuncture — roughly coinciding with the passage from the nineteenth century to the twentieth century — from which the closet seems to date as the strategy of containment, as the instrument of oppression, and as the site of production par excellence of same-sex desire in modern Western culture, that conjuncture that here will bear the name of modernity itself.[2] Dickinson's image of the deterritorialized "Brain" of the closet "going round" in voyages of intensity will be the guiding light of this chapter. All the invocations of the closet within the rich array of recent and ongoing investigations of same-sex desire notwithstanding, its queer political *potentia* has yet to be fully acknowledged, let alone unleashed. For (Dickinson's poem seems to be saying) you can "shut me up in" the "Closet," but then you no longer have control over the blazing and uncontainable star-like *potentia* that can be produced in it, thus effectively exceeding it and abolishing it from the inside.[3] It is such a *potentia* that we will now take more than a peep at, as we will watch and participate in the unfolding of the spectacle of the sublime of the closet in Conrad's *The Secret Sharer*. This chapter, thus, constitutes a series of notes toward an investigation of the closet as the privileged *locus* of an as yet untapped excess of same-sex desire.

We return here to Michel Foucault's concept of heterotopia —

intended as a special type of space that simultaneously represents, contests, and inverts all other spaces in culture — and to his claim that the ship has been "the heterotopia *par excellence*" of Western civilization. In chapter 1, I pointed out that the crisis of the ship as the crucial heterotopia in Western cultural discourse came to full fruition during a period — that very same passage from the nineteenth to the twentieth century — when a pervasive crisis in the conceptualizations of gender and sexuality was also rapidly unfolding. I argued there that such crises intersected each other in ways such that the ship, while its place in culture was being fatally put into question, turned into one of the most apt stages for the dramatization of paradigm shifts in conceptions of sexuality. Conrad's *The Secret Sharer* is an exemplary text of the encounter of such crises: here, I will focus on the conflation that this text makes inevitable between the already residual heterotopia of the ship and the fully emergent heterotopia of the closet (whose emergence was one of the main by-products of precisely those paradigm shifts). Although the concept of heterotopia will not be explicitly present in the course of the ensuing discussion, it may be useful here to further elaborate Foucault's sketchy theorization of such a concept by stating that heterotopias are always structured by the potential for their own supersession. They constitute the sites for the production of those desires — and their attendant practices of pleasure — that are at once indispensably exploited by the normative as well as lethally threatening to it if not closely monitored and strategically contained. It is in this sense that the closet is a heterotopia: this chapter wishes to investigate the mechanisms by which the closet always already functions at the limen of its own supersession.

And if preliminary is that which stands at the limen, then I would like to conclude these preliminary remarks by anticipating that the closet is itself such a zone of liminality, that the closet always potentially marks the threshold of an other-becoming. Such a process of becoming is what I find attractive in the closet in the first place: in the end, these meditations on the closet shall be revealed as having nothing to do with the closet at all. It is for its explosive, if fleeting, moments of virtual self-erasure, as well as for the sublime *potentia* of those moments, that the closet has been sought here — because, much like Dickinson, who was the poet of the liminal par excellence, one knows one shall have the last laugh. It is with the echo of her sublime laughter that these pages wish to resonate.

One has always wondered about the pleasures of the closet. These are pleasures steeped in danger and regulated by a dialectical economy of desire. Such is that libidinal economy that instructs one to desire the pleasures of imminent danger (the pleasures derived from the possibility of getting caught) as well as the dangers of forbidden pleasures (the dangers involved in conceiving one's pleasures in ways counter to the norm). Powerful and necessary as it undoubtedly is, a dialectical economy of subversion that impels one to desire always in relation to the law is also entirely beside the point: it constitutes that point beyond which the present pages wish to take us. Beyond such an economy lies an excess of representation incorporated in the very word "closet." The textual and other effects of such otherwise unrepresentable excess are what I will try to reconstruct here.

If the closet has been the crucial *locus* of production, containment, and oppression of same-sex desire and of its attendant practices of pleasure in modern Western culture, it has also constituted an image for other pleasures to come. These pleasures are not attainable either in or out of the closet; they are attainable, rather, in that social space where the very structure of the closet would be radically circumvented and at that time when its historical conditions of possibility would be completely eradicated. One has at times felt in the closet an incommensurable intensity of enclosure, a joy of infinitely finite and crammed spaces, a claustrophiliac ecstasy of the flesh: such are the other and nonrelational pleasures that the closet from time to time suddenly mobilizes, thus threatening to exceed what has been identified as a specifically dialectical economy of desire. The closet always threatens to realize a form of pleasure whose existence will no longer be contingent on it and will indeed obliterate it as both a trope of discourse and a locality of power dispensation. Paradoxically, it is in the melancholy claustrophilia and sublime loneliness of the closet that one first dreams at once of a future world without closets, and without their peculiar pleasures, dangers, and oppressions, as well as of the world as it would have felt had there never been any of the questions to which the closet was the brutal answer and foregone conclusion, had there never been any reason for the closet to exist at all. And yet, this is not exactly just a dream: this is the unexpected materialization of the loneliness of the closet as communion and intercourse, of the fulminous coming-into-being of the sublime of the closet as a shared loneliness. It was in the closet that the desire of these questions first and transiently materialized: what if such a sublime could be shared with someone else—and not as if he were an other but inasmuch as he were the same? What if someone else could be let into one's own closet so as to share with him its loneliness—and not so as to mitigate it but in order to make such a loneliness all the more intense and the closet all the more self-enclosed, crammed, and sublime?

The sublime of the closet is *not* a coming out. It is, rather, an overcoming of the closet: a coming pure and simple. This is not to underestimate the immense force and dire necessity of coming out for any queer politics. This is merely to understand the act of coming out of the closet as that political scenario that the powers that keep one shut up in there can already foresee and hence prepare for—such a scenario, after all, is their worst nightmare. To the extent to which the act of coming out is regulated by the same dialectics of incarceration and liberation already implicit in the very functioning of the closet, such an act is precisely that form of resistance that has been recorded a priori in the heteronormative social contract. To come out of the closet also reaffirms the effectiveness and raison d'être of the closet, to the point that there can be no closet prior to the act of coming out—not the least because such an act is what one cannot but be forced at once to envision, desire, and dread when in the closet. Insofar as coming out always implies a coming-into-being and a coming-to-visibility as a specifically nameable body, it also turns one into a particularly vulnerable target once again.[4] Clearly, to claim an identity makes one identifiable; but, furthermore, to reclaim and capsize an identity for a political project antithetical to the norms that needed to produce the former avatar of that identity in order to function means also to run the risk of being continuously translated back into that previous identity formation (in other words, I can call myself queer and still be heard as saying that I am a fag—for as long as I call myself anything at all, I can always be recognized, interpellated, and treated as something antithetical to that which I called myself in the first place). This is not to say that such a risk should not be run—or, as Judith Butler has pointed out: "The mobilization of identity categories for the purpose of politicization always remain threatened by the prospect of identity becoming an instrument of the power one opposes. That is no reason not to use, and be used, by identity."[5] This is to say, rather, that just because the act of coming out of the closet becomes necessary and inevitable at a given conjuncture in both the life history of particular sexual subjects and in the larger-than-life history of modernity, it does not necessarily follow that such an act is the solution to the problem that produced the closet in the first place. This is to say that if to come out of the closet may turn out to be also the proverbial solution that feeds back into the very problem it was meant to solve, as it locks one into the vicious circle of a perpetually self-reproducing dialectical relay, other types of solutions need to be pursued at the same time. This is to say that a dialectical political strategy—no matter how indispensable and productive—ultimately may become the fuel rather than the extinguisher of a dialectical system of power, and that nondialectical strategies urgently demand our attention. This is why even though these characterizations of the dialectical double bind of the act of coming out are similar to some of Butler's formulations, my project in the end diverges from such formulations.[6] In offering the sublime of the closet as an escape from such a double bind, that is, as a nondialectical engagement with what are nonetheless highly dialectical dynamics, I am undertaking a project that shares neither her concern with the symbiotic questions of parody and of subversion—a concern that has been undoubtedly very productive, that has been also much trivialized by friends and enemies alike, and that she has repeatedly and importantly qualified—nor the skepticism toward claims of circumvention of the dialectic that informs her projects and that she outlined in *Subjects of Desire*.[7] But before proceeding any further, we need to pause for a moment precisely on the question of the dialectic and on its importance for any understanding of the closet, so as to clarify the nondialectical stance I have put forth here as well as throughout the rest of this book.

This is not the place to rehearse the multitudinous and ongoing debates on the dialectic—debates that are virtually synonymous with the history of Western philosophy at least since Plato's momentous discovery of the productivity of negation for thought. It may do well, however, to complicate the philosophical underpinnings of my project by making at least two points. (1) The dialectic intended as a specific form of thought is not only an epistemo-critical apparatus but also a historical-political problematic, and hence, even when its analytical effectiveness is found to be obsolescent or baleful *tout court*, its complex history still needs to be properly engaged with rather than either blissfully repeated or simply snubbed. (2) When at its most self-critical—which is perhaps to say, when at its most relentlessly dialectical—the dialectic can become uncannily similar, in terms of its powerful analytics, to some of the most rigorous of contemporary critiques of the dialectic (without, however, making such critiques entirely irrelevant.) This is why the nondialectical investigation of the closet that I have just begun owes a debt not only to the anti-Hegelian and nondialectical thinkers—such as Agamben, Negri, Deleuze, Foucault, and Althusser—that have repeatedly emerged throughout this book, but also to a thinker whose fiercely dialectical and yet anti-Hegelian energies make him particularly relevant to the matters at hand, namely, Theodor Adorno. Much in Adorno's project of a negative dialectic is of great importance for the present investigation. Here, I would like to draw attention briefly to Adorno's attempt to devise a dialectic that would enable one to think the nonconceptual exteriority of a concept while remaining within as well as continuing to think that concept, a dialectic that would enable one to register within a concept the very exteriority that at once escapes and determines it.[8] Such a negatively dialectical form of thought is peculiarly congruent with the onto-epistemological structure of the closet, since to exist in the closet necessarily entails some form of awareness of that unreachable heteronormative exteriority that needed and invented the closet in the first place. To think and indeed to be in the closet by definition means to think the exteriority of the closet without necessarily leaving the closet behind and without ceasing to be interpellated by all that the closet entails in terms of both outright oppression and relative safety. To be or even to have been in the closet is to be a consummate dialectician de rigueur. (Historically speaking, the dialectical converse of such a proposition would be that there exist also important interferences and zones of indiscernibility between a certain kind of dialectical project and the emergence of a subject of homosexuality: to historicize Adorno's eminently modernist project of a negative dialectic would also mean to understand such a project as one of those "major nodes of thought and knowledge in twentieth-century Western culture" that, according to Eve Sedgwick, are symptomatic of as well as structured by a "now endemic crisis of homo/heterosexual definition."[9]) In this Adornian context, the act of coming out would be seen as the circular lure of the Hegelian synthesis and as the easy way out of the closet. In this sense, the sublime of the closet needs to be understood as a not so easy and not so Hegelian way out of the closet that would instantiate the self-supersession of the closet from its very inside, that is, by exploiting it for all its queer political *potentia* rather than by treating it as a tyrannical *eidolon* that would surely vanish if one were to just say no to it — that ideological formations do not just disappear when we denounce them as being false or oppressive still remains, after all, one of Althusser's most valuable lessons. To put all of the above in terms more congruent with the investigations undertaken in the preface of this book: the sublime of the closet does not entail thinking the heteronormative exteriority of the closet; rather, it entails thinking that immanent outside that makes itself felt at once on the form of the closet and on the forms of heteronormativity, which are exterior to one another and which hence are both forms of exteriority. The sublime of the closet is a modality of being of the thought of the outside. To come out of the closet, on the other hand, is to mistake an exteriority for the outside, or, much like Ahab, to mistake yet another last limit for the other limit. Finally, I would like to conclude this brief excursus on the dialectics of the closet by venturing even further in my invocation of Adorno. First, I would like to note here Deleuze and Guattari's belated yet important acknowledgment of the fact that in some respects Adorno's negative dialectic is quite similar to such a thought of the outside and to their own definition of philosophy.[10] Second, the sublime of the closet may well turn out to be that unrepresentable "resurrection of the flesh" which Adorno believes to be the "great desire" and the dissolving "vanishing point" of historical materialism itself.[11]

      The sublime of the closet thus constitutes an attempt to envision an exit from the closet that would not also be a trap, that would actually be unnamable and unimaginable from the standpoint of all that needs the closet in order to continue to exist. If the closet is the material manifestation of the tyranny as well as the possibilities of the dialectic in the realm of sexuality, if the closet is indeed the paradigmatic structure of all modern dialectical sexuality—understood as that normative double bind which produces heterosexuality and homosexuality as the asphyxiating symbiotic structures through which alone one's multiplicity of sexual pleasures and affects can come into being and be recognized as pleasures and as affects at all within modernity—it is also the case that in the closet one may encounter other and sublime affects incorporated in the flesh as puncta of sexualities to come. In such sublime affects, one confronts the waste of dialectical processes—namely, those leftover energies that remain unusable and unrecognizable within such processes. In this sense, the sublime of the closet needs also to be understood as a certain excess of the dialectic.[12] But modernity itself can be seen as the moment of the apotheosis of the dialectic, as that historical conjuncture when the dialectic increasingly becomes the dominant mode of production of everything everywhere and hence also of sexuality. In the sublime of the closet one confronts nothing less than an excess of the onto-epistemological production of modernity. Such an excess constitutes an escape from modernity as we know it—a cunicular network of a subterranean history of the body threatening suddenly to erupt through the ground of modernity and to materialize that which never would or will be modern.

The closet and its sublimities aside, one has also overheard the underground rumblings of such an outside of modernity, of such a nonmodern history of the body, aboard ships. Earlier, I announced the main focus of this chapter to be the modern conflation between the residual heterotopia of the ship and the emergent heterotopia of the closet: those sublime affects of loneliness and claustrophilia, which are among the most intense pleasures of the closet, can be found to exist just as intensely aboard ships. Let us approach such a conflation via certain remarks of Roland Barthes on Jules Verne:

> Imagination about travel corresponds in Verne to an exploration of closure, and the compatibility between Verne and childhood does not stem from a banal mystique of adventure, but on the contrary from a common delight in the finite, which one also finds in children's passion for huts and tents: to enclose oneself and to settle, such is the existential dream of childhood and of Verne.... [T]he ship may well be a symbol for departure; it is, at a deeper level, the emblem of closure. An inclination for ships always means the joy of perfectly enclosing oneself, of having at hand the greatest number of objects, and having at one's disposal an absolutely finite space. To like ships is

first and foremost to like a house, a superlative one since it is unremittingly closed, and not at all vague sailings into the unknown: a ship is a habitat before being a means of transport. And sure enough, all the ships in Jules Verne are perfect cubby-holes, and the vastness of their circumnavigation further increases the bliss of their closure, the perfection of their inner humanity.[13]

Barthes finds in Verne's ships that secret passion that lives in the closet and that makes life at all possible in it: a longing for a condition of enclosure more perfect than one ever could have achieved even in one's own home, a longing for the home to house that body that the history of modernity forbids from having any home at all. The closeted subject is precisely a Captain Nemo: no one, nobody, not any — visible, recognizable, acceptable — body. *Nemo*, in fact, is the Latin word for nobody or no one, and Captain Nemo is the protagonist of Verne's *20,000 Leagues Under the Sea*. Captain Nemo declares:

> I am not what you would call a civilized man! I have broken completely with society for reasons only I have the right to appraise. I do not therefore obey any of its rules, and I suggest that you never invoke them in my presence.[14]

Throughout the novel, Captain Nemo functions as the indeterminable emblem of the ostracized, invisible, and subjectless subject par excellence (even though at the very end he makes a belated, incredible, and anticlimactic gesture toward unveiling his secret by describing it as a veritable national-familial hecatomb: "I am the oppressed, and there is the oppressor! It is through him that all those whom I loved, cherished and venerated, perished: my country, my wife, my children, my father and mother!")[15] Barthes's and Verne's bliss of infinitely finite and enclosed space seems also to be inextricable from a desire for invisibility. Barthes does not tell us either why anybody — either child or adult — would want to produce such a bliss of enclosure in the first place, or why anyone would want to produce it in huts, tents, or ships. Barthes writes: "perfectly enclosing oneself"; "perfect cubby-holes"; "perfection of their inner humanity." What he does not say is that the historical conditions of possibility for such a bliss must undoubtedly implicate highly imperfect and painful modalities of being-at-home. What need would there be otherwise to perfect the habitability of enclosure in the form of huts, tents, or ships if the given familial-societal habitats were able and willing to accommodate just any body? (And perhaps the image of the perfect home is at once the most longed-for and domestic as well as the most incomplete and domesticated image of the sublime of the closet: the longing for such an impossible home may indeed be the passion that allows one to live in the closet, and yet a passion that may also at times exceed itself and bring about an abolition of the historical desire for a home, an escape from the very concept of home and of belonging altogether.) Such suggestions may seem to stray far from Verne's seraphically bourgeois dreams of enclosure—dreams that are above all else about private property and about the subjugation of nature by the scientistic forces of *Aufklärung*.[16] Nonetheless, Barthes's and Verne's bliss of enclosure does not merely bear an uncanny family resemblance to the sublime of the closet: their bliss is also quivering with barely containable libidinal energies. Such a joy of perfectly finite spaces may function at once as the motor of a centrifugal libidinal economy of enclosures and as the gearing device that regulates such an economy and prevents it from exceeding its comfortable bourgeois limits and from crystallizing into a terminal and unexchangeable sublime of claustrophilia—the sublime that would mark the breakdown of that economy as well as the complete overcoming of those limits. Verne's and Barthes's joy of enclosures does not constitute a more general paradigm, of which the sublime of the closet is only a particular instance; nor is such a sublime simply the grafting of the libidinal shoot of same-sex desire into that paradigm. Ultimately, these two structures of desire need to be thought of as one and the same. These pages will attempt to seize upon the event of the emergence of these structures as one complex apparatus for the production of an excess of same-sex desire. Here, this event bears the name of *The Secret Sharer;* or, the ship as the sublime of the closet.

And I would like to conclude these introductory remarks by engaging more explicitly with the theoretical paradigm to which all of the above and all of the below is possibly most indebted—namely, Sedgwick's theorization of the epistemology of the closet—even though her project is primarily epistemological, while mine has unfolded primarily as ontological throughout this book. Much of the analytical power of Sedgwick's investigation derives from having constructed the closet as a relational structure (namely, as that structure of social relations through which knowledge—sexual and otherwise—is produced and circulated in modernity) rather than merely as a special *locus* in culture (through which preexistent knowledge would pass on its way toward official modes of selective dispensation).[17] Sedgwick's closet is the epistemo-sexual factory of the modern. In writing about the closet, however, I have been rather literal about it: here, the closet has been conceptualized as a site and an image, as a unique yet emblematic space of enclosure. Possibly the main stimulus for such a conceptual direction stems from an indefatigable amazement at the fact that what is undoubtedly a relational structure would be discursively expressed in spatial terms in the first place. To have constructed the closet as I have done—that is, primarily as a space—is at best something of a conceptual step backward and a conceptual step forward with respect to Sedgwick: it is only after one has understood the closet as a relational structure that one can rethink it also specifically as a space, that one can conceptualize those cases in which the structure fulfills the semantic and representational promises of the metaphor that is its very name. It is precisely when the closet is at once a spatial structure and a structure of social relations that the epistemology of the closet must confront the sublime pleasure of enclosures: in this case, the closet cannot refrain from sharing in a libidinal economy of enclosures, which is in turn especially relatable to same-sex desire. This is perhaps to say that I am attempting to capture the coming-into-being of same-sex desire and of claustrophilia as one and the same conceptual-affective cartography.

And now, I can read you a tale — not as a proof, but as an offering.

> On my right hand there were lines of fishing stakes resembling a mysterious system of half-submerged bamboo fences, incomprehensible in its division of the domain of tropical fishes, and crazy of aspect as if abandoned forever by some nomad tribe of fishermen now gone to the other end of the ocean; for there was no sign of human habitation as far as the eye could reach. To the left a group of barren islets, suggesting ruins of stone walls, towers, and blockhouses, had its foundations set in a blue sea that itself looked solid, so still and stable did it lie below my feet; even the track of light from the westering sun shone smoothly, without that animated glitter which tells of an imperceptible ripple.[18]

In between right and left, the narrator of *The Secret Sharer* stands as a cartographer of time. Often in Conrad, landscapes are cartographies of time, maps redolent of temporality, the sites at which the event of history happens. Here, that event comes into being as the absence of history, or, rather, as the visible trace of its flight "to the other end of the ocean." The narrator — who occupies a liminal zone of multiple beginnings: the beginning of his homeward journey, of his first passage as a captain, of *The Secret Sharer* as a whole — outlines with his surveying gaze and gestures the scenographic contours of the temporal stage on which this story is about to unfold: "On my right hand . . . [t]o the left. . . ." Such a gaze and such gestures map a space from which history has departed, leaving behind ruinous, deserted architectures and "crazy," illegible semiotic systems. Under the spell of the narrator's alien gaze, everything stands "solid," "still," "stable," without an "animated glitter" or "imperceptible ripple," as if suspended in time, as if time itself had migrated elsewhere. More than having departed from this space, time and history have been forcibly squeezed out of it by the narrator's peremptory gestures. If it is the case that landscape often constitutes in Conrad a conduit for historical meditations, it is also the case that different land-scapes can evoke remarkably different rhetorics of temporality and modalities of historical discourse in his texts. For example, whereas at the beginning of *Heart of Darkness,* the Thames is turned into the metropolitan runway of British and ancient Roman imperial histories, the nameless African river in the same novel is always shrouded in the inscrutable and timeless mists of wild, uninhabited, prehistoric na-ture.[19] At the beginning of *The Secret Sharer* the setting is much like the African river in *Heart of Darkness:* a "tropical," "incomprehensible," "crazy" landscape—namely, the Orient of "the Gulf of Siam."[20] And yet, in *The Secret Sharer* the rhetoric of tem-porality unravels according to different designs. Indeed, there exist different modal-ities of absence: while for the African river neither history nor time have ever existed, in the opening scenography of *The Secret Sharer* both time and history have suspended their indefatigable and ineluctable processes, have just been evicted so that some other atemporal and placeless event may now take place. We will soon see how this latter temporal modality is the one needed for this predictably and terminally Euro-pean tale about the sublime vertigoes of disintegrating, entropic, modern subjectiv-ity. This is a tale for which the Orient is not exactly a timeless backdrop but rather the site of a tidal withdrawal of temporality, of a temporarily suspended history.

Once these panoramic perusings have thus emptied out time from the stage on which the whole story is about to unfold, there is soon nothing left for the narrator's gaze but to recoil inward so as to focus now on the floating time-capsule on which he stands:

> She [the narrator's ship] floated at the starting point of a long journey, very still in an immense stillness, the shadows of her spars flung far to the east-ward by the setting sun. At that moment I was alone on her decks. There was not a sound in her—and around us nothing moved, nothing lived, not a canoe on the water, not a bird in the air, not a cloud in the sky. In this breathless pause at the threshold of a long passage we seemed to be measur-ing our fitness for a long and arduous enterprise, the appointed task of both our existences to be carried out, far from all human eyes, with only sky and sea for spectators and for judges.[21]

Absence of movement, of sound, of breath, of life. It is unclear whether the cosmic quiescence pervading both these passages has finally enveloped and boarded the ship, or whether, vice versa, the spatio-temporal suspension transfixing this ship in its state of awaiting has spilled over onto and colonized the whole universe and its forms. What is clear, however, is that in "this breathless pause at the threshold of a long passage" Conrad has already condensed and anticipated everything that is to follow. This truly breathtaking phrase does make one pause. This phrase encapsulates the most recurrent and determining corporeal state in the constitution both of this text and of the closet: this "breathless pause" constitutes a conceptual-affective plane that transversally cuts across both the closet and *The Secret Sharer* as a whole. This narrative, in fact, is intensely preoccupied with breathlessness: as we will see presently, in the crammed enclosure of the ship's cabin, the narrator and a hidden fugitive continuously talk under or completely hold in their breath so as to ensure that their relationship remains secret; furthermore, fear of discovery often makes them suddenly breathless at the sound of the steward's straying step or at the negligence of an unlocked door. Such a protracted, coercive, and anxiety-ridden state of breathlessness soon becomes the condition of possibility for an almost complete liberation from words, language, and representation, and hence also for the emergence of whole new realms of tactile intercourse, of unspoken understanding, of secret communication, of silent staring into one another's eyes, bodies, and thoughts. These are indeed very risky nonrepresentational experiments for someone as enamored of the mimetic magic of language as Conrad is. But it is precisely the risk constituted by the coming-into-being of such new realms of the sensorium that ultimately unfastens the sublime pleasures of the closet. In this respect, the contrast with Edgar Allan Poe, the writer who probably more than any other has pushed the conjoined preoccupations with such a corporeal state of breathlessness and such spaces of enclosure to a veritable ontological level, is enlightening. The author of such paroxysmal tales of breathlessness and claustrophobia such as, for example, "Loss of Breath" and *The Narrative of Arthur Gordon Pym of Nantucket* is particularly relevant here: in his works one can find all that I have been looking for in both the closet and *The Secret Sharer* as well as its absolute converse, that is, an asphyxiating impasse of desire, a terroristic regime of enclosures. In Poe, such an impasse and a regime are usually assailable only from the exterior of that asphyxiating enclosure or by breaking through such an enclosure and into that exteriority: his texts, hence, recoil in horror from or simply lack that revolutionary immanence which reverberates in the sublime avatar of the closet. Admittedly, such a characterization of breathlessness in Poe does not adequately account for a conceptual *tour de force* such as "Loss of Breath," in which that impasse and that regime reach a delirious excess such that they may indeed produce other and differently revolutionary affects. I will return to these questions. For the moment, it suffices to suggest that in both Poe and Conrad breathlessness is one of the few possible phenomenological manifestations of the desire for an other history of the body.

What is also clear is that in the "breathless pause" of the passage quoted above we are faced with a narrative prosody of indeterminate deferral: such a spatio-temporal hiatus is not exactly a narrative caesura but rather *the caesura as narrative*. This state of expectant, atemporal, and placeless suspension "at the threshold of a long passage" will soon exceed even the narrator's expectations and proceed to engulf this narrative in its whole length: "this breathless pause" is *The Secret Sharer* itself. *The Secret Sharer* is the expression of a narrative conundrum: how does one tell a tale and what kind of tale can one tell in and as a caesura? Or—to return to Melville's preoccupations and phraseology—what can one do "in a nick of time"? Conrad had already confronted such questions in *Heart of Darkness*, where the narratives—the narrator's as well as Marlow's—are entirely contained within a suspended state of awaiting the turn of the tide on a ship at anchor at the mouth of the Thames. But while in *Heart of Darkness* such a spatio-temporal state gives rise to the narrative of Marlow's recollections, in *The Secret Sharer* this state of awaiting unexpectedly produces a narrative of the present, a narrative of an other presence. In this respect, *The Secret Sharer* marks a breathless pause in Conrad's literary output, which is so often preoccupied with searching the shadow-lands of memory for those pivotal moments among the scattered pieces of past life that might redeem the amorphous and meaningless flux of time by turning it a posteriori into narrative forms. Such a nostalgia-driven preoccupation with re-membering and re-telling the past is the crucial structuring principle of at least *The Nigger of the "Narcissus"*, *Youth*, *Heart of Darkness*, *Lord Jim*, *The Shadow-Line*, *Amy Foster*, *Falk*, *The Mirror of the Sea*, and *A Personal Record*. Although, much like in these other works, the raw material for *The Secret Sharer* comes from Conrad's past life at sea, this short novel is nonetheless a text written against memory: this is a text intensely focused on an excess of presence, on the present's virtual overflow into unrepresentable futures of same-sex desire.[22] It matters little that *The Secret Sharer* is for the most part written in the past tense, much like some of those other works. The point is that while in those works the interrelated questions of memory, storytelling, and nostalgia for an irretrievable past constitute the prime narrative impetus, in *The Secret Sharer* these questions are momentarily superseded.[23]

      The Secret Sharer is the narrative of a particularly corporeal form of caesura. To open and announce this narrative as a "breathless pause" is also immediately to let it unfold as a tale of corporeality and to call it into being as a pneumatic suspension, as a hiatus in and of the body. Such a caesura constitutes an unexpected aperture onto other histories of the flesh. *The Secret Sharer* captures bodies about to disappear, summons and then ruthlessly squelches a particular *modus* of the body at the last moment when it is possible to register it, procures certain pleasures of the body for one last time before effacing them so as to clear a space for the coming-into-being of what the narrator accurately calls "the appointed task" of our existence. For such pleasures could have crystallized only in a space in which the breath of temporality had been postponed until further notice, only in a spatio-temporal lapse of bourgeois reason. What emerges from such a lapse is *the male body as event:* a threatened, trembling Venus born out of the melancholy waters of a perilous desire so as to be first loved and then immolated on the altar of a prescribed, "appointed" heterosexuality. Leggatt is the name of that event and the incarnation of that lapse. Leggatt emerges from the dark waters of this narrative as the epiphany of an endangered, naked body for the narrator to protect, hide, love, and kill.

Soon after the cartographic opening, the narrator, contrary to custom, dismisses the ship's crew for the night so as to remain alone on deck, ostensibly waiting for the wind that may allow them to set sail and start the passage, but actually "expect[ing] in those solitary hours of the night to get on terms with the ship of which...[he] knew nothing, manned by men of whom...[he] knew very little more," since this is his first day both aboard this particular ship and as a captain.[24] With the complicity of this nocturnal solitude, the narrator starts exploring the body of the ship: "as she lay cleared for sea, the stretch of her main-deck seemed to me very fine under the stars...[v]ery fine, very roomy for her size, and very inviting. I descended the poop and paced the waist."[25] Such a hetero-eroticization of the space of the ship is a staple ingredient in the narrative configurations of the sea novel as a genre, and it usually functions as a mediation in the highly charged sexual-disciplinarian plots unfolding aboard. Here, however, in view of what is about to happen, this hetero-eroticization is all the more crucially positioned within the narrative. Soon enough, the prelusive tête-à-tête between the narrator and the ship is brusquely interrupted by a ghostly visitation, as the narrator catches sight of a "ghastly, silvery" and "cadaverous" "naked body of a man" "floating very close to the [ship's] ladder."[26] As the mysterious naked body reveals himself to be alive and to bear a name, Leggatt suddenly appears in a narrative that henceforth will never be the same, since now it will have to unfold as a tortuous — if temporary — detour from a captain's natural communion with his ship and with the "appointed task" she incarnates. *The Secret Sharer* is the narrative of a caesura in the sense that, in following the trajectory of the narrator's obsession with Leggatt, it records and is wholly contained within the interruption of the normative and heteronormative relations between a captain and the body and world of his ship. *The Secret Sharer* is a "breathless pause" in the discourse of the law.[27]

After this visitation, the narrator loses no time in crossing the limen separating the space of the body of the ship from the space of the body of Leggatt. *The Secret Sharer* truly is a narrative of crammed spaces: we will soon enter the crowded enclosure of the narrator's cabin; we will see how the very air aboard the ship is packed with the anxiety of forever imminent hysteria and with the turbulence of a refractory desire. The semantic field of this text too cannot escape such a spatial logic of saturation: words and especially proper names often become enclosures of signifying and representational excess in it. A cursory etymological excavation of that enclave named Leggatt reveals it filled and resonating with two intertwined Latin echoes: *legatus* (messenger, harbinger, envoy, ambassador) and *ligatus* (bound, fettered, captured, confined).[28] In between *legatus* and *ligatus*, Leggatt stands as an imprisoned messenger. He is the envoy sent from the entropic undersides of bourgeois jurisprudence—and its attendant sexual epistemology—to an overzealous host, who welcomes and incarcerates him as a sacrificial hostage. The sacred law of diplomacy and of hospitality commands never to harm a heralding ambassador—no matter how odious the dispatch he comes to relate or how inimical the sending powers. *The Secret Sharer*, on the other hand, charts a dominion beyond the jurisdiction of that law. For Leggatt's visitation is one that articulates a double implosion: of the messenger and the message, which are both collapsed into Leggatt's body—a body to worship and to sacrifice; and of the sender and the receiver, which are both constituted by the narrator's inarticulable desire—a desire that calls its own object into being so as to dispel it and exorcise it all the more. Such an imploded process of transmission is regulated by other and draconian laws, which decree that the body of the messenger-guest be effaced along with the desire that invoked him and that he incarnates.[29] There can be no doubt that Leggatt's apparition is expected, desired, and called into being by the narrator. Even at the level of sheer plot devices, Leggatt—who is swimming away from his own ship, aboard which he has committed murder—is able to stop and rest by the narrator's ship thanks to a providential ladder that owes its unusual presence at the ship's side during nighttime to the narrator's anxieties regarding his condition of "strangeness" with respect to the ship, to the crew, and to himself in his new role of captain. Just before he sights Leggatt's body afloat, in fact, the narrator observes "that the rope side ladder... had not been hauled in as it should have been" because, by having so unusually dismissed the crew from duty, he had also "prevented things [from being] properly attended to," and, greatly vexed with himself, he now wonders "whether it was wise ever to interfere with the established routine of duties even from the kindest of motives."[30] It is the narrator's wish to remain alone with the ship that proves indispensable for Leggatt's apparition; it is the narrator's first and minor breach of naval etiquette that generates further and graver transgressions of the law, such as hiding a murderer aboard. It is Leggatt, though, who gives away the dynamics of desire at work in the narrator's convoluted orchestration of chance, oversight, and interference with customary practice. When, in the privacy of the narrator's cabin, Leggatt describes his feelings at being discovered floating at the ship's side, he is appointed as the voice of the narrator's desire and says what the narrator will never say:

> I didn't mind being looked at. I—I liked it. And then you speaking to me so quietly—as if you had expected me—made me hold on a little longer [...] I don't know—I wanted to be seen, to talk with somebody, before I went on. I don't know what I would have said....[31]

The flirtatious and titillating diction of these sentences—in which a naked man openly declares to another man that, far from minding "being looked at," he actually enjoys it—will be revealed to reign omnipresent in this text. For the moment, it suffices to note how in Leggatt's words ("as if you had expected me") this narrative acknowledges that somehow the narrator had been expecting Leggatt's arrival and had played an ambiguous yet decisive role in bringing about the epiphanic detour Leggatt would afford him.

If the narrator is the host whose desire constitutes both the sender and the receiver, and Leggatt is the guest whose body constitutes both the messenger and the message, the medium through which their interactions are negotiated becomes increasingly more unstable as the narrative unfolds. As soon as Leggatt surfaces into the narrative as the epiphenomenon of a double implosion that produces two separate and dichotomous assemblages (messenger-message and sender-receiver) out of what might have been instead the four distinct elements of a circuit of desire— as soon as, in other words, an implosion takes place at the inception of the narrative as its presupposition and motor—the conditions of possibility for the further implosion of the two resulting terms have already been established. What ensues is the spectacle of a total meltdown of subjectivity. For if Leggatt is an attractive object for etymological investigation, he escapes and reaches the narrator from the confines of an even richer and more undecidable etymological carrier, namely, the ship aboard which he was an officer up until the moment of his crime: the *Sephora*. This ship is laden with a heavy Latin and ancient Greek semantic cargo, which causes the ship to falter under its weight and makes the ship's course irregular and unpredictable.[32] *Sephora:* that which carries itself, transports itself (namely, an automobile); or, that which goes, proceeds, makes its way; or, that which carries apart, puts aside, transports elsewhere; or, that which conveys one's own self, that which relates, transmits, brings the self. Whatever the case may be with this carrier of etymological excess, Leggatt commits murder on and finally flees from a ship that at the very least is always transporting and bringing forth some form or other of self, some pronominal particle of a desire for the self. And if one adds to such an unstable mise en scène of subjectivity the further complication of Conrad's previous titles for *The Secret Sharer* (namely, *The Secret Self* and *The Other Self*), one knows then one has entered a haunted enclosure of desire in which Leggatt and the narrator will soon start looking increasingly alike, thus giving rise to sublime implosions, identifications, and interpenetrations.[33]

Excursus on That Faceless Object of Desire

The reader who wishes to follow the course of such implosions between Leggatt and the narrator without further delay can go to the other end of the following speculations, which start from a 1937 painting by René Magritte so as to retrace a path begun by Edgar Allan Poe.

The painting in Figure 1 revolves around the negated center of a face. This painting represents an event; or, more precisely, it represents two — perhaps even four — events as one and the same: the breakdown of representation (and hence of signification) as well as the breakdown of subjectification (and hence of subjectivity). Such a multiple event can be identified as the breakdown of ideology: what one sees here is that, when and where one can no longer represent or be represented, one is no one for any body at all; what one sees here is that there is no recognition and no interpellation without representation, no production of meaning without subjectification, and no ideology without a face. If the face is the privileged bottleneck and gateway of ideological processes, this painting charts a space that is — *and must be kept* — inaccessible to the work of representation and subjectification, namely, to the production of ideology. This spellbound space — toward which one is irreparably drawn, and in which one dissolves into two — is the space at which the face is *not to be reproduced*. For this is, in fact, the title of this painting: *La Reproduction interdite* — a title that spells a forbiddance, a warning, and a refusal.

Such an iconoclastic prohibition of the face resonates with Deleuze and Guattari's formulations regarding the interference of those two semiotic systems they call "signifiance" and "subjectification":

> Signifiance is never without a white wall upon which it inscribes its signs and redundancies. Subjectification is never without a black hole in which it lodges its consciousness, passion, and redundancies. Since all semiotics are

Figure 1. René Magritte, *La Reproduction Interdite* (Portrait of Edward James). Museum Boymans van Beuningen, Rotterdam, The Netherlands. Reprinted by permission of Giraudon/Art Resource, NY.

mixed and strata come at least in twos, it should come as no surprise that a very special mechanism is situated at their intersection. Oddly enough it is a face: the *white wall/black hole* system.[34]

The face is always an interface—between the body and a subject of meaning as well as between the body and the meaning of the subject. It is precisely such an interfacing that constitutes the object of Magritte's prohibition: this is a prohibition moved by a desire for a body after, or even prior to, or simply free from the tyranny of the subject. It is the subject, in fact, that is eliminated by denying and erasing the face. Here, Deleuze and Guattari seem again to agree with Magritte:

> Nor can there be any appeal to a preexisting subject, or one brought into existence, except by this machine specific to faciality. In the literature of the face, Sartre's text on the look and Lacan's on the mirror make the error of appealing to a form of subjectivity or humanity reflected in a phenomenological field or split in a structural field. *The gaze is but secondary in relation to the gazeless eyes, to the black hole of faciality. The mirror is but secondary in relation to the white wall of faciality.*[35]

There is something disturbingly nonhuman, phenomenologically counterintuitive, and structurally impossible in Magritte's painting, in which the gaze and the mirror are posited as even more secondary than they normally would have been, had the face not peremptorily refused to be reflected and seen. In this painting there are neither "gaze" nor even "gazeless eyes." There is here only sheer gazelessness, only the negation of faciality: the "black hole" has been filled up and has become imperceptible; the "white wall" has been overwritten and buried under an excess of signification. But what exactly takes place, and where, when one refuses to have a face? What body can this be, and how can one think it? In Magritte that place is a mirror and that body is double: a very secondary and weak mirror; and a nonhuman, asignifying, and asubjective redoubling.

We have, thus, returned to one of the main refrains of this whole book, as mirrors and their redoublings occupy a crucial place in Foucault's conceptualization of heterotopias:

> I believe that between utopias and these quite other sites, these heterotopias, there might be a sort of mixed, joint experience, which would be the mirror. The mirror is, after all, a utopia, since it is a placeless place. In the mirror, I see myself there where I am not, in an unreal, virtual space that opens up behind the surface; I am over there, there where I am not, a sort of shadow that gives my own visibility to myself, that enables me to see myself there where I am absent: such is the utopia of the mirror. But it is also a heterotopia in so far as the mirror does exist in reality, where it exerts a sort of counteraction on the position that I occupy. From the standpoint of the mirror I discover my absence from the place where I am since I see myself over there. Starting from this gaze that is, as it were, directed toward me, from the ground of this virtual space that is on the other side of the glass, I come back toward myself; I begin again to direct my eyes toward myself and to reconstitute

myself there where I am. The mirror functions as a heterotopia in this respect: it makes this place that I occupy at the moment when I look at myself
in the glass at once absolutely real, connected with all the space that surrounds it, and absolutely unreal, since in order to be perceived it has to pass
through this virtual point which is over there.[36]

Given that such spatial elaborations still presuppose and reiterate a phenomenological "I" while the painting's figurations negate any condition of possibility for the
emergence of such a seeing "I," it would seem that Foucault's and Magritte's mirrors
are only nominally related and that they are addressing altogether different conceptual formations. And yet, that failed gesture of interpellation which is Magritte's mirror exists also as an exemplary and deconstructive case of the interference between
heterotopian and utopian desires constituted by Foucault's mirror, inasmuch as the
former foregrounds the constitutive paradox of the latter by denying the counteracting capacity of heterotopias as well as by producing a utopian space that is merely
and exactly more of the same. In this painting, the mirror reproduces as if it were
placed behind rather than in front of the body, and the body's mirrored reproduction is not even inverted: here, one sees precisely what one sees again. Magritte's
mirror is to Foucault's mirror what the ship is to heterotopia as such, namely, its spatial-conceptual type par excellence—that moment of excess which constitutes at
once the perfect apex and the ultimate undoing of a concept and a space. Magritte's
mirror is at once more perfect and more limited than any other: on the one hand, it
reproduces perfectly, that is, without inversions or distortions; on the other hand, it
is unwilling and unable to reproduce the condition of possibility for any seeing "I."
In this sense, Magritte's painting emerges as the interference of two other aborted
interferences: in it, the interference of semiotic systems that is the face is denied
representation through a sabotage of the interference of spatial structures that is the
mirror. This body in front of the mirror is a shard of metal placed in the microwave
oven of desire: this is the object that exceeds the capabilities of certain desiring circuitries, thereby occasioning a meltdown of their whole apparatus as well as calling
into being an other beyond of desire. It is exclusively in front of this mysterious and
anonymous body in a black suit and short hair, whose face is not to be reproduced and
whom can be reproduced only from behind, that Magritte's mirror fails to function
like Foucault's mirror: on the lower righthand corner of the painting, in fact, one
sees a book on the marble mantelpiece being faithfully reflected in the mirror, just
like one would expect any body to be reflected in any mirror, that is, from the front
and inverted. It is this book that gives away that faceless, nameless, and redoubled

body as the foreign agent and saboteur in the painting: if it hadn't been for this book, the viewer might have had the mistaken impression of facing an idiosyncratic and miraculous mirror (in other words, if the book too were reflected in the mirror in the same way as the body, the viewer might attribute special powers to the mirror rather than see the mirror as it stands here, that is, failed in front of and secondary to a nonreproducible face). It is in this book that one faces again and again that body which is not one: its title is *Aventures d'Arthur Gordon Pym*, and its author is a certain Edgar Poe.

Suddenly, Magritte's painting unfolds also as an exegetical gesture: it offers the redoubled body as an emblem of certain narrative structures and desires; it identifies, isolates, and magnifies the obsession that lies at the heart of *The Narrative of Arthur Gordon Pym of Nantucket*. Poe's novel, in fact, unleashes and gives narrative form to a terrifying and irresistible desire of doubleness. This desire becomes specifically manifest through a twofold, dichotomous structure: the desire for a double, for an identical twin, as well as the desire for being double, for existing as an irreparably dehiscent body. In the novel's preface—an exceedingly intricate statement, signed by A. G. Pym, on the genre, genesis, and shared authorship of the following text—one learns that some parts of the narrative were actually written by Poe while the other remaining parts were written by Pym. Pym concludes thus his prefatory remarks:

> This *exposé* being made, it will be seen at once how much of what follows I claim to be my own writing; and it will also be understood that no fact is misrepresented in the first few pages which were written by Mr. Poe. Even to those readers who have not seen the [Southern Literary] Messenger [where Poe had first published parts of this narrative *"under the garb of fiction"*], it will be unnecessary to point out where his portion ends and my own commences; the difference in point of style will be readily perceived.[37]

The point is, of course, that (1) the text of the novel is constituted by a sequence of rather autonomous and self-enclosed narrative episodes—each of which uses a great variety of literary genres and modes of writing simultaneously such as diary entries, nautical-scientific lexicon, narratives of geographical exploration, tales of piracy and mutiny, detective-story devices, horror-story phantasmagorias, anti-rousseauian narratives of primitivism and savagery, and so on—so that the reader cannot even begin to fathom which episode or style may be attributable to whom; and (2) there is—such narrative acrobatics notwithstanding—no discernible change of register in the narrative voice, which remains fairly constant and monotonal throughout the novel. Poe and Pym—intended as authorial signatures for this text—are two, and yet the same.

The Poe-Pym narrative apparatus, however, is far from being the only structure of redoubling: much of the novel revolves around the mutual reflections and refractions of Pym and his best friend Augustus Barnard (because of whom Pym is drawn to the sea in the first place, and with whom Pym shares his misadventures aboard the *Ariel* and the *Grampus*); and after Augustus's death, such a machine of redoubling and mutual incorporation rapidly reassembles (albeit differently) around Pym and Dirk Peters. Of Augustus, Pym relates on the first pages of the narrative:

> Augustus thoroughly entered into my state of mind. It is probable, indeed, that our intimate communion had resulted in a partial interchange of character.[38]

What does not transpire from Pym's self-possessed diction is the simultaneous desire and horror, attraction and repulsion that are constitutive of all such redoublings, that is, the contradictory modalities of being of such an obsession with doubles. Only when Too-wit—the savage-chief—appears in the narrative is the full degree of all the anxieties and trepidations surrounding doubles allowed to crystallize, as he provides a convenient narrative figure onto which to displace the horror of being reproduced ad infinitum. The delegation of "savages" is allowed to board the *Jane Guy* and to stare in wonder at all of its foreign bodies:

> There were two large mirrors in the cabin, and here was the acme of their amazement. Too-wit was the first to approach them, and he had got in the middle of the cabin, with his face to one and his back to the other, before he fairly perceived them. Upon raising his eyes and seeing his reflected self in the glass, I thought the savage would go mad; but, upon turning short round to make a retreat, and beholding himself a second time in the opposite direction, I was afraid he would expire upon the spot. No persuasion could prevail upon him to take another look; but throwing himself upon the floor, with his face buried in his hands, he remained thus until we were obliged to drag him upon deck.[39]

Placed in between the two mirrors and in between madness and death, Too-wit reacts by forbidding his face at once from seeing and from being seen. And so it is also with Pym and his doubles: they all are gazeless bodies and faceless surfaces to the extent to which their faces—the appointed bearers of identity, the official carriers of

subjectivity—become indiscernible from one another, become the nonreproducible
and negated centers of a narrative that has discovered at once with amazement and
horror that doubles do not need either identity or subjectivity in order to function as
symbiotic cogs of an assemblage of desire.

        Suddenly, the redoubled, anonymous, and faceless body in Ma-
gritte's painting could alternately bear the names of Edgar Allan Poe and Arthur
Gordon Pym, or, Arthur Gordon Pym and Augustus Barnard, or, Arthur Gordon
Pym and Dirk Peters, or, . . . But so what? What do all of Magritte's and Poe's doubles want (besides each other)? What is one to do with them (besides being obsessed
with them at least as much as Magritte and Poe)? And can one speak of such a redoubled and faceless body as the eminent body of modernity, when it is also the sub-
ject-object of a desire at least as old as that Sumerian paean to doubleness which is
the epic of Gilgamesh? And what are the historical conditions of possibility and
modalities of being of such a desire—the desire for being double, the desire for a
double, the desire for a body beyond the subject, the desire for a body to be shared,
the desire for an other body of the same? And why do Poe, Pym, and all their doubles naturally gravitate toward ships at sea? Why are they produced and reproduced
within the crammed and breathless enclosure of the heterotopia par excellence that
is the ship, at the climactic and last moment of such a heterotopia that is modernity?
I will let *The Secret Sharer* try to address such questions. For the moment, I would
like to recast all of the above in temporal terms and to imagine that Magritte's painting also captures one in a moment of seeing oneself as one's own double across the
vast expanses of time past: for one remembers oneself always from behind—since
one can never remember one's own (or anybody else's) face; since the face is that
which supremely escapes memory and its mimetic apparatus; since the face is not
any thing or any body in particular, but is rather a constellation of black holes on a
white wall united by nonexistent coordinates, that is, a shimmering, flickering, and
intermittent mirage of time. To see oneself as a faceless double, to see oneself from
behind—this is also what Jean Genet faces at the very end of his life:

> And is it a privilege of my present age or the misfortune of my whole life
> that I always see myself from behind, when in fact I've always had my back
> to the wall?[40]

The road is now paved for the narrator of *The Secret Sharer* to cross yet another limen:
the one separating his self from the other that is Leggatt. Just before the discovery
of Leggatt's naked body, the narrator muses on the life of the sea:

> And suddenly I rejoiced in the great security of the sea as compared with the unrest of the land, in my choice of that untempted life presenting no disquieting problems, invested with an elementary moral beauty by the absolute straightforwardness of its appeal and by the singleness of its purpose.[41]

Events lurking just around the narrative corner shall prove each and every assertion in this paragraph to be patently inaccurate; more significantly, such an inaccurate account of life at sea is strategically situated in the text as the famous last words, and hence it constitutes an ironic structure signaling that some other immanent and indeterminate textual entity inhabits a privileged epistemological position vis-à-vis the unknowing narrator. Such a position and a privilege are henceforth shared with the reader. This paragraph thus establishes crucial criteria for the functioning of the epistemological economies of this text: the narrator's initial and misguided trust in "the great security of the sea" stands retroactively as a prefatory warning to the whole narrative, stating that from such a threshold onward the reader is allowed to realize that it is always possible and at times inevitable to know more than the narrator. Ultimately, this paragraph, due to its location in the text as much as to its soon-to-be-disproved content, needs also to be read as an auto-exegetical moment in the narrative. It is not an act of interpretation, in fact, to say that Leggatt's apparition, along with all of its repercussions on the narrator, is produced and understood in this narrative as not at all a manifestation of "the great security of the sea" but as precisely an event of "unrest" and a "disquieting problem" in a life that is far from "untempted," that is "invested with [no] elementary moral beauty," whose appeal has nothing straightforward—let alone straight—about it, and whose purpose cannot be contained within a "singleness" since here it will be revealed as a terminal desire of doubleness. Such an interpretative register already bears the imprimatur of the text, so that the reader's discovery of it can only indicate the cogency of the text's exegetical apparatus rather than the perspicacity of the reader who has merely discovered what the text itself wanted him or her to discover in the first place. As soon as one learns what this text knows about Leggatt, however, a whole series of other questions may suddenly emerge: if Leggatt is presented as the sign by which the life of the narrator is revealed as far from "untempted," it becomes necessary to ask what kind of tempter someone might be whom the tempted and unknowing narrator refers to as the secret sharer, the other self, the secret self.

Leggatt's entrance into the life of the narrator needs now to be reexamined. After the narrator discovers Leggatt, a brief exchange ensues between the two. Let us spy on these first few moments of their encounter:

A mysterious communication was established already between us two ... I was young, too; young enough to make no comment [to Leggatt's statement that he didn't know whether to let himself "sink from exhaustion, or—to come on board."] The man in the water began suddenly to climb up the ladder, and I hastened away from the rail to fetch some clothes.

Before entering the cabin I stood still, listening in the lobby at the foot of the stairs. A faint snore came through the closed door of the chief mate's room. The second mate's door was on the hook, but the darkness in there was absolutely soundless. He, too, was young and could sleep like a stone. Remained the steward, but he was not likely to wake up before he was called. I got a sleeping suit out of my room and, coming back on deck, saw the naked man from the sea sitting on the main hatch, glimmering white in the darkness, his elbows on his knees and his head in his hands. In a moment he had concealed his damp body in a sleeping suit of the same gray-stripe pattern as the one I was wearing and followed me like my double on the poop. Together we moved right aft, barefooted, silent.

"What is it?" I asked in a deadened voice, taking the lighted lamp out of the binnacle, and raising it to his face.

"An ugly business." ...

"Aha! Something wrong?"

"Yes. Very wrong indeed. I've killed a man."

"What do you mean? Just now?"

"No, on the passage. Weeks ago. Thirty-nine south. When I say a man—"

"Fit of temper," I suggested, confidently.

The shadowy dark head, like mine, seemed to nod imperceptibly above the ghostly gray of my sleeping suit. It was, in the night, as though I had been faced by my own reflection in the depths of a somber and immense mirror.[42]

Unsurprisingly, Leggatt had been expected and then materialized by the narrator so as to be immediately turned into his double here. What is surprising is the celerity and nonchalance with which the narrator starts referring to Leggatt as his own double, as if this were a most unremarkable conjuncture in the natural course of narrative events and as if indeed it had been exactly his own double and no body else whom the narrator had been expecting. What is even more surprising is the narrator's utter lack of surprise at Leggatt's declaration of having killed a man. The narrator is already so familiar with and so well predisposed toward Leggatt that he not only suggests right away that such an act on Leggatt's part could have been due only to what he minimizingly describes as a sheer "fit of temper" (thus implying that Leggatt would not be capable of premeditation and that this must have been a mere accident due to some excusable virile outburst any healthy young man is supposed to have once in a while) *but also suggests all of the above "confidently"*: " 'Fit of temper,' I suggested, confidently." In this adverb lies the crux of this whole passage: it is the carefully unexplained nature of the narrator's confidence that steers their trajectory directly toward the fated enclosure of his cabin. Such confidence finds its opposite and dialectical counterpart in the narrator's suddenly stealthy and cautious behavior as he ascertains that everyone is asleep while Leggatt climbs aboard. There is no ostensible reason either for that confidence in the face of a murderer he has known for no longer than a few minutes, or for the preceding paranoiac show of fear at being caught doing something he already feels is highly unbecoming of a captain even before it has actually become so, since at this point he does not yet know that Leggatt is a murderer. Given that welcoming a nearly drowning man aboard a ship is surely a commendable thing for a captain to do, the narrator's paranoid fear can be understood only in two not necessarily mutually exclusive ways: either the narrator somehow already senses that Leggatt is a murderer even before the latter confesses to be one, or the narrator is aware that in letting Leggatt aboard he is not acting disinterestedly but rather tendentiously and according to other desires that he knows will be censured if discovered. In either case, the only detectable reason for both that confidence and that fear is the narrator's compelling desire to construct Leggatt as his double—to construct him, however, not merely as just any double but rather as a morally excusable and honorable one and as an imprisoned and secret one. Having thus been set, the course of the whole narrative follows a predictable route—predictable except for its intensity, perhaps. From here onward, *The Secret Sharer* unfolds precipitously as the chronicle of an obsession for an idealized and secreted double.

The passage quoted above is only the beginning of a paroxysmal escalation of redoubling. This is a quantitatively and qualitatively exponential crescendo: not only is Leggatt increasingly alluded to with words such as "double" and "reflection" or with equivalent periphrases, but such periphrases also successively denote an increasing level of identification between Leggatt and the narrator. In the above instances—"he...followed me like my double"; it "was...as though I had been faced by my own reflection"—a thin grammatical dividing line is still being maintained between the two characters of this text by hypothetical prepositions such as "like" and "as though." On virtually each remaining page of this text, however, the narrator not only identifies himself with Leggatt ever more insistently and directly through expressions such as "my other self," "my secret self," "my second self," "the secret sharer of my life," "the double captain," "myself," "my very own self," but he also repeatedly presents the question of the double as the crux of his anxiety-ridden narrations.[43] Clearly, in electing a trope as overdetermined as the doppelgänger to fulfill the function of central narrative device, Conrad inevitably shaped the course of much future critical literature, which often corners itself into focusing on this trope de rigueur. In this sense, the question of the double in *The Secret Sharer* is a hermeneutical trap—but that is no reason to disregard it altogether.[44]

What is most interesting about this question, in fact, is the way that it is at once presented as the central focus of the whole narrative as well as suddenly abjured. In the midst of such urgent utterances of a desire of doubleness, the narrator exclaims:

> He was not a bit like me, really; yet, as we stood leaning over my bed place, whispering side by side, with our dark heads together and our backs to the door, anybody bold enough to open it stealthily would have been treated to the uncanny sight of a double captain busy talking in whispers with his other self.[45]

Nowhere else in this narrative will we encounter again such a disclaimer. However, this sole discordant note in the general orchestration of redoublings actually reconfirms the urgency of a desire of doubleness. In the midst of such a vertiginous process of identification, the belated confession that Leggatt is not at all "like" the narrator can only indicate that the narrator's will to double is so overpowering and arbitrary that it will obliterate any trace of difference or empty it out of any import so as to use Leggatt as if he were amorphous clay, so as to mold him into an exact double against all odds and appearances. And yet, what could it mean to say, in this same passage, that "anybody bold enough to open [the door] stealthily would have been treated to the uncanny sight of a double captain busy talking in whispers with his other self"? Just how many replicas of the narrator are being presented here if a "double captain" is talking "with his other self"? And, moreover, who might that "anybody bold enough to open [the door] stealthily" be? This is not just "anybody" but rather an "anybody" who knows exactly what spectacle of redoubling he is about to witness inside the captain's cabin: what reason could there be for such an "anybody" to open the door "stealthily" otherwise? Chances are that this "anybody" is yet another double of the narrator, and that, once the first process of redoubling has been put into motion, it is virtually impossible to keep it from reproducing itself yet again (and, after all, "stealthiness" is the term the narrator uses to describe his own modus operandi in the cabin).[46] What is at stake in this potentially infinite process of serial redoubling is the uncanny aura of the double: even though this is a decidedly "uncanny sight," the double who is followed by other doubles on this assembly line of desire — much like the Benjaminian work of art — loses the aura that characterized those uncanny and complementary doubles one finds, say, in Oscar Wilde's *The Picture of Dorian Gray* or in Robert Louis Stevenson's *The Strange Case of Dr. Jekyll and Mr. Hyde.* As soon as it is revealed that there is more than one double of the narrator, that these doubles do not complement each other because they are not each other's inverted opposites, and that there are only exact replicas without any original, it is the *Unheimlich* itself that thins out and eventually dissipates much like a fog in which the narrative landscapes of this tale had up till then been steeped. This is all to suggest that this "anybody" (that is, this other double) does not seem to be a censuring and castrating superego but rather yet another invited, expected, and even welcome guest. But let me turn all of the above around yet again and point out that no matter who else that "anybody *bold enough* to open" the cabin's door is, he must also be the master of the *Sephora*, namely, Captain *Archbold*, who is very much a reprimanding figure since he is "very anxious" to find Leggatt and give him up to "the law."[47] Unless, given the narrator's rather comical and dismissive portrayal of this captain, one must surmise that Archbold would precisely not be "bold enough" to pose a real threat to anyone and that his name, hence, is ironically catachrestic. Whatever the case may be, in this sentence — "the uncanny sight of a double captain busy talking in whispers with his other self" — the narrator of *The Secret Sharer* is highlighting precisely that desire of doubleness which I identified earlier as a dichotomous formation in *The Narrative of Arthur Gordon Pym.* This sentence points to the sulcus that at once fractures and structures such an assemblage of desire: on the one hand, the desire for a double, for an other self, for a body of an other as the same, and, on the other hand, the desire for being double, for existing as an irreparably dehiscent body. Here the narrator reveals what ought to have been patent all along: for him, there is no such a body as Leggatt's; for him, there is no body else left but an anonymous body split in two by a desire for a body exactly like itself.

To look at such somersaults of desire through Magritte's looking glass means to see Leggatt not as an inverted reflection of the narrator but rather as the narrator materialized again, that is, as the embodiment of the narrator's own desire for a body of an other as the same. And are Leggatt and the narrator faceless? Yes. It is not only the case that often Leggatt's face is hidden.[48] More importantly, Leggatt and the narrator are without a face also in the sense that the reader is given to see exclusively their actions and is presented with one narrative fait accompli after another, without ever being faced by as much as the mere hint of a motive or of a facial and gestural expression that might materialize a motive without actually speaking it. The face they lack is the face that expresses the subject's attendant and constitutive accoutrements of self-knowledge, reason, will, and the like—the face as the traditional repository par excellence of subjectivity, as the site at which subjectivity happens. There is indeed something machinic about the narrator's way of articulating his own actions as if they were so obvious and self-evident as to not ever need any explanation, as if he was never actually going very much out of his way—that is, out of a prescribed and normative path of behavior—in welcoming and hiding Leggatt in the first place. The only face in this text is the face of the mirror of the sea: "[a] mysterious communication was established already between us two—in the face of that silent, darkened tropical sea."[49] This is a paradoxical face without a face, in which the narrator and Leggatt can both see themselves and each other as the same body: a face that constitutes the medium of the "mysterious communication" between them and that is uncoincidentally tropical and dark. In the next chapter, I will return to the question of the racial unconscious of the encounter between the narrator and Leggatt. Here, I want simply to seize upon that crucial adjective—"mysterious"—so as to remember it throughout the remaining pages: nowhere else in this text will we see the narrator concede that there is indeed something "mysterious" about his "communication" with Leggatt, and at no other point will this text sense and admit the existence of a gray area in the relationship between Leggatt and the narrator—an area that is to remain unquestioned and unexplored to the last.

It is crucial that such a redoubled body of desire be not only faceless but also nameless. Much is at stake in the act of naming for a narrative that is as suspiciously generous in lavishing the reader with geographical names[50] as it is peculiarly unforthcoming with names of people. Leggatt and Captain Archbold are the only characters named, and the name of the latter is even questionable, since the nameless narrator remarks that "it was something like Archbold—but at this distance of years I hardly am sure."[51] Furthermore, while the name of Leggatt's ship is disclosed almost immediately, the name of the narrator's ship is kept secret. Put differently, all the names in this narrative come from somewhere other than the stage on which the narrator's tale unfolds, namely, his ship—on which everything and everybody remains forever nameless. In *The Secret Sharer*, names irrupt from the exterior: the narrator has carved out for himself a perfectly anonymous space of enclosure that he is determined to keep unsullied from the act of naming and that seems even to preexist that very act. The narrator's reluctance in naming anything or anybody that either belongs in or that enters his floating closet of anonymity reaches epic proportions when it comes to Leggatt: Leggatt's name occurs only twice during the course of the narrative and both times it is pronounced by Leggatt himself and, strictly speaking, not aboard the narrator's ship, since he introduces himself while still in the water and later relates Captain Archbold calling him by his name aboard the *Sephora*. The fact that the narrator never once speaks Leggatt's name and yet insistently refers to Leggatt as his double or through myriad periphrases of doubleness several times on each and every page of *The Secret Sharer* suggests at the very least that these two forms of address are mutually exclusive and that they may correspond to altogether distinct modalities of being.

There is indeed something unnameable about a double. During an interruption in Leggatt's narration of his escape from the *Sephora*, the speechless and spellbound narrator remarks:

> His whisper was getting fainter and fainter...I had not interrupted him. There was something that made comment impossible in his narrative, or perhaps in himself; a sort of feeling, a quality, which I can't find a name for. And when he ceased, all I found was a futile whisper.[52]

In retrospect, such an inability to name Leggatt's *je ne sais quoi* strikes one also as a necessity. In order for his desire of doubleness to crystallize and for his tale to unfold, the narrator must not at all costs even look for, let alone find, a name that might represent, reveal, and put to rest such a "feeling" or "quality," and that hence might dispel that which is perhaps most attractive and indispensable in his double. But whose "feeling" and "quality," whose affects and attributes are these exactly? What is most remarkable in this passage is not so much the narrator's confession that he has rammed his head against the impenetrable wall of a certain unnameable "something" in Leggatt but rather that it is precisely this unnameable "something" that "made comment impossible." In other words, the very unnameability of Leggatt's affect in turn affects the narrator to the point of speechlessness. Unnameability is the other limit of language—a limit beyond which lie vast, sublime expanses of silence. In the closet of anonymity, language itself seems to be beside the point. As we will see, the language through which Leggatt and the narrator communicate once inside the cabin is a language that, properly speaking, does not say anything: this language at once defers as well as defers to the ineluctable primacy of the incommunicable, of that which there is no need whatsoever to communicate. Let us be rid of language at last: this is what these doubles seem to be saying to each other, while their very speech tapers off into almost inaudible whispers. I will return to such a language of whispers and to all that it enables. Here, it suffices to say that the

importance of whispers for *The Secret Sharer* lies not only in their proximity to silence but also in their critical quality of anonymity. To whisper, in fact, is not only to
speak in a lower volume but also to speak with a different kind of voice altogether —
namely, with a voice that has lost its recognizable uniqueness, that no longer belongs
to a specifically nameable body, that can be spoken and shared by anybody. The "fainter
and fainter" whisper of our breathless doubles is that anonymous voice that turns
anybody into a double of the same.[53]

Anonymity is the condition of possibility for the desire of doubleness. And for such an anonymity to remain undisturbed, the narrator needs not
only to refuse to name *tout court* but also to strip the body of its distinctive attributes
by making them unnameable — the voice being perhaps the most resilient and the
most uniquely personal among such attributes. In a pivotal moment before Leggatt's
boarding of the ship and before any mention of doubles, the narrator is suddenly
and simultaneously interpellated by the powers of the voice, of the name, and of the
self:

> "My name's Leggatt."
>
> The voice was calm and resolute. A good voice. The self-possession
> of that man had somehow induced a corresponding state in myself. It was
> very quietly that I remarked:
>
> "You must be a good swimmer."[54]

Contrary to what will immediately take place as soon as Leggatt climbs out of the
water and up the fatidical ladder, it is the narrator who begins to be turned into Leggatt's double here. To become a double of this Leggatt, however, would ultimately
mean not to be a double at all: to turn into such a vocal model of "self-possession"
would entail declaring one's own name and hence becoming (that is, possessing and
being possessed by) a specifically nameable self — and that is precisely what the narrator will refuse to either declare or become throughout the rest of the narrative. In
this context, the narrator's very quiet rejoinder — which constitutes an odd breach of
common forms of propriety prescribing that he likewise introduce himself at that
point, and which, in its quietness, already anticipates the anonymous whispering
made necessary by the ensuing situation of secret enclosure — also marks the immediate arrest and sudden reversal of such a "corresponding state" of "self-possession"
in himself. Far from being doubled by the narrator, Leggatt's "good," "calm and resolute" voice that stakes a claim to a nameable self is precisely the voice that shall be
stifled by being harbored in the narrator's closet of anonymity. Here, we witness the
last call for the passage to the adult bourgeois subject, after which the narrator embarks

on a different voyage. This is all that is firmly left behind—only to return venge-
fully at the very end—as soon as the narrator leads Leggatt into the cabin that,
Circe-like, turns them both into anonymous, whispering, and breathless doubles of
each other, into copies of a common sameness without any original. For this cabin is
the black sun toward which the whole narrative turns its heliotropic desires: this is
the crammed and sublime closet to which even we must now turn.

> It must be explained here that my cabin had the form of the capital letter L,
> the door being within the angle and opening into the short part of the letter.
> A couch was to the left, the bed place to the right; my writing desk and the
> chronometers' table faced the door. But anyone opening it, unless he stepped
> right inside, had no view of what I call the long (or vertical) part of the let-
> ter. It contained some lockers surmounted by a bookcase; and a few clothes,
> a thick jacket or two, caps, oilskin coat, and such like, hung on hooks. There
> was at the bottom of that part a door opening into my bathroom, which
> could be entered also directly from the saloon. But that way was never used.
>   The mysterious arrival had discovered the advantage of this particu-
> lar shape. Entering my room, lighted strongly by a big bulkhead lamp swung
> on gimbals above my writing desk, I did not see him anywhere till he stepped
> out quietly from behind the coats hung in the recessed part.
>   "I heard somebody moving about, and went in there at once," he
> whispered.
>   I, too, spoke under my breath.
>   "Nobody is likely to come in here without knocking and getting
> permission."[55]

In between right and left, the narrator of *The Secret Sharer* stands as a cartographer
of letters. In between the short (horizontal) and the long (vertical) parts of the letter,
Leggatt stands as the secret treasure buried in the island of L: he is the X marking
the intersection of the coordinates of the narrator's hidden desire on the map of language. One enters here a space of enclosure in which the very possibility of Leggatt's
shelter and imprisonment is directly dependent on the spatial conformation of what
is at once an alphabetic image and a linguistic sign: the "mysterious arrival had discovered the advantage of this particular shape." One is thrown here into a linguistic
space that seems to have been specifically fitted for and shaped around Leggatt's arrival: the very shape of this cabin seems to fit Leggatt to the letter; or, L stands for
Leggatt.[56] The narrator's cabin had been waiting for this arrival in order to realize
its full potential, in order to come into being as that which it had been meant to be
all along: an amorous alcove, a safe if fragile haven for the narrator's desire to find its

own language. It is ultimately a particular language of desire that this enclosure enables. There comes Leggatt out of a closet within a closet—"[e]ntering my room . . . I did not see him anywhere till he stepped out quietly from behind the coats hung in the recessed part"—and the narrator will now speak to and about him with words and gestures plucked from the trashy language of romance.

The most unstable and productive narrative faultline in *The Secret Sharer* must surely lie in the jarring dialectic between its explicit thematics—which revolve around a proto-existentialist crisis in moral codes of honor, duty, discipline, responsibility, courage, and so forth—and its gushy, sigh-ridden poetics of sentimentalism. To listen attentively to the subterranean murmurs of ideology by placing one's ear onto the uneven terrain of just such faultlines is the approach adopted by Fredric Jameson for registering how Conrad's text functions. Of Conrad's writing, Jameson states that it is always "spilling out of high literature into light reading and romance."[57] This formulation is accurate in more ways than one, since "spilling out" is also precisely the mode through which Conrad's language of romance and poetics of sentimentalism function: this is a mode of overspill and excess.[58] Differently from what Jameson argues regarding *Lord Jim*, however, such a language and such a poetics in *The Secret Sharer* do not derealize and reify but actually defamiliarize the ostensible subject matter and its specific tropes, namely, the thematics and rhetorics of a crisis in moral codes.[59] In *The Secret Sharer*, the stylistic diction of sentimentalism and romance in effect brings out and realizes the male homoerotic desires that structure those constitutionally homosocial and homophobic codes and their ever-so-productive crises.

The point is that, whatever else *The Secret Sharer* may be in terms of genre, tropology, stylistics, thematics, narrative structures, and so on, it is *principally* a same-sex romance. In this regard, it is enlightening to read, in a letter to his literary agent, Conrad's own characterization of *The Secret Sharer*, which was first published in a collection that also included *Freya of the Seven Isles*:

> I daresay Freya is pretty rotten. On the other hand The Secret Sharer, between you and me, is *it*. Eh? No damned tricks with girls there. Eh? Every word fits and there's no single uncertain note.[60]

Freya of the Seven Isles and *The Secret Sharer* are positioned here at the opposite poles of a spectrum in which misogyny, homophobia, and male homoerotic desire are all produced as the symbiotic structures of a single libidinal economy. "Freya is pretty rotten," Conrad declares emblematically: the direct personification of the object of his *ressentiment* in a woman's name reveals that such an object is not constituted merely by an unsuccessful piece of writing but rather by the purported cause of such a failure of writing, namely, the presence and question of woman itself. This is a convoluted and yet no less typical and devastating instance of blaming the victim: *Freya of the Seven Isles* by definition cannot but be "pretty rotten" because it is about and is even named after a woman.[61] In *The Secret Sharer*, on the other hand, Conrad plays the kinds of "tricks" at which he is so good, namely, tricks with boys — and hence this narrative "is *it*." Such an italicized "*it*" marks here that unspoken, goes-without-saying, no-need-to-mention event that happens "between you and me," that takes place between two men. For "*it*" *is* the sublime of the closet itself. What is indeed most remarkable in the unfolding of this narrative is that each and every situation in it is incidental and instrumental vis-à-vis the narrator and Leggatt's "secret partnership"[62] in the crammed enclosure of the cabin. *The Secret Sharer* is a text concerned above all else with formulating the following question: what kind of narrative somersaults are needed for two men to share a cabin and a life?[63] It seems that a murder had to be committed; that an extraordinary escape had to take place;[64] that an entirely fortuitous encounter had to occur; that a murderer had to be hidden for inexplicable reasons, at high personal risk, and against all established norms and common sense; that this same murderer had to be arbitrarily transformed into a double; that, in other words, the ruse of a highly complex and unlikely narrative apparatus had to be mobilized so that two men could be put legitimately and secretly in the same bed. Such are the textual acrobatics performed by Conrad so as to behold the spectacle of a male-male romance without any fear of getting caught either by himself or by the reader since, according to the text's own criteria, this spectacle can always be claimed, if need be, to not be such a romance. Such a spectacle is constituted by its offering at once a narrative of romance and a caricature of such a narrative. Jameson reveals precisely such a dynamic in the jarring narrative break within *Lord Jim:* "in the second half of the novel Conrad goes on to write precisely the romance here caricatured both by himself and ... by [Flaubert]."[65] There are several analogous instances of self-distancing and self-caricature in *The Secret Sharer*, such as, for example, the moment when Leggatt asks the narrator to be secretly marooned. To Leggatt's request, the narrator replies: "Maroon you! We are not living in a boy's adventure tale." But Leggatt's "scornful" rejoinder is: "We aren't indeed! There's nothing of a boy's tale in this."[66] The point is, of course, that the narrator *will* ultimately maroon Leggatt, that they *are* living precisely in a boy's tale of romance and adventure, and that even if they do not know they are living in such a tale, the text itself evidently does. Let us then watch this spectacle of romance and learn its language of desire.

One needs to start from the providential physical constraints afforded by the perilous situation in which the narrator and Leggatt find themselves: the captain of a ship is hiding a runaway murderer in his cabin, and the eventuality of accidental discovery would spell disaster for both. This conjuncture of secrecy and enclosure—which spans all of *The Secret Sharer* except for a few pages at the beginning and at the end, so that virtually the entire narrative is contained inside the narrator's cabin—necessarily gives rise to a narrative of whispers and touch:

> "I reckoned it would be dark before we closed with the land," he continued, so low that I had to strain my hearing near as we were to each other, shoulder touching shoulder almost.
>
> "Why didn't you hail the ship?" I asked, a little louder.
>
> He touched my shoulder lightly. Lazy footsteps came right over our heads and stopped. The second mate had crossed from the other side of the poop and might have been hanging over the rail for all we knew.
>
> "He couldn't hear us talking—could he?" My double breathed into my very ear, anxiously.
>
> It would not have been prudent to talk in daytime; and I could not have stood the excitement of that queer sense of whispering to myself.
>
> It was a rather high bed place with a set of drawers underneath. This amazing swimmer really needed the lift I gave him by seizing his leg. He tumbled in, rolled over on his back, and flung one arm across his eyes. And then, with his face nearly hidden, he must have looked exactly as I used to look in that bed. I gazed upon my other self for a while before drawing across carefully the two green serge curtains which ran on a brass rod...I was extremely tired, in a peculiarly intimate way, by the strain of stealthiness, by the effort of whispering and the general secrecy of this excitement.
>
> Later in the afternoon we had a cautious try at whispering. The Sunday quietness of the ship was against us; the stillness of air and water around her was against us; the elements, the men were against us—everything was against us in our secret partnership; time itself—for this could not go on forever.[67]

Such are the fragments of a lover's discourse, the tantalizing utterances of a barely contained desire. The actions of these passages are repeatedly modified by taunting, teasing adverbs: "shoulder touching shoulder almost"; he "touched my shoulder lightly"; my "double breathed into my very ear, anxiously." And the "excitement" of all this touching, "whispering," "stealthiness," "secrecy," and of the hypersensitized modality of being to which they provide access, becomes the electric current that runs at high voltage through the circuitries of this whole text and that makes them vibrate with an energy much akin to sexual arousal. In this context, the "peculiarly intimate way" in which the narrator feels "extremely tired" by the tension and exertion of all this "excitement" begins to remind one very much of postcopulative exhaustion. At the very least, these passages outline the quintessential and most stereotypical situation of romance, as the narrator resorts to the platitudinous, Romeo-and-Juliet language of the story of a forbidden passion and of the love against all odds: "everything was against us in our secret partnership; time itself—for this could not go on forever."

Time itself is against this spectacle. Illicit love is said to have a perennially conflictual relation vis-à-vis time: never enough time spent together, never enough time before inevitable discovery, never enough time to stop time altogether so as to love with a love *sub specie aeternitatis*; or, at any rate, such is the story told by the narrative and linguistic conventions of romance. Earlier, I referred to the narrative of *The Secret Sharer* as a "breathless pause," as a particularly corporeal form of caesura. Now I can add that the narrator and Leggatt's "secret partnership" inside the enclosure of the cabin needs precisely such a space of temporal absence in order to survive and indeed constitutes the collective body of such a caesura: this is the body of a love that can exist only as long as one does not breathe, only as long as one arrests time in the body in the first place. The love that dares here speak its name through a language of romance needs all the time in the world and all the time all at once: a time of the event beyond and outside all time, all signification, all representation. Such is the temporal paradox that the narrator acknowledges and yet feels finally obliged and even eager to terminate: "for this could not go on forever." This sentence at once already decrees, prejudges, and rushes the end as well as acknowledges an immanent tendency in this "secret partnership" to stretch and reach toward a time without the end, toward a time altogether exceeding time. To exclaim—either regretfully or thankfully, or both—that "this could not last forever" is already to image by converse and to actualize virtually that other time in which the "breathless pause" of the narrator's secret and secreted love for Leggatt would last no more and no less than forever. Once the end is thus anticipated by the narrator, the language of romance suddenly ascends to higher plateaus of atemporal breathlessness and homoerotic intensity.

After several near-discoveries, the decision to maroon Leggatt becomes inevitable, and the rest of the plot is preoccupied with the plan to achieve this end secretly and successfully. Much will be said later about how the narrator is just as quick in decreeing and accepting Leggatt's dire fate (he is going to be stranded near some deserted "islands off the Cambodge shore")[68] as he had been at first in welcoming him as the messenger of a desire so uncompromising as to imperil for a time all the narrator has (namely, his position in life as a sea-captain and his "communion" with the world and body of the ship.) What needs to be highlighted now is that, from the moment the decision to get rid of Leggatt is made, virtually every interaction between the two is overdetermined by the nearing end and is thus turned into a scene of farewell. The farewells of lovers, after all, are always repeated several times, and each time they last for the briefest of eternities:

> "...The Last Day is not yet—and...you have understood thoroughly. Didn't you?"..."As long as I know that you understand," he whispered. "But of course you do. It's a great satisfaction to have got somebody to understand. You seem to have been there on purpose." And in the same whisper, as if we two whenever we talked had to say things to each other which were not fit for the world to hear, he added, "It's very wonderful."
>
> We remained side by side talking in our secret way—but sometimes silent or just exchanging a whispered word or two at long intervals.

> He kept silent for a while, then whispered, "I understand."
> "I won't be there to see you go," I began with an effort. "The rest... I only hope I have understood, too."
> "You have. From first to last"—and for the first time there seemed to be a faltering, something strained in his whisper. He caught hold of my arm, but the ringing of the supper bell made me start. He didn't though; he only released his grip.

> Our eyes met; several seconds elapsed, till, our glances still mingled, I extended my hand and turned the lamp out. Then I passed through the cuddy, leaving the door of my room wide open. . . .

> We were in the sail locker, scrambling on our knees over the sails. A sudden thought struck me. I saw myself wandering barefooted, bareheaded, the sun beating on my dark poll. I snatched off my floppy hat and tried hurriedly in the dark to ram it on my other self. He dodged and fended off silently. I wonder what he thought had come to me before he understood and suddenly desisted. Our hands met gropingly, lingered united in a steady, motionless clasp for a second. . . . No word was breathed by either of us when they separated.[69]

One will never know exactly what it is that each of the two understands the other to have understood. Leggatt and the narrator "had to say things to each other which were not fit for the world to hear." Thus, throughout *The Secret Sharer* they remain "side by side" talking, whispering, or silently glancing at each other in their "secret way." The language of reciprocated love is often thought to be encrusted with eloquent silences, secret understandings, significant glances. The conventions of romance present this mythic language as an ad hoc semiotic system constituted by a series of secret codes that only they, the lovers, in the oblivious and passionate isolation of their love, can understand — except that there is no such isolation ever for any body anywhere. Such a secret language is ultimately dependent on the presence of a third body: the ever onlooking, eavesdropping social body of the "world" that, on the one hand, is not "fit . . . to hear" or understand such things as the lovers have to communicate to each other, and, on the other hand, constitutes that alien presence the lovers need to image as being by definition excluded from their secret language, if their secret is to be a secret and if their language is to function at all. In order to become intelligible to each other within the parameters of such a secret language, lovers not only need to produce themselves as unintelligible to the "world" but also need to do so in full view of it: Leggatt and the narrator must repeatedly confirm their implicit understanding of each other in front of a reader who will never be told what there is to understand if they are to believe that they understand each other at all. This is all to say that a secret is by definition an open secret, and that whatever needs to be excluded from a semiotic system so that such a system may function is also automatically included in it by virtue of that necessity: the "world" inhabits the language of romance as that transcendence-in-immanence that forever rearranges the syntax of such a language with its sudden demands and interventions.[70] "He caught hold of my arm, but the ringing of the supper bell made me start." The world of the ship — with its strictly observed routines, its highly regulated time in which there is no time for their "secret partnership" — suddenly disrupts the language of that partnership, and yet such a disruption at the same time structures that language as the latter exploits it for its own most heightened and intense affects. In other words, "the ringing of the supper bell" here is not unlike the quintessential narrative device of 1940s Hollywood romances in which the two protagonists — a man and a woman — are suddenly face-to-face with nothing else to say and with nothing else to do but to come closer and closer to each other's eyes and to each other's lips till the inevitable, passionate kiss seems finally to be about to . . . but the maid knocks at the door, the telephone rings, the jealous dog barks, the chauffeur walks in, the wind slams a door, the whole world suddenly intrudes to remind the startled, disappointed lovers that *it had been there watching them all along.* All this notwithstanding, the most significant aspects of the romance between the narrator and Leggatt still wait to be attended to. Their romance, after all, cannot be structurally equivalent mutatis mutandis to the supposedly heterosexual genre of romance, even though it needs to use the latter's linguistic and narrative conventions. For *their* romance — unlike the Hollywood one — is not going to have a happy ending.

Before attending to these specificities, a clarification is in order regarding the question of romance. *The Secret Sharer* reformulates a very old question: what language is one to use when one wants to express a desire that no available language can express, a desire whose very name marks the impossibility for that desire to exist in language *(illum crimen horribile quod non nominandum est)?* The answer is just as simple as its ramifications will turn out to be complex: *one always makes do with what one has* (in this text's specific case, with the conventional language of romance); *but* (and here come the ramifications) *what one has shall then be revealed never to have been what one thought it was in the first place.* I would venture to suggest that Conrad's engagement with the linguistic and narrative conventions of romance, far from constituting a mere adaptation of those conventions, reveals instead that there never was such a genre as a definitionally *heterosexual* romance to begin with, since its conventions are shot through with refractory shards of that unmentionable desire and with the very matter of its unrepresentability. In this context, *The Secret Sharer* could be said to show that the modern genre of romance is a series of linguistic and narrative conventions whose primary problematic consists of, on the one hand, the dialectical symbiosis between a representable, prescribed heterosexual desire and an unrepresentable, illicit same-sex desire, and, on the other hand, the necessary deployment of homophobia as the main regulative articulation of both these inextricable desires and of all the regimes of production and control that such desires are made to service. And if I have tended to conflate two distinct connotations of the term "romance" — namely, romance intended as the narrative of heterosexual desire and romance intended as the narrative genre of adventure related to the picaresque — that is so because *The Secret Sharer* comes into being precisely as a repeated slippage between these two connotations, as a zone of indiscernibility between the two.

To return to Leggatt and the narrator. Whatever it is that they tell each other by whispers or silent glances, whatever it is that they secretly understand about each other, whatever it is that makes Leggatt exclaim that "it's very wonderful" — an exclamation that is the unhindered utterance of a perilous desire that, according to the narrator, is "not fit for the world to hear" and that the narrator himself will never voice—whatever it is, in other words, that will forever remain concealed from the reader, their mise en scène of the unrepresentability of that "it" takes place in scenes replete with touching, groping, gripping, mingling, and clasping. "He caught hold of my arm, but the ringing of the supper bell made me start. He didn't though; he only released his grip"; "[o]ur eyes met; several seconds elapsed, till, our glances still mingled"; "[o]ur hands met gropingly, lingered united in a steady, motionless clasp for a second"; and so on. For whose glances "mingle" and whose hands meet "gropingly" and linger "united in a steady and motionless clasp" except the glances and hands of lovers? For one has indeed seen nothing yet in the passages quoted above if one has not also lingered to watch the intense physical intimacy of these two male bodies about to be permanently separated from each other. As a matter of fact, it may be necessary to linger just a while longer on their last moment together:

> We were in the sail locker, scrambling on our knees over the sails. A sudden thought struck me. I saw myself wandering barefooted, bareheaded, the sun beating on my dark poll. I snatched off my floppy hat and tried hurriedly in the dark to ram it on my other self. He dodged and fended off silently. I wonder what he thought had come to me before he understood and suddenly desisted. Our hands met gropingly, lingered united in a steady, motionless clasp for a second.... No word was breathed by either of us when they separated.

This hat, which will return crucially to haunt the last page of *The Secret Sharer*, constitutes the catalytic element of a scene bristling with ambiguities. Ostensibly, the narrator suddenly imagines that Leggatt will be at high danger of sunstroke once he reaches the islands toward which he is about to swim and hence gives him his own hat—except that there is nothing particularly ostensible about the ways in which such a simple narrative score is orchestrated. Take, for example, the felicitous choice of verb for expressing the giving and putting into place of a hat: "I ... tried hurriedly in the dark to ram it on my other self"—a verb that commonly, whether one is talking about medieval warfare or whether one is listening in on locker-room exchanges, expresses violent penetration and whose penetrative semantic aim is here deflected in extremis by the preposition "on." Or, consider the narrator's surprise at Leggatt's reaction: "I wonder what he thought had come to me before he understood and suddenly desisted." This "I wonder" is one of the rare instances of a present tense in a narration that otherwise is written almost entirely in the past tense. A gate is thus opened in the text through which one sees the narrator (in the present of his narration of past events) wondering about what Leggatt (in the past of those events) thought the narrator meant by his ramming "it on." Through this temporal aperture in the text, the narrator's action is suddenly also allowed to look like something other than the placing of a hat on Leggatt's head. There might be a causal relation between the narrator's specific choice of verb and his sudden wondering about what he evidently did not wonder about in the past of those events: it seems as if that choice—itself already inextricable from a specific recollection of the events—might be what suddenly causes the narrator to distance himself from that recollection and wonder in the present about what it was all about. In the end, however, all that is left is the trace of this temporal shift without any sign of either its cause or its result, without any sign of what the narrator undoubtedly and fleetingly sees in those events "at this distance of years" that he could not have seen or did not want to see then. On the other hand, the text actually allows for only two possible kinds of auto-exegesis. Whatever the narrator thinks now that Leggatt may have thought then, Leggatt evidently felt that the narrator's action in the darkness of the sail locker was, after so much mutual trust and secret understanding, something from which he ought to defend himself, *either* because it seemed to go against all that trust and understanding and hence signaled an inexplicable betrayal, *or* because it precisely did not seem to go against all that had been between the two of them and hence constituted an excess, a going beyond certain unspoken limits, a coming together and a becoming visible at the final hour of all that they had not so far allowed to be spoken or represented, of all that love their "secret partnership" was also all about. But such either/or narratives of desire have an alluring, deceptive quality: in the end, the narrator's action will turn out to have been both an ultimate act of love and an act of ultimate betrayal.

Before such an end, however, it needs to be stressed that if it is in this passage that *The Secret Sharer* comes as close as it ever will to representing what the narrator and Leggatt need to think they have been concealing from "the world," it is also here that this text produces in its most excessive form that punctum-like yet endless spatio-temporal suspension, that unrepresentable "breathless pause" within which this desire can exist at all. "Our hands met gropingly, lingered united in a steady, motionless clasp for a second.... No word was breathed by either of us when they separated." Within the clasp of this ellipsis, invisible enactments of desire forever unfold onto an offstage of signification and representation. This ellipsis is all *The Secret Sharer* was written around and for: it is the most uncompromising form this text has for thinking itself (as the narrative of a corporeal caesura); it is the site of an unrepresentable desire that has intensified and exceeded the enclosures of language and of the closet. Such an ellipsis marks the visible effect of an excess of desire that can be present only as the absent cause immanent in its own effects. Through the door left open by such an excess, both language and closet are stretched from the very inside and are turned into the immanent, atemporal, and limitless plateaus of the other limit: they become the secret pipelines leading to the outside; they emerge as the sublime events of a body yet to come. The asignifying and non-representational silence of this ellipsis is not at all the silence of which Foucault writes in *The History of Sexuality*, namely, that silence which speaks louder than words and which is part and parcel of discourse.[71] This silence is the silence of the outside. In one of his most inspired and inspiring essays — "La pensée du dehors" — Foucault writes:

> When language arrives at its own edge, what it finds is not a positivity that contradicts it, but the void that will efface it. Into that void it must go, consenting to come undone in the rumbling, in the immediate negation of what it says, in a silence that is not the intimacy of a secret but a pure outside where words endlessly unravel.[72]

In *The Secret Sharer*, the intimacy of a shared and open secret — where the trope of the secret is a screen hiding a sharing — turns language and the closet inside out like gloves, and opens the door to this "pure outside" in which it is possible to share in the open and without being seen. The only secret in *The Secret Sharer* turns out to be that there is no secret in it anywhere: in this text, the secret is the invisible bone thrown to the well-trained dogs of hermeneutics who run eagerly in its pursuit — thereby leaving Leggatt and the narrator rid of all chaperons and to their sharing.

> "... You don't suppose I am afraid of what can be done to me? Prison or gallows or whatever they may please. But you don't see me coming back to explain such things to an old fellow in a wig and twelve respectable tradesmen, do you? What can they know whether I am guilty or not — or of *what* I am guilty, either? That's my affair. What does the Bible say? 'Driven off the face of the earth.' Very well, I am off the face of the earth now. As I came at night so I shall go."
>
> "Impossible!" I murmured. "You can't."
>
> "Can't? ... Not naked like a soul on the Day of Judgement. I shall freeze on to this sleeping suit. The Last Day is not yet — and ... you have understood thoroughly. Didn't you?"
>
> I felt suddenly ashamed of myself. I may say truly that I understood — and my hesitation in letting that man swim away from my ship's side had been a mere sham sentiment, a sort of cowardice.[73]

In between sham and cowardice, the narrator of *The Secret Sharer* stands as a cartographer of betrayal. This is a text shot through with the sublime pleasures of betrayal. Jean Genet—who knew such pleasures well—has written of betrayal as "erotic exaltation" and has declared that anyone "who hasn't experienced the ecstasy of betrayal knows nothing about ecstasy at all."[74] *The Secret Sharer* culminates with such an ecstasy and with that attendant "cowardice" that constitutes its infinite courage. But let the narrator spell out one by one the letters of this betrayal: let him pronounce Leggatt's death sentence. For this passage is at once the turning point at which the narrator quickly overcomes what had been only a very fleeting "hesitation in letting that man swim away" and also the only moment when he reflects on such a "hesitation." This turning point is marked by a swift reversal of affects and by the sudden onset of shame: this is a shame caused by the coming to visibility (in the form of that "hesitation") of a desire for an incompossible narrative universe (other than, parallel, and contiguous to the one of *The Secret Sharer*) in which Leggatt could have been kept indefinitely in the enclosure of the cabin. The narrator—now caught in the act of such a desire—quickly covers his tracks by a thorough retroactive indictment of whatever had made him want to protract ad infinitum that sublime narrative of the closet. The narrator thus reconstructs his desire for Leggatt and for that narrative as a sham, as altogether not a desire at all—thereby obliterating any future possibility of even imaging an other narrative universe outside of this one in which to love Leggatt is necessarily to leave him. It is, however, such a virtual and unthinkable universe that for one last time disturbs the narrator's resolve, as he realizes the great dangers involved in bringing the ship at night as close as possible to the island's rocky coast so that Leggatt may hope to reach it:

> ...and I realized suddenly that all my future, the only future for which I was fit, would perhaps go irretrievably to pieces in any mishap to my first command.[75]

The unthought of this sentence lies in the implied possibility that there may indeed exist futures different from the one in which the narrator will commune with the body and world of the ship as a successful captain: such futures, however, are the ones for which he is not fit. Or—rewriting Kafka—there is hope, but not for him. The narrator's only possible future is posited as mutually exclusive with any future in which Leggatt would not be "driven off the face of the earth." And once the narrator's *alea jacta est* has thus been pronounced, there is no turning back from the path of total betrayal.

In the very end, the narrator attempts to exorcise all that Leggatt had allowed to crystallize in the enclosure of the cabin. Leggatt must be "driven off the face of the earth." But where exactly is that? Leggatt is going to be swimming toward some "islands off the Cambodge shore":

> The east side of the gulf is fringed with islands . . . Unknown to trade, to travel, almost to geography, the manner of life they harbor is an unsolved secret. There must be villages — settlement of fishermen at least — on the largest of them, and some communication with the world is probably kept up by native craft.[76]

These islands are precisely not on "the face of the earth": for if they "probably" have "some communication with the world," they must clearly be outside of it. To be of the world means to be known to white man's "trade," "travel," and "geography" — it means to be within the circuitries of capital and of modernity. To be "driven off the face of the earth" means actually to be driven among the "natives" and among their as yet "secret" ways "of life," modes of production, and communication. It is, then, only appropriate that the narrator's own secret would go join these otherworldly secrets and take along with it a desire that seems to be at least as incompatible with the world of modernity as these islands for the moment still are. However, it does not suffice to let Leggatt go, to regain control over the body of the ship, and to resume the straight and mandatory course of modernity: the whole narrative of desire of this text needs also to be rewritten over the traces of that body that has been "driven off the face of the earth." These are the triumphant pages of that rewriting:

> The great black mass [of the island] brooding over our very mastheads began to pivot away from the ship's side silently. And now I forgot the secret stranger ready to depart, and remembered only that I was a total stranger to the ship. I did not know her. Would she do it? How was she to be handled?
> I swung the mainyard and waited helplessly. She was perhaps stopped, and her very fate hung in the balance, with the black mass of Koh-ring like the gate of the everlasting night towering over her taffrail. What would she do now? Had she way on her yet? I stepped to the side swiftly, and on the shadowy water I could see nothing except a faint phosphorescent flash revealing the glassy smoothness of the sleeping surface. It was impossible to tell — and I had not learned yet the feel of my ship. Was she moving? What I needed was something easily seen, a piece of paper, which I could throw overboard and watch . . . All at once my strained, yearning stare distinguished

a white object floating within a yard of the ship's side. White on the black water. A phosphorescent flash passed under it. What was that thing?...I recognized my own floppy hat. It must have fallen off his head...and he didn't bother. Now I had what I wanted—the saving mark for my eyes. But I hardly thought of my other self, now gone from the ship, to be hidden forever from all friendly faces, to be a fugitive and a vagabond on the earth, with no brand of the curse on his sane forehead to stay a slaying hand...too proud to explain.

And I watched the hat—the expression of my sudden pity for his mere flesh. It had been meant to save his homeless head from the dangers of the sun. And now—behold—it was saving the ship, by serving me for a mark to help out the ignorance of my strangeness. Ha! It was drifting forward, warning me just in time that the ship had gathered sternway.... Already the ship was drawing ahead. And I was alone with her. Nothing! no one in the world should stand now between us, throwing a shadow on the way of silent knowledge and mute affection, the perfect communion of a seaman with his first command.

Walking to the taffrail, I was in time to make out, on the very edge of a darkness thrown by a towering black mass like the very gateway of Erebus—yes, I was in time to catch an evanescent glimpse of my white hat left behind to mark the spot where the secret sharer of my cabin and of my thoughts, as though he were my second self, had lowered himself into the water to take his punishment: a free man, a proud swimmer striking out for a new destiny.[77]

One has seldom witnessed a more staggering betrayal, as *The Secret Sharer* ends amidst the deafening fanfare of the restoration and apotheosis of normative order. Everything in this narrative—each and every whisper, glance, and secret understanding between Leggatt and the narrator; each and every expression of their desire—is here effortlessly hollowed out of any import and indeed obliterated in the face of the narrator's final reunion with his long lost and first love: the female body of the ship. That "breathless pause" that was the narrative of their "secret partnership" is here grotesquely reduced to some sort of stag party prior to the bridegroom's first night, and constituted ex post facto as a mere deferral of a "communion" that is finally consummated on this last page. The narrator's exclamation that "no one in the world should stand now between" him and the ship evidently implies that Leggatt already had stood in between them for far too long. Here, *The Secret Sharer* reveals itself more patently than ever before to be a tale of homophobic triangulation. This is a tale in which the price readily paid for the sudden materialization of sublime counternarratives of same-sex desire at the threshold of "the perfect communion of a seaman with his first command" is that such counternarratives and such a desire be just as suddenly dispelled when the last call to normative and heteronormative duty is finally heard. The price the narrator is only too willing to pay for resuming that "communion" is ultimately the very body of Leggatt: the final insult added to the injuries already munificently bestowed upon Leggatt's body on this last page is that "the hat" that "had been meant to save his homeless head" is fortuitously used for "saving the ship" instead. And yet, Leggatt's body has not been successfully disentangled from the hat and still lingers hauntingly in this final page of *The Secret Sharer.* In this passage, in fact, a recurrent flash of phosphorescence surrounds the hat: "I could see nothing except a faint phosphorescent flash revealing the glassy smoothness of the sleeping surface. . . . All at once my strained, yearning stare distinguished a white object floating. . . . A phosphorescent flash passed under it . . . I recognized my own floppy hat." This "phosphorescent flash"—along with the peculiarly "sleeping surface" that it reveals—have returned here from the opening pages of *The Secret Sharer,* where they had been enveloping the naked body of Leggatt floating on the water: "Before I could form a guess a faint flash of phosphorescent light, which seemed to issue suddenly from the naked body of a man, flickered in the sleeping water. . . . The phosphorescence flashed in the swirl of the water all about his limbs."[78] This phosphorescent trace of Leggatt notwithstanding, the moment when this hat is sighted by the narrator marks simultaneously the saving of the ship and the possibility of Leggatt's death by sunstroke (or, at least, the ultimate failure and undoing of the narrator's "sudden pity for his mere flesh"). The very fact of such a simultaneity signals just what powerful threats Leggatt's body and the desire it embodies continue to pose even after he has left the ship: it indicates just what overzealous and hermetic closure is needed at once for that body and all its traces to be finally erased as well as for this denouement of terminal homophobia to have the last and lethal laugh.[79]

But the cacophonous flourishes of victorious normativity cannot overwhelm the murmurs of a much betrayed desire. And here I ought to explain what I meant earlier by saying that the "cowardice" of such a betrayal is also its infinite courage. This text may seem to be taking highly calculated risks vis-à-vis the explosive matter of desire: after all, the narrator's inexplicable involvement with Leggatt is, on the one hand, presented as the narrative centerpiece and, on the other hand, retroactively excused as a momentary lapse and a necessary rite of passage unfolding at the critical limen of the narrator's full initiation into the bourgeois world of adult duties and responsibilities. The narrative form of the rite of passage—a liminal crisis that is usually narrativized as a caesura, as an inexplicable lapse into highly questionable practices and behaviors, and that marks at once the beginning of adulthood as well as the prescribed and irreparable loss of all that preceded it—was emblematically dear to Conrad (see, for example, works such as *The Shadow Line*, *Youth*, and *Lord Jim*). The most significant and attractive characteristic of this narrative form for Conrad is that it allows him, on the one hand, to concentrate all narrative energies specifically and solely on desires, practices, and proclivities that are strictly unacceptable to the normative order, and yet, on the other hand, to finally dismiss all such desires and their instantiations as isolated episodes that have now been transcended and whose exclusive function was to introduce the normative desires of adulthood. This type of narrative, in other words, can never be directly blackmailed as having roamed indulgingly the lands of the illicit, since its terminus is always an oath of abjuration. Open-ended, decentered, and unstable as Conrad's narratives often are, they are, in this sense, also just as hermetically sealed and airtight. *The Secret Sharer* is such a narrative of liminal crisis—but one in which the narrative mechanisms ultimately backfire. This text tries to ride the turbulent waves of a crisis of same-sex desire so as to reach the terra firma on which prescribed forms of closely monitored homosociality go hand in hand with mandatory heterosexuality: this text behaves as if this sexuality and that desire were as separate as land and sea, as if they were diachronic stages in the narrator's sexual-political passage. Here lies the attempted onto-epistemological *Aufhebung* of *The Secret Sharer:* this text wants to mobilize the crisis that is same-sex desire so as to make it at once productive of, realized in, and ultimately abrogated by the constitution of what I identified earlier as modern dialectical sexuality. (We have come full circle, in other words, to the lessons that we learned from Marx and Melville about crisis: a capital ingredient that—depending on whether or not one uses just the right amount of it—will make or break the dialectic.) But here also lies *The Secret Sharer*'s failure—and such a failure is its infinite courage. The attempt to force the hand of a refractory crisis so as to produce a dialectical resolution also provokes such a crisis to get out of hand and to result in an excess of crisis. Ultimately, this text unleashes far more desire than it can process and than its narrator can abjure. For the loving whispers, silent glances, and mingling bodies of *The Secret Sharer* will not be forgotten or betrayed just because this text decrees that they be forgotten by fiat or just because this narrator needs to betray them. For no acrobatics of homophobia can ever take back the claustrophiliac ecstasies of these two male bodies and the spectacle of their secret sharing. For the sublime of the closet comes when the time comes—and that coming cannot be exchanged, cannot be erased.

But it can be shared. Or, rather, the sublime of the closet can *only* be shared: it can only come into being as a sharing, as the being-in-common of those who have nothing in common. When in the cabin, Leggatt and the narrator are neither different from each other nor identical to each other. In that cabin, rather, they become other-as-the-same: they are no longer the captain and the murderer, and they share each other as the same — that is, as other than and in the stead of what they were outside the cabin in the first and in the last place. While continuing to exist in relation to the ship, to the world, to the law, to the unavoidable betrayal, and to the inevitable end, in that cabin they also no longer belong to any of these things or even to each other. They belong only to their sharing in that event that is the sublime of the closet — and such a sharing is precisely a mode of unbelonging. In the end, I would like to offer the sublime of the closet as a fleeting instance of a community of unbelonging, as a provisional form of what Georges Bataille describes as "the community of those who do not have a community."[80]

F   I   V   E

The Labor of Race; or,
Heterotopologies of the Third Man

IN THE END is the beginning, and we return full circle here to the sea narrative that opened these investigations, namely, *The Nigger of the "Narcissus"*. We return to this text, however, not without casting yet another parting glance in the direction of *The Secret Sharer*. When reflecting on the previous chapter, one has the strange feeling of having written oneself into the corner of the very text one wanted to open up for all to see, of having written all around oneself a textual closet in which to be alone with one's own redoubled selves, of having obeyed *ad litteram* the injunctions of *The Secret Sharer*. Far from abjuring the desires of that chapter much like the narrator of *The Secret Sharer* abjures the desires of his own narrative in the end, I wish to push his and my desires also in a different direction here. To undo *The Secret Sharer* in a different manner entails no less than rethinking the sublime of the closet by articulating its historical-political conditions of possibility within modernity. Whereas the previous chapter focused primarily on the modalities of being of the romance between the narrator and Leggatt, I want now to investigate the narrative presuppositions of that romance: in that chapter, I read what was there on the page for all to see rather than what had already taken place behind the narrative scenes. Here, we turn to the question of Leggatt's murder: it is about that murder—about whom, why, and how Leggatt killed—that questions need to be formulated so as to read

The Nigger of the "Narcissus" as the racial unconscious and the political archaeology of *The Secret Sharer*.

This murder constitutes as much of a *fons et origo* as *The Secret Sharer* will ever have: it is because Leggatt has killed a man that he runs away from his ship and into the eager arms of the narrator in the first place. So eager is the narrator, and for so long must he have been awaiting one such as Leggatt, and so well predisposed is he already to his arrival, that the news that Leggatt is a murderer makes the latter not only more attractive to the narrator but also altogether more like the narrator. You might also recall how "confidently" the narrator excuses Leggatt's murder, that is, how "confidently" the question of this crime is at once allowed to emerge in the narrative and evaded thereafter: " 'Fit of temper,' I suggested, confidently." The narrator's omnipotent confidence nonetheless does need this murder for his infinitely paranoiac imagination to be triggered into motion and for all the ensuing plots of romance to get off the narrative ground. It is amusing to see such a confidence in a character who has no self to speak of—let alone self-confidence—and whose self-described hysteric countenance is constantly on the brink of physical and mental collapse. It is crucial to emphasize, in other words, how it is precisely and only about the conjoined questions of Leggatt's murder and moral integrity that the narrator can have any confidence at all. Paranoia is henceforth Conrad's preferred and indeed obligatory narrative form.

Why should this murder be posited as the primal scene of such a form? Let us pose this question to Leggatt himself:

> "...[The murdered sailor] was one of those creatures that are just simmering all the time with a silly sort of wickedness. Miserable devils that have no business to live at all. He wouldn't do his duty and wouldn't let anybody else do theirs....You know well enough the sort of ill-conditioned snarling cur...."
> And I knew well enough the pestiferous danger of such a character where there are no means of legal repression. And I knew well enough that my double there was no homicidal ruffian. I did not think of asking him for details, and he told me the story roughly in brusque, disconnected sentences...
> "It happened while we were setting a reefed foresail, at dusk. Reefed foresail! You understand the sort of weather. The only sail we had left to keep the ship running; so you may guess what it had been like for days.... He gave me some of his cursed insolence at the sheet. I tell you I was overdone with this terrific weather.... I believe the fellow himself was half crazed with funk. It was no time for gentlemanly reproof, so I turned round and felled him like an ox. He up and at me. We closed just as an awful sea made

for the ship. All hands saw it coming and took to the rigging, but I had him by the throat, and went on shaking him like a rat, the men above us yelling, 'Look out! look out!' Then a crash as if the sky had fallen on my head.... It was a miracle that they found us, jammed together behind the forebitts. It's clear that I meant business, because I was holding him by the throat still when they picked us up. He was black in the face. It was too much for them. It seems they rushed us aft together, gripped as we were, screaming 'Murder!' like a lot of lunatics.... They had rather a job to separate us, I've been told. A sufficiently fierce story to make an old judge and a respectable jury sit up a bit."[1]

And so it is that a narrative of male homoerotic tenderness and affection has its origin and complement in a narrative of brutal violence between men. All that touching, holding, and gripping each other in the sublime closet of the narrator's cabin has its grotesque and just as homoerotic counterpart in this strangulation—a strangulation that is furiously protracted well beyond the call of duty ("I had him by the throat, and went on shaking him like a rat"; "they found us, jammed together"; "[i]t's clear that I meant business, because I was holding him by the throat still when they picked us up"; "gripped as we were ... [t]hey had rather a job to separate us"). Leggatt—who, mind you, is "no homicidal ruffian"—revels nonetheless in recounting in graphic and gruesome detail the frenzied horrors of the macho prowess of which he seems to be quite frankly proud: his feat, after all, is a "sufficiently fierce story to make an old judge and a respectable jury sit up a bit." The most arresting horror in Leggatt's edifying vignette of robust virility is the fact that his unrepentant and defiant pride is met by the narrator with an attitude of complete understanding and indulgence, which makes it abundantly clear that the narrator thought this to be a perfectly excusable and justified use of violence, even though such a violence is most significantly characterized by unaccounted intensity, vehemence, frenzy, and hysteria that make it well congruent with that systemic homophobic violence identifiable as homosexual panic.[2] Leggatt constitutes the shared element, the pivotal hinge, and the translating apparatus between these two complementary narratives—namely, the narrative of his murder and the narrative unfolding in the enclosure of the cabin—that belong thus in a continuum of gender and sexual production. This is a continuum in which Leggatt can afford openly to express affection for and be physically intimate with another man only because he has already amply proven himself to be a man, as well as gained that other man's respect, by killing a third man, who is one of those "[m]iserable devils that have no business to live at all," that is, who does not deserve to exist because he is all that a man must at all costs not be.

Who *is* this third man who, on the one hand, defies so despica-
bly the normative definition of masculinity, and, on the other hand, is indispensable
for this romance to take place, since it is precisely his murder that brings the narrator and Leggatt together (each as double of the other, and both as perfect replicas,
examples, and incorporations of that normative definition of masculinity)? Who is this
sailor who "is simmering all the time with a silly sort of wickedness," who "wouldn't
do his duty and wouldn't let anybody else do theirs," who is an "ill-conditioned
snarling cur" constituting a "pestiferous danger...where there are no means of legal
repression?" One has surely met him before, in an earlier novel. His name is Donkin.
His ship is the *Narcissus*. And this is his story:

> Another new hand—a man with shifty eyes and a yellow hatchet face...ob-
> served in a squeaky voice: 'Well, it's a 'omeward trip, anyhow. Bad or good, I
> can do it on my 'ed—s'long as I get 'ome. And I can look after my rights! I
> will show 'em!' All the heads turned towards him....He stood repulsive and
> smiling in the sudden silence. This clean white forecastle was his refuge; the
> place where he could be lazy; where he could wallow, and lie and eat—and
> curse the food he ate; where he could display his talents for shirking work,
> for cheating, for cadging; where he could find surely someone to wheedle
> and someone to bully—and where he would be paid for doing all this. They
> all knew him. Is there a spot on earth where such a man is unknown, an omi-
> nous survival testifying to the eternal fitness of lies and impudence?...He
> was the man that cannot steer, that cannot splice, that dodges the work on
> dark nights; that, aloft, holds on frantically with both arms and legs, and
> swears at the wind, the sleet, the darkness; the man who curses the sea while
> others work. The man who is the last out and the first in when all hands are
> called. The man who can't do most things and won't do the rest. The pet of
> philanthropists and self-seeking landlubbers. The sympathetic and deserving
> creature that knows all about his rights, but knows nothing of courage, of
> endurance, and of the unexpressed faith, of the unspoken loyalty that knits
> together a ship's company. The independent offspring of the ignoble freedom
> of the slums full of disdain and hate for the austere servitude of the sea.[3]

If, as Jameson suggests, Donkin is "the epitome of the *homme de ressentiment*" and
"*The Nigger of the 'Narcissus'*...may be characterized as one long tirade against *ressentiment*," such a tirade—of which this passage is an exemplary moment—seems to
borrow its acrimoniousness from the very *ressentiment* against which it is directed.[4]
The reactionary virulence of such a philippic is as relentless as Leggatt's murderous
violence—and they are both aimed at the same historical subject. At the very end of

The Nigger of the "Narcissus", the narrator—who turns out to be an officer aboard the *Narcissus*—actually imagines Donkin "who never did a decent day's work in his life, no doubt [to be earning] his living by discoursing with filthy eloquence upon the right of labour to live."[5] Donkin, the "independent offspring of the ignoble freedom of the slums," is the personification of an urban proletariat in social ascent through its increasing involvement in the politics of unionism and socialism—a politics that saw its confrontational and official culmination in the arena of British public discourse with the foundation of the Labour Party in 1900, three years after the publication of *The Nigger of the "Narcissus"*. Donkin is the compendium of all the proclivities, behaviors, and beliefs that for Conrad are antinomial to any definition of masculinity and that can be conveniently summarized as the refusal to work, as the rejection of the mystique of labor. In Conrad, real men work. Donkin—the modern political subject of an antagonistic working class that is "full of disdain and hate for the austere servitude of the sea," that, in other words, is determined to resist ruthless exploitation—resurfaces at the beginning of *The Secret Sharer* in the guise of the nameless murdered sailor, so as to be promptly sacrificed as a body of aberrant masculinity on the altar of a consecrated male-male romance whose spectacle is about to unfold. In this respect, *The Secret Sharer* completes what in *The Nigger of the "Narcissus"* constituted an unfinished project. In Conrad, a nostalgic as well as reactionary mystique of labor and a homoerotic as well as homophobic mystique of the male body are produced as one set of discursive practices. Donkin is the epitome of that emergent subject who—even though he is a man...but not really, and even though he is a worker...but not fully—can no longer be forced to work for either of those two symbiotic mystiques.

The real men—that is, the men like Leggatt, the men who proudly and silently endure their hard fate as well as "the austere servitude of the sea," the men both the narrator of *The Nigger of the "Narcissus"* and the narrator of *The Secret Sharer* love to love—are a dying race:

> [Singleton, the *Narcissus*'s oldest sailor] was only a child of time, a lonely relic of a devoured and forgotten generation. He stood, still strong, as ever unthinking; a ready man with a vast empty past and with no future, with his childlike impulses and his man's passions already dead within his tattooed breast. The men who could understand his silence were gone—those men who knew how to exist beyond the pale of life and within sight of eternity. They had been strong, as those are strong who know neither doubts nor hopes. They had been impatient and enduring, turbulent and devoted, unruly and faithful. Well-meaning people had tried to represent those men as whining over

every mouthful of their food; as going about their work in fear of their lives. But in truth they had been men who knew toil, privation, violence, debauchery—but knew not fear, and had no desire of spite in their hearts. Men hard to manage, but easy to inspire; voiceless men—but men enough to scorn in their hearts the sentimental voices that bewailed the hardness of their fate.... Their generation lived inarticulate and indispensable.... They were the everlasting children of the mysterious sea. Their successors are the grown-up children of a discontented earth. They are less naughty, but less innocent; less profane, but perhaps also less believing; and if they had learned how to speak they have also learned how to whine. But the others were strong and mute; they were effaced, bowed and enduring, like stone caryatides that hold up in the night the lighted halls of a resplendent and glorious edifice. They are gone now—and it does not matter. The sea and the earth are unfaithful to their children: a truth, a faith, a generation of men goes—and is forgotten, and it does not matter! Except, perhaps, to the few of those who believed the truth, confessed the faith—or loved the men.[6]

What can one add to such an infantilizing, patronizing, romanticizing, effacing, and yet stunning elegy to the laboring male body? What can one ask of the eloquent and sentimental heights that are reached here in order to speak of these "strong and mute" "caryatides" and "voiceless men" who were "men enough to scorn in their hearts the sentimental voices that bewailed the hardness of their fate"? And how is one to understand the relations that bind in secret partnerships the quasi-religious reverence for silence, the passionate veneration of masculine strength, and the contradictory position that this garrulous narrator occupies vis-à-vis that reverence and that veneration, since he, unlike those "strong" men who are silent and don't need to speak, is the one who does so much talking and representing? Here, I would like to rupture further the already uneven historical faultline that is the political voice of the narrator in *The Nigger of the "Narcissus"*—a faultline that will be restaged even more unevenly in the narrator of *The Secret Sharer*. In between these two generations of men and the two eras of labor and masculinity to which they belong—the first and premodern one constituted by the men who are "strong and mute," and the second and modern one constituted by the men who, having "learned how to speak," had "also learned how to whine"—stand "the few of those," like the narrator of *The Nigger of the "Narcissus"*, who remember, because they "believed the truth, confessed the faith—or loved the men." The men in between are inextricably caught in that modern double bind of representation within which to remember and to write longing elegies in honor of the "forgotten" laboring male body of yore is already to be its historical executioner. (This, of course, is the double bind that had been already painfully sensed by Melville in his narrative somersaults around the disappearing world and bodies of whaling in *Moby-Dick*.) But if the narrator of *The Nigger of the "Narcissus"* is in between these different bodies as well as in between these apparently mutually exclusive eras of labor, if he is constituted as a faultline between the Donkins and the Leggatts and their respective worlds, he is not as yet constituted as a faultline between the nostalgic as well as reactionary mystique of labor and the homoerotic as well as homophobic mystique of the male body. In *The Nigger of the "Narcissus"*, these two mystiques can still come into being as completely coextensive strata of ideology, since the narrator is able, for the most part, to deploy successfully both of them at the same time and in the same space without as yet unleashing their explosive contradictions. In *The Nigger of the "Narcissus"*, these mystiques somehow can still usefully exploit each other for the realization of a common ideological capital. It is in *The Secret Sharer*, instead, that a new interstitial position is added to the previous ones and that the narrator becomes a more uneven faultline between increasingly irreconcilable libidinal economies. The narrator of *The Secret Sharer* is precisely in between Leggatt and the ship and is constituted as the unstable interference between suddenly antinomial worlds: on the one hand, the world of Leggatt, of the "strong and mute" men who devoted their lives to the sea and its ships, of the homoerotic as well as homophobic passions for such men, and, on the other hand, the world of the ship, of its demands of labor and discipline, of its heteronormative as well as homophobic adult libidinal forms. In *The Nigger of the "Narcissus"*, both these worlds were the symbiotic halves of a whole apparatus of labor and desire: there, to love the men was in no contradiction whatsoever with and was actually indispensable to the world of the ship and its injunctions. In *The Secret Sharer*, however, the narrator is split by the opposite vectors of precisely these two trajectories of desire: while according to his definitions and expectations these trajectories should have been perfectly compatible with each other, they now seem at once increasingly semiautonomous and mutually exclusive as well as increasingly bound to each other's fates. The narrator of *The Secret Sharer* marks the intuition of a profound and perhaps ultimately indomitable modern crisis in the mode of production: this is a crisis in which the production of bodies and of their desires proceeds by enlarging the distance as well as by intensifying the antagonism between — at once increasingly self-enclosed and atomized, and increasingly interdependent and interrelated — libidinal economies such as labor and capital, and such as homosexuality and heterosexuality. The narrator of *The Secret Sharer* constitutes the ever-widening gap between the opposite polarities of the dialectic that are produced more and more as both monads *and* fragments, as both spaces of absolute enclosure *and* spaces of absolute relation-ality, as both times of the event *and* times of the teleological: he embodies the ten-dentially unexchangeable, unexploitable, and unco-optable crisis of modernity.

Let us return now one last time to Leggatt's murder, so as to begin, in the end, to tell yet another story. In *The Secret Sharer*, Conrad rewrote an event that at the time had caused quite a sensation in the maritime world of East Asia: the murder of a sailor by an officer aboard the *Cutty Sark*. Conrad often refers to that event as one of the sources for *The Secret Sharer*. In a letter, for example, he writes:

> [Leggatt] himself was suggested to me by a young fellow who was 2d mate (in the '60) of the *Cutty Sark* clipper and had the misfortune to kill a man on deck. But his skipper had the decency to let him swim ashore on the Java Coast as the ship was passing through Anjer Straits. The story was well re-membered in the Merchant Service even in my time.[7]

This last recollection is possibly even more chilling than Leggatt's own account of the murder. In between misplaced "misfortune" and misplaced "decency," Conrad stands here as a cartographer of capital and disciplinary power: in the end, he is al-ways on the side of the officers. In Conrad's rewriting of this event in *The Secret Sharer* as well as in his letters, however, there is a crucial omission: the murdered sailor was black. In *The Log of the Cutty Sark*, we learn not only that the murdered sailor was black but also that the officer who murdered him "was apparently a despotic character with a sinister reputation"—a far cry, in other words, from the narrator's portrayal of Leggatt—and that the incident culminating in the murder had started as the black sailor's attempt to challenge the officer's authority.[8] This sailor was a re-sistant black man—and it was as such that he was killed. The fact that the enabling event of a narrative of romance between two white men is the murder of a sailor who was not only the embodiment of the antithesis of Conrad's definitions of the la-boring male body but also a resistant black man—such a fact marks the emergence of same-sex desire in *The Secret Sharer* also as the articulation of lethal anxieties about racial difference.

      Furthermore, the fact that the matter of race is thoroughly erased in Conrad's rewritings of the murder also indicates the extent to which *The Secret Sharer* is a completion of the projects of *The Nigger of the "Narcissus"*. In the latter, in fact, there was a sailor whose isolation and ostracism lubricated the delicate machin-ery of labor, discipline, and homosocial cohesion even better than the isolation and ostracism of Donkin. That sailor's name is James Wait—the only black sailor aboard a ship of white men, to whom the title of the novel refers. Around his illness, agony, and death, the other sailors coalesce as one cohesive, compliant, efficient, and homo-erotically charged body of labor. Conrad, who was an officer aboard the *Narcissus*, thus remembers James Wait in the preface to the novel's American edition:

> FROM that evening when James Wait joined the ship...to the moment when he left us in the open sea, shrouded in sailcloth, through the open port, I had much to do with him. He was in my watch. A negro in a British forecastle is a lonely being. He has no chums. Yet James Wait, afraid of death and making her his accomplice was an impostor of some character—mastering our compassion, scornful of our sentimentalism, triumphing over our suspicions.
>
> But in the book he is nothing; he is merely the centre of the ship's collective psychology and the pivot of the action. Yet he, who in the family circle and amongst my friends is familiarly referred to as the Nigger, remains very precious to me. For the book written round him is not the sort of thing that can be attempted more than once in a life-time.

As Conrad only too precisely puts it, *The Nigger of the "Narcissus"* is indeed "written round" James Wait—who is at once "nothing" and "merely the centre of the ship's collective psychology and the pivot of the action." But what does it mean for some-body to be at once "nothing" and "the centre" of everything but that these two distinct modalities of being are nonetheless mutually determining and dialectically de-termined? And yet, what could it possibly mean to write that this "nothing" is not only "the centre" and "the pivot" but also "merely" so? How can anything and even a "nothing" be "the centre" and "the pivot" "*merely*"? This dialectic is decidedly tilted: while the condition of being "nothing" is given as pure and unqualified, the condition of being "the centre" and "the pivot" is qualified by an adverb that retracts at least as much as it concedes, and that hence expresses a certain reluctance and am-bivalence at having to grant that James Wait is "nothing" precisely to the extent to which he is not only the most important element in this narrative but also "very pre-cious" to Conrad after all this time. With the insertion of this adverb, Conrad attempts a reversal of this dialectic as soon as he realizes that he has cornered himself into ad-mitting that this dialectic is actually reversed the other way around. In other words, rather than being "the centre" because he is "nothing," James Wait is turned into "nothing" precisely because he is "the centre."

Ultimately, Conrad's preface to *The Nigger of the "Narcissus"* is more accurate as a description not of this novel but rather of *The Secret Sharer*. This preface indexes an as yet unfinished project that comes to its logical and complete fruition only in *The Secret Sharer*. In *The Nigger of the "Narcissus"*, after all, James Wait still *is* something and somebody, Conrad's claims to the contrary notwithstanding. In *The Nigger of the "Narcissus"*, the explosive question of racial difference is still allowed to be present as no less than the historical-political condition of possibility for the complex apparatus of labor, discipline, and same-sex desire—even if such a presence takes the form of a reiterated process of sublation. *The Secret Sharer* does what *The Nigger of the "Narcissus"* could not yet do: it entirely erases the body of racial difference, it completely elides the fact that it is over a murdered black body that white men stand to love each other. An inverse proportionality guides the passage from the first to the second novel: as the representation of sexual desire between white men emerges more clearly and crystallizes into a full-fledged narrative in the second text, the elision of the racial condition of possibility of such a narrative becomes increasingly successful to the point of its absolute disappearance from the representational field of that text. It is regarding *The Secret Sharer* that one can say what Conrad had already claimed regarding *The Nigger of the "Narcissus"*: there, the male body of racial difference is really "nothing" and yet all the more "the centre" of everything. Or, more accurately, in *The Secret Sharer*, the male body of racial difference is that negated "nothing" that constitutes "the centre" of everything that matters to the white body. There is finally something far more pernicious about the way in which *The Secret Sharer* negates the dialectical whirlwind of the *Aufhebung* that relentlessly sweeps the decks of the *Narcissus*. While *The Secret Sharer* is able to short-circuit and circumvent all sorts of dialectical processes—as I tried to show in the previous chapter—nonetheless it is not able to circumvent the dialectics of racial constitution: in *The Secret Sharer*, we witness a negation of this dialectic rather than an escape from it—and this is a negation that reasserts the power of such a dialectic all the more ruthlessly in the end. (By contrast, to the extent to which the very different romance between Ishmael and Queequeg constitutes a nondialectical engagement with and an escape from such dialectics of racial constitution, Melville is largely successful precisely where Conrad fails.) The faint and nonetheless overpowering trace of such a negation can be sensed in the textual fabric of *The Secret Sharer* only as a foundational and peremptory gesture of effacement, that is, only as violence and murder. *The Secret Sharer* brings back from *The Nigger of the "Narcissus"* both Donkin and James Wait so as to incorporate them into one single, negated body of labor and racial difference: it is the murder of such a body that enables the coming-into-being of what is nonetheless a liberating narrative of same-sex desire.

Such ruinous and productive double binds make it imperative for us to think an other history of the body, in which one's own body's sublime moments of liberation would not be bought at the price of an other body's obliteration—and would be neither bought nor sold at any price at all. This would entail moving beyond the *do ut des* formula that has so far structured the political strategies of liberation within modernity—a formula derived from and determined by the logic of exchange, a formula according to which the price for my liberation is always already being paid by some body else. This would entail nothing less than moving beyond the concept of liberation altogether. For this concept is more than ever useless for thinking and living that present and existent political *potentia* that I can now—at last and without hesitations—call *communism; or, the unexchangeable sharing in that excess of crisis that is the body as gift.*

Notes

Philopoesis

1. In producing and presenting the concepts of
literature and philopoesis, I will be following a double
logic — that is, at once a paleonymic and a neologistic
logic — that echoes and combines the methodological-
stylistical procedures of two philosophers for whom the
question of literature has always been a critical question,
namely, Jacques Derrida and Gilles Deleuze. For a suc-
cinct encapsulation of what Derrida calls "the logic of
paleonymics," see his "Signature Event Context" in *Limited
Inc*, trans. Samuel Weber (Evanston, Ill.: Northwestern
University Press, 1988), 20–21 — and I will return to
these pages. For Deleuze's thoughts on concepts and
their names, see, among the other places, "On *A
Thousand Plateaus*" in *Negotiations*, trans. Martin Joughin
(New York: Columbia University Press, 1995), 31–32.

2. Gilles Deleuze and Félix Guattari, *What Is Philosophy?*,
trans. Hugh Tomlinson and Graham Burchell (New
York: Columbia University Press, 1994). What follows
makes no pretense of being an impartial, accurate, or
comprehensive discussion of this work, and constitutes,
rather, an unfaithful selection and monstrous metamorphosis of a series of concepts in it. Such a methodology
of irreverent selectivity and loving betrayal, of course, is
omnipresent in Deleuze's own works — especially in his
philosophical monographs — from which I hope to have
learned even minimally. On this matter, see Michael
Hardt's discussion of Deleuze's method in his *Gilles

Deleuze: An Apprenticeship in Philosophy* (Minneapolis:
University of Minnesota Press, 1993), especially xix.

3. *What Is Philosophy?*, 2, 24, 117, and 164, respectively.

4. *What Is Philosophy?* is structured throughout by the
conceptual as well as tonal tensions between detached
serenity and furious passion — tensions that are most
poignantly articulated, perhaps, in the moving first
paragraph, in which the affective state of this whole work
is revealed as one of "quiet restlessness." I will return to
this paragraph. Such paradoxical symbioses, I believe,
are rooted in a particular understanding of the relation
between Friedrich Nietzsche and Immanuel Kant — in
which the former is seen at once as engaging and radical-
izing the latter's project of critique — an understanding
that is everywhere implicit in *What Is Philosophy?* and that
was most explicitly articulated by Deleuze in his *Nietzsche
and Philosophy*, trans. Hugh Tomlinson (New York:
Columbia University Press, 1983), see especially 87–94.

5. Deleuze and Guattari, *What Is Philosophy?*, 12. For
the clues warranting such an interpretation of this work,
see especially 10–12, 97–113, and 144–50, in which they
engage in scathing denunciations of the usurpatory
claims of capital on philosophy as well as on art and
science. See also Fredric Jameson's assertion "that
Deleuze is alone among the great thinkers of so-called
poststructuralism in having accorded Marx an absolutely
fundamental role in his philosophy — in having found in

the encounter with Marx the most energizing event for his later work." To this assertion, which is persuasively supported by an astute reading of the presence of Marx and Marxism in Deleuze and Guattari's *Anti-Oedipus* and *A Thousand Plateaus*, I would like to add that perhaps it is precisely there where Marx is least present, namely, in *What Is Philosophy?*—in which he is mentioned only twice in passing—that he has sunk most into the very fabric of their thought and become completely indiscernible there. Jameson, "Marxism and Dualism in Deleuze" in *A Deleuzian Century?*, ed. Ian Buchanan (Durham, N.C.: Duke University Press, 1999), 15.

6. Deleuze and Guattari, *What Is Philosophy?*, see the whole last chapter, "Conclusion: From Chaos to the Brain," 201–18, and especially 216–18.

7. Gilles Deleuze, *Cinema 2: The Time Image*, trans. Hugh Tomlinson and Robert Galeta (Minneapolis: University of Minnesota Press, 1989), 280.

8. Gilles Deleuze, and Félix Guattari, *A Thousand Plateaus: Capitalism and Schizophrenia*, trans. Brian Massumi (Minneapolis: University of Minnesota Press, 1987), 203. Translation modified.

9. Deleuze and Guattari, *What Is Philosophy?*, 217.

10. For a discussion of the concept of heterotopia, see also the introduction and chapter 1.

11. Walter Benjamin, "Theses on the Philosophy of History" in *Illuminations*, trans. Harry Zohn (New York: Schocken Books), 253–64, and especially 261–63.

12. Deleuze and Guattari, *What Is Philosophy?*, 60.

13. Ibid., 59. See also Deleuze's discussion of the concept of the outside in Michel Foucault and Maurice Blanchot, about which I will say more below, in Gilles Deleuze, *Foucault*, trans. Séan Hand (Minneapolis: University of Minnesota Press, 1988), 70–123 and especially 83–90 and 94–99.

14. For an extended discussion of the plane of immanence, see *What Is Philosophy?*, 35–60.

15. Deleuze and Guattari, *What Is Philosophy?*, 41.

16. Ibid., 59.

17. Ibid., 59–60.

18. I am referring here more to Derrida's reading of Plato's *Timaeus* in "*Khora*" than to the *Timaeus* per se. Jacques Derrida, "*Khora*," in *On the Name*, trans. Ian McLeod (Stanford: Stanford University Press, 1995), 87–127; especially relevant to the question of the relation between philosophy and the outside are 95–96, 103–4, 119–21, 125–27.

19. Deleuze, *Foucault*, 86.

20. Ibid., 87.

21. Ibid., 90.

22. Deleuze and Guattari, *What Is Philosophy?*, 218.

23. See the section entitled "Baby with the Bath-water" in *Minima Moralia*. Theodor Adorno, *Minima Moralia: Reflections from Damaged Life*, trans. E. F. N. Jephcott (London: Verso, 1978), 43–45.

24. Deleuze and Guattari, *What Is Philosophy?*, 1–2.

25. In articulating the concept of immanent interference, I have readapted one of the crucial dualisms in Deleuze's philosophy, namely, the relation between the virtual and the actual. For Deleuze's discussion of this relation, see at the very least his *Bergsonism*, trans. Hugh Tomlinson and Barbara Habberjam (New York: Zone Books, 1988), especially 42–43 and 51–72, as well as his *Cinema 2*, 68–83; but see also Hardt in *Gilles Deleuze*, 15–19, and Brian Massumi in his *A User's Guide to Capitalism and Schizophrenia: Deviations from Deleuze and Guattari* (Cambridge, Mass.: The MIT Press, 1992), especially 34–46 and 167–70. For a passionate critique of Deleuze's deployment of this conceptual pair, see Alan Badiou's *Deleuze: The Clamor of Being*, trans. Louise Burchill (Minneapolis: University of Minnesota Press, 1999), especially 43–53.

26. Friedrich Nietzsche, "Sils Maria," in *The Gay Science*, trans. Walter Kaufmann (New York: Vintage Books, 1974), 371. The last two lines of the poem are: "Da, plötzlich, Freundin! wurde eins zu zwei—/—Und Zarathustra ging an mir vorbei..." [Then, suddenly, friend, one turned into two—/And Zarathustra walked into my view.]

27. Marx and Melville—as we will see in the second section of chapter 3—in essence imparted this very same lesson even before Nietzsche. For Nietzsche's formulations on this matter, see at the very least section fourteen of Book One of *The Gay Science*. It would be impossible to give here even a summary account of the twentieth-century engagements with the impossible relation between love and ownership—and one would have to look more in literature than in philosophy for such engagements. It might be possible, however, to give a very schematic bibliography of the philosophical texts that echo specifically with Nietzsche's remark in *The Gay Science*, even though many more echoes are also heard in them: Georges Bataille's "The Sorcerer's Apprentice" in *Visions of Excess: Selected Writings, 1927–1939*, trans. Allan Stoekl (Minneapolis: University of Minnesota Press, 1985), 223–34, and especially 228–29; Adorno's *Minima Moralia*, see especially 78–80; Adorno and Max Horkheimer's *Dialectic of Enlightenment*, trans. John Cumming (New York: Continuum, 1987), see especially 72–73; Derrida's *Politics of Friendship*, trans. George Collins (London: Verso, 1997), see especially 61–74; Deleuze and Guattari's *What Is Philosophy?*, see especially 2–5, 70–71, and 106–8; Jean-Luc Nancy's "Shattered Love," in *The Inoperative*

Community, trans. Lisa Garbus and Simona Sawhney (Minneapolis: University of Minnesota Press, 1991), 82–109; Blanchot's *The Unavowable Community*, trans. Pierre Joris (Barrytown, N.Y.: Station Hilll Press, 1988), see especially 21–56; Giorgio Agamben's *Idea of Prose*, trans. Michael Sullivan and Sam Whitsitt (Albany, N.Y.: State University of New York Press, 1995), 61, and *The Coming Community*, trans. Michael Hardt (Minneapolis: University of Minnesota Press, 1993), see especially 1–2, and 23–25. What I have been calling the love of potentiality owes much to all these texts and above all to Agamben's *The Coming Community*.

28. Walter Benjamin, "Unpacking My Library," in *Illuminations*, 59–60 and 67.

29. Ibid., 60.

30. Ibid. See especially 60–61.

31. For similar formulations, see Thomas Pepper's important essay on Paul de Man entitled "Absolute Constructions: An Essay at Paul de Man," in his *Singularities: Extremes of Theory in the Twentieth Century* (Cambridge, Mass.: Cambridge University Press, 1997), 88–172, but see especially 170–72.

32. I am briefly adopting here Deleuze's distinction between copy and simulacrum, only to part ways with it in a moment. See Deleuze's *The Logic of Sense*, trans. Mark Lester with Charles Stivale (New York: Columbia University Press, 1990), 253–79, and especially 256–59 and 261–63.

33. Jorge Luis Borges, "Pierre Menard, Author of Don Quixote," in *Ficciones*, trans. Emecé Editores (New York: Grove Press, 1962), 51. I have commented elsewhere on Pierre Menard's enterprise with regards to the relation between Pier Paolo Pasolini's *Edipo Re* and both Sophocles's and Freud's versions of the Oedipus myth; see my "Oedipus Exploded: Pasolini and the Myth of Modernization," *October* 59 (1992): 27–47.

34. Here and throughout this book, the nonmodern is intended as the immanent outside of the modern. While the premodern is that which can always be dialectically sublated by the modern, the nonmodern is at once that which preexists and coexists with the modern as well as that which cannot be subsumed by the modern. In this respect, the nonmodern is similar to what Antonio Negri has called at times the antimodern and is even closer perhaps to what Timothy Murphy has recently called the amodern. For Negri's definition of the antimodern, see his discussion of Spinoza's antimodernity and of Hegel's and Heidegger's modern reelaborations of Spinoza in *Spinoza Sovversivo. Variazioni (in)attuali [Subversive Spinoza. (Un)timely Variations]* (Rome: Antonio Pellicani, 1992), 129–51. For Murphy's thoughts on the amodern, see his excellent *Wising Up the Marks: The Amodern William Burroughs* (Berkeley: University of California Press, 1997), 1–3 and 16–45.

35. For an analysis of the relation between isomorphism and heterogeneity under capital, see Deleuze and Guattari's "7000 B.C.: Apparatus of Capture" in *A Thousand Plateaus*, 424–73, and especially 436 and 464–66. For an analysis of the dialectic of identity and difference in postmodernity, see Fredric Jameson's "Antinomies of Postmodernity," in *The Seeds of Time* (New York: Columbia University Press, 1993), 1–71.

36. Jacques Derrida, "Signature Event Context" in *Limited Inc*, 21.

37. If Derrida's warnings still serve, Deleuze's strategy analogous to the deconstructive double gesture of reversal and displacement—and here "analogous" is meant in the strict sense of similar in function but not in origin or structure—consists in a careful circumvention of the binarism of identity and difference altogether. Such a strategy also entails producing whole series of other conceptual dualisms that presumably are not regulated by dialectical laws—given that the two concepts in the dualism remain throughout radically distinct in nature and yet indiscernible from each other—and that hence cannot, strictly speaking, be thought of as binarisms. For Derrida, on the other hand, "it seems necessary to retain, provisionally and strategically, *the old name*" of the concepts in question even after the double gesture of deconstruction has been performed, and hence to deploy such concepts paleonymically as "the structure of the *graft*." See "Signature Event Context," 21; but see also his discussion of the binarism of nature and culture in Claude Lévi-Strauss in his "Structure, Sign, and Play in the Discourse of the Human Sciences," in *Writing and Difference*, trans. Alan Bass (Chicago: University of Chicago Press, 1978), 278–93 and especially 284. For Deleuze's circumvention of the binarism of identity and difference, see in particular his *Difference and Repetition* (trans. Paul Patton [New York: Columbia University Press, 1994]), which constitutes a wealth of philosophical and political resources that remain still largely untapped.

38. For similar formulations, see Hardt in *Gilles Deleuze*, ix–x. Even though it appears in the context of a discussion of contemporary legal and political theories of the state, the following passage from Hardt and Negri's *Labor of Dionysus* should nonetheless clarify much of the above: "The liberal and moral refusal of teleology and the affirmation of right over good leads quickly to a philosophical refusal of ontology, because ontology itself is presumed to carry with it a transcendental determination of the good and a preconstituted structure of human action. 'Deontology' is thus advanced as the only philosophical position that can support a liberal society open to a multiplicity of ends. This is one point that marks a real confluence between liberalism and postmodern political theories. Liberal and postmodern thinkers who reason in this fashion, however, have in effect too easily accepted the Platonic and Hegelian claims about the

2

necessary connection between ontology and social tele-ology, and, despite considerable posturing about their rejection of dualism, they move too quickly to affirm the polar opposite position. (See in this regard Foucault's refusal of 'the blackmail of the Enlightenment' in 'What is Enlightenment?' pp. 42–45). The rejection of an ideal, necessary order of being does not require the acceptance of radical contingency; the refusal of an ontological vision that determines a conservative, closed society does not require a deontological vision. One need not make this leap to the opposite pole and reject ontology *tout court* in order to affirm the openness of ends in society.... [T]he tradition of modern metaphysics and politics is not of a piece, it is not a monolithic block, but rather contains within itself radical alternatives." The "radical alterna-tives" to which Hardt and Negri refer here are identified above all with Spinoza and Marx. *Labor of Dionysus: A Critique of the State-Form* (Minneapolis: University of Minnesota Press, 1994) 286–87, but see also all of 283–95.

39. Jacques Derrida, "Marx & Sons" in *Ghostly Demarcations: A Symposium on Jacques Derrida's "Specters of Marx"*, ed. Michael Sprinker and trans. G. M. Gosh-garian (London: Verso, 1999), 261, but see also 257–62 as well as endnote 89, 269.

40. I take Martin Heidegger's assessment regarding the inaptitude of his time for ontology understood as the primary question of philosophy to be axiomatic and still fully relevant for our time—since, in this respect, his time is still very much our own. See Heidegger's *Being and Time* (trans. John Macquarrie and Edward Robinson [New York: Harper and Row, 1962]) at the very least 19–22. In more recent times, this assessment has been reiterated most forcefully perhaps by Agamben; see, for example, *The Coming Community*, 89. Badiou, however, writes, "Our epoch can be said to have been stamped and signed, in philosophy, by the return of the question of Being.... When all is said and done, there is little doubt that the century has been ontological, and that this destiny is far more essential than the 'linguistic turn' with which it has been credited." *Deleuze: The Clamor of Being*, 19. Compelling as this polemical corrective to historio-graphical clichés undoubtedly is, I also think that it is ultimately right by being completely wrong. As far as philosophy is concerned, I would rather say that surely ontology in this century has been repeatedly put into question; that to put ontology into question, however, is not at all necessarily an ontological enterprise per se, especially since such a putting into question of ontology has often occurred on epistemological, phenomenological, or logical-analytical grounds; that, in some ways, the outright forgetting of ontology can be much more of an ontologically driven enterprise than even the explicit questioning of it; and hence that—since I believe in any case that much of contemporary philosophy has been characterized more by such a forgetting than by such a

questioning—Badiou's assessment is correct in the end. Moreover, Badiou carefully states that what he thinks as "the return of the question of Being" has occurred specifically "in philosophy"—and he is right in doing so because, as I am suggesting, other practices of thought, such as the theory and criticism of the text, have certainly witnessed such a return even less than philosophy has.

41. See, for example, Fredric Jameson's incisive discussion of de Man in "Theory: Immanence and Nominalism in Postmodern Theoretical Discourse," in his *Postmodernism; Or, The Cultural Logic of Late Capitalism* (Durham, N.C.: Duke University Press, 1991), 181–259 and especially 246–47, as well as John Guillory's account of de Man and his disciples in his *Cultural Capital: The Problem of Literary Canon Formation* (Chicago: University of Chicago Press, 1993), 176–265 and especially 227–30.

42. See, for example, Tom Cohen's trenchant account of the turn away from "high theory" in the 1980s and 1990s in his *Anti-Mimesis from Plato to Hitchcock* (Cambridge: Cambridge University Press, 1994), 1–8.

43. Such an understanding of self-representation is common even among those who are otherwise very critical of the rhetoric of multiculturalism. See, for example, Peter Hitchcock when he writes that "[a]t the present time, multiculturalism signifies both an impetus towards a more democratic cultural politics and a drive for more efficient late capitalist corporate strategies." I largely agree with this assessment, but I cannot agree with the conclusions that Hitchcock ultimately draws from it: "If the marginalized and the oppressed become the agents of their self-representation, then we might have a multiculturalism worthy of the name." The reasons for my disagreement will become clear presently in this preface, but see also the first section of chapter 4 as well as more generally the rest of that chapter for a critique of that form of self-representation which is the politics of coming out. Peter Hitchcock, "Workers of the World—!" in *Marxism beyond Marxism*, 87 and 82; for similar formulations, see also his "Multicultural Materialism" in *Rethinking Marxism* 5 (spring 1992): 78–79.

44. Agamben, *The Coming Community*, 53–56. Translation modified.

45. Montaigne's remark is quoted by Derrida as an epigraph to "Structure, Sign, and Play in the Discourse of the Human Sciences," in *Writing and Difference*, 278.

46. For a critique of New Americanist critical discourse that touches also on Dimock and that is at least as ontologically minded as my own, see William Spanos, *The Errant Art of Moby-Dick* (Durham, N.C.: Duke University Press, 1995), 38 as well as 36–42. Spanos's work is doubly relevant here, as it emphasizes the centrality of the question of ontology for any practice of reading much like I have done above—even though it appeals to a different understanding of ontology from the one I have outlined—and as it focuses on *Moby-Dick*.

47. Wai-chee Dimock, *Empire For Liberty: Melville and the Poetics of Individualism* (Princeton: Princeton University Press, 1989), 6.

48. It is important to note, however, that Dimock's work is particularly effective in both reversing and displacing a related and crucial binarism, namely, the binarism of "empire" and "liberty." In this respect, her account of how "Melville dramatizes the very juncture where the logic of freedom dovetails with the logic of empire, or (which is the same thing) where the imperial self of Jacksonian individualism recapitulates the logic of Jacksonian imperialism" is extremely valuable. Ibid., 10, but see also 7–11.

49. Ibid., 7.

50. The main point of reference in Nietzsche for the concept of the untimely is the second of his *Untimely Meditations*. For the interpretation of the untimely outlined above, I draw above all from Deleuze and Guattari's *What Is Philosophy?*, see especially 110–13 and 96, and to a lesser degree also from Deleuze's *Nietzsche and Philosophy*, 138–41 and from Foucault's famous essay "Nietzsche, Genealogy, History," in *Aesthetics, Method, and Epistemology: Essential Works of Foucault 1954–1984, Volume 2*, trans. Donald F. Brouchard and Sherry Simon, amended by Robert Hurley (New York: The New Press, 1998), 369–91.

51. The concept of the synchronicity of the non-synchronous, which I discuss in more detail with regards to *White-Jacket* in chapter 2, is found in Bloch's "Non-Synchronism and the Obligation to its Dialectics," *New German Critique* 11 (1977), originally written in 1932.

52. For such an immanentist interpretation of the Leibnizian concept of incompossibility, see Deleuze's *The Fold: Leibniz and the Baroque*, trans. Tom Conley (Minneapolis: University of Minnesota Press, 1993), 59–82 and especially 59–61 and 80–82. Let me also add here that this implicit leap is finally made explicit in the stunning appendix to *The Coming Community*, which has provided me with the filter through which I read the passage quoted above. See Agamben, *The Coming Community*, 89–106 and in particular 90, 92, and 102.

The Sea of Modernity

1. Hardt and Negri, *Labor of Dionysus*, 283–84. See also Hardt and Negri's *Empire* (Cambridge, Mass.: Harvard University Press, 2000), especially 69–83.

2. Benjamin, "Theses on the Philosophy of History," 257.

3. The literature on the question of the emergence of modern capitalism is vast. See at the very least, Karl Marx's *Grundrisse*, trans. Martin Nicolaus (London:

Penguin Books and *New Left Review*, 1974), especially 459–514, *Capital, Volume I*, trans. Ben Fowkes (New York: Vintage Books, 1977), especially 873–940; Paul Sweezy's *The Theory of Capitalist Development* (New York: Monthly Review Press, 1942); Karl Polanyi's *The Great Transformation* (Boston: Beacon Press, 2001); Maurice Dobb's *Studies in the Development of Capitalism* (New York: International Publishers, 1964); the critical exchanges collected in *The Transition from Feudalism to Capitalism*, ed. Rodney Hilton (London: Verso, 1976); Ferdinand Braudel's *Capitalism and Material Life 1400–1800* (New York: Harper Collins, 1973); Eric J. Hobsbawm's *Industry and Empire* (London: Penguin Books, 1990), especially 23–108; Immanuel Wallerstein's *The Modern World System* (New York: Academic Press, 1997); Étienne Balibar's "From Periodization to the Mode of Production" and "Elements for a Theory of Transition," in Louis Althusser and Balibar's *Reading Capital*, trans. Ben Brewster (London: Verso, 1997), 209–24 and 273–308; Deleuze and Guattari's "1227: Treatise on Nomadology—The War Machine" and "7000 B.C.: Apparatus of Capture," in *A Thousand Plateaus*, 351–473 and especially 452–53.

4. See Hobsbawm's *Industry and Empire*, especially 106–7, 227, and 231–33.

5. See Hobsbawm's *The Age of Empire: 1875–1914* (New York: Vintage, 1989) 50–51, but see also 350. For the merchant marine as an index of economic power in eighteenth-century Great Britain, see Hobsbawm's *Industry and Empire*, 24–25.

6. The shift from the share system—which had dominated ancient and medieval shipping and which allotted seamen with a proportional share of the profit—to the wage system occurred during the sixteenth century as part of a wider shift in property law. See Marcus Rediker's wonderful study *Between the Devil and the Deep Blue Sea: Merchant Seamen, Pirates, and the Anglo-American Maritime World, 1700–1750* (Cambridge: Cambridge University Press, 1987), 78–79, 116–52—especially 118—and 289–91.

7. See Rediker's *Between the Devil and the Deep Blue Sea*, 294 and 297. But see also Paul Gilroy's immensely productive formulation of the Black Atlantic as a trans-cultural and international zone of political contestation among America, Europe, West Africa, and the Caribbean that emerged in the wake of the slave experience, that continues to persist in our time, and that has left an indelible mark on—and, indeed, that has been crucially constitutive of—the cultures of modernity. Paul Gilroy, *The Black Atlantic: Modernity and Double Consciousness* (Cambridge, Mass.: Harvard University Press, 1993), especially 15–19.

8. "Nonsynchronism and the Obligation to Its Dialectics," *New German Critique* 11 (1977); originally published in 1932.

9. Quoted in Paul Gilroy's *The Black Atlantic*, 1. Indeed, it is precisely because of this "double consciousness" that Gilroy—in the wake of C. L. R. James and W. E. B. Du Bois, among the others—argues that blacks were "the first truly modern people, handling in the nineteenth century dilemmas and difficulties which would only become the substance of everyday life in Europe a century later." *The Black Atlantic*, 221. Clearly, I am making a similar and parallel argument with regards to the anticipatory and indeed prophetic conception of modernity as crisis that the sea narrative produced in the nineteenth century.

10. On this proliferation, see at the very least Thomas Philbrick's *James Fenimore Cooper and the Development of American Sea Fiction* (Cambridge, Mass.: Harvard University Press, 1961) and Bert Bender's *Sea-Brothers: The Tradition of American Sea Fiction from Moby-Dick to the Present* (Philadelphia: University of Pennsylvania Press, 1988.)

11. The interference between the pictorial and the literary representations of the sea in the nineteenth century was considerable. For the influence of the visual arts on Melville, see Stuart M. Frank's *Herman Melville's Picture Gallery: Sources and Types of the "Pictorial" Chapters of Moby-Dick* (Fairhaven, Mass.: Edward J. Lefcowicz, Inc., 1986) as well as the collection *Savage Eye: Melville and the Visual Arts*, ed. Christopher Sten (Kent, Ohio: Kent State University Press, 1991). For Melville's influence on the visual arts in the twentieth century, see at least Sam Francis's paintings. The relations between Conrad and Impressionism are just as rich.

12. On the privileged relations that the *Bildungsroman* had to the question of modernity, see Franco Moretti's important study *Il romanzo di formazione: Goethe e Stendhal, Puskin e Balzac, Dickens e Flaubert: La gioventù come forma simbolica della modernità nella narrativa europea* (Milan: Garzanti, 1986) as well as, of course, Georg Lukács's *The Theory of the Novel: A Historico-Philosophical Essay on the Forms of Great Epic Literature*, trans. Anna Bostock (Cambridge, MA: The MIT Press, 1971).

13. Michel Foucault, "Of Other Spaces," trans. Jay Miskowiec, *Diacritics*, 16 (spring 1986): 22–27. See also the "Preface" to *The Order of Things: An Archaeology of the Human Sciences* (New York: Vintage Books, 1994), xviii.

14. Foucault, "Of Other Spaces," 24.

15. Ibid.

16. See above all Edward Soja's *Postmodern Geographies: The Reassertion of Space in Critical Social Theory* (London: Verso, 1989) and "Heterotopologies: A Remembrance of Other Spaces in Citadel–LA, *Strategies* 3 (1990): 6–39; but see also Georges Teyssot's "Heterotopias and the History of Spaces," *Architecture & Urbanism* 121 (1980): 79–100, Edward Relph's "Post-Modern Geographies,"

Canadian Geographer 35 (1991): 98–105, as well as Derek Gregory's *Geographical Imaginations* (Oxford: Blackwell, 1994). Fredric Jameson's concept of cognitive mapping is in some ways also related to the form of spatial representation Foucault sketches here; see Jameson's *Postmodernism; or, The Cultural Logic of Late Capitalism* (Durham, N.C.: Duke University Press, 1991), 1–54 and especially 50–54.

17. Foucault, "Of Other Spaces," 24–26.

18. Ibid., 27.

19. Deleuze, *Foucault*, 96–97.

20. Deleuze, *Cinema 2*, 72, but see also 68–74.

21. Foucault, *The Order of Things*, xviii.

1. Of Monads and Fragments

1. Joseph Conrad, *The Nigger of the "Narcissus"* (Harmondsworth, England: Penguin Books Ltd., 1987, first published 1897), 21.

2. Ibid.

3. Joseph Conrad, *Heart of Darkness* (Harmondsworth, England: Penguin Books Ltd., 1985, first published 1902), 41.

4. Ibid., 31–32.

5. Ibid., 57.

6. Conrad, *The Nigger of the "Narcissus"*, 120.

7. Ibid., 120–21.

8. Foucault, "Of Other Spaces," 27.

9. Herman Melville, *White-Jacket; or, The World in a Man-of-War* (Evanston: Northwestern and Newberry, 1970, first published 1850), 23.

10. For a reading of the ship as metaphor of the world in *White-Jacket*, see also F. O. Matthiessen's *American Renaissance: Art and Expression in the Age of Emerson and Whitman* (London: Oxford University Press, 1941), 402–8.

11. Melville, *White-Jacket*, 226.

12. Ibid., 210–12. For the question of the exotic picaresque, see the third section of the introduction.

13. Ibid., 396.

14. Ibid., 115.

15. Ibid., 10.

16. Ibid., 7.

17. Ibid., 11.

18. A. R. Humphrey's discussion of Melville's debt to Tobias Smollett's works supports my suggestion that it is the historically specific Scotchman of the clearances and of early industrialization to whom Melville is referring here: "[Smollett's] *Roderick Random* seems to prompt many a touch...like the 'Sawney stare' of the callow Scot in London (p. 12) [which seems] to echo the taunts of 'Sawney' which greet Roderick and Strap in the capital (Melville deleted the words 'in King James's time', which appear in the London edition, perhaps reflecting that he had later Scots in mind.)" See Humphrey's "Introduction" to the 1966 Oxford University Press edition of *White-Jacket*, xvi.

19. Melville, *White-Jacket*, 35.

20. Ibid., 46.

21. Ibid., see especially 283–84, 175 and 383, 160, 90–91, 155, 252–64 and 325–31.

22. Ibid., 110, 336, 339, 361, respectively.

23. Ibid., 74–75.

24. Michel de Certeau, *The Practice of Everyday Life*, trans. Steven Rendall (Berkeley: University of California Press, 1988), 130.

25. This historical hypothesis on paradigms of sexuality, as well as some of the following speculations, owe their primary inspiration to Foucault's seminal *The History of Sexuality. Volume I: an introduction* (New York: Pantheon, 1978) and to Eve Kosofsky Sedgwick's theses in *Epistemology of the Closet* (Berkeley: University of California Press, 1990), see especially "Introduction: Axiomatic," 1–63.

26. For readings of *Billy Budd*'s intricate networks of power and sexuality, one should turn to—among others—W. H. Auden's *The Enchaféd Flood: Three Critical Essays on the Romantic Spirit* (New York: Vintage Books, 1950), 141–46; F. O. Matthiessen's *American Renaissance*, 500–14; George-Michel Sarotte's *Like a Brother, Like a Lover: Male Homosexuality in the American Novel and Theater from Herman Melville to James Baldwin* (New York: Doubleday-Anchor, 1978); Robert K. Martin's *Hero, Captain, and Stranger: Male Friendship, Social Critique, and Literary Form in the Sea Novels of Herman Melville* (Chapel Hill: University of North Carolina Press, 1986), 107–24; James Creech's *Closet Writing/Gay Reading: The Case of Melville's "Pierre"*, especially 7–19; and Sedgwick's *Epistemology of the Closet*, 91–130. The reference to the deployment of "male-male desire" as the "glue" and/or "solvent" of order aboard *Billy Budd*'s ship is from *Epistemology of the Closet*, 94.

27. Melville, *White-Jacket*, 375–76.

28. Herman Melville, *Clarel: A Poem and Pilgrimage in the Holy Land* (Chicago: Northwestern University Press and The Newberry Library, 1991), 2: 36; 96 and 44 respectively.

29. Melville, *Clarel*.

30. Melville, *Clarel*, 2: 35; 7, 8, 11, 15, and 14 respectively.

31. Melville, *Clarel*, 2: 35; 11 and 12 respectively.

32. Melville, *Clarel*.

33. I was alerted to the particular Piranesi images to which Melville refers in canto 35—he never actually mentions the title of these "rarer prints"—by the "Discussions" included in the "Editorial Appendix" to *Clarel*, coauthored by Walter E. Bezanson, Harrison Hayford, Alma A. MacDougall and G. Thomas Tanselle, 789–91.

2. In the Nick of Time

1. Melville, *White-Jacket*, 282. This is the opening of chapter 68 "A Man-of-war Fountain, and other Things."

2. See especially chapters such as "Flogging," "Some of the evil Effects of Flogging," "Flogging not lawful," "Flogging not necessary," 138–58, but also "Monthly Muster round the Capstan," "The Genealogy of the Articles of War," "Herein are the good Ordinances of the Sea...," 305–19. For the relations between *White-Jacket* and contemporaneous discourse on naval discipline, see Charles Roberts Anderson's *Melville in the South Seas* (New York: Dover, 1966), 431, John Samson's *White Lies: Melville's Narratives of Facts* (Ithaca, N.Y.: Cornell University Press, 1989), 133–48, as well as Christopher Sten's *The Weaver-God, He Weaves: Melville and the Poetics of the Novel* (Kent, Ohio: The Kent State University Press, 1996), 115–33. For the relations between the question of flogging in *White-Jacket* and the question of slavery, see Samuel Otter's *Melville's Anatomies* (Berkeley: University of California Press, 1999), 50–100, and especially 50–58 and 77–96, as well as David Suchoff's *Critical Theory and the Novel: Mass Society and Cultural Criticism in Dickens, Melville, and Kafka* (Madison: The University of Wisconsin Press, 1994), 99–108.

3. Edgar Allan Poe, *The Complete Tales and Poems* (New York: The Modern Library, 1938), 118.

4. An epiphany reveals to the narrator that the ship is on a voyage of discovery and that its quest is the South Pole. See Poe, *The Complete Tales and Poems*, 123–26.

5. Ibid.

6. Jacques Derrida, "Freud and the Scene of Writing" in *Writing and Difference* (Chicago: The University of Chicago Press, 1978), 230.

7. See Sigmund Freud's "A Note upon the Mystic Writing Pad" in *General Psychological Theory*, trans. Philip Rieff (New York: Collier Books Macmillan, 1963), 207–12 and Derrida's "Freud and the Scene of Writing" in *Writing and Difference*, especially 221–31.

8. Benjamin, "Theses on the Philosophy of History," in *Illuminations*, 254.

9. Melville, *White-Jacket*. This is the final paragraph of the chapter "The Manning of Navies" which deals predominantly with the iniquities of impressment in the English Navy and with other similar American practices, 385.

10. See the first chapter "The Jacket," but also chapter 60, "Of the Pockets that were in the Jacket," chapter 19, "The Jacket aloft," chapter 25 "The Dog-days off Cape Horn," chapter 92, "The Last of the Jacket," etc.

11. Melville, *White-Jacket*, 282–86.

12. Ibid., 282.

13. See F. O. Matthiessen on *White-Jacket* in his *American Renaissance: Art and Expression in the Age of Emerson and Whitman*, 409.

14. See *The Oxford English Dictionary*, 2nd ed., v.14, under "scuttle-butt."

15. See particularly the opening of chapter 91 "Smoking-club in a Man-of-war, with Scenes on the Gun-deck, Drawing near Home," 386–87.

16. Walter Benjamin, "The Storyteller. Reflections on the Works of Nikolai Leskov," in *Illuminations*, 84–85.

17. Melville, *White-Jacket*, 79.

18. In a chapter titled "Towards an Industrial World," in *The Age of Revolution: 1789–1848*, Eric Hobsbawm argues that already in the 1830s it "was reasonably certain that the USA would eventually be considered … a serious competitor to the British," whose economy was "effectively industrialized by 1848," and, furthermore, that no "economy expanded more rapidly in this period [1830s and 1840s] than the American" (New York: New American Library, 1962) 204 and 214. See also Bernard Bailyn, *The Great Republic: A History of the American People* (Lexington, Mass.: D. C. Heath, 1992), 1, 425–565, and John M. Blum, *The National Experience: A History of the United States to 1877*, 4th ed. (New York: Harcourt Brace Jovanovich, 1973), 187–91 and 197–201.

19. For a full discussion of boredom as a condition of possibility for storytelling, see Benjamin in "The Storyteller," 91.

20. About such tales Wai-chee Dimock remarks: "The very presence of those battle scenes is something of an incongruity, because the *Neversink* [the ship aboard which *White-Jacket* takes place] never engages in any actual combat, and properly speaking has no war stories of its own. Battle scenes have to be imported as 'told stories,' recollections by war veterans, or simply fantasies." See Wai-chee Dimock's *Empire For Liberty*, 104–5.

21. Benjamin, "The Storyteller," 87.

22. Melville, *White-Jacket*, 283.

23. Nathaniel Hawthorne, "A Rill from the Town Pump," in *Twice-Told Tales* (Boston and New York: Houghton Mifflin Co., 1882), 165–72.

24. See George Parsons Lathrop's "Introductory Note" to the *Twice-Told Tales*, 9.

25. From Hawthorne's 1851 "Preface" to the *Twice-Told Tales*, which were written during the 1830s. Ibid., 16–17.

26. Benjamin, "The Storyteller," 87.

27. Even though here I am anticipating issues whose intense urgency and impact are not yet fully registered in the text of *White-Jacket*, it is clear from Melville's letters that such issues (as, for example, the impossibility of finding a public for the kind of writing he desired most to develop) were already prominent concerns of his before and during the writing of *White-Jacket*.

28. The reference to Valéry is in Benjamin's "The Storyteller," 93. I take Valéry and Benjamin to mean that time, of course, always mattered, but very differently — and I will touch on that difference shortly.

29. Benjamin, "The Storyteller," 87.

30. Several of the conceptual shortcuts I am taking here owe much to E. P. Thompson's seminal theorization of the emergence of a specifically industrial-capitalist temporal ethics — which conceives of time as a currency with immanent value to be spent, bought, and, above all, never wasted — as opposed to the temporal structures, organized around tasks and cycles, constitutive of those earlier — pastoral, agricultural, and artisanal — formations which were the repositories of the traditions of storytelling. See E. P. Thompson's "Time, Work-Discipline and Industrial Capitalism," in *Customs in Common* (New York: The New Press, 1991), 352–403.

31. Herman Melville, *Moby-Dick* (Evanston: Northwestern and Newberry, 1988), 572.

32. Benjamin, "Theses on the Philosophy of History," 257.

33. This is also the time that Perry Anderson reconfigures as that "homogeneous historical time" of theories of modernization which is the very "temporality of the market and of the commodities that circulate across it." See his "Modernity and Revolution" in *Marxism and the Interpretation of Culture* (Urbana and Chicago: University of Illinois Press, 1988), especially 321–22. For Benjamin's thoughts on the time of historicism as opposed to the time of historical materialism one can turn in particular to theses VII, XIV, XVI—XVIII in "Theses on the Philosophy of History," 256–57 and 261–64.

3. White Capital

1. References to imminent crisis abound throughout Marx's writings in volumes 11 to 13 of Karl Marx's and Frederick Engels's *Collected Works* (New York: International Publishers), which span from 1851 to 1855. See especially "Political Consequences of the Commercial Excitement," *Collected Works, Vol. 11*, 364–68; "The Crisis in Trade and Industry," *Collected Works, Vol. 13*, 571–78; and "The Commercial Crisis in Britain," *Collected Works, Vol. 13*, 585–89. Marx wrote for the *New-York Daily Tribune* from 1852 to 1861. For more information on Marx's journalistic writing about the United States, see Saul K. Padover's "Introduction" to *The Karl Marx Library, On America and the Civil War, Vol. 2* (New York: McGraw-Hill Book Company, 1972), xi–xxxi.

2. Marx and Engels, *Collected Works, Vol. 11*, 362–63.

3. Eric Hobsbawm points out that this "was probably the first world slump of the modern type." For an analysis of the 1857 financial crisis as the first of its kind, see Hobsbawm's *The Age of Capital: 1848–1875* (New York: Penguin Books, 1986), 69–70.

4. Antonio Negri, *Marx beyond Marx: Lessons on the Grundrisse*, trans. Harry Cleaver, Michael Ryan, Maurizio Viano (Brooklyn, N.Y.: Autonomedia, 1991), 12.

5. Negri, *Marx beyond Marx*, 1–2.

6. On this point, see Negri, *Marx beyond Marx*, 16.

7. Negri, *Marx beyond Marx*, 12 and 18; but see also the whole first chapter ("The Grundrisse, an Open Work"), 1–19.

8. Melville, *Moby-Dick*, 256.

9. Ibid., 457.

10. Ibid., 346. An entire chapter—"The Prairie"—is spent in the futile attempt to describe the whale's face; see, 345–47.

11. Ibid., 566.

12. "To scan the lines of his face, or feel the bumps on the head of this Leviathan; this is a thing which no Physiognomist or Phrenologist has as yet undertaken. Such an enterprise would seem almost as hopeful as for Lavater to have scrutinized the wrinkles on the Rock of Gibraltar." Ibid., 345.

13. Ibid., 243.

14. From the chapter on "Cetology." Ibid., 136 and 145, respectively.

15. Adorno, *Minima Moralia*, 50.

16. Cited in Hershel Parker's "Historical Note" to *Redburn* (Chicago: Northwestern University Press, 1969), 321.

17. Ibid., 322.

18. Ibid., 323.

19. On the question of mixed narrative forms in *Moby-Dick*, see Sheila Post-Lauria's *Correspondent Colorings: Melville in the Marketplace* (Amherst: The University of Massachusetts Press, 1996), 101–22.

20. Quoted in Edwin Haviland Miller's *Melville* (New York: George Braziller, 1975), 185.

21. Ibid.

22. Benjamin, "Theses on the Philosophy of History," 257.

23. After the sinking of the *Pequod*, and on the last page of the novel, one learns that Ishmael had been "floating on the margin of the ensuing scene, and in full sight of it."

24. One ought to bear in mind that the 1857 crisis also marked the crucial watershed in the history of United States whaling. On this question, see J. T. Jenkins's *A History of the Whale Fisheries* (Port Washington, N.Y.: Kennikat Press, 1971), 235–36. I will return to this matter.

25. To my knowledge, only Charles Olson has hinted at the fact that *Moby-Dick* was being finished while Marx was writing for the *New-York Daily Tribune*. See Olson's *Call Me Ishmael* (Baltimore: The Johns Hopkins University Press, 1997), 24.

26. Melville, *Moby-Dick*, 64.

27. To say that *Moby-Dick* is not an epic is not to overlook Melville's ventriloquism of the plethora of expansionist and imperialist discourses of antebellum United States in rhetorical flights such as the ones quoted above—and one does come across even higher degrees of chauvinism in Melville (see especially *White-Jacket*, 150–51). I have taken up these questions in an essay titled "Empire of the Limitless" that begins precisely from this passage in *Moby-Dick* and that constitutes the beginning of a future project. For the moment, I refer the reader to Wai-chee Dimock's very persuasive reconstruction of Melville's troubled and essential involvement with such emergent imperialist discourses in *Empire for Liberty*, see especially 3–41.

28. Melville, *Moby-Dick*, 7.

29. Melville has a peculiar sense of humor. Nowhere must one take Melville more seriously than when he is at his most frivolous and lighthearted, than when he thinks he is being funny. What is most endearing about such moments in Melville is the fact that he systematically fails to be funny: one is usually left with a polite and sad smile as when faced by a well-meaning but nonetheless hapless and awkward attempt at humor. The sadness here has to do with having sensed within such an attempt a tremulous note of apprehensiveness and expectation, a desperate desire to openly manifest something that—precisely because it is too dear and important to be laughed at and not to be taken seriously—can be revealed only as a humorous aside, can be told only hurriedly (in the way in which dangerous truths are uttered) and can be disclosed only as something not meant to be taken seriously at all (so that the reader's inevitable laughter or amusement will have been less caustic, as it had been coated in advance by Melville himself with a patina of legitimation and propriety.) Humor in Melville is at once confession, apology, and disclaimer.

30. Edgar Allan Poe, *The Narrative of Arthur Gordon Pym of Nantucket* (New York: Penguin Books, first published in 1836), 57.

31. Melville, *Moby-Dick*, 7.

32. Ibid., 105.

33. Ibid., 70.

34. Ibid., 69.

35. See also Wai-chee Dimock's excellent discussion of this passage and of the question of fated narrative in *Moby-Dick* in *Empire For Liberty*, 109–39, but see especially 115–18. Dimock here argues that Ahab is constructed as the self-willed victim of *Moby-Dick*'s fated narrative, and that such a construction is enabled by the rhetoric proliferated about Native Americans at the time. I will return to this convincing argument. For the moment, I wish to focus instead on the construction of the practice of whaling—rather than on Ahab—as the victim of self-willed "extinction."

36. Melville, *Moby-Dick*, 456.

37. See specifically chapters 53 ("The Gam"), 60 ("The Line"), 62 ("The Dart"), 63 ("The Crotch"), 67 ("Cutting in"), 72 ("The Monkey-Rope"), 84 ("Pitch-poling"), 89 ("Fast-fish and Loose-fish"), 94 ("A Squeeze of the Hand"), 96 ("The Try-Works"), 98 ("Stowing Down and Clearing Up"), 107 ("The Carpenter"), as well as many other instances of description and explanation of the nitty-gritty of whaling activities and equipment that occupy the better part of numerous other chapters.

38. Melville, *Moby-Dick*, 278.

39. Ibid., 395.

40. Ibid., 289.

41. The specific danger lurking in the whale-line consists in the fact that at one end it is attached to the harpoon while the rest lies in the boat, enfolding the latter "in its complicated coils, twisting and writhing around it in almost every direction"; often, once the harpoon is fastened to the whale and once the whale starts to escape at high speed, one (or more) among the boat's oarsmen may get caught in the whale-line shooting outward with the harpoon and is thus strangled or drowned. This, of course, is Ahab's final fate. Ibid., 280–81.

42. See Jenkins, *A History of the Whale Fisheries*, 234; but see also Elmo Paul Hohman's *The American Whaleman* (New York: Longmans, Green and Co., 1928), 41 and 289–90.

43. See Jenkins, *A History of the Whale Fishery*, 234–43 and Hohman, *The American Whaleman*, 289–301.

44. Melville, *Moby-Dick*, 162.

45. Marx, *Grundrisse*, 196–97.

46. Melville, *Moby-Dick*, 7.

47. Ibid., 164–66.

48. Ibid., 549–51.

49. Marx, *Grundrisse*, 197; but see also the rest of the page and the following one.

50. Dimock, *Empire for Liberty*, 120, but also 117–24.

51. C. L. R. James, *Mariners, Renegades and Castaways: The Story of Herman Melville and the World We Live In* (London: Allison & Busby, 1985), especially 11–13.

52. Marx, *Grundrisse*, 115–256. For a brilliant discussion of the importance of the question of money in the *Grundrisse* and in Marx's work as a whole, see Negri's analysis in *Marx beyond Marx*, 21–40, to which I shall return.

53. Marx, *Grundrisse*, 229.

54. Ibid., 221.

55. Ibid., 197–98.

56. Ibid., 197.

57. Ibid., 211–12.

58. Melville, *Moby-Dick*, 195. A whole of chapter in *Moby-Dick* ("The Whiteness of the Whale") is spent discussing the matter of whiteness, 188–95.

59. "The epitome of all things." Marx, *Grundrisse*, 218. Marx borrows this definition of money from the seventeenth-century French economist Pierre le Pesant Boisguillebert. See the latter's *Dissertation sur la nature des richesses, de l'argent, et des tributs*, 399.

60. Marx, *Grundrisse*, 218.

61. Friedrich Nietzsche, *Beyond Good and Evil* (New York: Random House, 1966), 89.

62. See among others, Charles Feidelson's seminal *Symbolism and American Literature* (Chicago: University of Chicago Press, 1953), especially 30–31 and 243; Paul Brodtkorb's *Ishmael's White World* (New Haven: Yale

University Press, 1965), especially 115–19; Harold Beaver's "Introduction" to *Moby-Dick* (New York: Penguin, 1986), especially 27; Leon Seltzer's *The Vision of Melville and Conrad: A Comparative Study* (Athens, OH: Ohio University Press, 1970), 55–56; Bryan Short's *Cast By Means of Figures: Herman Melville's Rhetorical Development* (Amherst: The University of Massachusetts Press, 1992), 104–8; Bainard Cowan's *Exiled Waters: Moby-Dick and the Crisis of Allegory* (Baton Rouge: Louisiana State University Press).

63. For a decidedly nonhumanist reading of the question of whiteness in *Moby-Dick*, see Spanos's *The Errant Art of Moby-Dick*, 269–70, although at the very least 140–45 are also relevant to my discussion.

64. Negri, *Marx beyond Marx*, 24. I could not synthesize better than Negri how intimately money and value are related in the *Grundrisse* when he writes: "*the route leads immediately from money to value:* value is presented there under the form of money. Value is thus the same shit as money.... In addition we are not before value; we are in it: we are in that world made of money. Money represents the form of social relations; it represents, sanctions, and organizes them. Perhaps this immediacy of the approach, not to value, but to value under the form of money, as if money exhausted all possible value, is too naive? Yet the world represents itself thus, a world of commodities which money represents completely, determining, through itself the valorization of commodities.... Money has the advantage of presenting me immediately the lurid face of the social relation of value; it shows me value right away as exchange, commanded and organized for exploitation...money has only one face, that of the boss." Ibid., 23.

65. Marx, *Grundrisse*, 228.

66. Negri, *Marx beyond Marx*, 35.

67. On this matter, see most importantly Toni Morrison, *Playing in the Dark: Whiteness and the Literary Imagination* (New York: Vintage Books, 1993). The last paragraph of page 59 is particularly relevant here.

68. Melville, *Moby-Dick*, 188–89.

69. Ibid., 159. The expression "Descartian vortices" is here used in a different context.

70. Guillory, *Cultural Capital*, 302 and 303. The whole chapter on "The Discourse of Value" is relevant to my discussion, 269–340.

71. Negri, *Marx beyond Marx*, 94. But see also the whole chapter "Profit, Crisis, Catastrophe," 85–104.

72. Ibid., 100.

73. Marx, *Grundrisse*, 407–8.

74. Negri, *Marx beyond Marx*, 105.

75. Marx, *Grundrisse*, 410. Deleuze and Guattari's understanding of capitalism derives to a great degree from the insights found in this passage; see, for example, *A Thousand Plateaus*, 463.

76. The last limit and the other limit are similar to Deleuze and Guattari's concepts of limit and threshold; see *A Thousand Plateaus*, 438–39.

77. Melville, *Moby-Dick*, 163–64.

78. Melville, after his public literary career was over, became a customs inspector in New York City from 1866 to 1885.

79. Maurice Blanchot, "The Song of the Sirens: Encountering the Imaginary" in *The Gaze of Orpheus*, trans. Lydia Davis (Barrytown, N.Y.: Station Hill, 1981), 111. Deleuze and Guattari write similarly of Ahab's metamorphosis when discussing his "irresistible becoming-whale"; see *A Thousand Plateaus*, 243–45. My account of Ahab's encounter with the white whale places its emphasis differently from both Blanchot's and Deleuze and Guattari's accounts. In the end there is no metamorphosis for Ahab, or none of which one can write: he just dies — even though he dies of a death useful to capital's own metamorphosis. The question for me, ultimately, is not to reconstruct what happens to Ahab in that encounter or what that encounter is to Ahab, but rather to understand what that encounter does to everybody and everything but Ahab.

80. Melville, *Moby-Dick*, 281. See also my discussion of this passage in the second section of the present chapter.

81. Marx, *Grundrisse*, 411.

82. Antonio Negri, "Twenty Theses on Marx: Interpretation of the Class Situation Today" in *Marxism beyond Marxism*, 167.

83. Melville, *Moby-Dick*, 202. See also Jonathan Arac's excellent discussion of this chapter in his "Narrative Forms" in *The Cambridge History of American Literature, Volume 2: 1820–1865*, ed. Sacvan Bercovitch (Cambridge: Cambridge University Press, 1995), 729–30.

84. Melville, *Moby-Dick*, 471.

85. See especially the chapter entitled "The Candles," 503–8. On this matter, see also C. L. R. James in *Mariners, Renegades and Castaways*, 16–17.

86. This is that autonomy from capital which Samir Amin calls "delinking" and which he advocates for the countries of what used to be called the Third World. Amin writes: "The concept of delinking is a simple one, the direct opposite of that of adjustment. Adjustment means that you adjust *yourself* to the global laws of capital expansion. The notion of delinking, by contrast, is that revolts against actually existing capitalism in the areas which have been victimized by global polarization have to take the form of a development which is relatively autonomous from the laws of the global expansion of capitalism. Delinking, in other words, implies that you submit your external relations with the dominating capitalist world to your needs for internal change." In this sense, the Third World still constitutes today one of the most turbulent stages for the sudden crystallizations of the exogenous and immanent other limit of capital — and both Melville and Marx had already sensed the emergence of such global redefinitions of dependence and autonomy. The former does so in his acute awareness of the international and multiracial constitution of the labor force upon which the whaling industry depends (see *Moby-Dick*, especially 120–21). The latter does so in his insistence that the "tendency to create the *world market* is directly given in the concept of capital itself" (*Grundrisse*, 408) and in his discovery that exchange — through which such a world market would be constructed — is by definition unequal exchange and that, thus, what circulates in capitalist circulation is crisis in its virtually indomitable state. Samir Amin, "The Growing Sophistication of Northern Control," *Socialist Review* 20 (1990), 22, cited in Kenneth Surin's " 'The Continued Relevance of Marxism' as a Question: Some Propositions" in *Marxism beyond Marxism*, 192–93.

87. For Ahab's unmistakable feelings about the bourgeoisie, see his contempt for "the accountants [who] have computed their great counting-house the globe, by girdling it with guineas, one to every three parts of an inch." Melville, *Moby-Dick*, 163.

88. Ibid., 480–81.

89. *Mariners, Renegades and Castaways*, 46.

90. The English word "absolute" derives from the Latin "*absolutus*," the past participle of the verb *absolvere*, namely, to free, to absolve.

91. This suggestion might seem to corroborate Leslie Fiedler's famous intuition that the "form of *eros*" most central to the American novel is a "love passing the love of women, which binds together in the New World wilderness a pair of males, one white, one nonwhite." What one is attempting to present here, however, could not be farther removed from the homophobia in which such a courageous intuition was nonetheless rooted: for Fiedler, in fact, it is the "failure of the American fictionist to deal with adult heterosexual love" that led him — for in this case it is definitely a "him" he has in mind — to an "obsession with death, incest and innocent homosexuality." One wonders whose failure it is to deal with what here, as well as what exactly a noninnocent homosexuality might be. Leslie Fiedler, *Love and Death in the American Novel* (New York: Anchor Books, 1992), 509 and 12 respectively.

92. Luce Irigaray, "Love Between Us," in *Who Comes After the Subject?*, ed. Eduardo Cadava, Peter Connor, and Jean-Luc Nancy (London: Routledge, 1991), 167.

93. Leo Bersani, *Homos* (Cambridge: Harvard University Press, 1995), 128.

94. Marx, *Grundrisse*, 295.

95. Ibid., 267.

96. Ibid., 282–83.

97. Ibid., 298.

98. Ibid., 295–96.

99. Ibid., 268–69.

100. Jean Baudrillard, "For a Critique of the Political Economy of the Sign," in *Selected Writings* (Stanford: Stanford University Press, 1988), 72–73, but see also 63–73.

101. On this point, see also Negri in *Marx beyond Marx*, 70.

102. Baudrillard, "For a Critique of the Political Economy of the Sign," 67.

103. Ibid., 71.

104. Baruch Spinoza, *The Ethics and Selected Letters* (Indianapolis: Hackett Publishing Company, 1982), 106, but see also all of Part III and IV, 103–201.

105. See my discussion of Melville's discovery of this same kind of temporality earlier in this chapter.

106. Marx, *Grundrisse*, 300.

107. Ibid., 266.

108. Ibid., 271–72.

109. Ibid., 296–97.

110. Negri, *Marx beyond Marx*, 70.

111. Melville, *Moby-Dick*, 15.

112. Ibid., 7

113. Ibid., 480.

114. Marx, *Grundrisse*, 266.

115. As soon as they rolled in, the sailors "made a straight wake for the whale's mouth — the bar — when the wrinkled little old Jonah, there officiating, soon poured them out brimmers all round . . . The liquor soon mounted into their heads, as it generally does even with the arrantest topers newly landed from sea, and they began capering about most obstreperously." Melville, *Moby-Dick*, 15.

116. Negri discovers these same dynamics in Marx; see *Marx beyond Marx*, 189. But see also the *Grundrisse*, 421.

117. Ishmael explains that Ahab, having revealed the real purpose of the voyage, had laid himself open to what would have been a legally defensible mutiny. Melville, *Moby-Dick*, 213.

118. Ibid., 167, but see also all of 160–66.

119. James, *Mariners, Renegades and Castaways*, 46.

120. Ibid., 30 and 46.

121. Ibid., 11–39.

122. An exception to so many critical discussions that do not adequately engage with the complex economics of power aboard the *Pequod* is Donald Pease's important reading of "The Quarter-deck" chapter, which he finds exemplary of what he calls the "scene of cultural persuasion." Even though this reading is still structured around Ahab as *subject* of persuasion and posits Starbuck (the first mate) and at most Ishmael as the objects of such a persuasion rather than the crew as such, Pease is able to use this crucial moment in the novel as a springboard for what has rightly become an influential theorization of the Cold War cultural politics that informs the canonization of *Moby-Dick* and in particular the most emblematic work of such a canonization, F. O. Matthiessen's *American Renaissance*. See Pease's *Visionary Compacts: American Renaissance Writings in Cultural Context* (Madison: University of Wisconsin Press, 1987), especially 236–40.

123. Melville, *Moby-Dick*, 179.

124. Ibid., 186.

125. See Postone's powerful study *Time, Labor, and Social Domination: A Reinterpretation of Marx's Critical Theory* (Cambridge: Cambridge University Press, 1993), 37, but see also 3–42.

126. James, *Mariners, Renegades and Castaways*, 49 and 54.

127. Melville, *Moby-Dick*, 186–87.

128. Ibid., 179–87.

129. Ibid., 184–86.

130. Ibid., 185–86.

131. Sigmund Freud, *Civilization and Its Discontents*, trans. James Strachey (New York: W. W. Norton & Co., 1961), 17, but see also 16–19.

132. Melville, *Moby-Dick*, 542–45.

133. See Deleuze and Guattari's arguments concerning an "exaggerated Oedipus" in *Kafka: Toward a Minor Literature*, trans. Dana Polan (Minneapolis: University of Minnesota Press, 1986), especially 9–10, but also 9–15. See also Charles Olson's compelling discussion of the question of paternity in the above passage and in the whole novel, *Call me Ishmael*, 81–85, as well as John Wenke's reading of this passage in terms of an ontology of Ahab in *Melville's Muse: Literary Creation and the Forms of Philosophical Fiction* (Kent, Ohio: The Kent State University Press, 1995), 134–36 and more generally pp. 131–46.

134. For some excellent remarks on the vicissitudes of this philosophical distinction as well as for a very interesting notion of abandon, see Paolo Virno's brilliant essay "The Ambivalence of Disenchantment," in *Radical Thought in Italy: A Potential Politics*, ed. Paolo Virno and Michael Hardt, trans. Michael Turits (Minneapolis: University of Minnesota Press, 1996), especially 28–33.

135. Giorgio Agamben, *Means without End*, trans. Vincenzo Binetti and Cesare Casarino (Minneapolis: University of Minnesota Press, 2000), 9–12.

136. It is also worth quoting from Agamben's definition of this concept: "By the term *form-of-life* . . . I mean a life which can never be separated from its form, a life in which it is never possible to isolate something such as naked life . . . A life which cannot be separated from its form is a life for which what is at stake in its way of living is living itself. What does this formulation mean? It defines a life — human life — in which the single ways, acts and processes of living are never simply *facts* but always and firstly *possibility* of life, always and firstly power *[potenza]*. Each behavior and each form of human living is never prescribed by a specific biological vocation nor is it assigned by whatever necessity; instead, no matter how customary, repeated and socially compulsory, it always retains the character of a possibility, that is, it always puts at stake living itself. That is why human beings — as beings of power *[potenza]* who can do or not do, succeed or fail, lose themselves or find themselves — are the only beings for whom happiness is always at stake in their living, the only beings whose life is irremediably and painfully assigned to happiness. But this immediately constitutes the form–of–life as political life." Agamben, *Means without End*, 3–4.

137. Melville, *Moby-Dick*, 1.

138. Ibid., 51.

139. Ibid., 507. See, however, the whole chapter and, in particular, 505–8.

140. Ibid., 507.

141. Ibid., 506.

142. Ibid., 423.

143. Gilles Deleuze and Félix Guattari, *Anti-Oedipus: Capitalism and Schizophrenia*, trans. Robert Hurley, Mark Seem, and Helen R. Lane (Minneapolis: University of Minnesota Press, 1983), 3–5.

144. Melville, *Moby-Dick*, 423.

145. Deleuze and Guattari, *Anti-Oedipus*, 5; but see also all of 5–7 as well as Gilles Deleuze and Claire Parnet's discussion of the use of the conjunction "and" in the English language and in Anglo-American thought in their essay "On the Superiority of Anglo-American Literature" in *Dialogues*, trans. Hugh Tomlinson and

Barbara Habberjam (New York: Columbia University Press, 1987), especially 56–59. The latter essay in particular is symptomatic of one of the main reasons why Deleuze and Guattari have repeatedly emerged in these pages as a philosophical point of reference: many of the crucial concepts in their thought, in fact, are directly derived from — or, at least, related to — Anglo-American literary practices. This is all to say that Deleuze and Guattari are not really being invoked here as a way of helping us understand what Melville had in any case already put forth eloquently enough but as a way also of insisting on the necessity of reading Melville's work not at all as the product of isolated genius but rather within a heretical tradition of materialist ontology in Western metaphysics. The indebted affinity of Deleuze's thought to Melville in particular should never be underestimated: over and beyond the numerous references to Melville that are to be found both in his works and in the ones he cowrote with Guattari, it should be remembered that one of the very finest critical texts on Melville is Deleuze's late essay "Bartleby; or, The Formula" in *Essays Critical and Clinical*, trans. Daniel W. Smith and Michael Greco (Minneapolis: University of Minnesota Press, 1997), 68–90.

146. Melville, *Moby-Dick*, 422.

147. Ibid., 423–24.

148. Ibid., 424–25.

149. Melville, *"Billy Budd, Sailor" and Other Stories* (New York: Penguin Books, 1986), 322–26. For a similar reading of this passage in *Moby-Dick*, see Caleb Crain's "Lovers of Human Flesh: Homosexuality and Cannibalism in Melville's Novels," *American Literature*, 66 (March 1994): 25–53, and especially 40.

150. Marx, *Grundrisse*, 269.

151. Ibid., 361.

152. Leo Bersani, "Incomparable America," in *The Culture of Redemption* (Cambridge: Harvard University Press, 1990), 146.

153. Bersani, "Incomparable America," 145–47.

154. For the full version of these arguments, see my essay — coauthored with Saree Makdisi and Rebecca Karl — "Marxism, Communism, and History: A Reintroduction" in *Marxism beyond Marxism*, 1–13, but see especially 3–5 and 12.

155. Bersani, *Homos*, 6–7 and 10.

156. Ibid., 128.

157. Melville, *Moby-Dick*, 105.

158. Ibid., 480, 319, 319–20, 343, 476, 227, respectively.

159. Ibid., 214.

160. Ibid., 214–15.

161. Ibid., 215.

162. Ibid., 320.

163. Arac, "Narrative Forms," 731; but see also the rest of his discussion of agency and individuality in *Moby-Dick*, 729–34.

164. Louis Althusser, "*Une philosophie pour le marxisme: 'La ligne de Démocrite'*" in *Sur la Philosophie*, my translation (Paris: Gallimard, 1994), 40–42. This interview took place in Paris during the winter of 1983–1984, and the interviewer was the Mexican philosopher Fernanda Navarro. See Althusser's preface, 27–28.

165. Marx, *Grundrisse*, 162.

166. Melville, *Moby-Dick*, 51.

167. Bersani, "Incomparable America," 146.

168. Melville, *Moby-Dick*, 54.

169. Ibid., 10.

170. Ibid., 14.

171. Ibid.

172. Ibid., 16.

173. Bersani, "Incomparable America," 146.

174. See the end paragraph of chapter 6, in which Ishmael sings the praises of New Bedford women's beauty. Melville, *Moby-Dick*, 33.

175. Ibid., 18; but see all of 16–26.

176. Ibid., 22.

177. Ibid., 23–24.

178. On the complex relations between the discourses of cannibalism and of same-sex desire, see Caleb Crain's "Lovers of Human Flesh: Homosexuality and Cannibalism in Melville's Novels" as well as Geoffrey Sanborn's *The Sign of the Cannibal: Melville and the Making of a Postcolonial Reader* (Durham, N.C.: Duke University Press, 1998), especially 138–41.

179. Melville, *Typee*, 200–5.

180. Melville, *Moby-Dick*, 56.

181. Ibid., 25.

182. Ibid., 50–52.

183. Ibid., 53–54.

184. In the first few pages of the "Epistemo-Critical Prologue" to *The Origin of German Tragic Drama*, we see Benjamin contending with two different forms of philosophical writing and thinking. Here, Benjamin laboriously yet unmistakably announces the main purpose of his work: to rescue the philosophical form of the treatise from historical oblivion and to uphold it against that other philosophical form that was perfected in and that has become dominant since the nineteenth century, namely, the "system." For Benjamin, the latter "weaves a spider's web between separate kinds of knowledge in an attempt to ensnare the truth as if it were something that came flying in from the outside" and hence constitutes no more than "a guide to the acquisition of knowledge." "Knowledge"—Benjamin tersely asserts—"is possession. Its very object is determined by the fact that it must be taken possession of—even if in a transcendental sense—in the consciousness." In sharp contrast to the ultimately reifying relation that the philosophical system establishes between knowledge and truth, the philosophical treatise strives towards "the representation of truth." Benjamin further elaborates: "In the canonic form of the treatise the only element of an intention—and it is an educative rather than a didactic intention—is the authoritative quotation. Its method is essentially representation. Method is digression. Representation as digression—such is the methodological nature of the treatise. The absence of an uninterrupted purposeful structure is its primary characteristic. Tirelessly the process of thinking makes new beginnings, returning in a roundabout way to its original object." I quote these reflections as my hubristic confession of what it is that I have been trying to do in much of the present project. On these matters, see also my preface to this book. Walter Benjamin, *The Origin of German Tragic Drama*, trans. John Osborne (London: Verso, 1985), 27–29.

185. Agamben, *The Coming Community*, 23–25. Translation slightly modified. The English word "ease" and the Italian word *"agio"* both originate from the Provençal *aizi*. For a more detailed discussion of the concept of "whatever singularity," see the first chapter of *The Coming Community*, 1–2.

186. For a trenchant critique of the conflation between political-legal and philosophical-aesthetic modes of representation as well as for a useful discussion of their relations in Marx, see Gayatri Chakravorty Spivak's "Can the Subaltern Speak?" (in *Marxism and the Interpretation of Culture*, ed. Cary Nelson and Lawrence Grossberg [Urbana: University of Illinois Press, 1988], 271–315). But see also Jameson's discussion of this problematic in the "Preface" to *The Political Unconscious*, 9–14, and, in particular, 13. Indeed, the latter could be thought of as a monumental elaboration of that problematic.

187. Ludwig Wittgenstein, *Tractatus Logico-Philosophicus*, trans. C. K. Ogden (London: Routledge, 1992), 189.

188. Bersani, "Incomparable America," 145–46.

189. Melville, *Moby-Dick*, p. 264.

190. For a discussion of such representations in *White-Jacket* and *Clarel*, see chapter 1.

191. Bersani, *Homos*, 113.

192. The chapter entitled "Wheelbarrow" contains several such moments. Melville, *Moby-Dick*, especially 58 and 60.

193. Ibid., 415–16.

194. Ibid., 25–26 as well as 51.

195. I am referring here to Freud's speculations on the "oceanic feeling" with which he opens *Civilization and Its Discontents*.

196. Monique Wittig, *The Lesbian Body*, trans. David Le Vay (Boston: Beacon Press, 1986), 89.

197. Bersani, "Incomparable America," 145.

198. Melville, *Moby-Dick*, 185. This passage was discussed earlier in this chapter.

199. Ibid., 416.

200. I therefore disagree with Sanborn's reading of the conclusion of this passage as Ishmael's acknowledgment that such pleasures of touch "could only be possible in heaven" and that such a pleasure "is in the end a solitary pleasure, in which the squeezer is left alone with his (or her) incommunicable sensations and sentiments." Sanborn, *The Sign of the Cannibal*, 137–38. The rest of Sanborn's reading and his insistence on the question of touch, however, is congruent with my arguments; see 135–38.

201. The question of the dialectical formation of sexuality will be taken up in more detail in the next chapter.

202. Michel Foucault, *The History of Sexuality; An Introduction. Volume One*, 157.

203. Foucault, *The History of Sexuality; An Introduction. Volume One* , 155–57.

204. Marx, *Grundrisse*, 284–85.

205. Ibid., 285. For the full argument regarding both forms of self-denial, see also all of 284–89.

206. Ibid., 286–87.

207. Negri, *Marx beyond Marx*, 71.

208. Ibid., 72.

209. Antonio Negri, *Pipe-Line. Lettere da Rebibbia*, my translation (Turin: Einaudi, 1983), 94–95. This volume collects twenty letters that Negri wrote to the same friend between 1981 and 1982 from Rome's Rebibbia prison, in which he recollects the salient chapters of his political and philosophical education from the 1950s to the 1980s. In the letter to which this postscript is added, Negri writes of the 1962 workers' revolts in Turin.

4. The Sublime of the Closet

1. Emily Dickinson, *The Complete Poems of Emily Dickinson*, ed. Thomas H. Johnson (Boston: Little Brown and Company, 1960), 302

2. Such I take to be the further implications of Eve Kosofsky Sedgwick's epoch-marking encounter with Michel Foucault's *History of Sexuality, Volume I* in her *Epistemology of the Closet*; see especially 1–22 and 67–73.

3. Whether in Dickinson's poem the "Closet" of "Prose" is coextensive with the closet of same-sex desire is not strictly relevant to the present discussion. I am placing this poem here as a heuristic cluster of conceptual figures for the ensuing investigation of the closet in Conrad, and hence these passing remarks are by no means meant as a sustained engagement with the poem itself.

4. For similar arguments, see Bersani, *Homos*, in particular 11–12.

5. See Judith Butler's 1999 preface to the tenth anniversary edition of *Gender Trouble* (New York: Routledge, 1999), xxvi.

6. I am referring here to formulations such as the ones found in Butler's "Imitation and Gender Insubordination," in *Inside/Out*, ed. Diana Fuss (New York: Routledge, 1991), 13–31 and especially 15–17, as well as *Bodies that Matter* (New York: Routledge, 1993), especially 226–30. For a critique of these positions, see Bersani, *Homos*, 48–51.

7. For her positions on parody and subversion, see the whole third section as well as the conclusion of *Gender Trouble*, 101–90. For further clarifications of such positions, see *Bodies that Matter*, 223–42 as well as her aforementioned 1999 preface to *Gender Trouble*, especially xxii–xxiv. For her positions with respect to the question of the dialectic, see *Subjects of Desire* (New York: Columbia University Press, 1987), 183–84.

8. Theodor Adorno, *Negative Dialectics* (New York: Continuum, 1973), especially 11–15 and 138–43. See also Fredric Jameson's brilliant recuperation of Adorno for the postmodern moment in his *Late Marxism: Adorno, or, The Persistence of the Dialectic* (London: Verso, 1990), especially 25–34.

9. Sedgwick, *Epistemology of the Closet*, 1.

10. Deleuze and Guattari, *What Is Philosophy?*, 99–100.

11. Adorno, *Negative Dialectics*, 207.

12. Here, I borrow loosely from Georges Bataille's formulations of a "*general economy*" — as opposed to a restricted one — which "*makes apparent that excesses of energy are produced, which, by definition, cannot be utilized*" and which "*can only be lost without the slightest aim, consequently without any meaning,*" quoted in Arkady Plotnitsky's *In the Shadow of Hegel: Complementarity,*

History, and the Unconscious (Gainesville: University Press of Florida, 1993), 10, Bataille's emphasis; but see also Bataille's "The Notion of Expenditure" in *Visions of Excess*, 116–29. Much is at stake here in the past participles "utilized" and "lost," which ultimately face us with a false choice. Neither utilized nor lost, that excess of the dialectic that is the sublime of the closet unfolds in a realm of potentiality.

13. Roland Barthes, "The *Nautilus* and the Drunken Boat," in *Mythologies* (New York: Hill & Wang, 1983), 65–66.

14. Jules Verne, *20,000 Leagues under the Sea*, trans. Mendor T. Brunetti (New York: New American Library, 1981), 72.

15. Verne, *20,000 Leagues under the Sea*, 371.

16. Barthes says something to this effect several times throughout his essay. Barthes, "The *Nautilus* and the Drunken Boat," 65.

17. See Sedgwick, *Epistemology of the Closet*, especially 1–2 and 67–75.

18. Joseph Conrad, *The Secret Sharer*, in *Heart of Darkness and The Secret Sharer* (New York: New American Library, 1983; first published in 1910), 19. This is the opening passage of the short story.

19. Conrad, *Heart of Darkness* in *Heart of Darkness and The Secret Sharer*, see especially 66–69, 71, 102–5.

20. Conrad, *The Secret Sharer*, 20.

21. Ibid.

22. For the autobiographical aspects of *The Secret Sharer* — to which I will return — see Norman Sherry's *Conrad's Eastern World* (Cambridge: Cambridge University Press, 1966), 253–69.

23. Here and throughout the rest of this chapter — when reflecting on the relations between the history of modernity and the spatio-temporal and conceptual-affective constitution of enclosures — I have been much inspired by Saree Makdisi's excellent *Romantic Imperialism: Universal Empire and the Cultures of Modernity* (Cambridge: Cambridge University Press, 1998). See especially his detailed analysis of William Wordsworth's "spot of time," which bears an uncanny and uncoincidental resemblance to Conrad's breathtaking enclosures in *The Secret Sharer*. Makdisi, *Romantic Imperialism*, 23–44 and in particular 42–44.

24. Conrad, *The Secret Sharer*, 23.

25. Ibid., 23.

26. Ibid., 24.

27. In the critical literature on *The Secret Sharer*, this predicament is often construed in terms of divided allegiance: in between Leggatt and the ship, the narrator is seen as being torn by irreconcilable allegiances to, on the one hand, the world of community (namely, the ship, its men, its laws, etc.) and, on the other, the world of the individual (namely, Leggatt, his pride, his having taken the law into his own hands, etc.) See, most influentially, Albert J. Guerard's remarks in his *Conrad the Novelist* (Cambridge, Mass.: Harvard University Press, 1958), 23–24—remarks which are still echoed in as recent a study as Robert Hampson's *Joseph Conrad: Betrayal and Identity* (New York: St. Martin's Press, 1992), see especially 191–95. Much could be said about how it is indicative of a certain humanist ideology of individualism to conceive of community and of the individual in ways such that they must then inevitably be presented as antinomial to each other. It is precisely in the sharing of this ideology that Conrad and many of his critics become each other's secret sharers—with the crucial difference that Conrad is always ready to betray them by way of a linguistic excess capable of shattering such an ideology from the inside. Here, it suffices to say that the narrator in *The Secret Sharer* needs to be understood as being at once split and constituted not by mutually exclusive allegiances to community and to the individual but rather by allegiances to *two different communities*—the one incorporated in the ship and the one embodied in his bond with Leggatt—that is to say, two altogether different ways of conceptualizing and living the question of community.

28. And isn't that beautiful narrative fiction that goes by the name of etymology itself eminently a discourse of the closet—a discourse that images and probes words as if they were enclosures always filled with hidden signification, a discourse always on the verge of the paranoiac, as it must presuppose, detect, unveil, and denounce the secret lexical lives, histories, and desires of language? Hasn't this been all along a discourse and an economy of "outing"? And shouldn't we, therefore, rewrite the political history of philology intended as a discipline and as a disciplinarian regime regulating the production and circulation of the ultimate *etymon* of language—that is, regulating the production and circulation of the fantasy of an original historical atom of signification—whose identification and capture might also enable one to finally seize, determine, control, and mortgage the whole future life of language?

29. Eleanor Kaufman has taught me everything I know about the propriety of such most improper law of hospitality. See her *The Delirium of Praise: Bataille, Blanchot, Deleuze, Foucault, Klossowski* (Baltimore, Md.: Johns Hopkins University Press, 2001), especially the conclusion; but see also her "Klossowski; or, Thoughts-Becoming" in *Becomings: Explorations in Time, Memory, and Futures*, ed. Elizabeth Grosz (Ithaca, N.Y.: Cornell University Press, 1999), 141–57, and especially 143–45.

30. Conrad, *The Secret Sharer*, 23–24.

31. Ibid., 35.

32. The pronominal particle *se* in Latin is most commonly dependent on reflexive verbs or prepositions (in which cases it can be translated as "itself," "himself," "herself," "themselves," etc., according to the specific context) and is also often found in sentences with indefinite subjects (where it means "oneself" or "one") as well as in sentences expressing reciprocity (where it can be translated as "each other"). However, *se* is also a prefix that, when added to verbs, takes on the meaning of "apart," "aside" (see English cognates such as "to secede," "to seclude," etc). The Latin verb *fero, ferre*—derived from the ancient Greek verb *pherein*—also has a vast array of meanings such as "to carry," "to transport," "to take" (said often, but not exclusively, of ships or other vehicles), "to cause to go," and hence "to make one's way," "to proceed" (when it is used as a reflexive verb, often in sentences with *se*), "to have on or in it," "to contain," "to bring news of," "to convey meaning," "to relate," "to speak of," etc. The name *Sephora* seems to me to resonate with combinations of several of these different meanings of *se* and *fero*. An entirely different etymological investigation, however, may direct us to ancient Hebrew: *Sephar*, in fact, is the name of one of the boundaries of the territory of the sons of Joktan in *Genesis*, and in postbiblical Hebrew seems to have had the general meaning of "border country"; furthermore, *Sepharad* is the name of the place to which some inhabitants of Jerusalem were exiled (and it is probably from *Sepharad* that Sephardic Jewry derived its name). Whether *Sephora* is in any way relatable to these ancient Hebrew names, both liminality and exile are central to *The Secret Sharer* and indeed to Conrad's work in general. However, see also Tom Cohen's suggestion of *Sephora* as related to the "cabalistic *sephira*" in his *Anti-Mimesis*, 187–88. For the Latin and ancient Greek etymology I have consulted *The Oxford Latin Dictionary*, ed. P. G. W. Glare (Oxford: Oxford University Press, 1983), while for the ancient Hebrew I have consulted *The Anchor Bible Dictionary, Vol. 5*, ed. David Noel Freedman (New York: Doubleday, 1992).

33. Zdzislaw Najder writes: "Several titles were considered: 'The Secret Self,' 'The Other Self,' or 'The Secret Sharer'—'but that,' Conrad wrote of the last, 'may be too enigmatic.' It appears that [James B.] Pinker [Conrad's literary agent] made the final choice." Zdzislaw Najder, *Joseph Conrad: A Chronicle* (New Brunswick, Rutgers University Press, 1984), 353.

34. Deleuze and Guattari, *A Thousand Plateaus*, 167.

35. Ibid., 171; but see also the whole preceding paragraph.

36. Foucault, "Of Other Spaces," 24.

37. Poe, *The Narrative of Arthur Gordon Pym*, 44–45.

38. Ibid., 57.

39. Ibid., 191.

40. Jean Genet, *Prisoner of Love* (London: Picador, 1990), 29.

41. Conrad, *The Secret Sharer*, 23.

42. Ibid., 26–27.

43. Ibid., 35, 37, 38, 57, 37, 55; but see also 27–31, 34, 40–42.

44. In this sense, I agree only partially with Cohen's assessment of the question of the double in *The Secret Sharer* as a "screen"; see Cohen, *Anti-Mimesis*, 183, 186, and 188. If the question of the double in this text is a "screen," it may also function as a screen of itself: just because a narrative device constitutes a screen hiding something else, it does not follow necessarily that it may not at the same time be part and parcel of that which it hides. It is precisely as a screen of itself that this question interests me here. Unsurprisingly, much critical literature has approached the Leggatt-narrator dyad also from psychoanalytic perspectives that often lead directly into the aforementioned hermeneutical trap. For the more interesting among the many psychoanalytic accounts, see Barbara Johnson and Marjorie Garber's "Secret Sharing: Reading Conrad Psychoanalytically," *College English*, 49 (October 1987): 628–40, as well as Josiane Paccaud's "Under the Other's Eyes: Conrad's 'The Secret Sharer'" *The Conradian* 12 (May 1987): 59–73.

45. Conrad, *The Secret Sharer*, 30–31.

46. Ibid., 35.

47. Ibid., 39 and 40; my emphasis.

48. Ibid., 35 and 38.

49. Ibid., 26.

50. Ibid., see especially 19, 20, 22, 23, 27, 29, 31, 32, 51, 54. Each page number refers to the first occurrence of one or several geographical names; many of them, however, are repeated several times.

51. Ibid., 39.

52. Ibid., 33.

53. The link between whispers and anonymity was suggested to me by Yonatan Touval, who in his *The Anti-American: Criticism and Antipathy in Everyday Life* (unfinished dissertation) writes that "when whispering, all boys are the same."

54. Conrad, *The Secret Sharer*, 25–26.

55. This passage, which follows immediately after the narrator has secured Leggatt in his cabin, stands as a counterpart to the opening of the whole narrative. Here, too, there is the mapping of a space: while that space was one of vast openness marked by (temporal) absence, this one is a tiny and entirely self-enclosed space marked by the crowding and crowded presence of the narrator's belongings and desire. Ibid., 30.

56. Many critics comment on the letteral shape of this cabin. See, most interestingly, Cohen, *Anti-Mimesis*, 193.

57. See Fredric Jameson's *The Political Unconscious: Narrative as a Socially Symbolic Act* (Ithaca, N.Y.: Cornell University Press, 1981), 206; but see also all of chapter 5, 206–80.

58. While revising this section of this chapter, Catherine Sustana's excellent *Letters in Excess: Cross-Genre Investigations in Sentimentality, Feminist Poetics, and Counterhistory* (unpublished dissertation) has also made me ponder the relations between "excess" and "sentimentality" — relations to which I will return.

59. Jameson, *The Political Unconscious*, 210–14.

60. Conrad's letter is quoted in Najder, *Joseph Conrad: A Chronicle*, 380.

61. For an interesting psychoanalytic discussion of the question of gender in *The Secret Sharer* in relation to *Freya of the Seven Isles*, see Monika Elbert's "Possession and Self-Possession: The 'Dialectic of Desire' in *Twixt Land and Sea*," *The Conradian* 17 (spring 1993): 123–46, and especially 132–33 and 143–45.

62. Conrad, *The Secret Sharer*, 45.

63. The narrator at times refers to Leggatt as "the secret sharer of my cabin" as well as "the secret sharer of my life." Ibid., 41 and 38.

64. Ibid., 31–34, in which Leggatt relates the feats of his escape.

65. Jameson, *The Political Unconscious*, 213.

66. Conrad, *The Secret Sharer*, 51.

67. Ibid., 31, 34, 38, 35, 45, respectively.

68. Ibid., 51.

69. The third passage describes the moment when the narrator lets Leggatt out of his cabin and into the sail locker from which the latter will swim away, and the fourth one is their last moment together before Leggatt finally escapes the ship via the sail locker and into the sea. Ibid., 52, 55, 56 and 57, respectively.

70. The tireless dialectical gymnastics of the "open secret" as constitutive of the at once "liberal" and "carceral" subject have been best revealed by D. A. Miller in "Secret Subjects, Open Secrets," in *The Novel and the Police* (Berkeley: University of California Press, 1988), 192–220. Particularly reminiscent of many of the dynamics at work in *The Secret Sharer* is the problematic confronted in the following remarks: "the fact that the secret is always known—and, in some obscure sense, known to be known—never interferes with the incessant activity of keeping it." And again: "In a mechanism reminiscent of Freudian disavowal, we know perfectly well that the secret is known, but nonetheless we must persist, however ineptly, in guarding it. The paradox of the open secret registers the subject's accommodation to a totalyzing system that has obliterated the difference he would make — the difference he does make, in the imaginary denial of this system 'even so.'" Miller, *The Novel and the Police*, 206 and 207. Here, I am writing in the hope that the liberal subject who at once is incarcerated and produced in his own "open secret" might escape subjectification altogether by pumping up the volume of his incessantly repeated avowing disavowals to a deafening, sublime pitch. See also Sedgwick's acknowledgment of Miller's importance for her formulations in *Epistemology of the Closet*, 67–69.

71. Foucault, *The History of Sexuality, Volume I*, especially 27.

72. Michel Foucault, "The Thought from Outside," in *Foucault/Blanchot*, trans. Jeffrey Mehlman and Brian Massumi (New York: Zone Books, 1990), 22; but see also 15–19.

73. This passage follows immediately after Leggatt's decision to be marooned. Conrad, *The Secret Sharer*, 51–52.

74. Genet, *Prisoner of Love*, 59. See also Bersani's compelling discussion of the question of betrayal in Genet, in which he focuses on *Funeral Rites* rather than on *Prisoner of Love*. Bersani, *Homos*, 151–81 and especially 151–55.

75. Conrad, *The Secret Sharer*, 54.

76. Ibid., 53.

77. Ibid., 59–61.

78. Ibid., 24–25.

79. It is only at this point that I would like to disclose — like the proverbial rabbit out of the hat — a piece of biographical information that I have kept concealed till now lest it become the primary interpretive tool in reading the interactions between Leggatt and the narrator. Conrad wrote *The Secret Sharer* in 1909 shortly after a spell of acute depression that coincided with his final quarrels with Ford Madox Ford, ending the eleven-year intimate friendship and literary collaboration between the two writers. One could embark on a detailed and even persuasive reconstruction of *The Secret Sharer* as Conrad's final exorcism of his whole involvement with Ford: in such a reconstruction, Leggatt would impersonate Ford, while the ultimately traitorous and triumphant narrator would be a Conrad who had needed to bring back to life for one last time his "secret partnership" with Ford in the cabin of *The Secret Sharer* in order to better recant and overcome that partnership and all it had enabled. It would be more compelling, however, to corroborate the parallel between Leggatt and the narrator's "secret partnership," and Conrad and Ford's

relationship. This is how Wayne Koestenbaum writes of the homoerotics of their friendship and literary collaboration: "Conrad and Ford, however, enjoyed this sensation of transgression [caused by their collaboration on the novel *Romance*], and proudly labeled their work criminal. Conrad wrote, 'You cannot really suppose that there is anything between us except our mutual regard and our partnership — in crime'; and Ford remembered Conrad shuffling the manuscript pages of *Romance* 'distastefully as if they had been the evidence of a crime.' Their collaboration was criminal because its ambitions were so revolutionary: they meant to alter the techniques that fiction used to represent masculinity. Working with Conrad on *Romance* at night, Ford recalls whispering 'in a conspiracy against the sleeping world.'" The narrator and Leggatt's "secret partnership" is also a "partner-ship — in crime"; they also "alter the techniques that fiction used to represent masculinity"; and their whispers at night in the enclosure of the cabin are uncannily similar to Conrad and Ford's nocturnal and conspiratorial ones. In other words, I find this biographical anecdote useful only insofar as it helps to articulate the relations between writing intended as a social institution and the sublime pleasures of the closet intended here as the scene of writing. Wayne Koestenbaum, *Double Talk: The Erotics of Male Literary Collaboration* (New York: Routledge, 1989), 168 but see also 166–73.

80. Quoted in Maurice Blanchot's *The Unavowable Community*, 1.

5. The Labor of Race

1. Conrad, *The Secret Sharer*, 27–28.

2. The analytic category of "homosexual panic" is homonymous with the psychiatric term at times used in trials so as to advocate leniency for gay-bashers; see Sedgwick, *Epistemology of the Closet*, 19–21, but see also 200–201 and more generally 182–212 for a discussion of the dangers involved in using "homosexual panic" as a central category of an antihomophobic inquiry.

3. Conrad, *The Nigger of the "Narcissus,"* 19–21.

4. Jameson, *The Political Unconscious*, 215–16.

5. Conrad, *The Nigger of the "Narcissus,"* 143.

6. Ibid., 31–32.

7. See Appendix A in Norman Sherry, *Conrad's Eastern World*, 295; but see also Conrad's "Author's Note" to *'Twixt Land and Sea* (Harmondsworth: Penguin Books, 1978), 10.

8. See Norman Sherry's summary of Basil Lubbock's *The Log of the Cutty Sark* in *Conrad's Eastern World*, 256–57; for a more extensive account of Conrad's sources in *The Secret Sharer*, see also 253–69.

Index

Cesare Casarino is associate professor in the Department of Cultural Studies and Comparative Literature at the University of Minnesota. His essays have been published in *October*, *boundary 2*, *Social Text*, *Raritan*, and *Arizona Quarterly*. He is a coeditor of *Marxism beyond Marxism* and the translator (with Vincenzo Binetti) of *Means without End: Notes on Politics*, by Giorgio Agamben (Minnesota, 2000).